Rick Porter

PSYCHOLOGY
A SOCIAL APPROACH

DAVID F. WRENCH

PSYCHOLOGY
A SOCIAL APPROACH

McGRAW-HILL BOOK COMPANY

New York   St. Louis   San Francisco   Toronto   London   Sydney

CHAPTER FRONTISPIECES

1. *Perspective painting by Hogarth. Courtesy of The Bettmann Archive.*

2. *Photograph by Robert Paul, Portland, Oregon. Reproduced by kind permission of Mr. Paul.*

3. *Dr. Edward Tolman in his laboratory. Photographed by Herbert Kling, Berkeley, California. Reproduced by kind permission of Mr. Kling.*

4. *Spider web-building. Photographed by Dr. Peter N. Witt, North Carolina Department of Mental Health. Reproduced by kind permission of Dr. Witt.*

5. *Photograph taken and copyrighted by David Gahr, New York City. Reproduced by kind permission of Mr. Gahr.*

6. *Damaged child, Shacktown, Elm Grove, Oklahoma, 1936. Photograph by Dorothea Lange. Reproduced by permission of the Dorothea Lange Collection, Oakland Museum.*

7. *Immigrant man studying for citizenship. Reproduced by permission of Wide World.*

8. *East German rebellion. Photographer unknown. Reproduced by permission of Wide World.*

9. *Slave poster. Courtesy of The Bettmann Archive.*

10. *First World War Meuse-Argonne offensive, 1918. Reproduced by permission of the U.S. Army.*

11. *Photograph by the author.*

PSYCHOLOGY: A SOCIAL APPROACH

Library of Congress Catalog Card Number 68-8667
71915

1 2 3 4 5 6 7 8 9 0   H D M M   7 5 4 3 2 1 0 6 9 8

to John W. Thibaut

PREFACE

This book is entitled *Psychology: A Social Approach*, rather than simply *Psychology*, because it emphasizes those findings and theories of psychology which aid in the understanding of socially significant human behavior. Most theoretical areas in psychology developed in the hope that they would ultimately contribute to the understanding of man as he lives in a social and cultural environment. Frequently, however, this hope has been imperfectly realized. Research has raised interesting questions, and they have been pursued because they were interesting in their own right. The results of the investigations, however, have not been brought back out of the laboratory and applied to the more general questions about human behavior which provided the original impetus to the research. In this book the various areas of psychology are emphasized to the extent to which they can currently contribute to our understanding of human behavior on a social level. The content of the book is developed around three major themes: man as an information processor, man as a motivated organism, and man in relation to social groups. While all major areas of psychology are surveyed, the strongest emphasis is on those areas which are most related to these major themes.

Most new textbooks are written because the author is dissatisfied with the existing books in his field. This one is no exception. It was first conceived when the author was teaching introductory psychology at a school where the introductory course was only a single semester long. At that time he discovered that those parts of psychology dealing with man functioning in his environment were usually relegated to the end of the introductory text and that the text was often so long that the courses ended before those parts were covered. As a social psychologist, he resolved to write an introductory text which was either especially oriented toward complex human behavior or else short enough so that the students would finish it. This book is both.

As soon as the decision is made to write a book, the author must decide for whom he is writing and what his priorities are. The present book is very much a student's textbook. The author has assumed that the reader has no familiarity with statistics and thus has avoided complex methodological discussions. The use of technical vocabulary has been kept to a minimum, and the technical terms which have been employed are defined in a glossary for the convenience of the reader.

The book is intended to be used as the sole textbook for a one-semester course in introductory psychology or used in conjunction with other materials in a longer course. There are now many excellent supplementary materials available for use in introductory psychology courses. It is the author's belief that these materials have made the single large introductory psychology textbook outdated. The present book is intended to provide a theoretical framework for the integration of supplementary materials when used in a longer course.

I should like to express my appreciation of the ideas which I have obtained from my colleagues and students, often without remembering their original sources. My special thanks are due to my wife, Chris Wrench, for her help in putting my ideas into words.

David F. Wrench

CONTENTS

PSYCHOLOGY
A SOCIAL APPROACH

INTRODUCTION

The Definition of Psychology

A chimpanzee sits in a cage looking at a banana. The banana is on the ground outside the cage. The chimp tries to reach it with a stick, but the stick is not long enough. Suddenly the animal gets up and runs to the back of the cage where there is another stick. The sticks are made of bamboo, and the end of one will fit into the end of the other in the same way that a jointed fishing rod fits together. The chimpanzee fits the sticks together and pulls in the banana.

The study is a classic one done by the psychologist Wolfgang Köhler and described in a book entitled *The Mentality of Apes*.[1] For the duration of the First World War, Köhler was unable to leave the island of Tenerife. He spent the years doing naturalistic learning experiments with chimpanzees, and concluded that they did not learn by blind trial and error as general theories of learning current at that time proposed. Instead, he felt, they were able to analyze relationships and think out solutions to problems. This type of learning he called *insight* learning.

The interpretation of Köhler's results, however, is not a clearcut matter. He did not know the history of his animals before he acquired them. Is it possible that the animal was not solving a new problem, but simply remembering something it had learned earlier, perhaps even learned by trial and error? The issue raised is the basic one of what it is that is learned when learning takes place, which we shall consider at length when we look at the field of learning. For the moment, however, let us simply look at two other studies in the field of psychology. By seeing how they are similar to each other and how they differ, we shall take a first step toward defining the field of psychology.

The first of these is one of the studies which have led a majority of psychologists to conclude that there is no evidence of racial differences in intelligence. At first glance there would seem to be, for some cultural groups of apparently homogeneous racial type make higher average IQ scores than others do. These differences, however, seem to be due to the impossibility of making a test which will accurately compare individuals who have grown up under different cultural conditions. The scores of different groups are thus related to their cultures, but not to their race. This conclusion is supported by many studies, some of which are reviewed by Klineberg in *Race and Psychology*, published in 1958.[2] Our study under consideration here, done by J. H. Rohrer,[3] deals with the average intelligence quotient of an American Indian group, the Osage Indians.

The history of the American Indians is long and complex, for there existed quite dissimilar Indian cultures and each had different experiences in its contacts with non-Indian groups. In the end, all of them came to live on reservations which were definitely separate and clearly not equal in terms of opportunity to learn about the dominant culture. There they became more or less assimilated to that culture, usually less, depending to a large extent on how compatible their former culture was with it. Living under conditions of both cultural impoverishment and culture conflict, most Indian groups make, on the average, considerably lower scores on intelligence tests than do non-Indian groups. (This does not mean that there are not wide individual differences within each group.)

Are these low average scores, around 80 in comparison to 100 for the population in general, due to heredity or to environment? The question could be answered if it were possible to find an Indian group that did not live under conditions of cultural and physical deprivation. Rohrer found such a group in the Osage Indians, who enjoy a standard of living comparable to non-Indian groups in the United States. Biologically, the Osage Indians are undoubtedly closely related to other American Indian groups. That they have a higher standard of living is the result of a quirk of fate—the worthless land they were given as a reservation was later found to have oil under it!

The discovery of oil led to what has been called a *natural experiment*, one which has not been performed intentionally for research purposes but which did what a researcher would have wanted to do had he been able to. It eliminated for the Osage Indians the material disadvantage that most Indian groups live under. A comparison is thus possible. If the low scores of most Indian groups are due to race, then the Osage Indians should have scores averaging about 80, since they are racially similar to other Indian groups. If the low scores of most Indian groups are due to the restricted *environment* of the reservation, then the Osage Indians should average around 100, since they do not have restricted cultural advantages. The latter is the case: Rohrer found average scores of 100 and 104, depending on which of two tests was used. The results are clearly consistent with a cultural, rather than a racial, interpretation.

Culture affects Mentality

Already we can see some differences among the studies we are considering. One difference is in the *source of data*. While the Rohrer study deals with human beings, the Köhler study concerns infrahuman organisms, chimpanzees. As we shall see when we look at the history of psychology, this is one of the major factors which has influenced approaches to the field. Theories based primarily on animal experiments have, not too surprisingly, differed from those based largely on the study of human beings. Despite this difference, however, the studies are similar in one way as regards the source of data. A major distinction in psychology has been whether theories were based on the observed *behavior* of organisms or on their reported *experience*. Both the studies we have looked at so far have been studies of behavior as it appears to an outside observer, rather than the experience which an inside observer reports.

However, there is a second major difference in the studies. It concerns the extent to which they have been concerned with formulating general laws which will apply to all individuals or, on the other hand, the extent to which they are interested in studying the way in which individuals differ. This is such a major difference in psychological theories that terms have been devised for the two types. _Nomothetic_ theories are theories which apply to all members of a species, or even across different species. A simple example would be that the rods in the retina of the eye do not perceive the differences among colors. This generalization applies to tall people and short people, Arabs and Eskimos, or even rats and lemurs. But it is possible to draw generalizations about a single individual. Consider this generalization: "Whenever Tom gets involved with a girl he thinks up a good reason why he should not marry her." The principle might only apply to one person, but as long as it did apply to him, it could still be a valuable generalization. It would enable us to predict his future behavior in certain circumstances. We could, for example, predict that he would never get married. This type of principle is called _ideographic._

It is an oversimplification to class theories as either wholly nomothetic or wholly ideographic, for in reality there is a continuum between these two poles. A generalization about a group of people is more ideographic than a generalization about all people but less ideographic than a generalization about a single person. The two studies we have considered so far differ on this dimension. The first study, by Köhler, attempted to discover general principles of learning which would apply not only to all people but also to all primates. Studies such as the second one, by Rohrer, look at differences among various groups, rather than just ways that all people are the same. The second is thus more ideographic, though less so than a study investigating the behavior of a single individual. Whether theories of psychology attempt to draw nomothetic or ideographic generalizations is again one of their major differences.

A third typical study in the field of psychology will help to illustrate the variety of material found in the field. Some areas of the human brain are clearly used in the representation of the senses. If one of these areas is stimulated electrically when a person is undergoing brain surgery, the person will report a sensation, such as a flash of light, a sound, or a taste. Those parts of the brain are thus called _sensory_ areas. Other parts of the brain equally clearly serve for the control of muscular movements. If one of these _motor_ areas is stimulated electrically, the person will make a muscular movement. Besides the sensory and motor areas, there are other areas that do not have clearly defined sensory or motor functions. These areas apparently serve functions in higher thought, in integrating patterns of behavior, or in other activities which are not yet clear to investigators. The third experiment we shall look at, performed by James Olds,[4] investigated the functions of one of these apparently functionless areas of the brain.

Needless to say, most studies of brain functioning use animal subjects, for only a limited amount of information can be gathered from human subjects during surgery. The necessity of using animal subjects, by ruling out the possibility of the subject reporting what he experiences, is a serious limitation on this type of research. If you stimulate an area of the brain of an animal and the animal doesn't do anything, how do you know what function that area serves? Olds conceived the interesting idea of letting the animal stimulate its own brain. Whether it did so or not might then tell something about what it was experiencing.

Using rats as subjects, Olds surgically implanted electrodes in the *septal* region of the brain of each of them. This involves a minor operation, carried out under anesthetic, from which the rat rapidly recovers with no apparent ill effects. After recovery, the rat was placed in a box with a lever in it. The lever was wired up so that each time the rat pressed the lever, its brain would be briefly stimulated. Under these conditions, the rats pressed the lever rapidly and repeatedly, sometimes as frequently as two thousand or three thousand times per hour. The results clearly supported Olds's contention that he had discovered *pleasure centers* in the brain. Further research indicated that the rats would do work and learn things in order to receive the electrical stimulation, so that the areas of the brain were apparently not merely centers for lever pressing, as some people had suggested.

So far we have seen that studies in psychology differ in whether they use human or animal subjects and in whether they are concerned with general laws or the study of individual differences. Olds's study is animal and nomothetic. It also illustrates a third way in which psychological studies differ, for it has a different *unit of analysis* than either of the other studies we have looked at. Psychology used to be described as the study of the individual, but it has now come to study everything from individual nerve cells through the behavior of large groups of people. The three studies we have looked at focus on individuals, as representatives of all primates, on cultural groups, and on portions of the brain. Psychology is clearly broader than simply the study of individuals.

Now that we have looked at some typical psychological studies and the ways in which they differ from each other, we are ready to face the problem of trying to define what psychology is. The task will not be an easy one, for among other things psychology is an historical accident. Some areas of study are included within the field because famous psychologists in the past happened to be interested in them, while others are excluded simply because nobody has yet pointed out their relevance for the field. In the next section we shall see some of the ways in which contemporary psychology is a product of its history.

How, then, should the field of psychology be defined? The usual definition is that it is the science of human behavior. This definition is too broad in some ways and too narrow in others. It is too broad in that all the social sciences study human behavior and they all aspire to be sciences just as psychology does. The definition does not distinguish psychology from anthropology, political science, or economics. At the same time the definition is too narrow in limiting the field only to the study of behavior. Despite the historical impact of behaviorism as a school of psychology, most psychologists are still interested in whether the mental patient feels good or bad or whether a person would feel pleasure if his pleasure centers were stimulated. Although the emphasis has been first on one and then on the other during its history, psychology is apparently interested in human experience as well as human behavior.

Psychology cannot be defined in a few words in a way which will both include the things it has historically included and distinguish it from the other social sciences. It can, however, be described in terms of what it usually is. The description will not fit all studies done by psychologists, but it will fit most of them. Psychology, then, is the study of human experience and behavior based on research with animals and with technologically advanced cultures. It includes both nomothetic and ideographic approaches and units of analysis ranging from the nerve cell to the society. It uses experimentation and statistical control as its major research methods.

Even this description leaves some overlap with the other social sciences, and this overlap does in fact exist. When a political scientist concerns himself with the behavior of politicians rather than ideal systems of government or when a sociologist investigates small-group behavior, he is working in an area and a way that could equally well typify a psychologist. The social sciences differ in what they usually do, but all of them overlap in their interests. Psychology usually, but not always, uses experimental methods, studies individuals, and limits itself to American and Western European cultures.

Is it not a limitation of psychology that it is based more on some cultural groups than on others? It is, just as it is a limitation of anthropology that it usually does not have representative samples of the populations it studies, or a limitation of sociology that it seldom uses experimental methods in checking its results. Each field, then, is only a partial view of reality from a particular perspective. The perspective in this book will be that of social psychology. The primary focus will be on human interaction, and such areas of psychology as learning and perception will be studied primarily from the point of view of how they influence the relations of individuals and groups to each other.

1
The History of Psychology

THE BRITISH ASSOCIATIONISTS

Although it is possible to trace speculation about man's nature back into antiquity, probably the first group to have sufficient impact on the emerging field of psychology to be numbered among its ancestors was a group of British philosophers. The two most important aspects of their beliefs are referred to in the two different names they are sometimes given. Sometimes they are called *empiricists*, because they believed that ideas are not inherited, but learned from experience, and sometimes they are called *associationists*, because of their interest in how ideas are associated with each other. It is, of course, possible to be an empiricist without being an associationist or to be an associationist without being an empiricist. John Locke and his followers, however, were generally both. In being both empiricists and associationists, they raised the central problem of the future field of psychology and provided an answer to it.

The problem was where ideas come from. It became a problem when they were not assumed to be inherited, as many earlier philosophers had believed. Plato, for instance, held the position that we had once known everything, but that our memories were a bit bad and we needed to be reminded. This was, for him, a strong argument in favor of believing in reincarnation: if we had not lived before, how could we know so much? Similarly, Descartes held that there were some ideas which did not come from experience but which yet presented themselves to the mind with such certainty that they had to be believed. The rejection of innate ideas is the central theme of Locke's "An essay concerning human understanding," published in 1690, and is the step which made a field of psychology necessary.[5] This point is made clear in the best-known quote from Locke's essay:

> 2. All ideas come from sensation or reflection—*Let us then suppose the mind to be, as we say, white paper, void of all characters, without any ideas; how comes it to be furnished? Whence comes it by that vast store which the busy and boundless fancy of man has painted on it with an almost endless variety? Whence has it all the materials of reason and knowledge? To this I answer in one word, from experience. In that all our knowledge is founded, and from that it ultimately derives itself. Our observation, employed either about external and sensible objects, or about the internal operations of our minds, perceived and reflected on by ourselves, is that which supplies our understanding with all the materials of thinking. These two are the fountains of knowledge, from whence all the ideas we have, or can naturally have, do spring.*[6]

It will be noticed in this quotation that Locke did not carry empiricism as far as some of the later members of the school. While ideas were not inherited, the capacity for perceiving the world was, and a person could learn by paying attention to the operations of his mind. Others, such as George Berkeley and David Hartley, developed the positions that we must learn to perceive and that all ideas are compounds of ideas of sensations. No longer was observing the operations of the mind a source of knowledge.

"Compounds of ideas" provides the clue to the other important role which associationism was to play in the history of psychology. Ideas were associated with each other, and on the basis of this association complex ideas were built up out of simple ones. The answer to the question of where ideas came from was thus to look for the laws of association. Consciousness, like a chemical compound, could be analyzed into elements, and the laws of association were thought to govern how the elements combined to make the compounds. On the basis of introspection, the associationists suggested what the laws might be. For Hume, for example, there were three—resemblance, contiguity, and cause and effect. For automobile tires to make you think of doughnuts would be an example of associating ideas because of similarity of shape. Associating salt with pepper would follow a law of contiguity—associating things because they are frequently found together. If turtles make you think of turtle soup, you may be associating cause and effect.

NINETEENTH-CENTURY PHYSIOLOGY

The associationists did not carry out experiments or carefully controlled observations, but based their conclusions on thinking about their everyday experiences. Thus, while they anticipated the subject matter and some of the principles of later psychological theories, they did not anticipate their experimental methods. These methods were more a legacy from a second major forerunner of the field of psychology, the investigation of the physical nature of man by anatomists and physiologists. A publication of Charles Bell in 1811 will serve as an example.

While speculation about man is old, systematic study of him is not. It is perhaps not fanciful of anthropologists to suggest that the reason animals are represented in considerable anatomic accuracy in cave paintings, while men are either very crudely represented or not shown at all, is that early man had strong religious taboos against any representation of human beings. (This type of belief can be seen more recently in the notion that an image of a person would give a witch power over him.) In any case, man has been the last thing subject to scientific investigation. At the time Bell wrote, some people were just beginning to feel that perhaps man's anatomy might be amenable to scientific investigation. There still are many people who believe his thoughts, impulses, and emotions are outside the sphere of science. The novelty of studying even man's anatomy in the early nineteenth century is shown in this quote from Bell's "Idea of a new anatomy of the brain":

> I have found some of my friends so mistaken in their conception of the object of the demonstrations which I have delivered in my lectures, that I wish to vindicate myself at all hazards. They would have it that I am in search of the seat of the soul; but I wish only to investigate the structure of the brain, as we examine the structure of the eye and ear. It is not more presumptuous to follow the tracts

of nervous matter in the brain and to attempt to discover the course of sensation, than it is to trace the rays of light through the humours of the eye, and to say, that the retina is the seat of vision. Why are we to close the investigation with the discovery of the external organ?[7]

Bell is most remembered today for being one of the discoverers of the Bell-Magendie law, which distinguished between the sensory and motor nerves connecting with the spinal cord. The sensory nerves, which carry impulses toward the brain, connect with the cord through the dorsal roots (toward the back); the motor nerves, which carry impulses away from the brain, emerge as the ventral roots from the cord. More important than this specific discovery, however, was the role which Bell and others like him played in introducing systematic observation and experimentation as methods of studying living organisms. In Magendie's rediscovery of Bell's law, for example, he utilized an experiment:

> *Magendie cut the posterior root, could get no movement by pricking or pressing the limb, and was about to conclude that the limb was paralyzed when the animal moved it spontaneously. Magendie concluded that the limb was not paralyzed but anesthetic. Then Magendie tried cutting the anterior root and found that he then had paralysis, for he could get no movement in it at all, whether the posterior root was cut or not, unless he stimulated the distal end of the anterior cut.*[8]

PSYCHOPHYSICS

A third forerunner of the field of psychology was a growing literature on the operation of the senses. Thomas Young had proposed a theory of color vision as early as 1802, and it was elaborated by the physicist von Helmholtz in 1860. More important, Weber and Fechner established the area of study known as *psychophysics*. The impact of their work on psychology was so great that E. G. Boring, in his standard history of experimental psychology, views Fechner as the founder of the field:

> *We come at last to the formal beginning of experimental psychology, and we start with Fechner: not with Wundt, thirty-one years Fechner's junior, who published his first important but youthful psychological study two years after Fechner's epoch-making work; not with Helmholtz, twenty years younger, who was primarily a physiologist and a physicist but whose great genius extended to include psychology; but with Fechner, who was not a great philosopher nor*

at all a physiologist, but who performed with scientific rigor those first experiments which laid the foundation for the new psychology and still lie at the basis of its methodology.[9]

The view that Fechner founded psychology is based on two things. He applied experimental methods such as those employed by physics and physiology, and he applied them to problems which were definitely psychological, rather than physical or physiological. The problems dealt with the relationship between the physical stimulus a person was exposed to and the sensation he experienced. Weber had observed that the change in a stimulus which can be noticed is approximately a constant fraction of the value of the stimulus. In other words, if a 30-ounce weight must be changed in weight by an ounce for you to be able, on the average, to notice the difference, then a 30-pound weight would have to be changed by a pound for the change to be equally noticeable. This can be crudely observed in everyday life. If a room is illuminated only by moonlight coming through the windows, turning on even a 15-watt bulb will make a very noticeable difference in how bright the room seems. If sunlight is streaming through the windows, the change in illumination when the 15-watt light is turned on may not even be noticeable.

Fechner considerably extended Weber's work, both experimentally and theoretically. He extended it to other senses than those Weber had worked with, and he conceived of using the *just-noticeable difference* in stimulation as a unit in terms of which any sensation could be measured. Fechner thus did extensive work in psychology, yet the honor of founding the field is more commonly given to Wilhelm Wundt, who came later. This is partly because of disagreement on just how important Fechner's work was. Boring quotes William James as having written of it:

But it would be terrible if even such a dear old man as this could saddle our Science forever with his patient whimsies, and, in a world so full of more nutritious objects of attention, compel all future students to plough through the difficulties, not only of his own work, but of the still drier ones written in his refutation. Those who desire this dreadful literature can find it; it has a "disciplinary value;" but I will not even enumerate it in a foot-note. The only amusing part of it is that Fechner's critics should always feel bound, after smiting his theories hip and thigh and leaving not a stick of them standing, to wind up by saying that nevertheless to him belongs the imperishable glory, of first formulating them and thereby turning psychology into an exact science,

> " 'And everybody praised the duke
> Who this great fight did win'
>   'But what good came of it at last?'
> Quoth little Peterkin.
>   'Why, that I cannot tell,' said he,
> 'But 'twas a famous victory!' "[10]

Probably a more important reason why Wundt is usually considered the founder of psychology, however, is that it was his students who became the leaders in the new field. Fechner may have created part of the field of psychology; Wundt created psychologists. In addition Wundt, unlike Fechner, set out intentionally to create a new field of study.

The field of psychology thus began imperceptibly. Some psychological research, such as that of Weber and Fechner, was done before Wundt founded his psychological laboratory in 1879. James even had a laboratory at Harvard for performing psychological experiments prior to Wundt's. Wundt is usually considered the founder of the field, however, because he defined it in a systematic way and because he had disciples. His work was no single piece of research, but the creation of a field. He adopted consistent positions on what the subject matter of the field should be, what methods should be used to study the subject matter, what assumptions needed to be made in order to utilize the methods, and what problems it was important to attack first in terms of the theoretical approach. His psychology is worthy of our attention, for even today the various approaches to the field are based on the answers given to the questions Wundt raised. The history of psychology is largely a history of accepting or rejecting various aspects of Wundt's psychology.

WUNDT'S PHYSIOLOGICAL PSYCHOLOGY

Wundt's psychology was just what one would expect it to be on the basis of its antecedents. From the associationist philosophers came the tasks of the new field—the analysis of consciousness into elements and the determination of the laws of connection of these elements. Also from the associationists came introspection as a method, but this was combined with the experimental method of the physiologists. The method adopted was thus experimental introspection! This method is not a contradiction in terms, for it is the method employed by Fechner. The experiment consists of creating various stimulus conditions, and the subject then introspects and reports his experiences.

Wundt was very clear about what psychology was and was not. It was the science of experience, and concerned only with the experiences of the normal, adult, human mind. Other sciences were possible, but they would not be psychology. Similarly, the introspections of trained observers were the only source of acceptable data. Anything else would be unscientific. Finally, the basic task of the new science was to break down experience into elements. Wundt's system was a mental chemistry which hoped, like the science of chemistry, to find lawfulness by finding basic elements and seeing how they combined into compounds. Like chemical compounds, the mental compounds might show properties different from those of the elements making them up, an idea which had also been suggested by one of the later associationist philosophers, John Stuart Mill. It was this search for a molecular structure of consciousness which led the derivatives of Wundt's system to be named *structuralism*.

In 1859 Charles Darwin published the book of the century, *The Origin of Species*.[11] That psychology today is not structuralism is probably due more to this remarkable work than to any other single cause. Later, Freud's writings were to have their effect, yet even today contemporary psychology probably shows the impact of evolutionary theory more clearly than that of psychoanalysis. What exactly was it that Darwin did? He was not the first to propose an evolutionary theory—his own grandfather Erasmus Darwin had been one of those who had proposed evolutionary theories before him. Instead, he was the first to propose a plausible mechanism by means of which evolution might have taken place, and such a wide variety of evidence that his ideas had to be either accepted or disproved—they could not simply be ignored.

Before Darwin wrote, men were familiar with some of the evidence on which his theory was based. That some species which had previously been found on the earth were there no longer was evident from research in paleontology. Their disappearance was accounted for in terms of some great cataclysm rather than unsuccessful competition for survival. That new breeds of domestic animals, such as the Percheron horse, had been created by man was undeniable. These were merely breeds rather than species, however, and it was not considered possible that similar selective breeding might create new species. Species were held to have been divinely created, all at the same time, and forever unchanging. Finally, similarities of embryological development of different species were noted and used as a basis of classification of the species. They were not, however, seen as indicating that the species had evolved from common ancestors.

Darwin brought all of these sources of evidence into focus by showing their relationship to a mechanism of evolution—a mechanism of variation, differential survival, and resulting change of the population. His doing so created three new interests within the field of psychology. First, it led to an interest in the adaptive value of human thought and behavior. Instead of the contents of the mind, the basic question became the ways in which the mind helped man compete for survival. Second, evolutionary theory led to an interest in animal psychology. The mind of man and that of other organisms had been previously thought so different from each other that no comparison between them was possible. Evolution, in stating that man and primates descended from common ancestors, stressed their similarity and made a comparison of their mental capacities desirable. Finally, evolutionary theory led to the study of individual differences. If man's intelligence had evolved through variation and differential survival, then the variations in intelligence found among individuals became vitally important, for they were the stuff of which evolution was made.

FUNCTIONALISM AND BEHAVIORISM

All three of these interests in psychology primarily encouraged by evolutionary theory soon came to characterize American psychology. The approach which embodied them was too loose and eclectic to be considered a system of psychology in the sense that structuralism was; but to distinguish it from structuralism, it has been given the name *functionalism*. From it developed *behaviorism*, which was, like structuralism, a more rigidly defined theoretical system.

Because functionalism was more a general point of view than a well-developed theoretical approach, it cannot be identified with one man the way structuralism can with Wundt. It grew partly out of the work of William James at Harvard, and was influenced by work on individual differences done by Galton in England and Binet in France. It developed into a distinctive approach at Chicago under John Dewey and at Columbia under James McKeen Cattell. Even these two schools differed somewhat in their emphasis; the theoretical developments at Chicago led more directly to behaviorism, while the Columbia approach was more eclectic.

The central problem for functionalism, then, was how mental activity aided in adaptation to the environment. This included such subquestions as these: How do individuals differ in their adaptation? How do we develop the ability to adapt? What processes are common to the adaptation of animals and human beings? How may our knowledge be applied to help people adapt? As is obvious from these questions, Wundt's nomothetic pure science of human experience was expanded into the study of experience and behavior, of animals and people, of individual differences and common characteristics—to be applied as well as understood. Even this list does not exhaust the ways in which functionalism differed from structuralism. It also opposed the analysis of experience into elements by stressing, as James had, that experience is a continuous process which can only be broken down into elements at the cost of distorting it. We not only cannot step into the same river twice, we cannot step into it once, for it changes while we are acting.

This opposition to analysis into elements was not shared by behaviorism, which grew out of functionalism. Although it developed from functionalism, behaviorism regarded it as a compromise with an enemy which should have been slain. Behaviorism, as developed by John Watson and his followers, had as rigid rules about what psychology should be as structuralism did, even though the rules were almost diametrically opposed. For structuralism, psychology had been the study of experience; for Watson, only behavior was admissible data.

The study of behavior rather than experience is a natural consequence of an interest in animal psychology, since animals are unable to report their experiences. Watson's primary interests were in animal and child psychology, and he carried functionalism to its logical extreme of excluding all but behavior from psychology. The new school was to lean so heavily on experiments with animals that there was something prophetic in the title of Watson's doctoral dissertation, "Animal education: An experimental study on the psychical development of the white rat, correlated with the growth of its nervous system."[12]

It was also from animal experiments that the elements of the new approach came. After winning the Nobel Prize for his research on digestion, the Russian physiologist Ivan Pavlov became interested in the role of higher mental processes in salivation. A dog would salivate not only when meat was placed in his mouth, a simple reflex action, but also when his food dish was rattled. This latter behavior was not an innate reflex, but instead, Pavlov reasoned, a reflex which was conditional upon the training which the animal had received. By pairing a neutral stimulus, such as a bell, with the stimulus of meat powder in its mouth, Pavlov conditioned his animals to salivate to the bell. The extensive research which he did on these conditional, or conditioned, responses served as a major theoretical basis of behaviorism. Watson conceived of all learning as responses being conditioned to stimuli. The elements of the new psychology were not the sensations and images of structuralism or the ideas of British associationism, but the stimuli and responses of physiology.

INDIVIDUAL DIFFERENCES AND PSYCHOANALYTIC THEORY

In tracing the evolution of functionalism, we have neglected other aspects of it which were not central to behaviorism: its concentration on individual differences and its applied nature. These two characteristics, which had their own historical origins, led to the development of clinical psychology.

The role which evolutionary theory played in making psychology an ideographic science as well as a nomothetic one may be seen by looking at the pioneer of the study of individual differences, who was Darwin's cousin. Sir Francis Galton was a man of science of a type that is not found today, for today knowledge is so extensive and specialized that it is rare for anyone other than a professional in a field to make a basic contribution to it. Galton, on the other hand, was a dilettante who made basic contributions to anthropology, genetics, meteorology, psychology, physics, and statistics! He was a genius with an independent income who was productive without taking his work seriously. At one time he took a walking tour of the British Isles to determine where the girls were the prettiest. At another he established an anthropometric laboratory in London where he took physical and psychological measurements of thousands of people. While almost all psychologists since Galton's time have had to pay their subjects to participate in experiments, Galton charged his an admission fee.

It was an interest in evolution which made Galton interested in individual differences. He saw in intelligence a major factor in adaptation and survival, and was convinced that it was inherited rather than acquired. In individual differences in intelligence he saw evolution in progress. His major work in the area, *Inquiries into Human Faculty and Its Development*,[13] published in 1883, was the beginning of individual psychology.

If testing of individual differences began because of Galton's interest in evolution, it continued for more practical reasons. Binet and Simon published in 1905 the first practical intelligence test for schoolchildren, prepared at the request of the Paris school authorities. Mental testing was transplanted to Columbia by Cattell, who had been Wundt's first assistant but was more influenced by Galton. As Edna Heidbreder put it in her excellent book, *Seven Psychologies:*

> *In the early days of psychology at Columbia, the dominating figure was, beyond question, James McKeen Cattell. Cattell, it will be remembered, was one of Wundt's first students at the Leipzig laboratory. It has almost passed into legend that, at his own suggestion, he became Wundt's first assistant, and that in Wundt's laboratory, where the object of study was the generalized human mind, and where Wundt regularly assigned students the problems for their doctoral dissertations, Cattell suggested his own problem and included in his plan a study of individual differences. Wundt pronounced the program* ganz Amerikanisch, *and it is of great importance to psychology in the United States that Cattell remained* ganz Amerikanisch *and at the same time an active member of the Leipzig group.*[14]

Clinical psychology would have had no place in the nomothetic structuralism of German experimental psychology and at most a questionable place in the theoretically pure behaviorism of Watson. It was soon to play a major role in an American functionalism which was oriented toward individual differences, mental testing, and the application of psychology to practical problems.

Although he was a medical doctor rather than a psychologist, Sigmund Freud changed psychological conceptions of man as a personality as much as Darwin had changed conceptions of man as an animal. Again like Darwin, Freud was not completely original in his work, but was original in developing a unified theory with supporting evidence which had to be seriously considered. The use of hypnotism in the treating of mental disorder was an accepted technique before Freud, and William James was among those who used it to gather data on individuals with amnesia, publishing his observations in *The Principles of Psychology* in 1890.[15] Freud, however, made at least three major contributions. First, and perhaps most important in the long run, he expanded the scope of science to encompass new phenomena. He did not dismiss the behavior of children, slips of the tongue of adults, the symptoms of psychotics, and the myths of various cultures as accidental and meaningless trivia; rather, he viewed them as phenomena which a theory of man must explain. The second contribution was the theory that he evolved to explain these data—a theory stressing the motivation of behavior, the unacceptability of many motives to the conscience of the individual, and the consequent importance of repression and unconscious conflict. This theory will be explored at length later in the book. Finally, Freud contributed *psychoanalysis,* a method of treatment of mental illness which differed significantly from the hypnosis from which it was evolved. While hypnosis sometimes produced dramatic cures, it sometimes seemed to cure only the surface symptoms without getting at the underlying problems. The patient soon developed different symptoms after one set was cured. The psychoanalytic technique of therapy was evolved to lead people, while conscious, into discussing matters that they would usually reveal only under hypnosis.

Freud's approach served as a stimulus for the study of children, motivation, and individual differences. It was only through the testing movement, however, that clinical psychology evolved. Although some psychoanalysts were trained who were not medical doctors, the vast majority were, and eventually the precedent was established that only M.D.s would receive psychoanalytic training. The mainstream of psychoanalysis was obviously within medicine, and psychology was influenced only in the way it had been influenced by developments in philosophy, physiology, or biology. Psychologists, however, gradually developed two roles which were related to psychoanalysis. Through the development of mental testing they came to play a major role in psychiatric diagnosis, and through the development of research methodology they became the people most concerned with the evaluation of the effects of psychoanalytic therapy. While the former role placed them in a role subordinate to psychiatrists, the latter gave them an expertise which placed them at least on a basis of equality of status with the medical specialty. From the combination of the two roles and from the shortage of trained psychiatrists, clinical psychology developed into its present status of relatively independent quasi-medical practice. At the present time, approximately half of all psychologists in the United States are clinicians, and it is the clinical psychologist rather than the industrial, child, comparative, social, or physiological psychologist who is popularly thought of when the word "psychologist" is used.

GESTALT THEORY

The final school of psychology we shall consider is named _gestalt theory,_ after a German word which may be roughly translated as _"pattern."_ As its name implies, this school grew up as a protest against analysis and synthesis in psychology and stressed that there are emergent properties when elements are combined. A triangle is more than three straight lines. Triangularity is an emergent property which appears when they are organized in a pattern.

Gestalt theory arose as a theory of perception which was a reaction against the analysis of consciousness by German structuralism but became the chief alternative to the elementarism of behaviorism in the United States. In most ways the two theoretical approaches were opposed. Gestalt psychologists, who had come to the United States to flee Hitler's Germany, were strong advocates of psychology studying human values and social institutions, while behaviorism wanted to eliminate everything subjective from the field. Watson was a strong environmentalist, who maintained that anyone could become anything with the proper training; the gestalt theorists were nativists in perception, who stressed the innate organizing characteristics of the mind. Most important, however, the mind was for behaviorism a blank slate on which nothing but stimulus-response connections could be impressed, while for the gestalt theorists it was something wondrously complex. Behaviorism was simple and optimistic, with a simple theory to account for everything. Gestalt theory concentrated on destroying the simple explanations.

All the schools of psychology described here already existed when Heidbreder published her _Seven Psychologies_ in 1933. Why have there been no new schools of thought in the field in a third of a century? The reason seems to be that the field has become more mature, and as it has, knowledge has become more specialized. Just as evolutionary theory moved from early controversy over such general questions as whether evolution had taken place and whether acquired characteristics could be inherited to such specific research questions as the way in which pairs of chromosomes separate, psychology has moved from the clash of grand theories of human nature to the consideration of more specific research topics. This does not mean that there have been no new theories. Some, such as Festinger's theory of cognitive dissonance, will be discussed in this book. It does mean that the theories have been less broad in scope than, for example, those of Freud or William James.

In a sense, then, all the theories have been shown to be wrong. Neither the nativism of gestalt theory nor the environmentalism of behaviorism, the mental chemistry of Wundt nor the cultural universality of the Oedipus complex, has been supported by the very extensive research literature of the new field. Instead, each has proved sometimes right and sometimes wrong. The questions have changed, so that they no longer have the general nature of "Is man what he is because of heredity or environment?" but instead the much more specific pattern of "How do heredity and environment interact in the development of walking by the human infant?"

Few psychologists would be able to answer the question if asked to what theoretical school they belong. Yet even though psychologists do not consciously hold to specific theories, they are undoubtedly guided by implicit theories. One man will be more inclined toward the development of nomothetic theory, while another will be drawn toward individual differences. One will perceive the world as simple and incline toward explanations in terms of simple elements, while another will be emotionally a gestalt theorist, opposed to any simplification of the richness of human experience. The old theoretical questions, on which the schools had systematic and explicit differences, are often the ones which are found to characterize different explanations of more specific research findings, and theorists unconsciously carry the approaches of structuralism, psychoanalytic theory, and functionalism in new combinations to the problems they tackle. It is in this sense of the unverbalized theoretical biases which are part of the transmitted culture of psychology that the field remains the accidental product of its history.

Theory and Data in Psychology

THEORY

Psychology differs from most other fields in that all people hold psychological theories. If a superintendent of schools tries to decide whether a school budget will be approved by the voters, a boy estimates the probability of a girl accepting if he asks her for a date, or a husband attempts to figure out why his wife likes dances more than he does, each is operating on some kind of theory of human experience and behavior. Furthermore, each could point to evidence to support his theory. The superintendent of schools, for example, may argue that the school budget should be reduced on the basis that dissatisfaction over taxes is currently high and point to recent conversations with community leaders to support this generalization. How, then, do the theories of psychologists differ from common sense? Some of the main ways are that they are more explicit, are more internally consistent, and specify more clearly the relationships between the theories and the evidence they are based on. Let us look at each of these points in turn.

A person concerned with any area of human activity may develop a great deal of ability to predict events in that area without being able to communicate his expertise to anyone else. Thus if we asked the superintendent of schools mentioned earlier to predict the outcomes of ten successive budget elections, he might well predict accurately in most if not all cases. If he were asked how he made his predictions, he might say he predicted passage of the budget in one case on the basis of general satisfaction with the school program, failure in another case because of controversy over the buying of uniforms for the high school band, and passage in a third election because of a decline in political conservatism. The individual trying to learn from the expert how to predict the election outcome would be as puzzled after learning these predictions as he was before. He would not know how to combine and weight the various factors that seemed to be involved, or even what other factors might be involved in different elections. What should be predicted, for example, when people are satisfied with the educational program, there is strong political conservatism in the state, and the high school debate team has just won an award? The theory which has been communicated is not explicit enough to say. The development of theories which are explicit enough to state which variables should be looked at, how they should be measured, and how they should be put together in making predictions is one aspiration of the social scientist.

A second problem with commonsense theories is that they often seem to be self-contradictory. A self-made man, for example, who has risen from poverty to a position of wealth and power, may ascribe his success to the obstacles he has had to overcome. In explaining his own career he may attribute his success to the lessons learned in going hungry, fighting in the streets, and having to support himself from an early age. He may also give his children a home in the best residential neighborhood, enough money that they do not have to work in childhood, and an education at the best preparatory schools. Will he predict that they will be unsuccessful because of their not having the experiences which he says success depends upon when he explains his own career? In many areas of life, our commonsense theories may show similar apparent contradictions. Thus we can simultaneously believe "Out of sight, out of mind" and "Absence makes the heart grow fonder."

Some of this internal inconsistency in commonsense theories may be more apparent than real, however. If a person believed that "Out of sight, out of mind" applied when two people did not know each other well, but that absence did make the heart grow fonder after there were strong bonds of affection between them, then there would be no contradiction. In this case the commonsense theory would simply not be explicit enough through not stating when each principle applied.

Perhaps the greatest difference between formal and informal theories, however, is that the formal theories specify what observations are relevant to them. The two male protagonists in Mozart's opera *Così fan Tutte* debated whether women are faithful or not, a question which has been debated endlessly. They differed from others who have argued the matter in agreeing on what evidence they would use to settle the question—each would go away and return in disguise and try to seduce his fiancée. If he succeeded, it meant she was not to be trusted. In agreeing on just what evidence was and was not relevant to the question, they changed it from one which could not be answered to one which could be and formed the basis for a scientific theory, even if it was one limited to only two people.

Psychological theories, like Mozart's characters, specify how the concepts in them are to be related to operations or observations in the real world. To return to the case of the superintendent of schools mentioned earlier, imagine that he had the simple theory that people voted for school budgets when they had favorable attitudes toward the schools and against them when they had unfavorable attitudes toward the schools. After learning the outcome of any election, he would always be able to justify the results in terms of the theory, for he would always be able to find evidence of either favorable attitudes or unfavorable attitudes. In order to make an adequate test of the theory, he would need to specify a general method of gathering evidence on attitudes which was independent of his biases or knowledge of the outcome of the election. He might, for example, specify the following procedure: Collect all letters to the editor of the local newspaper (not just those printed) for the two months prior to the election. Have someone who does not know why the research is being done sort the letters into those favorable to the schools, those unfavorable to them, and those either ambiguous or irrelevant. Count the letters, and if there are more favorable than unfavorable letters, predict passage of the budget; otherwise predict its failure. While this might be a very crude method of assessing attitudes (the sample is biased in favor of people who read that particular newspaper, for one thing), it is a first step toward specifying the operations by which a particular concept may be measured and thus a first step toward making the theory testable.

DATA

The ideal of data gathering in psychology goes something like this: In order to study the effects of a variable, called the *independent variable, it is experimentally manipulated.* (If we wanted to study the effects of a drug, for example, different groups of people would be given different amounts of the drug.) The effects of the independent variable are assessed by measuring other variables which might be influenced by it, called the *dependent variables.* (In the drug study, these might include both physical measures such as pulse rate and psychological measures such as interpretation of ambiguous stimuli.) The various *experimental groups* would be given different amounts of the drug, while a *control group* would not be given the drug at all. The effects of other variables would be controlled by making the conditions for the experimental and control groups identical except for the differences in the level of the independent variable. (In the drug study, for example, the experimental and control groups should not differ in whether they think they have been given a drug or not. The control group should thus be given some inert substance which will have no physical effect, so nobody will know whether he has received the real drug or not.) The results of the experiment should be based on enough observations so that they are reliable, and would be similar if the experiment were repeated. They should only be applied under conditions similar to the experimental conditions, and to populations of people similar to the population of subjects.

These conditions are obviously impossible to create. If we want to study the effects of aspirin on people, we cannot start by getting a representative sample of the entire population of the world. Nevertheless, let us consider why the simple experiment has served as an ideal before we look at the ways in which actual research differs from the ideal.

The reason for varying only one thing at a time is easy to see. If more than one is varied, how is it possible to tell which one is responsible for the effects that are found? In the example of the drug study, if those who had taken the drug knew that they had while those in the control group knew that they had not, this second difference between the two groups might be what was responsible for any effects that were found. Even if the drug had no physical effect, people might convince themselves that it was affecting them. Similarly, it is clear that the experiment should be performed on a population of people similar to the one that the results were to be applied to, for it might have different effects on people of different characteristics. The drug, for example, might have quite different effects on diabetics and nondiabetics.

A somewhat more complicated point has to do with the levels of other variables during the experiment. All variables which influence the effect of the independent variable need to be kept at levels typical of the conditions the results are to be applied to. As a simple example, suppose you were studying the effects of large amounts of nitrogen fertilizer on corn. You tested the fertilizer on corn which was well watered and obtained more rapid growth. Then you applied your result by fertilizing corn which was poorly watered and killed most of it. Amount of water is a variable which *interacts* with amount of nitrogen in influencing the growth of corn. In other words, the effect of the nitrogen will depend on the amount of water. (Or it is equally true to say that the effect of the water will depend on the amount of nitrogen.) Failure to keep variables which interact with the independent variable at levels typical of the population which is being generalized to would, in this and many other cases, lead to very great errors. This is perhaps the most common error of research strategy and one which must constantly be kept in mind.

Finally, in our ideal experiment, it was specified that the results should be reliable and not due to chance. What is meant by this? Let

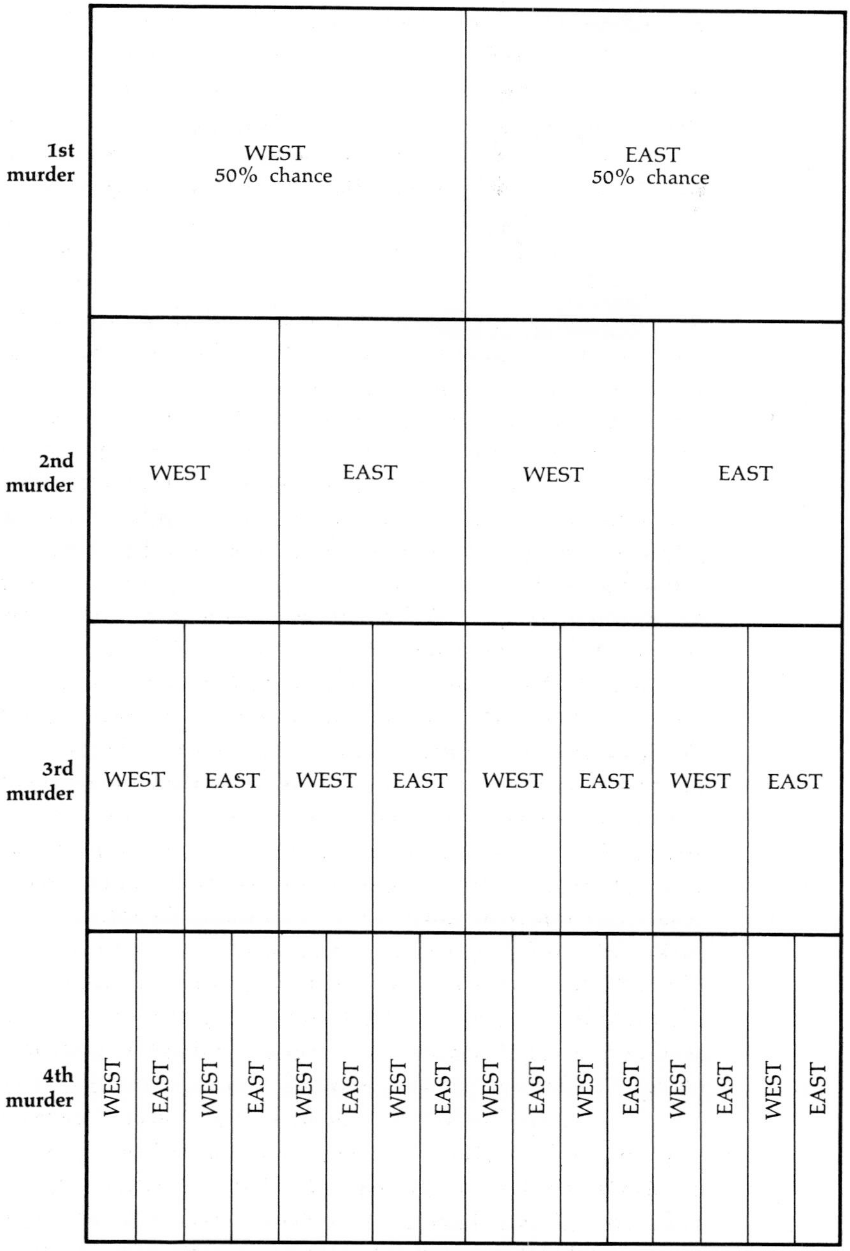

Figure 1 *All four murders being on the east side of the river is one of six-teen equally probable possibilities.*

us look at a very simple example. Imagine that half the population of Smogville lives on the east side of the river and half on the west side. A citizen of Smogville says that it is dangerous to go on the east side, for more murders are committed there than on the west side. In support of this argument, he produces statistics showing that during the preceding year four murders were discovered on the east side of town and none on the west side. Is his theory supported? The question is how many cases you need before you conclude that there is a reliable difference and not just a chance one. First let us see what we mean by *chance*.

By chance we mean all factors which have no relationship to the hypothesis we are testing. Each of the four citizens of Smogville was murdered, presumably for reasons which seemed adequate to the murderer at the time. If these reasons had no relationship to whether the victim was on the east or west side of town, then we may speak of them as chance. This is the sense in which it is a matter of chance to let the toss of a coin decide a question. Physical laws determine whether the coin will come up heads or tails, but these laws have no relationship to the question being decided. We can decide whether the murders support the theory that the east side of town is dangerous by determining how often the observed frequencies would occur by chance, that is, if they were determined by factors unrelated to geography. If that were the case, any given murder would be equally likely to occur on the east side of the river or on the west side. The probability of any given murder being on the east side would be one-half. On the average, half of the murders that were on the east side would be followed by second murders that were on the east side. In more general terms, the probability that two independent events will both occur is the product of their individual probabilities. The probability that all four of the murders will be on the east side simply through chance is (½) (½) (½) (½), or one chance in sixteen. This is illustrated in Figure 1. The evidence for the theory is weak but is some evidence. If we regularly accept theories on evidence this weak, we will be wrong, on the average, one time in sixteen in doing so.

The example we have considered is a very simple one. In most psychological studies, the rules of probability which must be applied to decide whether results are statistically significant are considerably more complicated than those in this example. These statistical models are beyond the scope of this book and will not be discussed. Following the usual convention, unless specified otherwise, results described as *significant* are results which have a probability of less than one in twenty of being a result of chance.

The importance of the simple experiment as an ideal is not that it can be realized, but that deviations from it must be justified. Suppose we were interested in the effects of extreme fear on individuals. We could not take a representative sample of the population of the world, divide this sample into experimental and control groups, and force the experimental group to undergo terrifying experiences! There are, however, a number of ways in which the problem can be approached. In each of them, the ways in which the study differs from the ideal point out additional points which the researcher must establish to make the research valid. Since we cannot sample all cultural groups in our research, for example, we will have to make do with a less adequate sample. In adopting this strategy, we place the burden of proof on ourselves to establish that cultural differences are unlikely to influence our results. If we can show that several radically different cultural groups react similarly, then we are probably justified in generalizing from only a few cultural groups.

Similarly, there are two basically different strategies we can adopt to cope with our ethical unwillingness to subject people to terrifying situations. One is to conduct an experiment using situations which are only slightly frightening. If we adopt this strategy, we must somehow manage to demonstrate that individuals do react to slightly and extremely frightening situations in basically the same way. The other strategy is to study individuals who are exposed to terrifying situations by circumstances beyond our or their control. Tornadoes, earthquakes, floods, fires, and all the ancient human disasters provide natural experiments which can be utilized. If this strategy is adopted, the researcher will find other ways in which his study deviates from the ideal, and he will need to demonstrate that differences of this type are unlikely to influence the results. It is unlikely, for example, that the research team will be ready and waiting at the time and place when disaster strikes. In what ways are the results liable to be influenced by the research being conducted after the fact rather than while the disaster is in progress?

By now it should be clear why there are few *critical experiments* in science, which by themselves provide conclusive evidence supporting or refuting a theory. While the statistical test of one hypothesis in one experiment can be done objectively, the theoretical interpretation of a body of literature remains a subjective matter of interpreting each experiment in the light of all the others. To each of us, reader as well as author, falls the fascinating task of seeking general explanations of apparently contradictory research results.

Summary

The field of psychology has become what it is partly through internal developments and partly through being influenced by major developments in other fields. Philosophy, medicine, and biology have had major influences through the development of associationism, anatomy and later psychiatry, and especially evolutionary theory. As psychology has changed partly in response to these influences, certain theoretical issues have tended to recur. Is the field primarily the study of the normal individual or of how individuals differ from each other? Should it be based on the study of internal experience or external behavior? What are the boundaries separating psychology from other fields? How do heredity and environment interact in influencing human experience and behavior?

The answers given to these recurring questions have changed with the dominance of various theoretical schools of psychology. Structuralism, the first formal school of psychology, was devoted to analyzing the consciousness of the normal adult male into elements through experimental introspectionism. Functionalism, behaviorism, and gestalt theory set different tasks for the field and set about solving them in different ways. Each of these schools may be partially described in terms of the answers it gave to the major theoretical questions listed above.

Despite the recurrence of some theoretical questions, the field of psychology today has little resemblance to the speculative notions about human nature from which it initially developed. During the last quarter of a century especially there have developed large bodies of data which theories must be able to explain if they are to be taken seriously. The theories which have been developed to account for these data differ from earlier commonsense theories through being more explicit, internally consistent, and testable.

One of the main tools of the psychologist in developing a scientific approach to man has been the study of experimental design. The ideal of experimental control is one in which one independent variable is actively manipulated, other relevant variables are controlled, and a dependent variable is accurately measured. Since this ideal is sometimes inappropriate to the study of variables in real-life situations, more complex statistical models for studying the inter-actions of multiple variables must frequently be employed.

Notes and Acknowledgments

1. Köhler, W. *The Mentality of Apes.* New York: Harcourt Brace & Company, Inc., 1925.
2. Klineberg, Otto. *Race and Psychology.* Paris: United Nations Educational, Scientific and Cultural Organization, 1958.
3. Rohrer, J. H. "The test intelligence of Osage Indians." *Journal of Social Psychology,* 1942 (16), pp. 99–105.
4. Olds, James. "Pleasure centers in the brain." *Scientific American,* October, 1956.
5. Locke, John. "An essay concerning human understanding" in Edwin Burtt (Ed.), *The English Philosophers from Bacon to Mill.* New York: Modern Library, Random House, Inc., 1939, pp. 238–402.
6. *Ibid.,* p. 248.
7. Bell, Charles. "Idea of a new anatomy of the brain" in Wayne Dennis (Ed.), *Readings in the History of Psychology.* New York: Appleton-Century-Crofts, 1948, p. 113. By permission of the publisher.
8. Boring, Edwin G. *A History of Experimental Psychology.* (2d ed.) New York: Appleton-Century-Crofts, Inc., 1957, pp. 32–33. By permission of the publisher.
9. *Ibid.,* p. 275. By permission of the publisher.
10. *Ibid.,* p. 294. By permission of the publisher.
11. Darwin, Charles R. *The Origin of Species by Means of Natural Selection.* New York: The Macmillan Company, 1927.
12. Watson, J. B. "Animal education: An experimental study on the psychical development of the white rat, correlated with the growth of its nervous system." Chicago: The University of Chicago Press, 1903.
13. Galton, Francis. *Inquiries into Human Faculty and Its Development.* New York: E. P. Dutton & Co., Inc., 1908.
14. Heidbreder, Edna. *Seven Psychologies.* New York: Appleton-Century-Crofts, 1933, p. 292. By permission of the publisher.
15. James, William. *The Principles of Psychology.* New York: Dover Publications, Inc., 1950.

Hogarth pinx.t   T. Cook & Son sc.t

FRONTISPIECE TO KERBY.

ONE

PERCEPTION

Let us begin our consideration of perception with a mystery. Fix your eyes on some point ahead of you, and have a friend hold up a photograph you have never seen before slightly to the left of your fixation point. Then have him hold it to the right of the fixation point. You will be able to recognize it as the same photograph and will probably not be surprised by your ability to do so. Yet it really is quite a surprising accomplishment, and one which commonsense theories of perception cannot account for. The lens of your eye forms an image on light-sensitive cells in the *retina,* and these *receptor cells* fire when stimulated. The puzzle in your recognizing the photograph is that since it has been moved, none of the same receptor cells are stimulated the second time you look at it. If different cells fire, how do you recognize the photograph as the same?

The commonsense theory of form perception is that there are places in the brain which correspond to places on the retina, so that a triangular image on the retina, for example, would form a triangular image in the visual cortex of the brain. If this were the case, however, you would not recognize the photograph as being the same. At some point in the brain's analysis of vision, the same pattern must be represented in the same way regardless of the part of the retina on which the image falls. The brain is an information-processing system, and it may transform the information into different forms, just as sound may be stored on recording tape in the form of magnetic charges. Location in space does not need to be represented by location in the brain, but may be represented in quite a different way. The actual mechanisms by which we perceive form are just starting to be made clear by recent research.

How the brain analyzes images can be studied in a number of ways, but probably the most direct is to study what makes nerve cells fire. Light falling on the retina of the eye stimulates the sensitive receptor cells there and makes them fire. The nerve impulse from these receptor cells is transmitted through half a dozen layers of the retina and a structure called the *lateral geniculate body* on its way to the many layers of the cerebral cortex of the brain. If the commonsense theory were correct, all these layers would do nothing but transmit the nerve impulse without changing it. At each level along the pathway, one given nerve cell would correspond to one of the receptor cells of the retina and would fire when its own receptor cell was stimulated. If analysis of the image is already being carried out at these levels, however, this will not be the case. If, for example, we analyzed the image in terms of circular patches, then each nerve cell in the cortex would correspond to a particular circular patch on the retina. Stimulation of the receptor cells within that patch on the retina would make the cell in the cortex fire more rapidly. In a program of research lasting over five years, D. H. Hubel and T. N. Wiesel of Harvard Medical School have explored the relationships between retinal stimulation and the firing of nerve cells within the brain.[1] Let us look at their research.

The basic approach of Hubel and Wiesel was to isolate a given cell in the visual cortex and then try out various stimuli to see what increased its rate of firing. Their results indicate that the first analysis of the image which takes place is to view the world as made up of straight lines oriented at different angles. The rate of firing of the typical cell in the cortex is increased by stimulation of receptor cells lying in a straight line on the retina. Furthermore, stimulation of any of the cells surrounding this line of cells slows down the rate of firing. Or, to use slightly different terms, the cortical cell has a central line of cells on the retina which turn it on and surrounding cells which turn it off. There are variations on this pattern: some cells are turned off by the central cells and on by the surrounding ones, and some correspond to edges with an on region on one side of the edge and an off region on the other side of the edge. On and off regions of typical cells are shown in Figure 1–1.

Besides these "simple" cells which responded to lines on the

Figure 1–1 *Simple cortical cells have receptive fields of various types. In all of them the on and off areas, represented by black and gray dots respectively, are separated by straight boundaries. Orientations vary, as indicated particularly at a and b. In the cat's visual system such fields are generally 1 millimeter or less in diameter. (Hubel[2])*

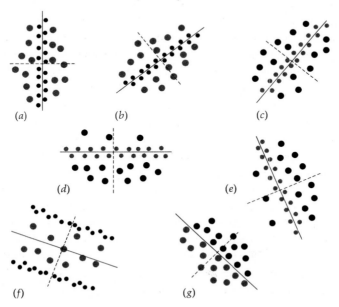

retina, Hubel and Wiesel also found "complex" cells which were most stimulated by moving images on the retina. They were differentially responsive to movement in different directions; some, for example, responded more to stimuli moving from left to right and others to stimuli moving from right to left. Even in the layer of the visual cortex which the nerve impulse enters first, then, considerable analysis of the image is already taking place. Response of a given nerve cell does not correspond to stimulation of one receptor of the retina, but instead corresponds to a line oriented at a particular angle or movement in a particular direction.

That some nerve cells seem to be specialized for the perception of movement should not surprise us, for the perception of movement is a basic function of perception, and one which has a good deal of adaptive significance. An object which is either moving more than its background, such as an animal in a forest, or less than its background, such as a rock in a stream, stands out immediately in our attention. More surprising, however, is research which illustrates that movement of our eyes is necessary for perceiving anything continuously.

Normally our eyes are in constant motion, making not only the large pursuit motions which are easy to see but also constant small tremor motions. While these motions cannot be stopped without damage to the eye, investigators have recently found ways of making a visual image remain relatively motionless on the retina. If a tiny slide projector is mounted to a contact lens, then the lens moves with the eyeball and the image remains at the same point on the retina, as long as the lens does not slip. When this is done, the slide which is projected into the eye is seen normally first, and then fades and reappears, sometimes as a whole and sometimes by parts. The changes in stimulation which eye movements bring are necessary to normal perception.

In looking at evidence on how the brain begins to analyze visual images, we have seen that motion of the image on the retina is necessary to the perceptual process and that the first steps of the analysis involve stationary and moving lines as the units of analysis. A question which arises at this point is the extent to which the process of analysis is learned or innate. Is our brain somehow wired up at birth to analyze vision in terms of lines, or do we learn how to do so on the basis of visual experience? Again, Hubel and Wiesel's research provides some indications.[3] They fitted a baby kitten with translucent contact lenses just as its eyes were beginning to open. The lenses permitted diffuse light to reach the eyes but did not permit pattern vision. When the kitten was sixteen days old, the retinal on and off regions of cortical cells were mapped. The results indicated that the analysis of perceptions in terms of lines is largely inherited, for the on and off regions were quite similar to those in adult cats with visual experience. They were not exactly the same, however. Many of the regions were less clearly defined than in the case of either adult cats or kittens of the same age with visual experience. Either the innate mechanism had started to deteriorate through lack of use, or else it is normally improved through visual experience. The perception of lines may be both innate and learned.

Thus far we have been looking at one of the interesting questions in the area of perception not only because the question of how we perceive form is important in its own right but also because it illustrates several general characteristics of perception. First, we have noted that there is more to explain in perception than there seems to be at first glance. Vision is not a simple matter of transmitting messages from the retina to the brain, but involves complex processes of recognizing objects when they are in different positions, turned at different angles, and differing distances from the eye. Although we take all these things for granted, they imply a complex system of analysis. Second, we have noted that perception is an active process. It involves not the mere passive recording of information, but the active seeking of stimulation through eye movements. Without activity on the part of the eye, the image fades. We shall see that this is only one of the ways in which perception is a dynamic process. Third, we have noted in looking at Hubel and Wiesel's work that information is transformed or coded by the nervous system. What we perceive as location is not represented by location in the brain, but instead in some other way. We have already noted that straight edges are coded by the firing of individual cortical cells in the brain, and not by any straight edge of cells. As Gibson has noted, "There is a naive theory of perception to the effect that the outer world somehow gets into the eye. Almost the first principle the beginning student learns is that nothing gets into the eye but light."[4]

Two of these three aspects of perception will form the remainder of this chapter. We shall be interested in perception as an active organizing process, and we shall consider the ways in which the perception differs from the raw excitation of the sense organ with which it starts. Besides these two major interests, we shall find one persistent question, the old question of heredity and environment. To what extent are our perceptual processes innate, and in what ways must they be learned?

Perception as an Active Process

The most obvious function of the sense organs is the passive recording of stimulation. The eye at first seems to be like a television camera, impartially transforming an image of whatever is before it into electrical stimulation for transmission to a center where the stimulation may be acted upon, and it is this model of passive transmission which was first developed in the field of psychology. At the time when psychology was being transformed from a speculative field into one based on data, it may be that any other conception of the sense organ seemed too mentalistic and subjective. An eye which noted some things and not others would be like a camera with a human operator to direct it, and seemed at first to imply a little man somewhere inside the brain who was interested in some things and not in others. Thus, while attention has usually been an important concept in commonsense theories of psychology, for a considerable time the most generally accepted position among professional psychologists was that all stimuli falling on the receptors would be equally effective as a basis for learning.

We can make many observations, however, which make it seem that we do pay attention to some things and not to others. If we think that we smell smoke, we sniff. If something moves on the right side of our visual field, we turn our eyes toward the right. Similarly, if we ring a bell in the presence of a dog that has not heard it before, the dog will prick up its ears. Motor adjustments of sensory receptors as a way of paying attention to some stimuli and not others are a commonplace aspect of behavior.

Is it only through motor adjustments that we pay attention? There is one well-known psychologist who is in the habit of startling his students by remarking during a lecture, "Don't look now, but your shoes are full of feet." Most people, on hearing this admonition, will suddenly become aware of the sensations arising from the pressure of their shoes. Myriad stimuli bombard our sense organs all the time; we are usually only aware of a few of them at any given time.

This is also demonstrated in what has been called the *cocktail-party effect*. If a person is exposed to several voices speaking at the same time, it is possible to listen to one and filter out the others. There would thus seem to be mechanisms of selective attention other than simply motor adjustments of the receptors.

SLEEP AND WAKEFULNESS

One of the first factors influencing perception is the extent of general alertness of the organism. While the regular alternation between sleep and wakefulness is one of the more striking things which happen to people, it is only recently that sleep has been very extensively studied. Two methodological developments have been important in allowing it to become a major research topic. The first of these, some years ago, was the development of the *electroencephalograph*. This is a device making a record, EEG, of the electrical activity of the brain. With an EEG, it is possible to objectively identify various stages of alertness ranging from deep sleep to excited attention. The second important methodological development was the discovery that eye movements during sleep are an almost perfect indication of dreaming. By recording electrical potentials to the eye muscles and waking the subject during periods of rapid eye movements, it is possible to obtain much more complete accounts of dreams than those which can be obtained if the person is permitted to finish the dream. Because this technique makes possible the production of many dreams under controlled conditions, it promises to provide objective data on psychoanalytic hypotheses on dreaming which had previously seemed to be outside the realm of experimental testability.

One of the earliest findings (1937) to emerge from the use of the EEG was that there are characteristic patterns of electrical activity in the brain of a person who is sleeping, awake but relaxed, or alert.[5] It was thus possible to use the EEG to study what it was that led to sleep or wakefulness, and a series of studies over a period of years gradually made it clear that there is a specific system in the brain which functions to maintain wakefulness. As common sense would suggest, external stimulation produces wakefulness. It does not do so, however, as might be suspected, because of the impulses transmitted to the sensory areas of the cerebral cortex. Instead, other nerve pathways lead into an area which has been named the *reticular activating system (RAS)*, and it is the activity of this structure which enables the organism to wake up. Moruzzi and Magoun[6] showed, for example, that stimulation of the RAS led to alertness, while Lindsley, Bowden, and Magoun[7] demonstrated that cutting the nerve pathways to the RAS led to an unending state of sleep in an animal. Since there are nerve pathways leading to the RAS from higher brain centers as well as from the sense organs, wakefulness may be caused either by external stimulation or by internal thought. Without activation stemming from one of these two sources perception could not take place.

While degrees of alertness in the waking organism may be unambiguously identified from EEG patterns, depth of sleep is more difficult to assess. The stage of sleep at which dreaming takes place has been called *paradoxical sleep*, and the paradox is that in some ways it seems to be the deepest stage of sleep while in others it is most similar to being awake. It is deep sleep in that the muscles are most relaxed and the person is more difficult to awaken than from any other type of sleep. It is similar to waking in the rapid eye movements which take place and in a pattern of electrical activity which is barely distinguishable from that of the waking brain. Dreaming is an activity which is unlike either waking or dreamless sleep in terms of the physical state of the organism. It should thus not be too surprising that different anatomic systems seem to be involved from those involved in waking activation of the nervous system, as demonstrated by Jouvet.[8]

A survey of the rapidly growing literature on sleep and dreaming is beyond the scope of the present book, and the reader is referred to Dement[9] for a comprehensive and readable overview of the area to 1965. Two studies, of which Dement was one of the authors, however, seem sufficiently important to consider at this point. The first considered the relationship between eye movement and the content of the dream.[10] The correspondence between the recorded eye movements and the content of the dreams was surprisingly good, especially for dreams which the subjects felt that they were able to recall accurately. In one example which the authors cited, the subject reported walking up five or six steps and looking up at each one. Five upward glances were clearly evident in the recorded eye movements! These results imply that the technique of waking the subject to record his dreams whenever he shows a rapid-eye-movement stage in sleep will give such accurate accounts of dreams that they may be studied in detail.

The other study implies that dreaming serves important psychological functions for the dreamer.[11] For several consecutive nights, each subject was awakened each time he or she started to dream, kept awake a few minutes, and then allowed to go back to sleep again. The procedure allowed the subject to obtain an almost normal amount of sleep but prevented almost all dreaming. To make sure that any results found were due to not dreaming rather than to being awakened a number of times a night, a control condition was also run. The same subjects were awakened repeatedly when they were not dreaming, disturbing their sleep equally but not interfering with dreaming. How did the subjects react to the dream deprivation? First, it became more and more difficult to prevent them from dreaming as the experiment proceeded. After several nights of dream deprivation, they would go into rapid-eye-movement sleep soon after falling asleep. An even more significant finding was that all the subjects showed deterioration of psychological functioning when they were deprived of dreaming, which they didn't show when they were simply awakened when they were not dreaming. In general, they became tired, irritable, anxious, and unable to concentrate. It is this evidence of the psychological importance of dreaming, combined with the indication that dreams may now be studied in detail, which has led to the recognition that dreaming is an important new area of perceptual research.

SELECTIVE ATTENTION

After the question of whether the organism is generally alert, the next important question in understanding the effect a stimulus will have on it is the extent to which it is paying attention to that stimulus. The definitive experiment illustrating the existence of selective attention was done by Raúl Hernández-Peón, Harald Scherrer, and Michel Jouvet.[12] Their results demonstrated that attention influences the sensations from a sense organ even before they reach the level of the brain. The experiment was an ingenious one done with cats. Recordings were made of electrical activity in each cat's *cochlear nucleus*, a neural center processing auditory stimuli in the brain. First recordings were made while a click was sounded in the cat's ear. Each time the click sounded, there was a large change in electrical potential of the cochlear nucleus. Then the click was sounded while the cat's attention was attracted by a stimulus using some other sense modality. In one case the smell of fish was used to attract the cat's attention, in another the sight of two mice in a jar. In each case, there was much less neural response to the sound of the click. In shifting its attention to a sight or a smell, the cat suppressed the neural activity resulting from the sound. (See Figure 1–2.) We are not only able to shut our eyes when we are listening to something; to some extent we are apparently able to shut off our ears when we are looking at something.

Before this striking confirmation of selective attention from the field of physiological psychology, the controversy over whether it existed or not had centered in the area of learning theory. In Clark Hull's theory of learning, which was the dominant theory in this area

Figure 1–2 *Direct recording of click responses in the cochlear nucleus. (Hernández-Peón, Scherrer, and Jouvet[13])*

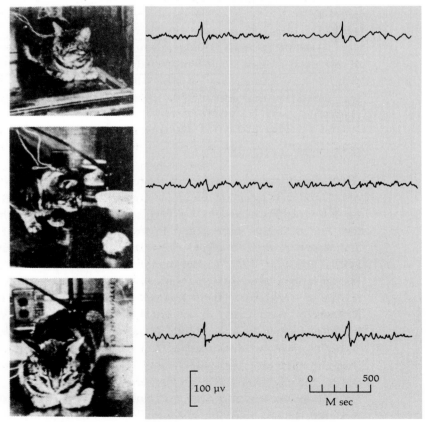

for a period of 20 years, selective perception was minimized. As Woodworth and Schlosberg concisely summarize his position, it was that:

1. All stimuli *acting on the receptors at the moment when a success-ful (reinforced) response is initiated become associated with that response.*
2. Every time *any stimulus is present when a successful response is being initiated, the particular stimulus-response association is strengthened. That is, the building up of an S-R association is a continuous, cumulative process.*[14]

Extensive research on the question, however, failed to support the Hullian position. In one study by K. S. Lashley,[15] for example, rats were first reinforced for choosing the larger of two circles. This step introduced a *set*, or tendency, to respond in a given way—in this case a set to choose the larger figure. A large triangle was then sub-stituted for the large circle for 200 trials, with the rats consistently rewarded for choosing the large triangle and not the small circle. By this time, according to Hullian theory, the rats should have learned to respond positively to triangles, since they had been reinforced for 200 trials for doing so. If, on the other hand, the rats had learned to pay attention to size rather than shape during the early trials, they might not have learned a preference for triangles even if they had been reinforced 200 times for choosing the triangle. Lashley tested what the rats had learned by presenting them with a choice between a triangle and circle of equal areas. The rats showed no preference between the two shapes. As this study and others demonstrated, rats as well as human beings may pay attention to some aspects of a stimulus situation and fail to learn anything about other aspects which they have not paid attention to.

In general, change and difference are the factors which most attract our attention. We notice a stimulus which is moving in front of a stationary background or stationary in front of a moving back-ground. A sound which starts and stops irregularly holds our atten-tion more than one which continues steadily. Similarly, in looking at a picture, we note the complex parts of the pattern which are most irregular and carry the most information rather than looking at straight lines and parts of the pattern which are predictable. Any-thing which contrasts with its background, in color, brightness, loud-ness, or rate, tends to attract attention. There are also differences between different species, however. A few pages from the history of comparative psychology will show the importance of keeping the nature of the organism in mind in securing his attention.

Discrimination learning, or learning to tell a correct from an incorrect cue, was first studied in the rat by use of a simple device patterned after one built by Yerkes around the turn of the century for studying the mouse. The rat ran down a corridor in the middle of a box. After some distance the corridor was divided into right and left sides, from the rat's point of view, by a narrow partition. At this point, where the rat made its choice, the two stimuli were ahead of it, one on either side of the dividing partition. The correct stimulus was sometimes on the left and sometimes on the right so that the problem could not be consistently solved simply by following a right- or left-hand turn tendency. Using this apparatus, it was possible to teach a rat to make a simple discrimination, such as between black and white, although even such a simple problem as this usually took between one and two hundred trials. During this period, the intelligence of the rat was not highly thought of by psychologists.

Probably the main difficulty with the apparatus was that rats are highly dependent upon the sense of smell, and they run with their noses to the ground. The stimulus cards were some distance ahead and slightly elevated—that is, in a position where they were not likely to attract the rat's attention. In 1930, considering this problem, Lashley devised a radically different piece of apparatus, now called the Lashley jumping stand after him. In this device the rat stands on an elevated platform and has nowhere else to go unless it jumps at one of two hinged doors presented some distance in front of it. The stimulus cards are attached to the doors, and only the door with the correct stimulus card is unlatched. If the rat chooses the correct card, the door opens and it finds itself on a feeding table with food. If it chooses the incorrect one, it bumps against a locked door and falls a short distance into a net below. With the invention of this piece of apparatus the intelligence of the rat radically increased, for it was now able to learn in four or five trials what had taken it a couple of hundred before.

Organization of Perception

Not only is perception an active process in seeking out some stimuli and ignoring others; it is active in that the stimuli which are perceived are organized and transformed in the process. When we look at a scene, we do not record all aspects of it impartially the way a camera does. Instead, some central objects stand out clearly in our awareness, while the rest of the scene recedes into a dim background. This phenomenon, which is known as a *figure-ground relationship*, is illustrated when the beginning photographer takes pictures without being aware of the subject's background. While he is only aware of the person he is photographing when he takes the picture, he finds that the tree behind the subject is equally recorded by the impartial camera. A more striking illustration is given by reversible figures, in which first one part and then another is seen as figure, while the other portion becomes background. In one well-known example of such a figure, either a vase or two profiles may be seen depending on whether the white or black part of the design is seen as figure. A more complex example is shown in Figure 1–3. Are the knights marching to the right or to the left?

Even more important processes of organization are those which enable us to perceive objects as remaining the same even though the stimulation we are receiving from them is changing. If you look at a plate lying on a table, you see it as round. Unless you are looking straight down on the table, the image on your retina is not round. Your ability to perceive an object as keeping the same shape, even though the shape of the retinal image is constantly changing, is known as *shape constancy*. Similarly, *size constancy* and *brightness constancy* are names for the perceptual processes which make an object seem to remain the same size even when it is moving farther away and the same color even though brightly or dimly illuminated. These types of organization are very important, for they enable us to perceive a world of stable objects, rather than a wonderland in which everything is constantly changing its size, shape, and brightness. Our perception thus manages to go beyond changing aspects of reality and observe stability behind them. In doing so, however, we make assumptions which are sometimes in error. While we are often unaware of the complexity of perception when it is accurate, the errors we make in interpreting perceptual illusions give some idea of the complexity of the processes which are always involved.

One of the most basic questions of perception is how we perceive objects at all. I look up and see a lamp standing in front of a bookcase. What is it that makes me assign some stimuli to the lamp and others to the bookcase—to perceive objects rather than simply a complex pattern of various hues and brightnesses? Part of the bookcase is hidden behind the lamp, yet I do not see it as ending where

Figure 1–3 (Escher[16])

the contours meet. How do I see the part that is behind the lamp?
These questions were raised by Max Wertheimer, and were basic for
gestalt psychology.[17]

Some of the main factors which gestalt theorists found to cause
stimuli to be grouped together are shown in Figure 1–4. Part *a* illustrates the principle of *proximity*. In the absence of any other factors
of grouping, we will group together things which are close to each
other. Part *a* is thus seen as sets of two dots each rather than just a
row of dots. Part *b*, however, illustrates that other factors such as
similarity can override proximity. Even though the figure has the
same spacing as in *a*, the small dots are seen as going together as are
the larger 0's. The second principle of how we organize our perceptions to see objects is therefore that we will perceive similar stimuli
as going together. In part *c* of the figure, two intersecting lines are

seen. In perceiving these lines, the observer assigns dots near the intersection point to the pattern they are in line with rather than to the one they are nearest. This illustrates the factor of _direction_ in perceptual organization. Finally, part _d_ shows our bias toward perceiving closed rather than open figures. Pairs of lines which are quite far from each other are seen as going together, illustrating the principle of _closure_.

These principles of what stimuli go together usually have _ecological validity_. That is, the nature of the world is such that assigning stimuli to the same or different objects on the basis of these principles will usually lead to accurate rather than inaccurate perceptions of where one object stops and another starts. To return to the example of the bookcase and the light, the different parts of the bookcase are similar to each other in color and are, on the average, closer to each other than they are to the parts of the light. There are few sharp changes of direction of outline of either object, and of course the outline of each forms a closed curve. By using the types of cues which the gestalt theorists have pointed out, I will correctly perceive the bookcase as one object and the light as another.

Where unusual conditions make the cues inaccurate, an _illusion_, or misperception, may occur. Some of the most interesting of these

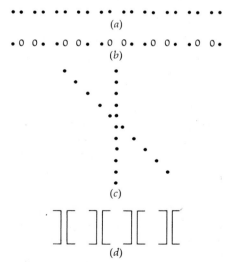

Figure 1–4

illusions were developed in a research program initiated by Adelbert Ames, Jr., and are called the Ames demonstrations in perception.

One of the Ames demonstrations presented by Ittelson and Kilpatrick utilizes playing cards held on stands.[18] By cutting a corner out of a card which is near to the observer so that the cutout just fits the corner of a card that is farther away, the impression is created that the faraway card is obscuring the nearer one. This impression leads to an inaccurate perception on the part of the observer of which card is closer. The illusion is an illustration of the misguided application of the gestalt principle of direction. The observer assumes that the outline of the card with the cutout does not change direction at the point where it intersects the outline of the whole card, and thus incorrectly perceives it as a rectangular card obscured by another rectangular card rather than an irregular card in front of a rectangular card. The observer "sees" the missing part of the card in the same way as I "see" the part of the bookcase which is behind the lamp. Under most circumstances such a perception, which is called a *completion effect*, leads to accurate results. It is quite improbable that the bookcase is actually nearer to me than the lamp but has a cutout to enable me to see the lamp through it. If that actually is the case, I will be in error in completing the bookcase.

The Ames demonstrations also make another important point about perception. Many of our perceptual processes are unconscious. When we look at the cards in Ittelson and Kilpatrick's demonstration,[19] we do not say to ourselves that one card must be farther from us because another card is interposed between ourselves and it. Instead we simply *see* it as farthest away and do not conceive of there being any other possibilities. This type of unconscious interpretation also characterizes social perceptions. Many qualities which we ascribe to other people are our own interpretations of ambiguous stimuli. When we meet someone who has a different interpretation, we do not understand how this is possible because we incorrectly believe that our interpretation is part of the stimulus.

INNATE AND LEARNED FACTORS IN PERCEPTION

Ittelson and Kilpatrick explained the illusions they studied by reference to the past experience of the observer. The observer of the cards which we have been considering has many times observed similar cases of the outline of one object being cut into by the outline of another. On all previous occasions, it has been because the latter object was between him and the former one. It is only the trickery of the experimenter which makes the application of his past experience to the present case incorrect. One way to explain the illusion is thus to say that the observer unconsciously interprets the stimulation as being caused by what has most frequently caused that type of stimulation in the past, or that he makes use of an *assumptive context* based on past experience. Such an explanation considers the interpretations of the subject, and thus his misperceptions, to be based solely on the learning which he has carried out during his lifetime. This is the empiricist theory of perception.

Standing in opposition to the empiricist theory have been nativist theories, which hold that many of the organizational processes in perception are inherited rather than acquired. The gestalt theorists were in this tradition and held that the perception of objects on the basis of cues such as proximity, similarity, direction, and closure is an innate ability of human beings. If this type of explanation is adopted, the validity of the cues we use in making accurate perceptions can be explained on the basis of evolution rather than individual learning. Organisms basing their perceptions on cues which were generally accurate would stand a better chance of surviving than those basing their perceptions on cues which were frequently inaccurate. Evolution would thus favor the use of valid cues, if the cues used are inherited rather than learned.

The question of how much of our perceptual ability is learned and how much is acquired is an old one, and many ingenious approaches to the problem have been devised. The question would be easy to answer if it were possible for a newborn infant to describe what he saw when he first looked at the world. Since this is not possible, a number of other approaches have been devised. First, there are various studies of perceptual learning. If we learn perceptual cues in infancy, then people in radically different cultures who have different experiences with the visual world may learn different things. Similarly, if we use distorting lenses to change the visual world later in life, we should be able to learn different ways of seeing. Along with these learning studies of human beings, there have been studies employing restriction of opportunities for perceptual learning which had to be done with lower organisms. Austin Riesen, for example, studied the effect on chimpanzees of raising them without an opportunity to see.[20] Also, natural experiments with human beings have been employed. Some individuals who were born blind have acquired vision through surgical operations. If the operation took place after the person had acquired language, he was able to describe what he saw when he looked at the world for the first time. Finally, there have been studies of infants which utilized the limited responses an infant can make. Even if he cannot talk, he can move his eyes. In a properly designed experiment, we can learn much from these eye movements. Thus, even though each of the studies has some weaknesses, the results from all of them combined are beginning to tell us how heredity and environment interact in influencing perception.

The result which is emerging from the various types of studies is that the truth is somewhere between the nativist and empiricist interpretations. Some perceptual organization of the type proposed in the gestalt principles above seems to be innate. As we will see when we look at research by T. G. R. Bower, even young infants show completion effects in their perception of objects. Experience, however, plays two essential roles. It not only modifies innate processes, it also is apparently necessary simply to maintain them. The importance of both native and environmental factors is well illustrated in a study by Gordon Allport and Thomas Pettigrew.[21]

Allport and Pettigrew's study employed one of the Ames demonstrations, the illusion of the rotating trapezoid. From most points of view, a rectangle makes a trapezoidal image on the retina. That we still see it as rectangular is an example of shape constancy. In the illusion of the rotating trapezoid, we incorrectly interpret a trapezoidal retinal image as signifying a rectangle when in fact the object itself *is* trapezoidal. In interpreting the object as rectangular, we make incorrect inferences about the relative distances from us to its long and short sides, seeing the short side as farther from us than it is and the long one as nearer. Finally, the effect changes as the trapezoid is rotated by a motor, so that the trapezoid is seen as swinging back and forth when it is actually rotating. The illusion is a compelling one, and even looking at the trapezoid and seeing its shape before the demonstration will not prevent a person having the misperception.

Allport and Pettigrew raised the question of whether we see the illusion because of our lifelong experience with rectangular walls, floors, windows, doors, boards, books, papers, etc., or whether the interpretation of trapezoidal retinal images as rectangles is a result of innate processes of perceptual organization. To investigate this, they compared two groups of Zulu children between the ages of ten and fourteen. One group was composed of rural children who had been raised in a cultural setting where they almost never saw rectangular forms. Their houses were beehive-shaped, with rounded doorways; their fields followed the contours of the rolling land. In their language there was no word for "square" or "rectangular." Many of this group had never seen a rectangular window before participating in the experiment. The other group was composed of urban boys, most of whom attended school and all of whom regularly came into contact with a *carpentered world*. If experience with rectangular forms viewed from an angle is what causes the illusion, then these groups should dramatically differ in what they experienced.

Whether or not a person experiences the illusion depends on the viewing conditions—the illumination and distance of the trapezoid and whether there are objects in the background. There were two main results of the experiment. Under optimum viewing conditions, all children saw the trapezoid as swinging back and forth instead of revolving. Under viewing conditions which were less conducive to seeing the illusion, the urban boys were more likely to see it than the rural boys. The results thus unambiguously rule out a purely nativist explanation. Experience has some effects, or the two groups would not have differed. It is more ambiguous whether a purely environmentalistic explanation is ruled out, for the experiment cannot discriminate between two possibilities. One is that the illusion can be caused by purely innate processes, but may be heightened by relevant experience. The other is that it depends on experience, but experience of a type which all people will have if they have vision. These two possibilities are very difficult to discriminate between by means of research. On the basis of what research there is, the most probable explanation might be that innate organizational processes enable rapid learning on the basis of experiences which all people have to some extent. Two men standing different distances from the observer form a trapezoidal image on the retina if the principles of similarity and closure cause the observer to view them as one object. In a sense, then, anyone with vision has had some experience with rectangles being represented by trapezoidal retinal images.

The theory that people show rapid perceptual learning on the basis of some built-in organizational processes is supported by research with adults seeing for the first time. Many earlier cases of individuals who had been born blind but given sight as adults were collected, but these cases need to be interpreted with caution. The state of medicine was such at that time that the operation which gave the person sight involved removing the lens of the eye, and vision could certainly not be considered normal afterward. Now that corneal transplants make it possible to give some congenitally blind individuals normal vision, the operation is not delayed until an age when the person can report his experiences on obtaining vision. One case, however, has been described by Gregory and Wallace,[22] and a brief account is also included in Gregory's excellent brief book on vision, *Eye and Brain.*[23] Because of doubts whether the corneal transplants would be successful, S. B. was not given them until the age of fifty-two. He was thus able to describe his experiences in detail when the operation was successful. Gregory describes the results as follows:

> *When the bandages were first removed from his eyes, so that he was no longer blind, he heard the voice of the surgeon. He turned to the voice, and saw nothing but a blur. He realised that this must be a face, because of the voice, but he could not see it. He did not suddenly see the world of objects as we do when we open our eyes.*
>
> *But within a few days he could use his eyes to good effect. He could walk along the hospital corridors without recourse to touch; he could even tell the time from a large wall clock, having all his life carried a pocket watch having no glass, so that he could feel the time from its hands. . . .*[24]

The learning was remarkably fast, but then S. B. was really quite unlike a child seeing from birth. He showed much transfer from things which he had already learned by touch, even recognizing block capital letters from having learned them by touch at blind school. On the other hand, he had to unlearn some past experience in coming to trust his new sense. In terms of what we have learned from visual-deprivation experiments with lower organisms, it is surprising that he could learn to see as well as he could. Hubel and Wiesel found that in the cat, the nerve cells which respond to straight lines did not function normally well if the animal had received only unpatterned light from birth.[25]

Turning to direct studies with infants, we find evidence of some quite specific innate factors in perception. Nevertheless, the amount of plasticity in human perception is a good deal greater than in many lower organisms. Sperry, for example,[26] cross-connected the eyes of an amphibian to the wrong sides of the brain, reversing left and right in the animal's vision. This caused the animal to snap toward its right at a fly when the fly was on its left. Such animals never learned to correct for this rearrangement of the nervous system. Despite innate factors, human perception is much more modifiable than that, and human beings adapt fairly rapidly to goggles which distort the visual field or even turn it upside down.[27]

Perhaps the most striking evidence of innate factors in perception is found in Eleanor Gibson's work with the *visual cliff*.[28] Mrs. Gibson wondered why infants did not more frequently fall off cliffs when they were old enough to crawl and wondered if there might be an innate mechanism to prevent this, a mechanism which would obviously have considerable adaptive significance for the species. To find out, she constructed a visual cliff—a level area and drop-off covered by strong glass. An infant placed on the glass can see the drop-off just as if the glass were not there, but if he actually does crawl over it, he will not fall and hurt himself. Using this apparatus, Mrs. Gibson found that young animals including human infants do avoid the cliff. Since they have not had experience of falling off things to teach them this avoidance, it is apparently innate.

Less clearly solely innate, but still very striking, is the evidence that young babies will spend more time looking at a representation of a face than at another pattern, even one made up of the same elements as the face but in a different arrangement.[29] While the preference would at first glance seem to be innate, there are other possibilities. It is impossible to test infants at the moment of birth, and we have seen evidence that perceptual learning may be very rapid. For example, an innate mechanism of paying attention to a moving object might cause the infant to look at faces as soon as he had any control over his eye movements. The preference for the representation of the face might thus be learned, but still learned on the basis of innate mechanisms of attention which would cause this particular learning to take place given normal experience with the world. This explanation would be consistent with what was observed in the case of S. B. when he received his corneal transplants. He did not recognize a face when he first opened his eyes, but it was the first thing that he looked at.

Some of the most significant experiments on perception in recent years are those of T. G. R. Bower,[30] who has come closer than anyone else to solving the old problem of how to investigate the world of the infant. Bower's techniques, which are based on Skinnerian methods of studying learning, make it possible to use subjects between one and two months old in perceptual experiments. Let us look at his procedures and results.

One of the classic ways of studying perception in organisms without language is by using the *equivalent-stimulus technique*. The animal is trained to respond to one stimulus in a given way, and then the extent to which it gives that response to other stimuli is investigated. To find out whether an animal had color vision, for example, it might be trained to respond to a red triangle. If it responded equally frequently to triangles of different colors (but always the same brightness), this would indicate that it did not discriminate color. Bower used this technique with infants, but to do so he needed to find first a response which the infant could make and then some way of reinforcing the response to encourage the infant to make it. (Since the topic of reinforcement will be considered at length in later chapters, it will suffice here to consider a reinforcer to be anything which will increase the probability of an organism making a response.)

The response which Bower taught the infant to make was a turn of the head to the side, which closed a microswitch and recorded the response on a data recorder. This is such a natural response that the infant can give it several hundred times without apparent fatigue. The reinforcer used was the sudden appearance of a woman's smiling face in the infant's field of vision, as in the game of "peekaboo." Infants as young as two weeks old found the "peekaboo" highly reinforcing, and learned to repeat whatever behavior they were engaging in when it was presented. The basic plan of Bower's experiments was thus as follows: (1) A "peekaboo" was given each time the infant turned his head *when the conditioned stimulus was present.* (2) The infant was taught to give the response to the stimulus with the "peekaboo" only presented one time in five on the average. (3) Various stimuli differing from the conditioned stimulus were presented, and the frequency with which the infant responded to each of them was tabulated. The stimulus to which the infant responded most frequently was considered most similar to the conditioned stimulus as the infant perceived the world. These procedures were so effective that they made it possible for Bower to use infants between one and two months old as experimental subjects.

Many of Bower's experiments dealt with size constancy and the perception of depth, topics which will be discussed in the next section. Especially interesting from the point of view of organizational processes in perception, however, was his study of completion effects. A wire triangle which was partly obscured by a metal bar passing in front of it was used as a conditioned stimulus. After training, the infant was tested on a complete triangle, a triangle with a gap where the bar had been, and a triangle above a trapezoid corresponding to the parts of the triangle which had been exposed. If the infant did not show completion effects, he should respond most to one of the incomplete triangles, which corresponded to what he could actually see of the triangle during training. Instead, the infant responded most frequently to the complete triangle. The infant also "sees" the part of the triangle which is obscured by something passing in front of it, even though he is less than sixty days old and has never seen a triangle before! This is certainly striking evidence in favor of some perceptual organization of the type studied by the gestalt theorists being built into the perceptual system by heredity.

The Stimulus Error

Because of the great complexity of the nervous system, we have as yet little understanding of just how information from sensory receptors is transformed as it passes through the nervous system. What we do have, however, is some knowledge of what the mechanisms accomplish. When the neural mechanisms are discovered, there are certain basic properties of perception which they will need to account for. The most important of these are constancy phenomena and depth perception. These have in common that they are cases where the perception matches the distal stimulus rather than the proximal one, that is, matches what is happening in the world rather than what is happening at the level of the sensory receptor. The two-dimensional image on the retina is transformed into a three-dimensional image in experience, and thus corresponds to the three-dimensionality of the real world.

This amazing ability of human senses to correspond to the nature of the real world rather than what is happening at the level of the receptor cell is here called the *stimulus error* after a phrase coined in the days of introspective psychology. At that time the task of the experimental subject was to report his experiences in a raw and uninterpreted form. This required considerable training, for his immediate reaction was to say, "I see a book," rather than to report the apparent color and form of the object without the learned interpretation that it was a book. For an introspector to report the nature of the object rather than the nature of the raw sensation was to commit the *stimulus error*. There is now increasing evidence that one of the most basic characteristics of perception is that it is constructed so as to commit the stimulus error. It is the object which is immediately given in experience, not the sensations on which the perception of the object is based, and Bower's experiments seem to indicate that this is true of young infants as well as adults. The raw sensations which introspective psychology was trying to recapture may never have existed.

One of the simplest of the constancies is the constancy of form when displaced. If you watch a man walk behind something which obscures him from view and then reappear on the other side of it, you have no difficulty in recognizing him as the same individual. Yet entirely different receptors are being stimulated on your retina. Apparently you are able to recognize the same pattern of stimulation regardless of where in your field of vision it is presented. More surprising are size, shape, and brightness constancy, which enable the observer to recognize an object as the same even though the retinal image changes as it moves farther away, is turned at a different angle so that the form of the image changes, or moves between light and shadow. The extent of brightness constancy may be seen from the oft-quoted example that a lump of coal in the sunlight reflects more light back to the eye than a white sheet does under dim illumination. That we still see the sheet as white and the coal as black shows that in brightness, as in form, we respond to relationships. As long as the coal reflects the least light of anything in our field of vision we will see it as black, even though the absolute amount of light reflected may be quite high.

Size constancy is not possible without accurate perception of depth, as is illustrated in a classic series of experiments by Holway and Boring.[31] The subject was required to adjust the size of a disk of light to try to make it the same physical size as another stimulus presented varying distances away. The cues to distance were varied in the various conditions. Viewing the stimuli with either two eyes or one eye, the subject had no difficulty adjusting the standard to the same size as the stimulus presented, even though the different distances involved meant that the retinal images of the two stimuli were different sizes when the adjustment was made. When depth cues were reduced by requiring the subject to view the scene through an artificial pupil, which removed the cues which may be obtained from head movements, then the subject was only partly able to maintain size constancy. Under these conditions, he adjusted the standard to a size which was between the physical size of the stimulus being matched and the size which would produce the same size image on the retina as the stimulus being matched. Some depth cues still remained, however, in the form of reflections from doors spaced along the corridor in which the experiment was conducted. When these cues were removed, the subjects had little idea how far away the stimulus was. Under these circumstances, they adjusted the standard stimulus so that it produced a retinal image approximately the size of that produced by the experimental stimulus, even though the stimuli were different distances away. Without adequate cues to depth, size constancy had broken down.

Holway and Boring's experiments also give indications of some of the cues used in perceiving depth. Two important cues are *binocular parallax* and *motion parallax*. The first is the differences in the images formed by the two eyes because of their being separated in space. It is the cue used in making pictures which appear three-dimensional when viewed through a stereoscope. Two photographs are taken by lenses which are separated just as the eyes are. When one is presented to each eye through the stereoscope, the differences in the two images give a clear impression of depth. Motion parallax, on the other hand, does not depend on having binocular vision. Move your head from side to side while looking at some scene. The objects closest to you are most displaced by the motion, while those farther away almost seem to be moving along with you as you move. This phenomenon also gives strong cues to depth.

Besides these two indicators of depth, however, there are many others which people can use. The artist trying to portray depth in a painting cannot use either binocular parallax or motion parallax in doing so. Yet he is able to make a striking portrayal of depth by using such cues as *linear perspective*, the convergence of contours with distance; *aerial perspective*, increased haziness of more distant objects; and *interposition*, the blocking of part of an object by something appearing in front of it. Perhaps the most complete discussion of these varied indicators of depth is that of Gibson in his comprehensive book *The Perception of the Visual World*. He lists thirteen ways in which depth is indicated, eight of which he regards as clearly important![32]

Of the thirteen possible indicators of depth, which do we really use? There is no one answer to this question, for we use different indicators depending on the circumstances. Size is a cue with known objects, for example, and we will see a ball as farther away if we are told that it is a billiard ball than if we are told that it is a ping-pong ball. Yet when size is overruled by a stronger cue, such as interposition, we will see even known objects as being of unusual size.

Even if different stimuli are used to infer depth under different circumstances, however, it is still possible to raise the question of which ones first signify depth as the organism develops. It seems quite likely that not all of them become effective at the same time, but that depth is first perceived on the basis of some cues and then others are learned on the basis of being associated with them. This was the major question to which Bower turned in his experiments on the perceptions of infants. He conditioned each infant to respond to a stimulus of a given size at a given distance. Then he tested him with a stimulus which was farther away but larger, so that the retinal image was the same size; one that was farther away but the same size; and one that was the same distance away but larger. If the infant had size constancy and could perceive distance, he should respond to both the stimulus which was the same size and the one which was the same distance away, but least to the stimulus which differed in both size and distance. If the infant had neither size constancy nor perception of depth, he should respond most to the stimulus which differed in both size and distance from the training stimulus, for that one projected a retinal image of the same size. Finally, if the infant perceived distance but did not have size constancy, he should respond to the object which was the same distance as the training object. The fourth possibility, of the infant's having size constancy without perceiving distance, was considered impossible on the basis that a perception of distance is necessary to size constancy.

How did the infants respond? They apparently had both size constancy and perception of distance, for they responded both to the stimulus which was the same real size as the training stimulus and the one which was the same distance away as the training stimulus. It was then possible for Bower to see on what cues the perception of depth was based by repeating the experiment with various possible depth cues eliminated. When the cues the infant was using were eliminated, the infant would start responding most frequently to the object which gave the same size retinal image as the training object. On this basis Bower found that young infants made most use of movement parallax in perceiving depth, next most use of binocular parallax, and least use of the types of cues which can be used by an artist in painting a picture. Bower's result is fascinating, for it shows young infants making use of what would seem to be the most complex cues to depth. Despite the complexity of the mental processes which must be involved, the infant perceives depth on the bases of the differences between the views of the two eyes and the ways in which the perception is transformed when the head is moved in space. It is to be hoped that further research will soon reveal how this feat is possible.

Summary

Nothing gets into the eye but light, yet we see objects in a three-dimensional world. This and other amazing achievements of our senses cannot be understood in terms of any simple commonsense theory of perception, but only through viewing perceptual processes as actively organizing information and coding it into different forms. The active nature of perception is apparent in the role of the reticular activating system in bringing about general alertness of the organism. It is apparent in the psychological and physiological evidence of selective attention which has accumulated from the early experiments of Lashley through the recent dramatic experimental work of Her-nández-Peón, Scherrer, and Jouvet. It is perhaps most strikingly demonstrated in the necessity of eye movement to normal visual perception.

The same information is represented in different ways as it passes through the nervous system. The first stage of the coding of visual information has been studied by Wiesel and Hubel in pioneering work on the reactions of single cells in the brain to visual stimulation of the eye. Principles of perceptual organization, such as those of proximity, similarity, direction, and closure, show the results of the coding processes. The use of conditioning techniques in studying the perceptual worlds of very young infants promises to reveal more about the contributions of heredity and environment to perceptual organization.

When an object is viewed from a different angle, the retinal image changes in shape. As it moves farther away and into shadow, the retinal image becomes smaller and less bright. Despite these changes in the image formed in the eye, the perceiver shows constancy phenomena and perceives the object as retaining its size, shape, and brightness. He also sees it as receding in depth although the image on the retina of the eye is two-dimensional. A wide variety of cues may be used in the perception of depth, including linear and aerial perspective and interposition. Recent research has indicated that even young infants make use of motion parallax and binocular parallax, two depth cues which had formerly been thought of as among the most complex and last to be utilized.

Notes and Acknowledgments

1. Wiesel, Torsten N., and David H. Hubel. "Effects of visual deprivation on morphology and physiology of cells in the cat's lateral geniculate body." *Journal of Neurophysiology*, 1963 (26), pp. 978–993.
   Hubel, David H., and Torsten N. Wiesel. "Receptive fields of cells in striate cortex of very young, visually inexperienced kittens." *Journal of Neurophysiology*, 1963 (26), pp. 994–1002.
   Wiesel, Torsten N., and David H. Hubel. "Single-cell response in striate cortex of kittens deprived of vision in one eye." *Journal of Neurophysiology*, 1963 (26), pp. 1003–1017.
   Hubel, David H. "The visual cortex of the brain." *Scientific American*, November, 1963.
2. Hubel, David H. "The visual cortex of the brain." *Scientific American*, November, 1963, bottom of p. 57. By permission of W. H. Freeman and Company.
3. Hubel, David H., and Torsten N. Wiesel. "Receptive fields of cells in striate cortex of very young, visually inexperienced kittens." *Journal of Neurophysiology*, 1963 (26), pp. 994–1002.
4. Gibson, James L. *The Perception of the Visual World.* Boston: Houghton Mifflin Company, 1950, p. 9. By permission of the publisher.
5. Rheinberger, M., and H. H. Jasper. "Electrical activity of the cerebral cortex in the unanesthetized cat." *American Journal of Physiology*, 1937 (119), pp. 186–196.
6. Moruzzi, G., and H. W. Magoun. "Brain stem reticular formation and activation of the EEG." *EEG and Clinical Neurophysiology*, 1949 (1), pp. 455–473.
7. Lindsley, D. B., J. Bowden, and H. W. Magoun. "Effect upon the EEG of acute injury to the brain stem activating system." *EEG and Clinical Neurophysiology*, 1949 (1), pp. 475–486.
8. Jouvet, M. "Recherches sur les structures nerveuses et les mécanismes responsables de différentes phases du sommeil psysiologique." *Archives Italiennes de Biologie*, 1962 (100), pp. 125–206.
9. Dement, William C. "An essay on dreams: The role of physiology in understanding their nature" in Frank Barron et al., *New Directions in Psychology II.* New York: Holt, Rinehart and Winston, Inc., 1965, pp. 135–257.
10. Roffwarg, H., W. Dement, J. Muzio, and C. Fisher. "Dream imagery: Relationship to rapid eye movements of sleep." *Archives of General Psychiatry*, 1962 (7), pp. 235–258.

11. Dement, W., and C. Fisher. "Experimental interference with the sleep cycle." *Canadian Psychiatric Association Journal,* 1963 (8), pp. 400–405.

12. Hernández-Peón, Raúl, Harald Scherrer, and Michel Jouvet. "Modification of electric activity in cochlear nucleus during 'attention' in unanesthetized cats." *Science,* February, 1956 (123), pp. 331–332.

13. *Ibid.,* p. 331. By permission of the American Association for the Advancement of Science.

14. Woodworth, Robert, and Harold Schlosberg. *Experimental Psychology.* New York: Henry Holt and Company, 1958, p. 593. By permission of the publisher.

15. Lashley, K. S. "An examination of the 'continuity theory' as applied to discrimination learning." *Journal of General Psychology,* 1942 (26), pp. 241–265.

16. Escher, Maurits C. "Knights on Horseback." By kind permission of the artist.

17. Wertheimer, Max. "Laws of organization in perceptual forms" in Willis D. Ellis (Ed.), *A Source Book of Gestalt Psychology.* New York: The Humanities Press, Inc., 1955, pp. 71–88.

18. Ittelson, William H., and F. P. Kilpatrick. "Experiments in perception." *Scientific American,* August, 1951.

19. *Ibid.,* p. 53.

20. Riesen, Austin. "Arrested vision." *Scientific American,* July, 1950.

21. Allport, Gordon W., and Thomas F. Pettigrew. "Cultural influence of the perception of movement: The trapezoidal illusion among Zulus." *Journal of Abnormal and Social Psychology,* 1957 (55), pp. 104–113.

22. Gregory, R. L., and J. G. Wallace. "Recovery from early blindness: A case study." *Experimental Psychology Society Monograph,* Cambridge, England, 1963, no. 2.

23. Gregory, R. L. *Eye and Brain: The Psychology of Seeing.* New York: World University Library, McGraw-Hill Book Company, 1966.

24. *Ibid.,* p. 194. By permission of McGraw-Hill Book Company.

25. Hubel, David H., and Torsten N. Wiesel. "Receptive fields of cells in striate cortex of very young, visually inexperienced kittens." *Journal of Neurophysiology,* 1963 (26), pp. 994–1002.

26. Sperry, R. W. "The eye and the brain." *Scientific American,* May, 1956.

27. Kohler, Ivo. "Experiments with goggles." *Scientific American,* May, 1962.

28. Gibson, Eleanor J., and Richard D. Walk. "The visual cliff." *Scientific American,* April, 1960.

29. Fantz, Robert L. "The origin of form perception." *Scientific American,* May, 1961.

30. Bower, T. G. R. "The visual world of infants." *Scientific American,* December, 1966.

31. Holway, A. H., and E. G. Boring. "Determinants of apparent visual size with distance variant." *American Journal of Psychology,* 1941 (54), pp. 21–37.

32. Gibson, James J. *The Perception of the Visual World.* Boston: Houghton Mifflin Company, 1950.

Robert Paul

TWO

SOCIAL
PERCEPTION

Attention

We have seen in the discussion of perception that the human infant has a preference for certain visual objects which either is innate or is brought about very rapidly by innate attention mechanisms. Infants from four days old had clear preference for looking at complex rather than simple patterns and at the pattern of a human face rather than a pattern made of the same features arranged not in a face.[1] Human perception of social events is thus given a head start from birth by innate mechanisms. While these innate factors influence the extent to which an individual will pay attention to various stimuli, learned interests and the characteristics of immediate situations become more important as one experiences more complex social situations. Especially important are the interests and attitudes learned by being a member of a culture, for the individual is likely to be unaware of these cultural characteristics since all his peers show them also. They are well illustrated in an informal experiment conducted by F. C. Bartlett when he was in Swaziland. To test the commonly held notion that individuals without a written language have especially well-developed memories, he asked an eleven- or twelve-year-old boy to carry a message to the other end of the village for him. Although the story was repeated twice to the boy and it took him 2 minutes to cross the village, he made three important omissions in repeating the story, about par for any eleven- or twelve-year-old boy asked to carry a message. The results were quite different, however, when Bartlett asked an individual to recall material in which he had a personal interest and which was of central importance to his culture. In this case he asked a herdsman to describe the cattle his employer had bought during a sale the previous year. His account was as follows:

> From Magama Sikindsa, one black ox for £4;
> From Mloyeni Sifundra, one young black ox for £2;
> From Mbimbi Maseko, one young black ox, with a white brush to its tail, for £2;
> From Gampoka Likindsa, one young white bull, with small red spots, for £1;
> From Mapsini Ngomane and Mpohlonde Maseko, one red cow, one black heifer, one very young black bull for £3 in all;
> From Makanda, one young grey ox, about two years old, £3;
> From Lolalela, one spotted five year old cow, white and black, for £3, which was made up of two bags of grain and £1;
> From Mampini Mavalane, one black polly cow, with gray on the throat, for £3;
> From Ndoda Kadeli, one young red heifer, the calf of a red cow, and with a white belly, for £1.[2]

The herdsman had been with the owner during the sale and had driven the purchased cattle back to the main farm, but there they had been separated and the animals sent to different sections so that the herdsman had not even seen them again. Only two details of his description were different from the owner's written records. One price was wrong by ten shillings, and the color of one animal was inaccurate. What Bartlett had demonstrated was not the superior memories of individuals without written language but the importance of interest to learning. If the Swazi herdsman could come to the United States and test the memories of some inhabitants, he would probably be amazed at our ability to tell at a glance the difference between a Buick and a Pontiac and to remember what make of car each of our friends owns.

Cultural attitudes and emphases thus have pervasive effects on what individuals pay attention to, and these emphases are often reflected in the number of terms that a given language has referring to some phenomenon. Thus the English speaker usually simply calls snow snow and a camel a camel, while the Eskimo has a multitude of terms in his language to refer to snow of various consistencies and the Arab has an equally great number of words to refer to camels of various types and in differing conditions. Besides these cultural emphases, however, there are also effects of long-standing interests of individual members of a culture. The skiing enthusiast distinguishes many types and conditions of snow even if he is an English speaker, and what is merely an automobile engine to most of us may be classed as a 2-liter double-overhead-cam engine with two dual-throat carburetors, five main bearings, and wedge-shaped combustion chambers by the interested individual.

The effects of differences in interest on the perception of other people are nicely illustrated in a study by Tajfel and Wilkes.[3] The individuals participating in the experiment were asked to make judgments of other people. Before doing this, however, the importance of various personal characteristics to them was investigated by having them give spontaneous descriptions of other people. Just as an artist might describe a person without ever mentioning his political beliefs, while a politician might describe his political attitudes without mentioning his physical characteristics, the attributes used by the judges in the spontaneous descriptions were used as an indication of the importance they ascribed to various characteristics. It was then predicted that in making ratings of others, individuals would make more extreme judgments on the characteristics which were important to them and less extreme judgments on the characteristics they did not care about.

This prediction also is in accord with everyday observations. If we do not care about the characteristics of horses, automobiles, or faces, we may describe a champion jumper as looking like an average brown horse, a classic Bugatti as an old-fashioned car, and the "Mona Lisa" as a woman smiling. The prediction was supported by the data, although more clearly for unfavorable ratings than for favorable ones. The judges tended to see more good characteristics than bad ones in the people they were judging and were especially reluctant to ascribe unfavorable characteristics except on attributes which were important to them.

As well as having certain sets as a result of his personal beliefs and beliefs in which he participates as a member of a culture, a person may have a readiness to perceive a certain aspect of the stimulus situation which is developed either by instructions or by the preceding stimulus situations. A number of different experiments illustrate this point. Rees and Israel,[4] using anagrams, and Luchins,[5] using a water-jug problem, showed that solving a number of problems which can all be solved in the same manner made it more difficult for subjects to see other ways of solving later problems even though they were not aware that they had learned any generalized procedures in solving the early problems. These studies thus show the importance of set on perception and make the equally important point that we are not necessarily consciously aware of all the processes involved in perception.

The importance of unconscious processes in perception is actually one of the older findings of experimental psychology, although it is only recently that the controversy over the use of *subliminal* cues in advertising has brought much publicity to the matter. In 1910 C. W. Perky[6] reported an experiment which is still worth mentioning today. She had subjects look at a white ground-glass screen and try to imagine a series of common objects. Without the subjects' realizing it, slides of these objects were at times faintly projected on the translucent screen from the other side. Since the objects were presented in unusual positions in the slides, it was possible to tell from the subjects' descriptions that they had actually been perceiving the slides. The images were so faint, however, that they thought they were only imagining them. The inability of individuals to tell the extent to which their perceptions reflect the actual situation they are perceiving and the extent to which they represent an unconscious interpretation based partly on their own ideas and experiences is a central fact in understanding the relation of the individual to the world, and one to which we shall return repeatedly in the remainder of the book.

We see, then, that the individual's perception of the world is selective, and what he pays attention to is governed by interests, cultural beliefs, and attitudes of which he may or may not be aware. Even those things he does pay attention to, however, are not merely

passively recorded, but are organized and, through being organiz
distorted. To these topics we must now turn.

Organization of Perception

As was seen in the last chapter, perception does not take place
through the passive recording of stimuli. Even the perception of
physical objects involves the active organization and interpretation
of information. As this is also the case with social perception, merely
knowing the extent to which an individual pays attention to various
aspects of a stimulus situation will not enable us to predict how he
will perceive that stimulus situation. It is also necessary to understand how he organizes his perceptions. While an individual's idiosyncratic characteristics and those he shares with other members of
his culture do influence what he pays attention to, they probably have
a greater impact on his perception by influencing how he organizes
and interprets those stimuli to which he does attend.

Consider, for example, how the perception of an item of behavior may be influenced by the social context in which it occurs.
Some behavior is so strongly called out by the nature of the situation
that it does not seem to an observer to reveal anything about the
person who is engaging in the behavior. If someone is solemn at a
funeral or sociable at a convention, it does not seem to reveal much
about him, for our society calls for those behavior patterns in those
situations. The person who is jovial at a funeral or solemn at a convention, on the other hand, may be seen as behaving in response to
his own inner needs rather than the requirements of the situation.

The expectations which a given society has about how a person
shall behave when he occupies a given position in that society are
referred to as the *social role* associated with that position. Each member of the society occupies many roles, so that a man is expected to
behave differently as an employee, as a husband, and as a friend.
(Sometimes the different roles are incompatible with each other, a
problem which will be discussed in a later section of the book.) Because there are these social expectations about how individuals should
behave when they are playing various roles, we may speak of behavior as being "in role" or "out of role." In-role behavior is behavior
which is expected by society from a person who is holding a given
position, while out-of-role behavior is behavior which is either op-
tional or forbidden to a person playing that role.

The differing perceptions which individuals have of behavior when it is in role or out of role are well illustrated in a study carried out by Jones, Davis, and Gergen.[7] The hypothesis they tested was the one suggested above, that out-of-role behavior would be perceived as revealing much more about the person doing the behaving than would in-role behavior.

The subjects in the experiment listened to tape recordings of individuals purportedly trying to obtain jobs as either astronauts or submariners. These two occupational roles were described in such a way that it was seen as being appropriate for submariners to be friendly, sociable, and conforming people, but for the astronauts to be independent and prefer solitude. It was thus in-role behavior for the potential submariner to stress his sociability or for the potential astronaut to stress his independence. The opposite combination, of independence from the submariner applicant or sociability from the astronaut, was out-of-role behavior.

As was predicted, the subjects listening to the interviews saw the out-of-role behavior as more revealing about the individuals. The potential submariner who stressed his sociability in the interview was seen as predictably answering that way in a sensible attempt to get the job, while the potential astronaut who stressed his sociability was perceived as revealing his true preferences. These perceptions markedly influenced ratings by the subjects as to how conforming and how sociable the individuals being interviewed really were! Furthermore, the greater impact of out-of-role behavior on the ratings was not due to its being better remembered. Probably partly because role expectations were used to guess at behavior which was imperfectly remembered, the in-role behavior was in fact better remembered than the out-of-role behavior. Cultural differences thus influence perception by influencing the interpretation of behavior, as well as by causing differences in attention.

The importance of the perceiver's interpretation of the nature of the stimulus was first investigated by Asch. Earlier research had indicated that statements were more favorably evaluated when attributed to highly thought-of authors than when attributed to authors that the subjects thought less highly of. Asch reasoned that this phenomenon of prestige suggestion might be due to a different perception of the meaning of the statement when it was attributed to a different author. He thus asked his subjects to respond to statements, not by rating how much they approved of them, but rather by saying in their own words what they thought the statements meant. One of the statements used was Jefferson's "I hold that a little rebellion, now and then, is a good thing, and as necessary in the political world as storms are in the physical." When the statement was correctly attributed to Jefferson, the subjects interpreted "a little rebellion" as meaning something quite mild—social change, political agitation, or any change in political opinions. On the other hand, when the statement was incorrectly attributed to Lenin, rebellion was generally taken to mean full-scale armed revolution and the qualifying "a little" was ignored. An occasional person correctly denied that Lenin made the statement, and quite a number paraphrased it without interpretation. The exact number of subjects responding in each of these ways is shown in Table 2–1.

Asch obtained similar results for other statements attributed to their actual authors and to other individuals. Especially interesting is his use of a labor plank from the Republican Party Platform of 1944. The experiment was run during the 1944 presidential campaign, using largely Democratic supporters as subjects. The plank reads as follows: "The Republican party accepts the purposes of the National Labor Relations Act, the Wage and Hour Act, the Social Security Act and all other federal statutes designed to promote and protect the welfare of American working men and women, and we promise a fair and just administration of these laws."

Of the subjects who were told correctly that the plank was from the Republican Party platform, 85 percent felt that the plank contradicted the principles of the party and 2 percent denied that the statement could come from the Republican Platform. Of the subjects who were told incorrectly that the statement was from the Democratic Platform, 83 percent felt that it was a straightforward expres-

Table 2–1 *Frequency of different forms of interpretation (in percent)*

	JEFFERSON ($N = 71$)	LENIN ($N = 56$)
Assimilation of "rebellion" to "agitation," etc.	59	9
Assimilation of "rebellion" to "revolution"	1	68
*Literal duplication**	39	23

* Included in this category were a few protocols the interpretation of which was ambiguous.
SOURCE: Asch[8]

sion of the policy of the party. In this experiment, the reinterpretation of the meaning of the statement involved a good deal of speculation about the motives of the authors of the statement.

Some reactions to the plank are shown in Table 2–2. In these responses we can clearly see the search for an interpretation which will make sense in terms of other beliefs. The image which the subjects had of the Republican party at that time made them question that the plank represented the party's true position on the issue. They thus interpreted the statement either as a concession to political reality at the time or as a blatant attempt to get votes, depending upon their political preferences.

Table 2–2 *Perceptions of the Republican plank*

IDENTIFIED AS REPUBLICAN PLANK	IDENTIFIED AS DEMOCRATIC PLANK
After the Democratic party has fought to improve the lot of the working man, the Republican party claims to accept its purposes.	*I trust this statement because it was the Democratic administration which brought about the passage of these acts, and has been enforcing them justly.*
We, the Republican party, have to accept these laws, since labor has organized to enforce them.	*If the Democratic party made this statement, they were sincere about it. But I do not like the word "accepts.". . .*

SOURCE: Asch[9]

Our perceptions are thus organized around what we consciously or unconsciously expect from our past experiences. An interesting technique devised by Allport and Postman[10] makes possible the study of how this organization takes place. Working in the context of civilian reaction to the Second World War, Allport and Postman were concerned to try to find the underlying dynamics of the transmission of the rumors which were so prevalent at that time. To do this they created rumors in the laboratory, by describing a scene to one subject and having him pass on the description to the next, who in turn relayed it to a third, and so on. As the description was transmitted, it was both shortened and distorted until it formed a concise and sloganlike whole which could be learned by rote by the remainder of the subjects. Three closely related types of distortion were found.

The first type of distortion, *leveling*, simply consisted of dropping out large numbers of details in the original description. By the time the message had been repeated four times, only about a quarter of the original details remained. As many details were dropped out, those remaining were *sharpened*, or further emphasized. This emphasis took many forms, including changing the description from the past to the present tense, exaggeration of size, and multiplication of the numbers of individuals involved. Sometimes the experimenters were able to detect the basis of selection of the items which were emphasized, as when police officers made a police officer in one scene the central figure in the description or when a group of women chose the dresses worn by a group of women to become central to their description. In other cases, however, items seemed to be selected either because they were mentioned early in the description and thus easily remembered or because they employed unusual and attention-getting words such as "remonstrating," or for reasons which were unclear to the experimenters.

The final type of distortion, *assimilation*, is perhaps the most interesting, for it involves changes to make the details of the story fit in better with the expectations of the subject and with the central theme of the story. In one battle scene, for example, people were reported as being killed, an ambulance became a Red Cross station, the amount of devastation was increased, and a chaplain was introduced. Assimilation to linguistic habits and to stereotypes was also found—a drugstore in the middle of a block became a corner drugstore, and a razor portrayed in the hand of a White man speaking with a Negro jumped in the telling into the Negro's hand in over half the experimental groups!

The fact that earlier information serves as a basis for the organization of information obtained later is one of the reasons why the initial impression which one person makes on another is especially important. In this area also, Solomon Asch[11] did pioneering research. In several experiments he presented subjects with a list of adjectives and asked them to write a description of the person portrayed by them. In one of the experiments two groups of subjects were given identical lists except that the order of the adjectives differed. In one list the favorable adjectives were presented first, while in the other the first part of the list was predominantly unfavorable. The majority of subjects who read the favorable adjectives first portrayed the individual in a basically positive manner, though with minor faults, while those who read the unfavorable adjectives first portrayed him as having basic deficiencies of character, though with some good points. In both cases the interpretation of what was meant by the adjectives later in the list depended upon the impression formed by the first part of the list.

The extent to which later impressions are dominated by the first impression depends to some extent on how basic the information obtained in the first impression is. Even where the initial information is not especially important, it, along with the last items of information obtained, tends to be better remembered than information in the middle of a message or series of encounters because of what is called the *serial-position effect* in learning. Where the initial information is trivial, however, it does not exert much influence on the organization of later information. In one variation of Asch's impression-formation experiment he presented identical lists of adjectives to the two experimental groups, except that the opposite of one of the adjectives was included in the second list. When the opposites dealt with what most people consider a central personality trait—for example, the words "warm" and "cold"—they considerably influenced the interpretation of the other adjectives. When they dealt with more peripheral traits—for example, the words "polite" and "blunt"—they exerted much less influence.

Since the publication of Asch's initial work, a number of similar studies have been done amplifying our knowledge of the impact of the initial impression. Especially interesting are studies by Luchins and by Kelley. Luchins[12] made the experimental task somewhat more realistic by presenting the subjects with descriptions of an individual's behavior instead of a list of adjectives for them to form their impressions from. Two paragraphs were used, one describing activities of someone named Jim that would lead one to feel that he was a friendly individual and one that would give the impression that he was unfriendly or shy. Sometimes one of these paragraphs was presented first and sometimes the other, so that the extent of the influence of the first versus the second part of the message could be assessed.

Luchins, like Asch, found a strong *primacy effect*, that is, the impressions the subjects formed of Jim were generally more influenced by the part of the description they read first. Two other findings are noteworthy, however. One is that the primacy effect could be overcome simply by warning the subjects that they should not jump to conclusions but wait until all the evidence was in. There is some difficulty about interpreting this finding, because it is possible that since experimental subjects are generally motivated to please the experimenter, they may have given more weight to the latter part of the description simply because they thought this is what the experimenter wanted. Since other studies using different techniques have reached similar conclusions, however, we may conclude that merely knowing that there are two sides to a story will reduce the amount we are influenced by the side which we happen to hear first.

The other interesting finding of Luchins is that many of the subjects formed hypotheses about Jim in order to try to explain the apparent inconsistencies in his behavior. In Allport and Postman's terms, these subjects did not assimilate their later to their earlier impression of Jim, but instead sharpened the contradictory impression and sought meaning in it. Some of the descriptions which were given are as follows:

> *Jim is essentially a friendly person and when he appeared to act in an unfriendly manner it was because he was tired, or because he had an unhappy day at school, or because the girl was a bore. . . . Jim is awkward with girls and needs to mix more. Jim acts differently at different times because he is at an awkward stage of development or because he is an adolescent, a moody person, a "nervous person," "a queer fellow," or a "strange character."*[13]

Kelley's experiment[14] is interesting because he managed to introduce considerably more realism into it. Essentially it was a replication of Asch's original experiment using "warm" and "cold," but done in a naturalistic setting. What Kelley did was have a friend deliver a guest lecture in each of two sections of a class. The friend had rehearsed so that he could give exactly identical lectures in the two sections. Kelley also gave identical introductions to the speaker in the two sections, except that he was introduced either as a very warm person or as a rather cold person. Questionnaires administered to the students at the end of the lecture revealed that they not only evaluated the lecturer more highly when he had been introduced as warm but also thought that he had given a better lecture and that they had learned more from it.

The results were similar, but not identical, to those which would be predicted from the well-known *halo effect* in judgment. According to this effect, if we know something good about a person, we are likely to perceive him as having other good characteristics, while if we know something unfavorable, we are liable to see other unfavorable things also. This effect, however, does not predict one important aspect of Kelley's results: Characteristics which are thought to be related to the favorable thing known about the individual are more influenced than things which are not seen as so related. A person who is introduced as warm is more likely to be seen as friendly than he is to be seen as, for example, a good high jumper.

The halo effect, incidentally, is a common source of error in the grading of student papers when the students are already known by the instructor and their names are on their papers. Without being aware of bias, the instructor may read more meaning into the ambiguous answer of a student who has done well in the past than he does into the similarly ambiguous answer of a student who has previously done poorly. The manipulative student is thus well advised to do well on the first quiz in classes where essay exams are used and names are not concealed during the grading process.

Perhaps, however, students do not need such obvious advice. Jerome Singer summarizes the results of a study he carried out on the manipulative strategies of students as follows:

> In an exploration of the utility and efficacy of manipulative strategies of behavior, positive relationships were found between Machiavellianism and students' grades with abilities held constant. Further studies demonstrated that this relationship held for men but not women, and that there were birth order effects: later-born males are more successful as manipulators than first-born. Evidence was presented that women also use manipulative strategies, those of physique. Again, there were birth order effects: there was a significant partial correlation between attractiveness and grades for first-born girls but not later-borns. It was then found that first-born girls are more concerned about their physique and are more apt to make themselves noticed.[15]

We have been looking at some of the ways in which our expectations influence our perceptions. Even where they do not influence what we perceive, they may influence our evaluation of it. Again an animal experiment offers a good illustration. Bananas are highly preferred food for monkeys and chimpanzees; carrots and lettuce are less highly preferred although still readily accepted. If one of these foods is placed under a tin cup within sight of one of these animals, it will take it out and eat it as soon as given the chance, even if it is temporarily taken out of sight of the cup during the intervening time. Tinklepaugh[16] tested the animals' reaction to an unexpected food substitution. He placed a banana under the cup within sight of a monkey. Then, while the monkey was out of sight of the cup, he removed the banana and substituted a piece of lettuce or carrot. When the animal was brought back, it went straight to the cup and lifted it. Instead of eating the piece of lettuce as a monkey normally would, it reacted with signs of surprise and frustration, engaging in such bits of behavior as continuing to search for the banana and shrieking at the experimenter. How satisfactory a reward is here clearly depends upon what level of reward is anticipated. This topic has been studied in human beings under the name *level of aspiration.*

If you ask a person attempting a task on which varying levels of success are possible what he hopes to achieve, he will usually cite a level just a bit higher that his usual performance. The bowler who usually rolls around 150 does not generally strive for a perfect game of 300 but does hope that he will manage to achieve around 175. His degree of satisfaction with his score depends, not on its absolute magnitude, but rather on its relation to his level of aspiration—the score he is trying to attain. A student who usually gets C's may be quite happy to get a B, while a student who usually achieves A's may be extremely disappointed to do so.

While the level of aspiration for familiar tasks is usually slightly higher than the typical performance, this is not always the case. What is the reaction of the student who usually gets D's and F's, the bowler who rolls around 90, or the golf player who goes around in a bit over double par? Such habitual failure to reach any normal level of aspiration may be very threatening to the individual. While it is always possible to give up bowling or golf, the student may not have reached school-leaving age. How may he protect himself from habitual experiences of failure? Two quite different methods may be employed. By setting an extremely low level of aspiration, failure may be avoided by exceeding aspirations. The student who aspires to obtain D's will, in all probability, succeed in doing so at least some of the time. The opposite strategy will also work, however. By setting an unrealistically high level of aspiration, failure may not be experienced when the goal is not attained.

Consider the poor golfer who is about to drive his ball. A realistic level of aspiration for him might be to hit it at least 50 yards without going out of bounds. Even achievement of this level is not very satisfying in comparison with the performance of others, however. He may thus decide that this is the time he is going to belt it 200 yards right down the center of the fairway. Failure to achieve this goal is not really experienced as failure, for it does not really make a person a bad golfer that he is unable to hit the ball 200 yards down the middle every time. The golfer, by concentrating on the fact that he did not hit the ball 200 yards, may avoid paying much attention to the fact that he did not hit it 100 yards either. The experience of failure is not as great as it would have been if he had been trying to hit it 100 yards. Thus studies by Jucknat[17] and by Pauline Sears[18] have indicated that schoolchildren who have habitually experienced failure tend to set either a very high or a very low level of aspiration.

Theories of Distortion

In the previous section we have seen that our perceptions of persons and events are greatly influenced by our expectations. The greatest distortions probably occur in situations which involve strong emotional reactions, and a number of fairly technical theories have been proposed to predict the types of distortion which will occur and the conditions under which they will be found. In this section we shall look at *balance* theories, which are primarily perceptual in nature, saving until later the discussion of *conflict* and *dissonance* theories, which are more theories of motivation.

Perceptions are balanced which seem internally consistent and reasonable to the perceiver, and imbalanced, or unbalanced, if they seem unreasonable. Some examples of imbalanced perceptions are:

> He always imitates people he dislikes.
> He hates q because q is similar to his friend o.
> He avoids people he likes.[19]

Another is

They think exactly alike so they hate each other.

The essence of balance theory is that imbalanced perceptions will be distorted by the perceiver to make them more balanced. In order to make precise predictions, however, it is necessary to note what perceptions will be imbalanced and how they will be modified. Let us look at some theories which attempt to do just that and some experiments in which their predictions have been tested out.

The single work which probably did the most to stimulate research on balancing was Fritz Heider's *Psychology of Interpersonal Relations.*[19] This work considers quite exhaustively the relations which may exist between two persons, two persons and an impersonal object, or three persons. (As we shall soon see, the basic ideas have since been extended to deal with perceptions of larger social systems.) Heider dealt primarily with two kinds of relationships that could exist between people. Sentiment relations, as the name implies, exist where they have positive or negative feelings toward each other.

Unit relations exist where two people are bound together in some way such that they must interact with each other; marriage and business partnership would be two examples. Sentiment relations are consistent when they are reciprocal. Thus if George is seen to love Ann and Ann to love George, nothing seems inconsistent to the perceiver about this idyllic relationship. If, however, George is seen to love Ann but Ann to hate George, the relationship is puzzling and seems to need further explanation. Why should George persist in his affection for a person who makes it clear that she despises him? Imbalanced relationships of this type are thought to involve a strain toward becoming more balanced both in reality and in the eye of the perceiver. That is, in the real world, it is thought that George would in time come to repent of so futile a passion, unless of course his suit were successful and he managed to inspire in Ann feelings similar to his own. More important for our purposes here, it is thought that a person observing such an imbalanced relationship between George and Ann existing over a period of time would modify his perception of the relationship so as to make it more symmetrical: Maybe Ann really loves George, and it is just an unfortunate personality characteristic of hers that makes her degrade him in public. Perhaps George does not really love Ann, and it is just a fear of women that makes him want to play the romantic role of the rejected lover.

Sentiment relationships are thus balanced when they are symmetrical and imbalanced when they are asymmetric. This means, of course, that if Ann and George both hate each other, there is no inconsistency in the relationship from the point of view of the perceiver, unfortunate as it may be in other respects.

Unit relationships are consistent when they are accompanied by positive sentiment relationships. George and Ann mutually hating each other may be a perfectly consistent state of affairs taken in itself, but if it is accompanied by their being married to each other, it again becomes a situation which doesn't seem to hang together. Again, the person perceiving such a situation is likely to modify his perception to make it more internally consistent, in this case probably by deciding that the couple must really care for each other despite having their little difficulties.

A strain is also involved if two persons bound together by positive unit and sentiment relations have markedly different sentiments toward some other person or object of importance to them. Returning to our unfortunate lovers, let us imagine that they are now both mutually in love and married to each other. The situation may still be less than perfect if Ann loves children while George detests them, Ann is a devout Christian while George is an athiest, or Ann is a Republican while George supports the Peace and Freedom Party. Important differences such as these exert strong forces toward attitude change, so that in the last example it is likely that Ann and George will either converge in their political beliefs, meeting perhaps about the middle of the Democratic party, or will turn away from political interests in order to avoid the area of disagreement. We shall return to this point, and some experimental evidence on it will be cited, when we come to the consideration of reference groups.

Useful as Heider's model is in making predictions about two or three people, it says nothing about larger social systems. Cartwright and Harary[20] thus extended the basic ideas to permit analysis of perceptions of larger social systems, using directed-graph theory as an analytic tool. Without going into the details of the theory, it may be summarized briefly as follows: Letters are used to represent people and things, and arrows between them to represent unit and sentiment relations. If A likes B, this is represented by an arrow of one color pointing from A to B. If dislike is being indicated, a different color is used. Unit relationships are viewed as always being positive, and are indicated by two-headed arrows, since if A is a unit with B, B is also a unit with A. A _semicycle_ is then defined as a collection of lines which when followed successively, regardless of the direction of the arrow, enable return to the point of origin. (A given arrow may participate in any number of semicycles.) The sign of the semicycle is the product of the signs of its component arrows, so that, for example, a semicycle composed of A liking B, B disliking C, and C disliking A would have a positive sign. The amount of balance in the system is the number of positive semicycles over the total number of semicycles in the system. From this it may be seen that our example of A, B, and C would be perfectly balanced if they comprised the total social system and there were no other relationships among them, since the only semicycle would be positive. Cartwright and Harary's system is useful in permitting an approximation of the amount of imbalance in various systems, but has limited usefulness because of two weaknesses. One is that it assumes that all relationships represented are equally important, which may not be the case,[21] and the other is that the variety of means of reducing imbalance makes prediction difficult for large systems.

One of the earliest and best studies of cognitive balancing was

Newcomb's study of the acquaintance process.[22] With a persistence in doing the impossible which is necessary to obtain good data, Newcomb obtained a rooming house and let students live there rent-free in return for participation in his research. Two groups of seventeen male transfer students were studied, each for an entire academic year. The students were selected so that at no time in their lives had any two of them lived in the same city, thus guaranteeing that they had never met.

Newcomb's theoretical model was basically similar to Heider's and dealt with the relationships between two persons and the other persons, objects, and events of importance to them. It was assumed that a balanced state of affairs existed when persons who were attracted to each other had similar orientations toward other things of importance to them or when two persons who disliked each other had different orientations. (The entire model is more complex than this, for predictions of what changes in perception would take place under conditions of imbalance involved considerations of what new information individuals were likely to acquire given the differences between their perceptions of events and the real nature of these events as known to the experimenters.) On the basis of this model, Newcomb predicted that early in the acquaintance process people would assume that the individuals they were attracted to were similar to themselves but that since the early attraction was based on so little information, it would be unlikely that this would actually be the case. Furthermore, he predicted that as the students came to know more about each other, their friendship choices would change until ultimately they would be most attracted to those individuals who were most similar to themselves in their basic value orientations.

These predictions were supported by the data on both groups studied. At the very start of the year, the students chose as friends the men who had been randomly assigned them as room-mates or who lived in the neighboring room, a result which could be predicted from Heider's unit relationships. After a few weeks went by, they managed to obtain superficial information about each other, and friendship choices were at least partially predictable from similarity in such matters as which college of the university they were enrolled in, their religious preferences, and whether they came from a rural or urban background. It was only after a considerable period of time that their friendship choices became predictable from their choices on the value-orientation questionnaires they had filled out before meeting each other.

Two aspects of these results are striking. The first is that it was possible for the experimenters to predict, from the value questionnaires given before the experiment started, which men would be friends by the end of the year. (The prediction was not perfect, of course, but it was much better than the subjects' own predictions early in the year of who their friends would be later on.) The other is that the predictions of distortion of perception made from the model were confirmed—early in the year the subjects thought that the men they chose as friends were similar to themselves in attitudes and values, even though in fact there was only chance similarity; that is, they were no more similar than the men who were not chosen. Newcomb's study thus provides strong evidence in favor of a balance model of perceptual distortion, with results which were obtained in a naturalistic setting and which were confirmed by repetition of the study a second year.

From Newcomb's study we can see that people will distort their perceptions in order to make them more consistent or balanced but also that there are constant pressures to make people modify their perceptions to reflect reality accurately. Even though it is possible to believe that the person you have chosen as a friend agrees with you when you do not know much about him, ultimately he will give you clear indications of whether he does or not. Cognitive balancing is thus not something which is done at one time in an informational vacuum; instead it is carried on constantly, using and responding to new information. Just as new information may lead to more imbalanced perceptions and require new balancing, the way in which the system can be most easily balanced makes us more or less willing to accept new information. A well-known study by Rosenberg and Abelson provides a good illustration of this point.[23]

Rosenberg and Abelson used three groups of subjects and confronted them with a role-playing situation. Each subject was asked to imagine that he was the manager of a large Midwestern department store and that as a department-store manager he had the following beliefs: (1) naturally, he strongly positively valued keeping the level of sales by the store as high as possible, (2) he was aware of research evidence showing that displays of modern art in department stores made the customers buy less, (3) he had been told that Fenwick, the manager of the rug department, intended to put up a display of modern art there, yet (4) he believed that Fenwick was a good department manager and had increased the volume of sales of the rug department in the past. Now intuitively we can see that this already presents the subjects with an imbalanced set of perceptions. If Fenwick is generally good at increasing sales, why does he now intend to do something which is bad for sales? There would not be any problem if Fenwick were generally a bad department manager—the store manager would simply fire him and get someone better. This situation, however, is not so simple.

To be useful, a balance model must not only say that a given situation is imbalanced but also point out how it is imbalanced and predict what perceptual distortions the imbalance will lead to. Rosenberg and Abelson's model does do these things, but to see how it does them, we must leave Fenwick and the rug department for the moment and look at the model. It is simpler than Heider's, for Rosenberg and Abelson do not distinguish between unit and sentiment relations, but instead class all the relations between cognitive elements (persons or things thought about) as simply positive, negative, or null. Positive relations would include not only liking and supporting but also things which Heider would classify as unit relations—using, being equivalent to, or bringing about. We can thus see that there is a postive relationship between, for example, Fenwick and modern art. Negative relations include the opposites of these terms, such things as disliking and hindering. There is thus a negative relationship between modern art and sales. Null relations are simply the lack of either positive or negative relations.

Because our description of the experimental conditions must now become somewhat complex, let us look first at only the first of the three experimental groups and use its instructions to illustrate a simple method of diagraming *cognitive structures*, or views of the relationships between persons and things. The subjects in the first group were told, in addition to the four things already mentioned, that they (1) liked modern art, and (2) liked Fenwick. Let us see how this situation may be represented.

Any cognitive structure must be represented through the eyes of the person who sees things that way, in this case the subject in his role as department-store manager. Whether this person has positive, negative, or null relations with the various objects is represented by where they are placed on a vertical scale ranging from positive at the top to negative at the bottom. Since the subjects in the first group have positive views of all three social objects—sales, modern art, and Fenwick—all three are placed at the top of the scale.

Figure 2–1 *(Brown[24])*

Lines between the various objects labeled p for positive or n for negative may then be used to represent the relations, other than null, existing among the objects (see Figure 2–2).

Rosenberg and Abelson's theory states that cognitive relations are balanced where (1) concepts of identical sign are positively linked, and (2) concepts of opposite sign are negatively linked. The theory predicts that structures will be balanced by making the smallest number of changes which will achieve this state of affairs. Let us see then what is predicted for the first experimental group. If the subject, in his role of department-store manager, convinced himself that Fenwick did not really plan to display modern art, the system would still be unbalanced because positively valued modern art would be negatively linked to sales and Fenwick, both of which are also positively valued. Trying out the various other possibilities, we see that there is only one way in which the structure can be balanced by making only one change. If the manager convinces himself that modern art

Figure 2–2 *(Brown[25])*

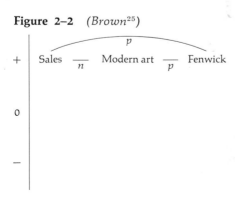

is really good for sales, then all the items will be positively valued and all will be positively linked, a state of perfect balance.

The basic design of the experiment was as follows: Each of the three experimental groups was given a slightly different state of affairs to imagine, so that while all were unbalanced, each could be most economically balanced in a different manner. All three groups were then exposed to messages, with each message designed to balance most economically the cognitive system of one of the three experimental groups. It was predicted that if people strive to balance their beliefs with the fewest possible changes, then it should be found that the subjects in each experimental group would be most receptive to the message which could do this for them.

We have already looked at the cognitive structure of the first group. Those for the second and third groups are shown below. It may be seen that the second group differs from the first in that here the manager does not like modern art. The cognitive structure may be balanced by making only one change if that change is to decide that Fenwick does not intend to display modern art. In the third group the manager does not like either Fenwick or modern art. This structure may be balanced by deciding that Fenwick is not actually a good salesman.

All subjects were given three communications. The art-sales (AS) communication contended that art displays actually increase sales volume; the Fenwick-art (FA) communication maintained that Fenwick did not plan to display modern art; the Fenwick-sales (FS) communication indicated that Fenwick had not maintained sales volume in the rug department. As predicted, the subjects in the first group reacted most positively to the AS message, those in the second

Figure 2–3 (Brown[25])

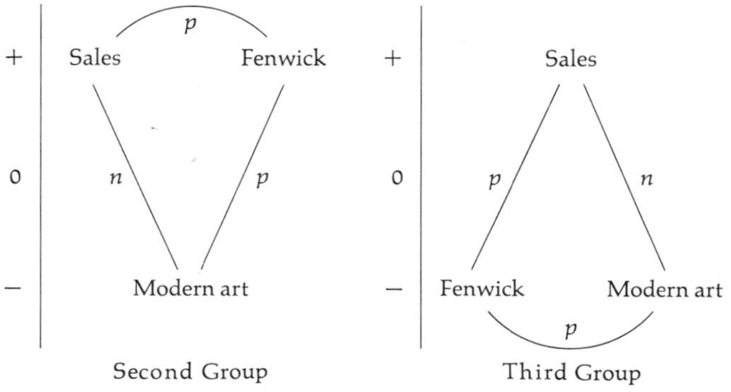

Second Group

Third Group

group to the FA, and those in the third group to the FS. This study, like Newcomb's, was repeated a second time with similar results, thus providing strong evidence that people are most easily persuaded by being told what they want to hear and that balance theory can point out what it is that they want to hear.

Rosenberg and Abelson's study not only supports balance theory but also makes the equally important point that balancing does not occur automatically. Subjects in the first group, for example, did not decide at the beginning of the experiment that art displays were good for sales, but waited until they had some evidence to justify that belief. Balancing thus takes place by making us selectively perceive our environment, accepting the evidence which will bring about a more balanced state and ignoring that which would increase our imbalance. In a complex and ambiguous social world, evidence in favor of most points of view can be found. Where it cannot, Rosenberg and Abelson propose other means of coping with imbalance. One of these is to redefine or differentiate one of the concepts. The subject might divide Fenwick into a competent part and an incompetent part by deciding that while he is usually good at selling rugs, he is a fool for modern art and this leads him into occasional lapses of judgment. Or he might differentiate modern art, deciding that some of it is extreme and drives away customers but some of it is good and a good man like Fenwick will choose the latter kind. The final method of coping with imbalance is to stop thinking and avoid being aware of inconsistent beliefs at the same time. This idea is similar to the psychoanalytic concept of repression, which we shall take up in the next chapter.

It would be pleasant to stop thinking about balance theory at this point, leaving ourselves with a positive view of balance theory and some evidence to support it. Unfortunately we would be ignoring some of the evidence if we did so. In a repetition of the Fenwick study which differed only slightly from the one described, Rosenberg and Abelson investigated not only the receptivity of the subjects to the three messages but also the extent to which they actually managed to achieve a balanced state after hearing them. While a majority of the subjects in the first experimental group did so, only a very few in the second and third groups achieved balanced cognitive structures, and a majority of those who did so achieved different structures from those which were predicted. These results are not as damaging to balance theory in general as they look at first glance, for the failure of the subjects in the third group to achieve balance is easily explained. Rosenberg and Abelson's initial conception of the cognitive structure which they had created in all the subjects ignored the fact that a unit relationship, in Heider's terms, exists between the manager and Fenwick—as a department manager, Fenwick stands just below the store manager, who depends upon him for running a major part of the store. Thus the subjects in the third group would not actually achieve a balanced state even if they did convince themselves that Fenwick was a poor department manager, for negatively valued Fenwick would still be tied to the subject by a unit relationship.

This explanation, however, does not account for the subjects in the second group deviating from expectations. Although it is not parsimonious to use a separate explanation for this, one is hinted at in the description of the experimental procedure. Some subjects had to be rejected at the start of the experiment because after receiving the original instructions, they saw modern art as being good rather than bad for sales. It may be that while the subjects had no prior views about Fenwick, they liked modern art and were unable to forget this belief in trying to play the required role, making the cognitive structure of some members of the second group more like that of the first group.

From this single study it would be difficult to conclude that there was any validity to balance theory. Different types of studies have been done, however, with different types of methodological weaknesses. In Chapter 8, on values, attitudes, and opinions, we shall look at a study by Rosenberg, in which attitudes are changed under hypnosis and changes occur in other attitudes as predicted by balance theory. That study suffers from the weakness that not all people can be hypnotized, so that a selected sample is used. Nevertheless, the frequency of positive results in tests of balance theory using different methodologies shows the value of further investigation of this theoretical framework. It is to the rapidly growing research literature on balance theory that the student must turn to assess the complexity of the issues involved.

Summary

Social stimuli are even more ambiguous than physical stimuli, and their perception is influenced by the context in which they occur. A statement has a different meaning when it is spoken by one person than when it is spoken by another, and the same behavior seems to signify different things when enacted by different people. A number of classic experiments have demonstrated how the interests of the perceiver, his previous knowledge about the person being perceived, and even the order of presentation of the same information may influence the initial perception of a stranger.

Rumor transmission provides a convenient method for studying the changes which inadequate perception and memory make in stimuli. These changes may be crudely described by saying that the stimuli are reproduced as if they had been compared with expectations; some differences exaggerated and other differences ignored. Allport and Postman described the process as involving leveling, sharpening, and assimilation.

In recent years a number of theories of perceptual organization have attempted to describe the ways in which perceptions change to become more internally consistent. The first of these balance theories was that of Fritz Heider. Heider proposed that for a perceptual system to be balanced, sentiment relations should be reciprocal and unit relations should be accompanied by positive sentiments. Individuals with positive bonds between them should have similar sentiments toward things of importance, while those with negative relations should have divergent sentiments. These simple principles have been extended by other theorists and applied in a wide variety of experimental situations. Balance of perceptions may be restored in several ways, and some novel results have been accurately predicted by the theories.

Notes and Acknowledgments

1. Fantz, Robert L. "The origin of form perception." *Scientific American,* May, 1961.
2. Bartlett, F. C. *Remembering.* London: Cambridge University Press, 1932, p. 250. By permission of the publisher.
3. Tajfel, Henri, and A. L. Wilkes. "Salience of attributes and commitment to extreme judgments in the perception of people." *British Journal of Social and Clinical Psychology,* 1963 (2), pp. 40–49.
4. Rees, H. J., and H. C. Israel. "An investigation of the establishment and operation of mental sets." *Psychological Monographs,* 1935 (46), no. 210.
5. Luchins, A. S. "Mechanization in problem solving: The effect of 'Einstellung.'" *Psychological Monographs,* 1942 (54), no. 248.
6. Perky, C. W. "An experimental study of imagination." *American Journal of Psychology,* 1910 (21), pp. 422–452.

7. Jones, Edward E., Keith E. Davis, and Kenneth J. Gergen. "Role playing variations and their informational value for person perception." *Journal of Abnormal and Social Psychology*, 1961 (63), pp. 302–310.
8. Asch, Solomon E. *Social Psychology*. Englewood Cliffs, N.J.: Prentice-Hall, Inc., 1952, p. 424. By permission of the publisher.
9. *Ibid.*, pp. 433–434. By permission of the publisher.
10. Allport, Gordon, and Leo Postman. *The Psychology of Rumor*. New York: Holt, Rinehart and Winston, Inc., 1947.
11. Asch, Solomon E. "Forming impressions of personality." *Journal of Abnormal and Social Psychology*, 1946 (41), pp. 258–290.
12. Luchins, Abraham S. "Primacy-recency in impression formation" in Carl Hovland (Ed.), *Yale Studies in Attitude and Communication*. Vol. I. *The Order of Presentation in Persuasion*. New Haven, Conn.: Yale University Press, 1957, chap. 4.
13. *Ibid.*, p. 47. By permission of the publisher.
14. Kelley, H. H. "The warm-cold variable in first impressions of persons." *Journal of Personality*, 1950 (18), pp. 431–439.
15. Singer, Jerome E. "The use of manipulative strategies: Machiavellianism and attractiveness." *Sociometry*, June, 1964 (27), p. 128. By permission of the author and publisher.
16. Tinklepaugh, O. L. "An experimental study of representative factors in monkeys." *Journal of Comparative Psychology*, 1928 (8), pp. 197–236.
17. Jucknat, M. "Leistung, Anspruchsniveau und Selbstbewusstsein." (Untersuchungen zur Handlungs und Affectpsychologie: XX. Edited by Kurt Lewin.) *Psychologische Forschungen*, 1937 (22), pp. 89–179.
18. Sears, Pauline S. "Levels of aspiration in academically successful and unsuccessful children." *Journal of Abnormal and Social Psychology*, 1940 (35), pp. 498–536.
19. Heider, Fritz. *The Psychology of Interpersonal Relations*. New York: John Wiley & Sons, Inc., 1958, p. 180. By permission of the publisher.
20. Cartwright, D., and F. Harary. "Structural balance: A generalization of Heider's theory." *Psychological Review*, 1956 (63), pp. 277–293.
21. The student should refer to Knox, Robert E. "The components of cognitive balance." Unpublished dissertation presented to the Graduate School of the University of Oregon, 1963.
22. Newcomb, Theodore M. *The Acquaintance Process*. New York: Holt, Rinehart and Winston, Inc., 1961.
23. Rosenberg, M. J., and R. P. Abelson. *Attitude Organization and Change*. New Haven, Conn.: Yale University Press, 1960.
24. This method of illustrating cognitive structures was developed by Roger Brown in his excellent discussion of balance and dissonance models entitled "Models of attitude change" in *New Directions in Psychology*. New York: Holt, Rinehart and Winston, Inc., 1962.
25. Adaptation of fig. 9 from "Models of attitude change" by Roger Brown from *New Directions in Psychology*, by Roger Brown, Eugene Galanter, Eckhard H. Hess, and George Mandler. Copyright © 1962 by Holt, Rinehart and Winston. Adapted and reproduced by permission of Holt, Rinehart and Winston, Inc.

THREE

PHENOMENA & THEORIES OF LEARNING

The general acceptance of John Locke's theory that the mind is a blank slate and that all knowledge comes from experience made learning the central issue of psychology. If all that we know and all that we are result from learning, then the principles governing that learning are the most basic statements which can be made about human beings. In the effort to discover such principles, psychologists have engaged in half a century of intensive research.[1] While this research has not resolved all the controversies about learning, it has built up an agreed-on body of data which any theory must be able to explain. In this chapter we shall first look at this body of data and then turn to the paradox that there should be disagreement about theory while there is agreement on the data which the theories are trying to explain.

The earliest work in an area is not always the most influential, and the two men who were most influential in shaping the development of modern learning theory were not the first to publish extensive work in the field. They were preceded by Ebbinghaus's extensive research on memorizing, which will be discussed in Chapter 7, and by a number of less extensive research programs. Nevertheless, it was with the research of Ivan Pavlov and Edward L. Thorndike that learning theory began. Although Pavlov was the elder of the two men, their work in psychology was roughly contemporaneous, for Pavlov came into the field rather late in his life. His first interest was in physiology, and in that field he won the Nobel Prize for his work on digestion. The work on digestion, however, led into the field of psychology, for what a person or animal thought influenced digestive processes. That a dog would salivate if food was placed in its mouth was a simple reflex. That it would salivate if it heard its food pan rattle was more difficult to explain. To this phenomenon of "psychical secretion" Pavlov turned his attention. In doing so, he was encouraged by knowledge of Thorndike's doctoral dissertation, published in 1898.[2] From 1903 to 1928, and regardless of the distractions of the Russian Revolution taking place around him, Pavlov published papers on the training of reflexes in dogs.

Pavlovian Conditioning

Pavlov's basic training situation was as follows: For any reflex act, there is a stimulus which will always call out the reflex response. A puff of air on the eyeball, for example, will cause the response of blinking the eye, or the stimulus of a bit of meat powder in a dog's mouth will cause the response of salivating. Using this latter response, Pavlov called the meat powder the *unconditional stimulus*, because its effect was invariant and did not depend on training. Besides this unconditional stimulus to salivation, there are other stimuli which may or may not cause the response depending on what training the animal has had. A stimulus of this type, which does not call out the response initially but will after the animal is trained, Pavlov called a *conditional stimulus.* (A conditional stimulus is also frequently called a *conditioned stimulus,* for this is the way the term was translated from the Russian in the earliest translation of Pavlov's work.) To train the animal, Pavlov first presented the conditional stimulus—the ringing of a bell, for example—and then the unconditional stimulus—such as the meat powder. After a while, the dog learned to salivate when it heard the bell without the meat powder being presented at all. This is the first stage of acquisition, or learning, of the conditional response.

Pavlov's theoretical conception of acquisition has frequently been interpreted as a theory of stimulus substitution, as if the animal learned to give the same response to the conditional stimulus as it had previously given to the unconditional stimulus. That conception is often shown diagrammatically as in Figure 3–1. In that figure R stands for response, *UCS* for unconditional stimulus and *CS* for conditional stimulus.

Stimulus substitution, however, is not complete. As Woodworth and Schlosberg have pointed out, the dog does not start to eat the buzzer instead of the meat. It is thus valuable to distinguish between the response given to the unconditional stimulus and that given to the conditional stimulus by calling them the *unconditional response* and the *conditional response,* respectively. This distinction is shown in Figure 3–2, where UCR stands for unconditional response and CR for conditional response.

Even if the animal does not completely substitute the conditional stimulus for the unconditional stimulus, in the sense of giving all the same responses to the two of them, there is one phenomenon which does seem to show a surprising amount of stimulus substitution. This is the phenomenon of *higher-order conditioning.* Suppose that the dog is trained to salivate to a buzzer. Then on a number of trials the following sequence of events is followed: a light is turned on, then the buzzer is sounded, but no meat powder is placed in the dog's mouth. After a number of trials, the dog will learn to salivate

Figure 3–1

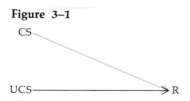

CS ⟶ CR

UCS ⟶ UCR

Figure 3–2

to the light presented alone *even though the light has never been paired with the meat powder.* In first-order conditioning, then, the animal learns to give a response to a new stimulus by that stimulus being paired with an unconditional stimulus for the response. In second-order conditioning, the animal learns to give the response to a stimulus by that stimulus being paired with another conditional stimulus which has come to call out the response through learning. While animals are not capable of higher orders than secondary, human beings may show even higher orders of conditioning.

Let us look at an example with human beings rather than dogs. If a person learns to salivate when he sees tables set for dinner, this is the first-order conditioning. If after learning this he gets a job working in a restaurant where he salivates at seeing the tables set even though he cannot eat at them, he is showing the effect of the past conditioning. If the restaurant has a player piano and he learns to salivate whenever he hears a player piano even though he never was allowed to eat in the restaurant where he heard it, that would be second-order conditioning. If he then went to a theater where a person wore a bowler hat and played a player piano and thus learned to salivate when he saw only a bowler hat, that would be third-order conditioning. Higher-order conditioning may not show great logic in this subject, but it is certainly a feat of learning. As we shall see later, it plays a crucial role in some motivational theories.

What happens if, after conditioning, the experimenter repeatedly gives the conditional stimulus without ever giving the unconditional stimulus, ringing a bell without ever giving meat, for example? As might be expected, eventually the dog stops salivating when it hears the bell. This process of losing the conditional reflex is called *extinction.* It is different from what we usually mean by forgetting, for it depends on the presentation of the conditional stimulus without presentation of the unconditional stimulus. Forgetting takes place much more slowly. If the dog is simply not presented with the conditional stimulus, it will show very little forgetting of the conditional response over a period of years.

Pavlov's first two principles of learning were thus a principle of acquisition and a principle of extinction. They have been concisely paraphrased by Skinner as follows: "The approximately simultaneous presentation of two stimuli, one of which (the 'reinforcing' stimulus) belongs to a reflex existing at the moment at some strength, may produce an increase in the strength of a third reflex composed of the response of the reinforcing reflex and the other stimulus." This was called Type S. "If the reflex strengthened through conditioning of Type S is elicited without presentation of the reinforcing stimulus, its strength decreases."[3]

The second principle is somewhat ambiguous as to whether the conditional reflex is lost or merely inactivated by extinction. That it is not completely lost is demonstrated by one of the more interesting phenomena of conditioning, *spontaneous recovery*. If an animal is first trained and then the response is extinguished, this will make it stop giving the response to the conditional stimulus. To use the concrete example of salivation, the dog stops salivating to the bell when it is repeatedly presented without being followed by meat powder. If, however, the animal is then given a period with no further training, the next time the bell is rung it will salivate again. It has spontaneously recovered the conditional response, indicating that the response had not been permanently lost, but at least partially inactivated.

The reappearance of the conditional response may at first glance seem puzzling. If what is learned during extinction is to not respond, however, then spontaneous recovery is consistent with other observations on learning and forgetting. Forgetting takes place most rapidly with recently learned material. Since the conditioning took place earlier than the extinction training, what was learned during conditioning is not being forgotten as rapidly during the rest period. The learning to not respond which took place during extinction, on the other hand, is very recent learning, and much of it will be forgotten during the inactive period. Thus it is quite reasonable that the tendency to not respond might be the stronger of the two at the beginning of the inactive period, while the tendency to respond might be the stronger at the end of it. This is illustrated in Figure 3–3.

Learning would not have much significance if it only showed its effects in situations exactly the same as those in which it took place. If being stung by a bee did not make us beware of wasps and yellow jackets or if being stung while standing up did not make us also cautious while sitting down, then learning about the world would be

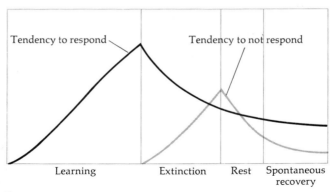

Figure 3–3

a more painful experience. As Pavlov's work showed, learning is applied in situations somewhat different from those in which it took place. A dog trained to salivate to a bell of a certain pitch will show *initial generalization.* That is, without further training it will also salivate to a bell of a different pitch. This is generalization because the animal responds as if it had generalized about bells, responding in the same way to all of them. The generalization is not complete, however. The more different the pitch of the new bell is, the less probable it is that the dog will salivate to it, and the less saliva it will produce if it does. While an animal may show generalization initially, it may also be trained to discriminate—to respond differently to similar stimuli. If one stimulus is followed by the unconditional stimulus while another similar stimulus is not, the animal will learn to give the conditional response to one and not the other.

Thorndike and the Law of Effect

In Pavlov's principles of learning, the word "reinforcement" is used in speaking of the strengthening of a conditional reflex. As used there, it means simply the strengthening which takes place when the unconditional stimulus is presented immediately after the conditional stimulus. The use of the term in that way is rather confusing, because Thorndike's work had the result of giving this term a more specific meaning—the bringing about of a state of affairs satisfying to the organism. Furthermore, theorists who believed with Thorndike that some type of reward was necessary to learning came to be called *reinforcement theorists*, while those who believed with Pavlov that contiguity, or stimuli being presented together, was sufficient for learning were called *contiguity theorists* or *nonreinforcement theorists*. Thus Pavlov, although he spoke of reinforcement, meant contiguity by it and was a nonreinforcement theorist! He assumed that his animals learned because conditional stimuli and unconditional stimuli were presented together. For a more hedonistic view of animals, let us turn to the work of E. L. Thorndike.

Thorndike's research is a good example of the impact evolutionary theory had on the development of the field of psychology. His work started with the major question which evolutionary theory raises—what is the relationship between the intelligence of animals and that of human beings? To answer this question he studied a variety of different animals, as well as adults and children. While some earlier authors had seen animals and human beings as similar because animals were so clever, Thorndike saw human beings as following essentially the same simple laws of learning as lower organisms. For him, learning was a blind and irrational process involving random variation of behavior and selection of what chanced to prove successful. Even the mechanism of learning, then, was similar to the mechanism of evolution. It did not imply direction, but simply variation and survival.

While Thorndike employed a wide variety of experimental situations, he is best known for his studies with cats in puzzle boxes. A hungry cat was imprisoned in a box which could be opened by pushing against a lever protruding into the box. The first time the cat was placed in the box, it engaged in various acts—spitting, clawing, exploring, etc. Eventually by chance it would happen to trip the lever, the door would open, and it would be released to find a plate of food waiting for it. The next time the animal was placed in the box, it would tend to do the same thing it was doing when it released the catch the first time. If, for example, the first time it had been sniffing in a corner and had backed into the lever, it would tend to go to the corner, sniff, and back up. Since it would not exactly repeat its former behavior, however, it might miss the lever and fail to be released. With repeated trials, its behavior became more and more stereotyped and its release more and more rapid.

The cat in the box seemed to Thorndike to be typical of much real-life learning in several ways. It did not involve reflexes which are invariably called out by certain stimuli the way Pavlov's experiments did, but instead responses which are normally emitted by the animal in the random variation of its behavior. Nor did the emitted behaviors need to be learned, the way a motor skill such as a golf swing does. They were normal and routine behaviors of the animal. Finally, the solution to the problem was not obvious from an examination of the situation, but was arbitrary from the animal's point of view. The experiment was thus a situation similar to that of a rat learning to go to where garbage is. Where the garbage is kept is purely arbitrary from the rat's point of view, but once the rat happens upon the garbage, it can go there again without learning any new motor skills. Much human learning also seems to be arbitrary. There is no logical connection, for example, between an object and the word which stands for it.

On the basis of arbitrary learning situations such as that of the cat in the puzzle box, Thorndike first formulated two basic laws of learning. As his research led him into new areas, he abandoned one of these principles and modified the other, as well as adding a number of subsidiary principles. The principle he abandoned was one which has caused untold misery to students, the *law of exercise*. This principle, which was widely accepted at the time when Thorndike wrote, held that practice made perfect regardless of the nature of the practice. Thorndike rejected this principle on the basis of experiments such as one by Trowbridge and Cason reported in 1932.[4] They had subjects practice drawing lines exactly 3 inches long without ever being told how long the lines were which they had drawn. Under these circumstances, there is negligible improvement with practice. Thorndike eventually concluded that practice only causes a significant amount of improvement through the operation of the other basic law, the *law of effect*.

Thorndike was one of the earliest stimulus-response psychologists. What was learned, according to his theory of learning, was a connection between a stimulus and a response. The law of effect stated that when a response was followed by a state of affairs satisfying to the animal, then the connection between that response and the stimulus which had preceded it would be strengthened. Conversely, if a response was made to a stimulus and was followed by an annoying state of affairs, then the connection between the stimulus and that response would be weakened. Reinforcement, in the form of satisfying or unsatisfying consequences for the organism, stamped in or stamped out correct or incorrect responses.

How is it possible to tell whether a state of affairs is satisfying or annoying for an animal? Thorndike's answer was that if the animal tries to continue it, it is satisfying, but if the animal tries to terminate it, it must be annoying. On hearing this answer, some critics complained that the law of effect was circular and said nothing: Why does an animal learn to do something? Because it is satisfying. How do we know that it is satisfying? Because he does it!

Careful inspection of this argument, however, will reveal its weakness. In judging whether a state of affairs is satisfying or annoying to an animal, its immediate reaction is used. Thus a person might conclude that a rabies shot was annoying to a cat because it struggled to get away when it received one. That observation, however, would be quite independent of observations on learning. After conclusions were drawn about what was satisfying or annoying to the animal, it would still be equally possible that what it learned would be dependent on its emotional state, as Thorndike proposed, or would depend solely on what responses it made, as Pavlov's theories would suggest. Rather than being circular, the law of effect proposed the very important principle that the same conditions which governed how the animal reacted to the immediate situation would govern what, if anything, it would learn.

In the first formulation of the law of effect, Thorndike saw reward and punishment as having equal and opposite effects. Reward stamped in the correct response, and punishment stamped out the incorrect one. On the basis of his own experiments he changed this view and decided that while reward strengthened a response, punishment did little if anything to weaken it. In one experiment reported in 1932,[5] for example, he had subjects guess which of five English words was the equivalent of a given Spanish word. In order to reward a subject on a given trial, the experimenter said "right." To punish the subject, the experimenter said "wrong." It was found that while the responses called right were more likely to be repeated on further trials, those called wrong were just as likely to be repeated as if they had not been punished.

Thorndike's conclusion that punishment is not as effective as reward in teaching has been supported by later studies, although they have not indicated that punishment has no effect. Punishment is probably most effective when it leads to responses which remove the possibility of future learning. An example of such a situation would be avoidance training. A rat is placed in a compartment with a barrier down the middle. A signal is given, such as a ringing bell, and then the rat is shocked through a grid on the floor. The rat will soon learn to climb over the barrier into the other end of the box when it hears the bell and thus avoid the shock. If the shock is no longer given when the bell rings, the rat will not be likely to learn this because it will leave the shock compartment before the shock is or is not turned on.

In the conditioned-avoidance situation just described, the animal has no positive motivation to remain in the compartment where it is shocked. Punishment is less effective where it is in conflict with reward. In one of a series of experiments on punishment, Estes first trained rats to press a lever in order to receive a pellet of food and then started extinguishing the response by not reinforcing it with food.[6] At this point the rats were divided into two groups, one of which was punished a number of times when they were near but not pressing the lever. The other group was not punished. The main effect of the punishment was a temporary suppression of the lever pressing. The animals that had been shocked pressed the lever less often immediately afterwards but made up for it by pressing the lever more later on. It took approximately the same number of responses for the response to extinguish, regardless of whether the animals had been punished or not. While some of Estes's other experiments indicated that responses may extinguish more rapidly if punished under some conditions, the main effect of punishment is to lead to a temporary suppression of the behavior, and not to eliminate it. If the temporary decrease in the punished activity is used to teach a new competing response, however, the punishment may serve a purpose. An analogy to child behavior may help illustrate these principles. A child at the seacoast who is punished for going into the water would be expected to show a temporary suppression of this behavior and stay away from it for a while. If there is nothing else to do, however, he may be expected to return to the water. If, on the other hand, he discovers something else to do while avoiding the water, he may not return to it. The effect of punishment depends upon the circumstances.

Perhaps the most striking effect punishment may have is to *increase* the probability of the punished response. This effect was demonstrated by Muenzinger and various colleagues[7] in a long series of experiments. The results of Muenzinger, Bernstone, and Richards provide an excellent example. Rats were run in a T-shaped maze. On each trial, one arm of the maze was lighted and the other was dark. If the rat ran to the lighted side, it found food. If it ran to the unlighted side, it reached a locked door instead. There were three groups of rats. One group received no electric shock; one group was shocked for the incorrect response of choosing the dark alley; and one group was shocked for the *correct* response of choosing the lighted alley. While the group which was shocked for errors learned more quickly than the group which was not punished, the group which was punished for making correct responses did also. The no-shock group required 107 trials to learn, on the average. The group which was shocked for errors only required 35 trials, and the group which was shocked for correct responses required 45. Punishment does not seem to have stamped out responses in this situation.

The explanation which Muenzinger gave for his results and which was supported by further research was that the shock made the rats engage in vicarious trial and error. That is, the shocked rats stopped at the junction of the T-maze and looked both ways before making their choices. The unshocked rats ran through more rapidly and paid less attention to the cues. Again the importance of attention in learning may be seen. The effects of punishment are not the opposite of the effects of reward, but instead seem to consist of (1) directing attention, (2) suppressing behavior, and (3) altering opportunities to learn. The way these factors will interact will depend upon the situation.

Learning theorists are in agreement on the phenomena described by the later version of the law of effect. Organisms do learn to behave in ways which are reinforced. Various theorists disagree, however, on two aspects of how this comes about. First, there is disagreement about what makes something a reinforcer, a question which will be discussed in the next chapter. Second, it is unclear just what it is that is changed by reinforcement. According to Thorndike's theory, it was the connection between a stimulus and a response which was strengthened by reinforcement. Some other theorists, such as Edward Tolman, believed that it was motivation which was changed by reinforcement rather than learning. A study by Tolman and Honzik[8] will help illustrate this position.

Tolman and Honzik ran rats through a multiple-unit T-maze in which each choice point was followed by a one-way door. That is, at the first choice point the rat would turn either left or right. If it made an incorrect choice, it would go into a blind alley and need to retract its steps. If it made a correct choice, then it would go through a door which would prevent its going back toward the starting point, and would proceed to the next choice point. Three groups of rats were run. Each rat in the first group always found food when it reached the end of the maze. Each rat in the second group never found food when it reached the end of the maze. Each rat in the final group ran through the maze ten times without finding any food and then found food every time after that. The important comparison is between the rats which always found food and those which did not find it until the eleventh day. If reinforcement simply strengthened the connection between a stimulus and a response as Thorndike believed, then the delayed-reinforcement group would not learn anything until the eleventh day. On the eleventh day it would start learning and would learn at the same rate as the group which had been reinforced from the beginning had learned.

That was not what happened. On the twelfth day, after being fed in the maze only once, the delayed-reinforcement group made as few errors as the group which had been fed in the maze eleven times. The delayed-reinforcement group had obviously been learning things during its first ten days of running the maze which had not shown in its performance until it was motivated. Reinforcement cannot have its effect solely by strengthening connections by stimuli and responses, but must act at least partly to motivate behavior. Experiments such as that of Tolman and Honzik are called latent-learning experiments, because the learning is latent rather than apparent in performance in the early part of the experiment.

There are two questions raised by latent-learning experiments, one of which is easier to answer than the other. The easy one is, "Does reinforcement only strengthen connections between stimuli and responses?" As we have seen, there is clear evidence from latent learning that reinforcement also has an incentive effect, making learning show in behavior which might otherwise go unobserved. The more difficult question is, "Can learning take place without reinforcement?" At first glance this question too would seem to be answered by Tolman and Honzik's experiment. The rats which did not receive food during the first ten runs through the maze did learn something during that period. While this is true, it is also true that they probably received some reinforcement. Their performance actually did increase a little bit before they started getting any food, and it may well be that being removed from the maze at the end was reinforcing to some extent. It is the difficulty in saying for sure that no reinforcement was present in any given situation that makes the second question about latent learning almost impossible to answer and accounts for the presence of both reinforcement theorists and nonreinforcement theorists. Reinforcement theorists such as Thorndike and nonreinforcement theorists such as Tolman agreed that animals came to do things for which they were reinforced. The reinforcement theorists believed this happened through reinforcement strengthening the connections between stimuli and responses. The nonreinforcement theorists believed it happened through reinforcement directing attention and altering motivation. They believed that if an organism noticed something, it would learn from that experience even though the learning might not show in performance until there was appropriate motivation.

Clark Hull's Behavior Theory

While the theories of Thorndike and Pavlov differed in a number of essentials, they had in common that they were stimulus-response theories. In each, what was learned was thought to be a connection between a stimulus and a response. While they were challenged by the expectancy theory of Tolman, which held that it was ideas which were learned rather than S-R connections, the two theories of learning which came to replace Thorndike's and Pavlov's were stimulus-response theories which combined various aspects of Thorndike's and Pavlov's approaches. These were the theories of Clark Hull and B. F. Skinner.

The most important combination of Pavlov and Thorndike in Hull's theory was the concept of secondary reinforcement, which combined the higher-order conditioning of Pavlovian theory with the law of effect. To appreciate the significance of this rather complex concept, it is necessary to look at the problem it was designed to deal with. Hull was a reinforcement theorist. To the question of what was reinforcing, his initial answer was that things were reinforcing which reduced biological drives such as hunger and thirst. Since he believed that reinforcement was necessary to all learning, the problem was to explain how learning took place in situations where drive reduction was not immediately apparent.

Consider a rat in a multiple T-maze where it must learn a series of perhaps a dozen different turns to reach the goal box. It is easy to explain the learning of the last turn in terms of reinforcement theory. The animal varies its response as Thorndike suggested. On those occasions when it makes the correct turn at the last choice point, the response is soon followed by eating, which reduces the hunger drive and is thus a reinforcer. On those occasions when it makes the wrong turn, its response is not reinforced for a much longer period of time. The response of making the correct turn is thus stamped in more than the response of making the incorrect turn, and the animal learns.

Explaining the learning of earlier turns in the maze is more difficult, for studies have indicated that reinforcement must come quite close in time to a response if it is to strengthen it. How can the rat learn the first turn, when it will not reach the food for quite a while whether it makes the right turn or the wrong one? The solution of the contiguity theorist would be to say that reinforcement is not necessary to learning and that the animal acquires expectancies about what leads to what in the environment. Hull proposed a solution which was consistent with his theoretical position that reinforcement is necessary to learning and that all learning is the strengthening of stimulus-response connections.

The solution was based on Pavlov's observations on higher-order conditioning, which Hull interpreted in terms of Thorndike's law of effect. The meat powder in the dog's mouth was obviously a reinforcer. If a conditional stimulus, such as a light, has acquired the ability to reinforce a new conditional response, as happens in secondary conditioning, then that conditional stimulus must itself have become a reinforcer—a satisfying state of affairs, in Thorndike's terminology. Speaking less precisely, it has become a symbolic reward which is valuable because of what it stands for, food. Hull felt that *secondary reinforcers* of this sort were what reinforced most learning. Except in learning experiments, it is very seldom that an action is immediately rewarded by, for example, food being placed in the subject's mouth.

Secondary reinforcement, because it was responsible for most human learning, was central to Hullian theory. To return to the rat running through the maze, the learning of earlier turns was accounted for in terms of secondary reinforcers. If the proposed mechanism had simply been that the sight of certain parts of the maze was rewarding to the organism because they were seen immediately before eating, then the model would be easy enough to understand. The explanation was more complex, however. As the animal approached the goal, it started prematurely giving the responses it would give when it got there. If it was running toward food, for example, it would start chewing and swallowing while it was still running through the maze. These *fractional anticipatory goal responses* were believed to serve as the secondary reinforcers. In Hull's system the stimuli arising from these anticipatory goal responses had the interesting properties of both reinforcing behavior, which would seem to imply that they reduced a physiological drive, and at the same time increasing motivation. This paradox is not as self-contradictory as it seems. What happens if you eat one salted peanut? Eating it is satisfying, yet your motivation to eat another may well be increased. It is perhaps perfectly reasonable that secondary reinforcers should at the same time be reinforcers and increase drive.

His development of a theory of secondary reinforcement is but one of the ways in which Hull modified the type of simple stimulus-response theory held by Thorndike in order to make it fit a wider range of phenomena. Hull's great achievement was that while only using relatively few concepts, such as drive, incentive, habit, and reaction potential, he developed a theory which gave a reasonably good approximation to the phenomena of learning in hundreds of different situations. It is difficult to devise a theory which will predict such diverse things as the tendency of a chicken to eat more if there is a large pile of grain in front of it rather than a small pile, the elimination of errors more rapidly at the start and finish of a long maze rather than in the middle, the speed at which a rat will run down a straight alley in order to reach food, and the learning of verbal material by human beings. To all these situations, and hundreds more, Hullian theory applied reasonably well.

In extending stimulus-response-reinforcement theory to apply to such diverse phenomena, however, Hull and his students made drastic modifications in all three basic terms of the theory. We have seen that reinforcement stopped being the simple matter of a cat getting or not getting a plate of salmon to eat, as it had been for earlier theorists, and became instead a complex matter of such unobservable things as fractional anticipatory goal responses. If the advantage of behaviorism is that it deals with observable phenomena, how are unobservable responses giving rise to unmeasurable stimuli superior to ideas as explanatory mechanisms?

Not only reinforcement was changed drastically from what it had been in early stimulus-response theories; the natures of the stimulus and the response were also. Both these changes made the theory a more accurate fit to the real world, but they did so at the cost of also making it more ambiguous and more difficult to apply.

Stimulus-response ideas about the nature of the stimulus changed to take account of experiments such as the *transposition* experiment. In this type of experiment, first reported by Köhler, an animal appears to respond to the relations between different stimuli rather than their absolute values.[9] While many variations on this type of experiment have been run, the basic design is as follows: An animal is trained to choose the lighter of two shades of gray. It is then tested with the lighter of the two shades used in training paired with a still lighter shade. The animal does not respond to the shade which was reinforced during training, but rather chooses the new lighter shade. This result is called transposition because the animal seems to be responding to the relationships between the stimuli regardless of changes in their absolute values, just as a musician keeps the relationships between notes constant in transposing music to a different key.

A simple stimulus-response theory, of course, would predict that the animal would choose the stimulus which it had been reinforced for choosing during training. Spence, however, developed an explanation which was consistent with a Hullian position.[10] In discussing Pavlov's work, we have seen that animals show *stimulus generalization.* That is, they respond to a lesser extent to stimuli which are somewhat different from those they were trained on. Spence used this phenomenon to evolve an explanation for the transposition phenomenon. During training, the animal would learn not only to approach the positive stimulus but also to a lesser extent to approach similar stimuli. Similarly, it would learn not only to avoid the negative stimulus but also to avoid to a lesser extent stimuli which were similar to the negative stimulus. By making assumptions about the extent to which learning fell off as the stimulus was changed, Spence devised a theory which predicted the transposition effect without assuming that the animal responded to the relationship between the stimuli. In fact, Spence's theory was able to explain something that Köhler's had not been able to, the decline in transposition when test stimuli considerably different from the training stimuli are used.

Spence's theory, however, was still not able to account for all the phenomena. An experiment by Baker and Lawrence,[11] for example, found that the transposition effect disappeared if the stimuli were presented one after the other instead of at the same time. According to Spence's theory, there is no reason why this difference in procedure should make any difference in the results. A different theory was thus proposed by Donald Riley, who provided strong experimental evidence in favor of it.[12] Riley pointed out that earlier work had ignored the background against which the stimuli were presented. The decline in the transposition effect which was found when stimuli far from the training stimuli were used might be due, not to the factors suggested by Spence's theory, but to the brightnesses of the stimuli having different relationships to the brightness of the background. Riley tested this idea by changing the brightness of the background, so that it had the same relationships to the brightnesses of the test stimuli as it had to the brightnesses of the training stimuli. When this was done, the transposition effect was just as strong with stimuli greatly different from the training stimuli as it had been with stimuli only slightly different from the training stimuli. The effective stimulus was in fact a relationship, as proposed by Köhler. Rather than being the relationship between the two stimuli, however, it was the relationship of each to its background.

The stimulus in stimulus-response theory has thus changed from being a concrete physical object which the experimenter designates as a stimulus to being instead the aspect of the situation which the organism perceives. This change has made the theory much more able to account for phenomena of attention as well as transposition but has also made the theory less concrete and explicit. A similar change has taken place in the conception of the response. In Watsonian behaviorism, a response meant a contraction of specific muscle fibers or secretion by a specific gland. A number of different types of study, however, show that the phenomena of learning cannot be accounted for in any simple way by the learning of simple muscular responses. Two of these types of study are studies of *motor impairment* and studies of *place learning*. A typical motor-impairment study is one by Lashley and Ball.[13] Rats were first trained on a maze, and then underwent an operation in which the nerve fibers carrying sensation from the muscles of the trunk and legs were cut. As a result of this operation, the rats not only lost the normal kinesthetic cues from the position of their limbs but also developed a very strange manner of walking. They dragged their legs and stepped on the back of the feet instead of the sole. Despite this change in method of locomotion, which made necessary very different muscular movements from those they had used in running the maze before, the rats were able to drag themselves through the maze with virtually as few errors as before. This result is very difficult to account for in terms of learning specific muscular responses, as is the result of a similar study by Macfarlane.[14] Macfarlane used a maze which could be flooded with water and tested the result of the rat changing between swimming and running through the maze. One group of rats was trained to swim through the maze and then tested running through it, while another was trained running and tested swimming. In neither case did the change markedly interfere with the rats' performance. Since very different movements are involved in swimming and running, the evidence is again strongly against the position that it is simple muscular movements which are learned.

The place-learning experiments were a series of studies, many of them carried out by Edward Tolman and his students, in which animals seemed to learn to go to the same place even though getting there might require different movements. Perhaps the most interesting of these is a more recent study by Gleitman[15] which is reported in a *Scientific American* article. In this study the animals did not run through the maze at all, but instead rode through the air in Plexiglas trolley cars. The journey was 10 feet long and took about 20 seconds, and they were given an electric shock all the way until they reached the end. After a number of such trips, the trolley line was dismantled and a T-maze was set up in its place, with one end at the starting point and the other at the ending point of the former trolley line. If the rats had learned anything from their previous experience, then in the maze they should have run to the end where the electric shock had stopped rather than the end where it had started. The vast majority of them did this, showing that they had learned the difference between a "good" place and a "bad" place without making appropriate responses at all.

While all these results would clearly contradict a simple stimulus-response theory of the Watsonian type, they could be reasonably well explained by the more sophisticated theory of Hull. The concept which enabled Hull's theory to deal with this type of result is that of the *habit-family hierarchy*. The idea of the habit-family hierarchy is that an organism learns multiple routes from the same starting point to the same goal, the quickest and easiest being preferred over the longer and more time-consuming. The different routes from *A* to *B* thus make up a whole family of habits, and they are called a hierarchy because the most preferred one will be tried first, then the next most preferred, and so on. The habits are transferred to situations similar to those in which they were learned. This concept enables Hullian learning theory to account for results such as those of Macfarlane on the basis that walking and swimming to a goal are alternate ways of getting there which have been learned in the past. When the most preferred habit of walking cannot be used, the animal falls back on the less preferred method of swimming.

Even conditioning cannot be explained as the learning of a simple response. Liddell[16] conditioned a sheep to flex its foreleg in order to avoid an electric shock. The sheep was then turned on its back, and the signal was given. Under these circumstances it did not flex its leg, but instead stiffened all four legs as it attempted to get up.

In summary, then, stimulus-response learning theory has been greatly modified to fit the results of experiments run by its critics. As a result of the modifications, it is now able to account for the experimental findings. This has been achieved, however, at the cost of making the theory both more complex and more ambiguous. The three fundamental concepts of stimulus, response, and reinforcement have all had to be changed. John Watson would hardly recognize contemporary behavior theory.

Attitudes toward Theory Construction

While there are still theoretical differences between stimulus-response theorists, who believe that only responses to stimuli may be learned, and cognitive theorists, who believe that people can learn ideas, these differences have become less differences about the nature of learning and more differences of opinion about the construction of scientific theories. A theory is essentially a set of symbols and rules for their manipulation. In order to translate events in the real world into the concepts of the theory, *rules of correspondence* are necessary, and these frequently take the form of a description of operations to carry out. Counting is an operation to map objects in the real world into the concepts of arithmetic. Not feeding a rat for 24 hours is a way of making the condition of the rat and the concept "hunger drive" correspond to each other.

Besides the rules for translating between the real world and the symbols of the theory, there must also be rules for how the symbols may be manipulated. The statements $2 + 1 = 3$ and $1 + 2 = 3$ are statements about the manipulation of the symbols rather than about the real world. They will permit deductions about the real world which will be accurate if that part of the world follows the theoretical model of arithmetic. Not all aspects of the real world do. A pint of alcohol mixed with a pint of water gives less than a quart total of liquid. If two parts of concentrated sulfuric acid are poured into one part of water, there is less likely to be a violent reaction than if one part of water is poured into two parts of acid. These examples should make clear that arithmetic principles are not true or false by themselves, but only when applied to some aspect of the world. The symbol system, however, can be criticized on two bases without knowing whether any aspect of the world corresponds to it. (1) It might be self-contradictory, or (2) it might be unclear.

When it is proposed that some aspect of the world corresponds to some theory, this may be tested by deducing things from the theory, carrying out the corresponding operations on the real world, and seeing if the results of the two processes correspond. To take a simple example, suppose that someone has proposed that the addition and subtraction of golf balls follows the rules of ordinary arithmetic (a proposition that no one is likely to disagree with). To test the theory, we might carry out a number of experiments. The theory suggests, for example, that two golf balls plus one golf ball give three golf balls. This is a deduction from the theory. How do we carry out corresponding operations on the real world to get an experimental result? First we create the situation of two golf balls and one golf ball by counting them into separate piles. We consider the "plus" to be the operation of combining the two piles. We then count the golf balls in the one resulting pile, and "Eureka!" there are three of them. We have been unable to disprove the theory that golf balls follow the rules of arithmetic.

While the example of the golf balls is so absurdly simple that it is difficult to conceive of the experiments as actually being experiments, the same principles apply to complex theories. We may see, for example, that the theory only says things about the real world to the extent that there are clear rules about what in the real world corresponds to what in the theory. We may also understand why it is that it is said that a theory may be disproved but cannot be proved. It is generally impossible to test all the deductions which may be drawn from any particular theory, so all that can be said is that the theory fits the facts that are known so far. Some new deductions and new theoretical results may be found to not correspond, so that the theory needs to be revised.

The classic example of theories which appeared to be perfect needing revision is the breakdown of the *conservation of mass* and *conservation of energy* with the advent of nuclear fission. The law of the conservation of mass, which said that matter could be transformed but not destroyed or made, and the law of the conservation of energy, which similarly said that energy could change from one form to another but could not be made or destroyed, both held for the facts which were known during the nineteenth century. In nuclear fission, however, mass is transformed into energy, violating both laws. They thus needed to be revised by being combined into a more general law of the conservation of mass and energy, which indicated that they could be transformed into each other. This new principle describes all the phenomena which were described by the earlier formulations, plus some which were not. More than one theory may explain the same results, and any theory may be superseded by a more general one.

While research has forced changes in Hullian theory, its supporters have pointed out that this could not have happened if the theory had not made explicit predictions. With a theory which is not as precisely stated as Hull's, it is not clear what the theory would predict, and any results may be made to seem in agreement with it. They hold that even a theory which is wrong is better than one which is ambiguous, for research will improve the inaccurate theory but not the ambiguous one. Critics of stimulus-response theory, on the other hand, maintain that it is not really all that precise and that decades of research have just started to bring it into agreement with what they have been saying all along. The difference really amounts to differences about when it is better to patch up a theory and when it is better to throw it out completely. The history of science is ambiguous on the point, so some theorists continue to hold each position.

These two positions do not exhaust the possibilities, for there is the third point of view that theories are neither necessary nor desirable. This has been most forcefully put by B. F. Skinner[17] and supported by some interesting evidence. Skinner's contention is that many of the concepts developed by learning theorists do not correspond to anything observable in reality and that greater progress would be made by keeping interpretations closer to the data. To emphasize this point, he has indicated that the abbreviation CNS, which psychologists have used to refer to the central nervous system, should really stand for "conceptual nervous system"—the nervous system which exists only in their own imaginations.

Skinner's position makes him in one way the most radical behaviorist, for he alone would report behavior with no theoretical interpretation at all. The conditions of the experiment would be described, the data would be illustrated in a graph, and there would be no hypothesis testing at all! Yet in another way, Skinner is similar to critics of radical behaviorism, who have objected to the overelaborateness of such theoretical concepts as fractional anticipatory goal responses and habit-family hierarchies.

Skinner may well be right that theorizing in learning theory has been more elaborate than was justified by the data. The neurologizing of early learning theorists did not stand up, for as more knowledge of the nervous system has been acquired, it has been found to be very different from the telephone switchboard between stimuli and responses which had first been imagined. It is therefore worthwhile to look briefly at Skinner's work to see where an atheoretical approach led him.

It may have been partly Skinner's aversion to a Procrustean bed of theorizing which led him to make the distinction which is most basic to his work, that between *respondent* and *operant* behavior. Respondent behavior is already familiar to us, for it is made up of responses which are called out by known stimuli—the unconditional responses of Pavlovian conditioning. While some learning theorists tried to make all behavior fit a Pavlovian model and proposed that there were always unconditional stimuli even when they did not know what they were, this seemed an unwarranted assumption to Skinner. Instead, he proposed separate laws of learning for behaviors which were simply emitted for unknown reasons. These behaviors, which are more common in everyday life than reflexes, he called operant.

While operant behaviors are not initially called out by any

known stimuli, they eventually come under the control of stimuli. If a pigeon, for example, is reinforced for pecking a key when a light is on but not when the light is off, it will learn to peck the key when the light is on, a response which is called a *discriminated operant*. Rather than being similar to Pavlovian conditioning, operant conditioning is similar to the trial-and-error learning of Thorndike, for the initial stimuli calling out the behavior are unknown, but the behavior is strengthened through reinforcement. Much of Skinner's work may be viewed as the elaboration of the law of effect.

Skinner's research has indicated the value of remaining open to novel observations, for some of his most important discoveries resulted partly from laboratory accidents.[18] Failures of equipment to deliver food pellets to his animals and reluctance on Skinner's part to spend his time making the food pellets led him to the study of extinction and of the effects of only reinforcing the animals part of the time. There are many different methods of reinforcement, and they lead to characteristic patterns of response on the part of the reinforced animal. On a *fixed-interval* schedule, for example, the animal is reinforced for the first response made after a given length of time has passed since the last reinforcement, while on a *fixed-ratio* schedule the animal is reinforced once each time it runs off a certain number of responses. Variable-interval and variable-ratio schedules are possible, as well as combinations of different schedules either with or without discriminable stimuli to tell when the schedule is changing. Skinner became so involved in studying the effects of different schedules that he coauthored an entire book entitled *Schedules of Reinforcement*.[19]

While, as suggested by Skinner, theories may be overly elaborate and far removed from the data, it is important to remember that they also have great value in presenting information in concise form. One equation may summarize thousands of experimental observations, and to simply acquire lists of everything any organism could possibly do under any conceivable circumstance would seem to be a hopelessly laborious task.

Unfortunately, if everything has *not* been observed, then conclusions will be drawn about specific situations which have not yet been observed. It is at this point that theorizing is taking place, whether consciously or not. When Skinner presents graphs of the operant behavior of his experimental animals, he is avoiding this; he is not making theoretical inferences. When he applies his results to human beings operating in a social environment, as he does in his book *Science and Human Behavior*,[20] he is assuming that the same variables control the behavior of complex organisms in a complex environment as control simple organisms in a simple environment. The only way to draw conclusions about human social behavior, without generalizing far beyond the data, is to study human beings in a social environment directly.

Tolman's Purposive Behaviorism

While stimulus-response theorists held that all learning was a matter of learning responses to stimuli, cognitive theorists believed that ideas could be associated directly with each other without any response intermediary. Perhaps the most influential of the theorists holding this position was Edward Tolman,[21] whose work on latent learning and place learning has already been mentioned. Tolman believed that there were half a dozen different kinds of learning, the majority of which had been largely neglected by psychologists. These included the learning of *cathexes*, that is, preferences for objects that reduce drives; *field expectancies*, or principles of what leads to what in the world; and *motor patterns*, the learning of skills rather than ideas.

Similarly, behavior is purposive. Tolman disagreed with Thorndike that learning was a blind mechanical process, feeling that it was instead motivated and guided by perception toward goals. To some critics of a cognitive point of view, it did not seem scientific to consider behavior as being purposive. It seemed to be reminiscent of earlier animal psychology, which had made unjustified inferences about what animals were thinking and feeling, and used them to argue that there was a divine purpose in life. Tolman had no such meaning in mind, but merely meant that behavior comes in sequences which are terminated by goals. Within each sequence it is predictable, but not from one sequence to another. A person who enters a restaurant at lunchtime will almost always obtain food and eat it. The whole of the sequence is quite predictable from its first steps. What sequence of behavior he will engage in after reaching the goal of satisfying his hunger is much less predictable.

In reaching goals, behavior is dependent upon perception. One difference between the learning studies run by Tolman and those run by Hull and his students was in the type of learning situation used.

While Hull and his students used alley mazes in which a rat ran down a narrow corridor and could not see anything, Tolman's group used elevated mazes which enabled the animal to look around. Each group was using a situation which would make more likely the type of learning it believed in. It is difficult to learn much more than a sequence of right and left turns while running through corridors with no distinguishing features, while it is much easier to learn general principles about the nature of the environment from an elevated viewpoint.

Tolman did not have a theory in the sense that Hull did—a highly formalized set of mathematically stated laws. His work is more a proposal for a theory, a framework in which the details are not yet filled in. Does it make sense to work out constants in equations dealing with reinforcement to four decimal places if we do not know whether reinforcement is necessary to learning? Should an entire learning theory be based on the learning of responses without first considering whether other kinds of learning are possible? Tolman started with some general principles about behavior to guide the development of theory. Since he did not live to elaborate the theory himself, the extent to which the program will be realized will depend upon his students.

Let us look at a typical piece of behavior as an illustration of some of the general properties of behavior which Tolman described. A man is going downtown to buy a phonograph needle. If his car won't start, then he will take the bus. If the street he plans to take is closed, then he will take a different one. What does this simple example illustrate?

First of all, behavior is *molar*. By this term, Tolman meant that behavior was more predictable when viewed in terms of large units than when viewed in terms of small ones. When the man sets out for the record store, the muscular movements he will use in getting there are not predictable, nor is his exact route. His reaching his destination is much more predictable. This is the same point which was made by the studies on place learning. The response is not a pattern of muscular responses, but the achievement of a goal.

Another general principle of behavior is that it is *modifiable*. If the man's car will not start, he will not continue trying to start it forever, but will turn to some other means of transportation or call the garage to come repair the car. This aspect of human behavior is so obvious that it would not be worth mentioning, except that the instinctive behavior of some species is not modifiable to any significant extent. The naturalist Fabre studied a type of pine caterpillar which follows a silken trail left by the first caterpillar in the line. By an accident, the leader laid down a circular path around the top of a large vase, and the entire troop of caterpillars walked around in a circle for over a week before managing to break out of the circle![22] We shall see more examples of the rigidity of instinctive behavior in the next chapter. Human beings, however, are much more flexible than the caterpillars and modify their behavior more easily on the basis of experience.

Finally, behavior *differs from one species to another*. Tolman believed that these differences were not just differences in degree, but differences in type of learning. Simple learning tasks are not carried out any more efficiently by human beings than they are by lower organisms, yet human beings are capable of feats of learning which other species cannot duplicate. Caution must therefore be used in generalizing from one species to another.

While Tolman did not devise a detailed theory of learning, his work is perhaps more relevant to the study of social behavior than any other learning theorist's. In order to consider the interaction of groups of individuals and not be overwhelmed by detail, it is necessary to describe behavior in molar rather than *molecular* terms. Molecular theories can only be applied by analogy. For that reason the point of view in this book is probably closer to that of Tolman than to that of any other learning theorist described in this chapter.

Summary

While there is still considerable disagreement among psychologists over theoretical interpretations of learning, much is known about the empirical phenomena which the different theories attempt to explain. The accumulation of empirical knowledge began in earnest with Pavlov's work on conditioning, which provided a model of behavior taken over by American behaviorism. Some of the important phenomena of learning which Pavlov investigated are conditioning, extinction, spontaneous recovery, generalization, and discrimination.

Pavlov's work, however, concentrated on reflex responses which were elicited by known stimuli. The study of responses which are not called out by any known stimuli represents a second line of development in learning theory, pursued by Thorndike and more recently Skinner. While there is disagreement among different theorists as to whether positive reinforcement is necessary to learning or whether it has its effects in other ways, such as by modifying motivation, there is no doubt that organisms learn to behave in ways that are rewarded. The effects of negative reinforcement are more complex. They are not, as Thorndike initially thought, equal and opposite to the effects of positive reinforcement.

The most ambitious attempt to develop a comprehensive learning theory to date has been that of Clark Hull. While basically a stimulus-response theory, Hull's modified the nature of the stimulus, the response, and reinforcement from the meanings these terms had in earlier and simpler theories. The concepts of secondary reinforcement, fractional anticipatory goal response, and habit-family hierarchy enabled the theory to relate to diverse phenomena of learning, but at the expense of some loss of concreteness. One's appraisal of the theory depends to a great extent on one's attitudes about the development of scientific theory, and this topic was discussed at some length in this chapter.

An approach to learning theory which stresses the complexity of human behavior is that of Edward Tolman, whose picture appears at the beginning of this chapter. The studies he and his students did of such phenomena as latent learning and place learning have contributed much to our understanding of human behavior, even though the theoretical position he held has not yet been as completely elaborated as that of Hull.

Notes and Acknowledgments

1. For a history of learning theory the student is referred to Boring, Edwin G. *A History of Experimental Psychology.* (2d ed.) New York: Appleton-Century-Crofts, Inc., 1957.

    For data on which learning theory is based he should see the somewhat outdated but extremely comprehensive Woodworth, Robert S., and Harold Schlosberg. *Experimental Psychology.* (Rev. ed.) New York: Holt, Rinehart and Winston, Inc., 1958.

    For the theories of learning he should read Hilgard, Ernest R., and Gordon H. Bower. *Theories of Learning.* (3d ed.) New York: Appleton-Century-Crofts, Inc., 1966.

2. Boring. *Op. cit.*, p. 637.

3. Skinner, B. F. *The Behavior of Organisms.* New York: Appleton-Century, 1938, pp. 18 and 19. By permission of the publisher.

4. Trowbridge, M. H., and H. Cason. "An experimental study of Thorndike's theory of learning." *Journal of General Psychology,* 1932 (7), pp. 245–258.

5. Thorndike, E. L. *The Fundamentals of Learning.* New York: Bureau of Publications, Teachers College, Columbia University, 1932.

6. Estes, W. K. "An experimental study of punishment." *Psychological Monographs,* 1944 (57), no. 263.

7. Muenzinger, K. F. "Motivation in learning: I." *Journal of Comparative Psychology,* 1935 (17), pp. 267–277.

   Muenzinger, K. F., A. A. Bernstone, and L. Richards. "Motivation in learning: VIII." *Journal of Comparative Psychology,* 1938 (26), pp. 177–186.

   Muenzinger, K. F., and R. F. Powloski. "Motivation in learning: X." *Journal of Experimental Psychology,* 1951 (42), pp. 118–124.

8. Tolman, E. C., and C. H. Honzik. "Introduction and removal of reward, and maze performance in rats." *University of California Publications in Psychology,* 1930 (4), pp. 257–275.

9. A history of this type of experiment is given in Riley, Donald A. "The nature of the effective stimulus in animal discrimination learning: Transposition reconsidered." *Psychological Review,* January, 1958 (65), pp. 1–7.

10. Spence, K. W. "The differential response in animals to stimuli varying in a single dimension." *Psychological Review,* 1937 (44), pp. 430–444.

11. Baker, R. A., and D. H. Lawrence. "The differential effects of simultaneous and successive stimuli presentation on transposition." *Journal of Comparative and Physiological Psychology,* 1951 (44), pp. 378–382.

12. Riley. *Op. cit.*

13. Lashley, K. S., and J. Ball. "Spinal conduction and kinaesthetic sensitivity in the maze habit." *Journal of Comparative Psychology,* 1929 (9), pp. 71–105.

14. Macfarlane, D. A. "The role of kinesthesis in maze learning." *University of California Publications in Psychology,* 1930 (4), pp. 277–305.

15. Gleitman, Henry. "Place learning." *Scientific American,* October, 1963.

16. Liddell, Howard S. "The conditioned reflex" in F. A. Moss (Ed.), *Comparative Psychology.* Englewood Cliffs, N.J.: Prentice-Hall, Inc., 1934, p. 273.

17. Skinner, B. F. "Are theories of learning really necessary?" *Psychological Review,* 1950 (57), pp. 193–216.

18. Skinner, B. F. "A case history in scientific method." *American Psychologist,* 1956 (11), pp. 221–233.

19. Ferster, C. S., and B. F. Skinner. *Schedules of Reinforcement.* New York: Appleton-Century-Crofts, Inc., 1957.

20. Skinner, B. F. *Science and Human Behavior.* New York: The Free Press of Glencoe, 1953.

21. A systematic statement of Tolman's position will be found in Tolman, E. C. *Purposive Behavior in Animals and Men.* Berkeley, Calif.: University of California Press, 1949.

A collection of his work, sponsored by his students and his colleagues, is Tolman, E. C. *Collected Papers in Psychology.* Berkeley, Calif.: University of California Press, 1951.

22. Teale, Edwin Way (Ed.). *The Fascinating Insect Word of J. Henri Fabre.* Greenwich, Conn.: Fawcett Publications, Inc., 1956.

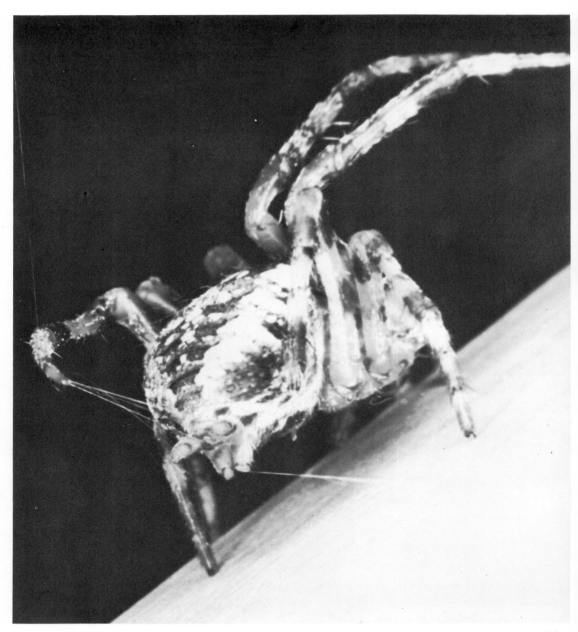

Peter N. Witt

FOUR

INNATE, LEARNED & MOTIVATED BEHAVIOR

If the ability of man to learn is incredible, perhaps it is no more incredible than the inherited behavior patterns of lower organisms which rely on instinct rather than learning. Let us join the great French naturalist J. Henri Fabre[1] in the middle of the nineteenth century as he observes the behavior of a solitary wasp, the Languedocian sphex. In doing so, we may broaden our view of learning and motivation from what it would be if we considered only human beings.

When ready to lay an egg, the sphex searches out a female of a grasshopper known as an ephippiger. It stings the grasshopper in the thoracic ganglia, an operation which removes the grasshopper's ability to use its legs without harming it in any other way. The sphex then drags the ephippiger toward the sphex's burrow. If the grasshopper struggles too much, the wasp may perform another delicate operation on it. Forcing open the nape of the grasshopper's neck, the wasp reaches in with its mandibles and squeezes the grasshopper's brain. This brings on paralysis but does not do permanent injury. An ephippiger which Fabre took home in that state recovered from the paralysis in a few hours.

Upon reaching its burrow, the sphex lays one egg at the root of the ephippiger's thigh. Although the ephippiger may live for a period of weeks, it is unable to dislodge or damage the egg because of the damage to the thoracic ganglia. In time the egg hatches, and the sphex grub proceeds to eat the still living but powerless ephippiger. The young wasp is guaranteed a supply of fresh food, and its chances of survival are increased.

How does the sphex learn to perform the delicate and complex acts necessary to providing its young with food? It has no opportunity to learn them, for as we have seen, the young wasp is born in isolation and is not reared by its parents. The entire pattern of behavior is innate. It is to this type of complex, unlearned behavior shown by all members of the species under appropriate conditions that the term *instinct* is properly applied.

Amazing as instinctive behavior may be, it does not have the flexibility of behavior which is learned. Fabre demonstrated this by a number of experiments which he performed with the insects he was observing. One of these experiments utilized a different variety of sphex which left a paralyzed cricket for its grub to eat. When the wasp had the cricket almost to the mouth of its burrow, it would leave the cricket for a moment and inspect the burrow. Fabre took advantage of its absence to move the cricket a little distance away again. When the wasp returned, it again dragged the cricket near to the burrow and then again went into the burrow. Each time Fabre moved the cricket away while the wasp was gone, and each time the wasp went mechanically into the burrow again as soon as it drew the cricket near. The instinctive behavior was not completely unmodifiable, for occasionally Fabre would find a wasp which would eventually abandon the final inspection and drag the cricket directly into the hole. The vast majority, however, would simply keep repeating the instinctive pattern even when it was no longer appropriate. This rigidity of behavior was also clear in other examples. In one, Fabre stole the sphex's egg and prey just as the wasp was about to close the entrance to the burrow. Although the wasp inspected the inside of the burrow after it was emptied, it then proceeded to close the entrance just as if the burrow had not been disturbed.

Some organisms obviously have brains which are far from being blank slates at birth. It may be that the caution of psychologists in regarding anything as innate in man is a result of psychological theorizing having gone too far in the other direction at one time. With complex instincts having been described in animals during the nineteenth century, a strong trend developed to explain human behavior in similar terms. Instincts were an important part of the theorizing of William James, and were given further impetus as an explanatory concept by the work of William McDougall. In a number of ways, McDougall was one of the important pioneers of the field of psychology. He was the author of one of the first two social psychology texts, published in 1908, and was a behaviorist before Watson, calling his general psychology text *Psychology: The Study of Behaviour*[2] in 1912. It is thus unfortunate that McDougall is remembered today only as a discredited instinct theorist.

McDougall used the term "instinct" in a more general way than we would today, so that in some ways it was more equivalent to what we would call a drive. He conceived of man as having a limited number of instincts, such as curiosity and gregariousness, and characteristic sentiments associated with these instincts. Since the expression of the instinct could be modified by learning, the instinct in McDougall's theory was something much less rigid than the behavior of one of Fabre's wasps. The ease of explaining behavior by attributing it to instinct, however, led to overuse of the term. L. L. Bernard,[3] in a survey of the literature in 1924, found that several thousand human actions had been described as instinctive by one writer or another! It soon became apparent that the explanation and labeling of behavior were being confused in saying that one boy fought because he had an instinct of pugnacity while another ran away from home because he suffered from too much wanderlust. As cross-cultural evidence was by then accumulating which showed that everything in human behavior varied radically as a result of different learning experiences in different cultures, instinct theory was discredited.

Reacting to the proliferation of endless numbers of instincts to account for human behavior, psychologists next reduced the number of human motives to an absolute minimum. The model of motivation which came to be generally accepted was that motives had their origins in the efforts of the organism to maintain a constant internal environment. While this view had earlier advocates, it was worked out in the most convincing detail by the physiologist Walter B. Cannon in his book *The Wisdom of the Body.*[4] For a human being to continue living, there are many internal conditions which must remain relatively constant. The temperature can only vary within fairly narrow limits, similarly the salt, water, and sugar contents of the blood. Each of these levels, as well as many others, is maintained by a combination of internal mechanisms and behavior. When blood sugar level falls, stored sugar is released into the bloodstream to restore it. Besides this internal adjustment, however, behavior plays a role in maintaining the level. The organism eats. Because of the active nature of this process of keeping conditions inside the body relatively stable despite changes in the external world, Cannon gave the process the name *homeostasis.*

Ideas of homeostasis were accepted and extended by other theorists. Virtually all human motivation came to be viewed as having its ultimate object in the maintenance of homeostasis. That behavior was influenced by such factors was shown by experiments such as those of Richter,[5] who showed that rats which had had their parathyroid glands removed would eat much more calcium than rats normally did and thus stay alive, while parathyroidectomized rats which were not given a chance to eat extra calcium would die in a few days. Similarly, an experiment by Davis[6] had shown that human infants allowed to choose their own foods over a period of months maintained a well-balanced diet. (Learned preferences for nonnutritious foods may break down this adaptive pattern in human beings, however.)

Obvious as it is that homeostasis plays an important role in human survival, how could all the various activities which human beings engage in be explained in these terms? What physiological balance is maintained by looking at a painting, going ice skating, or writing a letter to the editor? The solution to this problem which became widely accepted was that of secondary reinforcement in Hullian learning theory. As the young infant is cared for by his mother, satisfaction of his hunger need is associated with the presence of his mother's smiling face. Social approval by his mother, and by generalization by other people, should then become able to reinforce other actions which could be learned by higher-order conditioning.

The explanation was an ingenious one and was in accord with observations which show social approval to be a very important factor in human learning. It probably oversimplified, however, the basis of human motivation. If we look at human beings from an evolutionary point of view and expect them to have characteristics in common with other animals, then we will expect them to show some homeostatic drives, which do serve important functions in adaptation. There is no reason why all motives should be homeostatic, however. We have already seen in looking at Fabre's wasps that there are forms of animal behavior which are very adaptive for the species which have purposes quite different from the maintaining of an optimal level of some internal physiological system. Why should human beings be the exception in which all motives are based on homeostasis?

An ingenious experiment by Harry Harlow[7] casts serious doubt on the traditional explanation of the child's learning to love his mother on the basis of her feeding him. Harlow raised baby monkeys in the laboratory with surrogate mothers made of wire. One wire frame was covered with soft terrycloth, while the other was simply bare wire. Each of the frames was constructed so that a feeding bottle could be attached to it and so that the baby monkey could climb on it. According to the usual theory based on homeostatic drives, the baby monkeys should have preferred the "mother" which fed them. Instead, they preferred the cloth-covered frame regardless of which one they were fed on. Not only did they spend much time climbing on the cloth "mother" while they only climbed on the wire "mother" to eat, they also ran to the cloth "mother" for comfort when they were frightened! The *contact comfort* of the soft cloth was a more effective reinforcer than the drive-reducing food.

Harlow's study not only raised problems for the homeostatic drive model of motivation but also supported studies showing the importance of contact in developing social motivation in human infants. One of the better known of these was a study by Spitz[8] comparing nursery children with foundling-home children. While the children in both institutions had good food, housing, and medical care, the foundlings had only a minimum of contact with an adult. Each nurse was in charge of eight to twelve children and had little time to devote to each. In the nursery setting, each child had close relations with his own mother during a part of the day.

Because the children were compared at too young an age to permit the use of intelligence tests, they were compared on the Hetzer-Wolf baby tests. These test skills which infants normally develop during the first years of life. Because there is little relationship between a skill such as grasping a block of wood and what we mean by intelligence in adults, there is no relationship between developmental quotient at, say, age two and intelligence quotient at age twenty. On the other hand, the tests do measure the types of skills which are being developed during the early years.

The nursery children and the foundlings were first measured when they were only a few months old, and the foundlings had a slightly higher developmental age on the average, making an average score of 124 as compared to the nursery children's 102. With small groups of children and with scores quite variable at that age, the difference would not be significant, but it does make it very unlikely that the foundlings were initially retarded compared with the nursery children.

The longer the children stayed in the foundling home, however, the more their developmental quotients dropped. At the end of 1 year, the average developmental quotient of the foundlings was 72. At the end of 2 years it was only 45! They were hardly able to do anything at the age of two which they had not been able to do at the age of one. In contrast, the nursery children stayed about the same in developmental quotient, which, of course, is what people usually do. The severely deprived environment had radically retarded the development of the foundlings.

While there are some methodological questions about some of the early studies and some doubts as to which variables are most important in causing the effects, there is considerable evidence that severe early social deprivation has extremely deleterious effects on child development. A survey of studies by Bowlby[9] indicated that the effects of the deprivation were reversible if it did not last for too long a period but that social deprivation continued over a period of years could result in permanent mental retardation. These effects, like the results of Harlow's study, do not fit a homeostatic model of motivation.

The Blank-slate Hypothesis Reexamined

The homeostatic-drive model of motivation was the natural accompaniment of the blank-slate theory of learning. It provided an explanation of behavior based on a mind in which nothing was built in except the mechanisms for recognizing and correcting physiological imbalances. Furthermore, the research findings inconsistent with the homeostatic model are usually also inconsistent with the blank-slate theory. Whether it is a preference for soft objects, a tendency to explore a new environment, or a pattern of sexual behavior, something more than homeostatic drives is built into the organism according to each of the lines of research critical of the homeostatic-drive model of motivation. The accumulation of such research is thus an adequate reason to reexamine the question of what is innate in human behavior.

The question of the relationship between heredity and environment in human development has generally been disposed of by noting that an interaction of heredity and environment is always necessary for development. A human infant would not be human if it did not have the genetic composition of a human being rather than of some other organism. Equally, however, it would not be human without an environment within the uterus adequate for the development of its genetic potential. Without this initial interaction of heredity and environment no infant would result.

Despite the closeness of this interaction, however, it is still possible to ask the extent to which either heredity or environment usually limits development given certain developmental conditions. An analogy to a chemical reaction may help clarify this point. If hydrogen and oxygen are combined to form water, two *gram molecular weights* of hydrogen will combine with each gram molecular weight of oxygen. In any given reaction, if you know how much hydrogen and how much oxygen are present, it is possible to say whether the amount of water produced will be limited by inadequacy of one element or of the other. Similarly, just as both hydrogen and oxygen are necessary to form water but one may be the limiting factor in a given case, both heredity and environment are necessary for human development, but either one may limit development in a particular situation. Saying that heredity and environment interact does not say everything there is to be said about that interaction, for it does not say which is normally the limiting factor. For example, what we mean when we say that the grasshopper-stinging behavior of the sphex is innate is not that it will develop without any environmental supports, but that most of the time the environment will provide adequate supports. In that way it is radically different from behavior we call learned, which is behavior depending on environmental conditions which often do not exist. Most people, for example, never are exposed to the necessary conditions for learning Japanese.

The main impetus for the consideration of innate factors in the behavior of animals, as well as much of the data on these factors, has come from a group of biologists studying animal behavior and calling themselves *ethologists*. Since it sprang from a field different from comparative psychology, ethology has stressed both a different subject matter and a different methodology from comparative psychology, which is also devoted to the study of animal behavior. Ethologists have been more interested in behavior as adaptation and in studying a wide variety of organisms in their natural habitats. Psychologists have been more concerned with trying to find general principles of learning and with the control which laboratory experiments can give. While the two fields have become more similar as they have started to influence each other, there are still differences in point of view, and one of the most important differences is in the attention devoted to unlearned behavior. As Tinbergen has commented, "Ethologists consider that learning is a change in something, and that it must pay to study this something before the change occurs."[10] Let us look at some of the research of ethologists on the something before the change occurs in order to see what might be built into human beings if the slate should turn out to have writing on it.

The two most basic concepts of the ethologists in their work on instinct are the *fixed motor pattern* and the *innate releasing mechanism*. The first, as its name implies, is an organized muscular response which is inherited rather than learned. The second is a general mechanism enabling stimuli of a certain type to call out a response. (To speak of calling out a response perhaps gives the wrong impression. The ethologists speak of its being released instead, because the tendency of the animal to give the response is so great that it will sometimes go off in the absence of appropriate stimulation. They thus conceive of it as merely having to be released instead of called out.) A number of excellent examples of both fixed motor patterns and innate releasing mechanisms are given in a paper on the interaction of unlearned behavior patterns and learning by Eibl-Eibesfeldt.[11] Since they all are drawn from the behavior of mammals, they represent behavior more similar to that of human beings than the behavior of Fabre's wasps.

One of the examples dealt with nest building in rats. Earlier research had maintained that nest building and retrieving of young by rats were learned, as rats which had not had any opportunity to manipulate solid objects did not show these behaviors. Eibl-Eibesfeldt noted that in the earlier research the animals had been tested in a strange cage, where exploration would be expected to take precedence over other types of behavior. When tested under more appropriate conditions, the vast majority of the inexperienced rats did build nests.

To ask whether nest building as a whole is innate is inappropriate, however. The nest building of inexperienced rats is different from that of experienced rats. Both use a number of specific motor patterns which are the same in a number of species and which are unlearned and may therefore be called fixed motor patterns. These patterns include several motions which are used for digging in the earth, such as scratching, kicking backward, pushing, and pushing with the snout. While these motions are inappropriate to building a nest out of strips of paper on a cage floor, they often appeared in the inexperienced animals' nest-building activities. More appropriate were the grasping of materials, pulling them free, biting them loose, and carrying them to the nesting site and depositing them there. A number of other specific motions are then made in transforming them into a nest. The ability to carry out each of these motions seems to be innate, but their integration into a functional pattern of nest building improves with experience. The inexperienced rats eventually manage to fumble nests together, but they often employ motions out of sequence and when they are inappropriate to the conditions. Nest building as a whole should not be regarded as innate, but rather as a learned integration of innate elements.

While the rats displayed a number of fixed motor patterns, the killing of prey by polecats provides a better example of an innate releasing mechanism. Studies by Eibl-Eibesfeldt indicate that the killing itself is initially called out by the prey running away. An inexperienced polecat will not attack a rat, for example, as long as the rat stands its ground. When the rat runs, the polecat kills it. The sight of the fleeing prey thus seems to be the innate releaser for the instinctive attacking behavior. With experience, however, the cat learns to attack whether the rat runs or not. The learned behavior in this case extends the range of the more specific innate mechanism. The interaction of innate and learned factors is also seen in the part of the body in which the polecat bites its prey. A wild polecat may initially grab its prey anywhere it can, but then it rearranges its hold and kills it with repeated bites to the back of the neck. The motor pattern of repeated sharp stabbing of the *killing bite* is innate, but the location of the bite on the back of the neck is learned. Polecats which only have experience with defenseless prey, such as baby chickens, do not learn to locate the bite in a particular place. As soon as they have experience with an animal which can bite back, such as a rat, the cats learn to locate the bite on the back of the neck, a position which leaves the animal unable to bite them.

Many other examples of innate releasing mechanisms have been studied by the ethologists. Escape reactions of the type which ducks and geese have to birds of prey, for example, are released by the short neck of the predator as its shape passes overhead. A cardboard model of a bird with a long protuberance on one side of the wings and a short protuberance on the other side will call out escape reactions if moved through the air with the short extension going first so that it is shaped like a hawk, but will not call out the reactions if moved the other way so that it resembles a bird with a long neck and short tail such as a goose.[12] Similarly, fighting and courtship behavior of the three-spined stickleback (a small fish) are released by quite specific stimuli. Fighting is called out in males by the red abdomen and threatening vertical posture of another male, while courtship is called out by the swollen abdomen of the female. The male will court a model with little resemblance to a stickleback except for having a swollen abdomen and will not court a model of a female stickleback which is realistic in all ways except for lacking this one sign.[13]

These examples and others which have been studied indicate that there may be innate behaviors other than the sort of simple stimulus-response link represented by the salivation of Pavlov's dogs. It is possible for a sensitivity to a particular stimulus configuration to be built in, such as the stickleback's sensitivity to the swollen abdomen or the duck's reactivity to neck length. On the other hand, it is possible for an organized motor-reaction pattern to be built in without being closely tied to any releasing stimulus, such as the scratching reaction of the rat or the killing bite of the polecat. These innate motor patterns may go off with little environmental support, as in the case of the rat deprived of objects to manipulate which carries its tail around in its mouth.

This position is more consistent with a cognitive position in learning than with a stimulus-response position. Rather than all knowledge being a matter of stimulus-response connections, it implies that the mind of even a lower organism is more like a computer, having separate routines built in for stimulus identification and for response patterns, as well as for connecting stimulus with response. Both the stimulus-identification process and the motor-response organization may be either learned or innate. In the case of a duck reacting to a bird of prey, for example, the effective stimulus pattern is built in. For a child reacting to words, the effective stimulus pattern is learned. The killing bite of the polecat is an innate motor pattern, while the one we use in tying our shoelaces must be learned. Learning to give a response to a stimulus, far from being the simplest possible type of learning it was once thought to be, is actually quite complex, since it involves stimulus recognition, a response pattern, and the connection of the two. A simpler type of learning is the simple stimulus-recognition learning involved in realizing that a stimulus is familiar.

Motivation, then, is a way of bringing about behavior which is more complex and more flexible than that which can be programmed completely in advance. A motive, in the sense of goal-oriented behavior, would not be necessary for a simple reflex such as a knee jerk, for in that case the connection between one stimulus and one response could be innate. A motive would be necessary to bring about behavior which needed to change in unpredictable ways with changing circumstances, such as the finding of varied sources of different foods.

An interesting case of a behavior pattern in which almost, but not quite, everything is innate is *imprinting*. The young of some birds, such as the greylag goose, typically follow the mother bird around. While the reaction is innate, the recognition of the appropriate stimulus is not. Instead, the young gosling learns to follow the first moving object of approximately the right size which it sees after birth. The learning takes only one trial, does not extinguish, and does not lead to any reinforcer in the usual meaning of the term. It is a behavior pattern, however, which would generally be quite adaptive. As Deutsch has pointed out, building in the stimulus-recognition pattern would result only in the gosling recognizing geese in general and not its own mother, and might lead to some geese which most closely approached the ideal pattern being followed by all the goslings. Adaptive as imprinting usually is, it becomes maladaptive when the conditions it normally occurs in are changed. If the first moving object the gosling sees after hatching is Dr. Lorenz, it will follow him around and show the normal instinctive behavior toward him instead of toward geese.[14]

A process similar to imprinting may account for some of Harlow's observations on his monkeys raised with terrycloth surrogate mothers. When the monkeys reached maturity, it was almost impossible to get them to mate. The few that did succeed in mating did not show the normal instinctive mothering patterns toward their off-spring. If monkeys, like birds, depend upon an early learning experi-ence for recognizing the proper object of their instinctive reactions, then the failure of these reactions in Harlow's monkeys would not be surprising.

The research of the ethologists has been significant for a theory of motivation in at least three ways. First, it has demonstrated that there is much behavior which, while it clearly is of adaptive signifi-cance, equally clearly does not fit a homeostatic model. Second, the research has shown that both the stimulus-recognition and motor-organization functions in many instinctive acts are too complex to be taken for granted under the rubric of an S-R formulation. Finally, the research has shown an interaction between the internal and external control of behavior, in which these two factors assume differing amounts of importance in different instinctive acts. To this third contribution we must now turn.

Perhaps the best summary of the ethological research on the interaction of internal and external factors in behavior is a chapter by Tinbergen entitled "The internal factors responsible for the 'spon-taneity' of behavior." This discusses such examples as the *fanning* of newly laid eggs by the three-spined stickleback.[15]

The fanning is adaptive, since it provides a better supply of oxygen to the developing eggs. The amount of fanning normally in-creases gradually from spawning until the eggs hatch just over a week later. Is this pattern due to internal programming or to the perception of the condition of the eggs? It is partly controlled by external conditions, for artificial lowering of the oxygen content of the water increases the amount of fanning. Internal factors also play a role, however. If half-developed eggs are removed and replaced by freshly laid eggs, the fanning reaches a peak when the original clutch would have hatched, apparently showing a running off of an internal pattern of behavior. After this initial peak of fanning, a secondary peak is reached corresponding to the hatching of the second clutch of eggs, showing responsiveness to external conditions. If repeated sub-stitutions of eggs are carried out, the stickleback eventually stops exhibiting the fanning behavior, apparently in response to internal changes. The control of even quite simple behavior may thus involve a fairly complex interaction of internal and external factors, and the relation of these factors must be discovered in each separate case of motivated behavior.

One type of relationship between internal and external factors which is observed is that some behaviors are more and more easily called out with increasingly long periods of time since they were last released. In some cases, such as hunger and thirst, the increasing motive may be fairly clearly ascribed to homeostatic imbalance. This is less clearly the case with sexual behavior. Male rats, for example, need less and less instigation to mating behavior with longer and longer deprivation, although there is no known physiological imbalance which is corrected by the mating behavior.[16] Especially interesting are instinctive behaviors which, after a sufficiently long period of not being released, will go off in the absence of any apparent releasing stimulus. Lorenz observed this phenomenon in a captive starling which ran off the entire pattern of catching, killing, and swallowing insects without any insect being present![17] Similarly, Tinbergen observed a male stickleback going through the elaborate rituals of courtship while alone in a tank. These and other examples cited by Tinbergen are more complex examples of something which may be easily observed in everyday life. The play of animals, such as stalking and pouncing by kittens, carrying objects in the mouth on the part of dogs, and butting by young goats, usually involves the practice of motor patterns which are involved in adult instinctive behavior.

All the examples of instinctive behavior which have been considered so far are drawn from animals considerably less intelligent than human beings. Everyone knows that insects have instincts but that human beings have only a few simple reflexes! There are, however, patterns of human activity which do seem to have large innate components. These include the movements made by infants when held upside down or when placed in water, the development of grasping, and especially the development of locomotion. An excellent summary of the role of maturation in human development is that of McGraw.[18]

Maturation of some human activities shows two gradients of development of which the first seems to correspond to the development of *subcortical* control of the behavior and the second seems to correspond to its control by *cortical* areas of the brain. Young infants, for example, make well-coordinated swimming motions when placed in water. This innate pattern of behavior seems to be under control of subcortical areas of the brain. As the infant grows older, he stops showing the innate pattern and instead makes disorganized and random motions when placed in water. This change seems to correspond to increasing control of his behavior by the *cerebral cortex*; this change culminates in well-controlled voluntary movements.

Some aspects of behavior eventually come under more cortical control than others do. Innate factors in behavior are probably most marked for those activities which are oldest in terms of evolution and under control of the most primitive parts of the brain. These are generally functions which are similar over a wide range of living organisms. For example, routine maintenance functions such as the regulation of temperature, blood pressure, and blood sugar level are fairly similar in different species and are generally controlled at a subcortical level. Besides these internal activities, there are some gross body movements which are necessary to a wide variety of organisms and which have thus evolved control patterns at subcortical levels. Probably the most important of these, and thus the best candidates for being considered instinctive in human beings, are the control of posture and locomotion. The pattern by which human infants develop the ability to crawl has been intensively studied, and seems to depend on maturation much more than learning. As pointed out by McGraw,[19] the sequence of stages in the development of crawling not only is similar in different human beings but is almost identical in human beings and salamanders.

Postural adjustments also may have large innate components. This is illustrated more effectively for dogs than for human beings by a case observed by Katz.[20] A dog, because of being in an accident, needed to have one of its front and one of its hind legs amputated. As soon as the dog had recovered from the operation and was allowed to stand up, it was able to stand and run with no practice at all! Photographs of the dog are shown in Figure 4–1 and Figure 4–2.

Hormones and Behavior

In some cases the varying thresholds for release of a form of behavior have been traced to *hormones*, chemicals released into the bloodstream by the *endocrine glands*. These glands include the pituitary, the gonads, the thyroid and parathyroid glands, the adrenal cortex and adrenal medulla, and the placenta and corpus luteum in pregnant women. The chemicals produced by these glands influence many aspects of adaptation, but there is generally not a simple cor-

Figure 4-1 *Dog which had lost two legs. (Katz[20])*

Figure 4-2 *The same dog running at top speed. (Katz[20])*

respondence of one gland to one form of behavior. Most hormones have a number of effects, and generally more than one hormone is involved in any given piece of behavior. The maintaining of pregnancy, for example, involves hormones from the *pituitary, corpus luteum,* and *placenta.* The pituitary gland, especially, is involved in many functions and secretes hormones influencing several other glands.

The situation is further complicated by the wide variety of ways in which the hormones could act. As both Lashley[21] and Beach[22] have pointed out, it is possible that the hormones might (1) have general effects upon the excitability of the organism, (2) influence the development of the structures involved in response patterns, (3) stimulate sense organs so as to make them send afferent impulses to the central nervous system, or (4) act directly on portions of the central nervous system. The action on the central nervous system could be of any of three types: (*a*) the hormone might be necessary to the development of a nerve structure involved in producing the behavior, (*b*) it might lead to the periodic growth and decline of the structure, or (*c*) it might increase its sensitivity at the moment it was stimulated by the hormone. Nor are these possibilities logically exclusive of each other, so that it is not simply a matter of which one way hormones operate. Instead, they act in different ways in different mechanisms and often in more than one way in the same mechanism.

An example of a gland which has general effects throughout the organism rather than effects confined to some specific target organ is the *thyroid.* As is widely known, the secretions of this gland regulate the rate at which the cells of the body carry on metabolism. Insufficient output of the gland produces disorders related to too slow metabolism—apathy and reduced intelligence, dry skin, and puffy flabby muscles. On the other hand, *hyperthyroidism,* or an excess production, causes nervousness, a racing heart, and weight loss.

The hormone secretion of the thyroid gland consists of a mixture of compounds, and at least half a dozen major enzyme systems are involved in their production.[23] There are thus a number of different ways in which their synthesis may be inadequate, ranging from insufficiency of iodine in the diet to failure of the usual control of thyroid production by the pituitary gland and including failure of synthesis at each of the many steps involved. As this one example illustrates, simply the diagnosis and treatment of disorders of any one endocrine gland is an extensive field by itself.

Besides the effects which varying thyroid output has on the adult, there are different effects of thyroid insufficiency during development. In extreme cases, such as individuals born without any thyroid gland at all, *hypothyroidism* may cause a form of mental deficiency called cretinism, which is characterized by dwarfism and a very low level of intellectual functioning. While the effects of hypothyroidism in the adult are generally reversible by the administration of thyroid extract, the effects of insufficiency during early development are largely irreversible. The thyroid gland thus has two different types of effects.

Many of the endocrine glands are concerned primarily with maintenance of the proper internal environment. Such functions as regulation of the sodium and calcium levels in the blood, or even the maintenance of pregnancy, need not concern us here. More interesting is the study of the effects of the *gonads,* which are the most directly influential in controlling behavior.

The migration of birds is an activity which seems to be quite directly under hormonal control. While there are still unanswered questions about it, the general pattern seems to be that the length of the day influences pituitary activity, which causes seasonal changes in gonad development on which migration depends. Artificial manipulation of day length may cause migration out of season.[24] A number of other studies show the specific control of some forms of behavior by hormones in birds. Male chicks injected with testosterone propionate develop all the sexual-behavior patterns of adult cocks. Male hormones also cause aggressive behavior, which may result in an animal ranking higher in a dominance hierarchy.[25]

Sexual behavior, however, is not completely under hormonal control even in birds. While pigeons usually cease mating after castration, mating may be induced by particularly active female pigeons.[26] This continuation of sexual activity in the absence of the supporting hormone is more common in higher mammals than in pigeons. Similarly, sexual receptivity in women is not as dependent on variations in hormone level during the menstrual cycle as is the case with lower mammals. As we go up the phylogenetic scale, learned central-nervous-system control of behavior becomes more important. The most striking effects of hormones on behavior are thus shown by animals other than mammals.

The effects of sex hormones on behavior seem to involve not only current activation of structures but also differences in development. Animals castrated before maturity do not exhibit sexual behavior, while those castrated after maturity may continue to show it.[27] Similarly, capons and poulards behave differently after the same hormone treatment. These and other similar observations suggest that many of the more important influences of hormones on behavior are mediated not just by current activation but by the development of structures in the central nervous system. Later in this chapter a model of motivation will be presented which provides one explanation of how these two types of effect might come about.

In human beings, the study of hormones has led to dramatic explanations of physiological phenomena, which tend to support the view that there is no one-to-one correlation between a specific gland secretion and a certain emotion. Instead there is a growing awareness of the interaction between the endocrine system, the divisions of the nervous system, other body tissues, and the environment. Increasing knowledge of the constant interplay of physiological processes which adapt an organism to the demands of its environment has led to widespread adoption of a new view of medicine and disease developed by Hans Selye,[28] based on the whole-body reaction to extremely severe stress. He called this reaction the *general adaptation syndrome* (*GAS*). It means the body's physiological reaction to all severe threats to its continued existence, whether the stress is caused by burning of its flesh or by conflict in its central nervous system. The entire mechanism of the general adaptation to stress has not been completely discovered, just as knowledge of the hormone system as a whole is far from complete. The initial alarm message which calls it out may be, for example, a hormone secreted by the hypothalamus and received by the pituitary, or it may be a chemical state of the total body. But the clearest endocrine relationship in this stress adaptation is the upsetting of normal feedback between the pituitary secretion *adrenocorticotropic hormone* (*ACTH*) and the *corticosteroid hormones* which are produced by ACTH stimulation of fatty globules on the adrenal glands. Normally the ACTH stimulation of corticosteroid production is regulated by the presence of the hormones themselves in the blood. The general stress adaptation somehow stimulates the production of ACTH regardless of the volume of corticosteroids in the blood, allowing them to increase. They have the ability to wall off the sites of invading destructive microorganisms and perform other defensive functions, while some of them produce anti-inflammation effects. Prolonged reliance, however, on the very complex general adaptation syndrome causes physical damage to the organism, of a sort different from what would be caused by the stressor itself; e.g., burning of the animal's feet causes bleeding lesions in its stomach. Let us look at rats exposed by Selye to prolonged cold.[29] A hundred rats were put into living quarters kept at near-freezing temperature. After 2 days ten animals were sacrificed, and their physical changes were noted. The corticosteroid-producing fat bodies on their adrenals had been consumed, and their adrenal glands were enlarged by the process of making more. Their thymus glands were decreased, and they all had stomach ulcers. At this time twenty more of these rats were put into an even colder room with rats which had been living at comfortable temperature. The rats which had had the 2 days at near-freezing temperature were not able to stand this as well as the rats put straight into it from room temperature. Yet after 5 weeks in it, the rats from the original cold chamber were able to withstand conditions of extreme cold which rats directly from room temperature could not. Were they adapted to cold? Apparently they were adapted only in the sense that they were depending on their general adaption to stress mechanisms. Exhaustion eventually killed them.

The degree of stress which calls out this stress syndrome varies from a fatal shock to an amount which will call it out in one individual but not in another. Studies of the degree of psychological stress which produces the general adaptation syndrome in human beings have necessarily been difficult, from the point of view of rigid experimental controls. Many controlled observations of the phenomena have nevertheless been made.[30] One such study was done by Bunney et al.,[31] using level of corticosteroids as the dependent variable. Patients in a mental hospital who had depressive psychoses were tested for daily corticosteroid levels and independently rated on their state of psychological well-being. Experiences of the patients which they reacted to as being severely ego-threatening were also recorded, separately. When the patients were suffering a severe depressive psychotic crisis as observed by the psychological raters, coinciding on the record with at least three separate violently ego-threatening experiences, such as being told that they were not going to be relased from the hospital on their expected release date, their corticosteroid levels were almost three times the level of their average for the previous 3 months.

An unusually carefully controlled field experiment by Sachar et al.[32] gives a glimpse into the possible physical-survival value of mental illness. Corticosteroid levels in six psychiatric patients hospitalized for psychosis jumped to high levels during the active psychotherapeutically induced "working through" of a problem which they had been unable to face alone. Corticosteroid levels *after* resolution of the psychological conflict and subsequent recovery of a normally functioning mental state were very similar to levels while the patients were still psychotic but before the psychiatric disruption of their psychotic fantasies. One possible interpretation is that being in a state of organized psychosis—severe mental illness characterized by denial of reality—gives temporary protection from the physiologically destructive GAS. Another study on this topic will be discussed in Chapter 6.

Causality is usually regarded as a one-way street in which physical events cause psychological events. The regarding of physical events as somehow more basic than psychological events is somewhat similar to early attempts to reduce all medicine to anatomy. To the untrained observer, anatomy may seem more real than physiology—where there are physical structures of flesh and bone, no one can have any doubt about their reality. How much more concrete and satisfying they seem than gradients of ion concentration, which can only be inferred from sophisticated measurements. Yet it is now clear that anatomy is no more fundamental than physiology. In the development of the embryo, differences in ion concentration, which cannot be directly observed, cause anatomical differences which can. Similarly, psychological events can cause physical events as well as be caused by them. Sexual behavior provides a good example. Sexual excitement, from environmental stimulation, causes the pituitary to release *gonadotrophins,* which stimulate the production of androgens (male sex hormones) by the gonads.[33] A psychological state thus influences hormone production just as the hormones influence psychological states. This is especially clear in the case of anxiety, where a psychological state can call out stress reactions which have profound physical effects on the organism.

A Theory of Motivation

While there have been many theories of motivation proposed and probably no existing theory can account for all the data in the area, one of the most successful seems to be one proposed by Deutsch.[34]

Because it provides for separate systems for perceptual analysis and response pattern, it is more compatible with the observations of the ethologists than some theories. Similarly, it provides mechanisms for the activating of motives, which are at least not contradictory of the ways in which hormones operate. It has been applied by Deutsch specifically to some research areas, such as that of thirst, and is especially able to account for some of the effects of electrical stimulation of the brain which cause difficulties for other theories.

This great compatibility with the data, however, has come about to a large extent because the theory is not yet very complete or explicit. It is, rather, a schematic overall model which needs to be completed with more precise formulations of how it applies in different areas. Given the present state of knowledge of motivation, the programmatic nature of the theory is probably not a disadvantage. The whitening bones of discarded theories of motivation along the roadside should perhaps warn the theorist to proceed cautiously in this area.

Two distinctive features of Deutsch's model of motivation, besides its separate perceptual and response systems, are its proposal that it is some positive stimulation which terminates motivated behavior and its suggestion of separate arousal and reinforcement mechanisms. The former of these features is just the opposite of the latest revision of Hull's motivational model, which suggests that drive stimuli initiate and maintain motivated behavior while their absence terminates it, but is more similar to Tinbergen and Lorenz's[35] instinct model. Tinbergen noted that at least for some instinctive acts, the extent to which the act was performed would be a function of the length of time since the behavior was engaged in. In his system, then, it was not a reduction of drive stimuli which terminated the goal response. Instead, the response was simply run off in proportion to the amount of accumulated drive. Deutsch's model differs in specifying that feedback from the goal object is necessary to terminating the drive. In both theories the consummatory act may end independently of the ending of the stimulation which initiated that consummatory act.

For thirst, at least, it is clear that separate mechanisms initiate and terminate the drinking activity. First it was demonstrated that water entering the stomach was not necessary to the terminating of drinking. A dog with a *fistula* which prevented the water from entering the stomach still drank the appropriate amount of water for the length of time it had been deprived of water and then stopped drinking.[36] After a time of not drinking, the animal would again drink the appropriate amount of water. This result suggests that (1) the drinking is terminated by a mechanism which does not depend on the water actually being absorbed, but (2) the drinking is initiated by a mechanism which does depend on the absorption of an adequate amount of water to meet the body's needs, so that drinking will be initiated again when the fistula prevents the absorption of the water.

The separate mechanisms for initiating and terminating drinking are shown even more directly by the results of placing water directly in the stomach of a thirsty dog.[37] If the dog is allowed to drink right away, before the water can be absorbed, it will drink the same amount as it would have if the water had not been placed in its stomach. If there is time for the water to be absorbed before the animal is allowed to drink, then it will not drink at all. In the former cases the stimulation from drinking terminates the activity, while in the latter the mechanism initiating drinking is inactivated by removal of the water deficit.

Knowledge of thirst was furthered when Zotterman discovered the sensory structure involved in the termination of drinking. It is a fiber in the tongue which responds to salt and to water in the following ways: The fiber has a high spontaneous rate of discharge, and is thus constantly sending nerve impulses to the central nervous system. When salt, a hypertonic solution, is placed on the tongue, the fiber increases its rate of firing. When water, a hypotonic solution, is placed on the tongue, the fiber decreases its rate of firing.

Combining his own theory and Zotterman's findings, Deutsch suggested the following mechanism of thirst:[38] Drinking is initiated by the central nervous system in response to a deficit state. A separate mechanism terminates drinking, and this mechanism depends on a message indicating that water is being taken in, arriving at the brain in a sufficient amount to overcome the activity initiated by the deficit. In the case of drinking, however, the message is a negative one—the lack of stimulation from a structure which normally sends afferent impulses to the brain. Since Deutsch sees this mechanism as consistent with his theory, it is apparent that the message which terminates motivated behavior in his theory should be interpreted as a change from the normal state of stimulation, whether that change is an increase or decrease in the rate of firing of nerve cells.

Applying this model of thirst, Deutsch pointed out that it could explain the puzzling observation that rats would drink more dilute saline solution than they would pure water. This finding had previously been interpreted in terms of the rat preferring salt water. Deutsch pointed out that it could be due to the greater quantity of dilute saline needed to give the same amount of water message to the brain during drinking. Since the firing of the water-salt fibers is not inhibited as much by dilute saline as it is by plain water, more drinking of dilute saline would be necessary. From this point of view, then, salt water is diluted water.

Deutsch and Jones[39] tested this explanation by a series of experiments in which thirsty rats ran through a T-maze with plain water in one arm and salt water in the other. They learned to run to the plain water, showing that their greater drinking of salt water was not due to a preference for it. These results, as well as those of the earlier research, thus strongly support Deutsch's model as applied to thirst. Unfortunately, less is known about many other drives, and it is not yet clear that stimulation from the goal object is necessary to terminate all drives. It might be the case, for example, that some actions were terminated by feedback from performance of the act or even by the sending of the neural messages to perform the act without any feedback that this had been done. This latter case would most closely approximate the ethological model.

One example showing that different drives may act differently is that of hunger as contrasted with thirst. As we have seen, a dog with a fistula so that water does not enter its stomach will still stop drinking after lapping an amount of water appropriate to its water deficit. However, it does not stop eating when it has swallowed an amount of food appropriate to its hunger. In an experiment reported by Hull,[40] a dog weighing 10 kilograms and having a fistula ate 8 kilograms of food before pausing. In contrast to the case with thirst, apparently the mere act of chewing and swallowing food does not terminate eating. This result does not contradict Deutsch's theory, for appropriate feedback for terminating eating may be initiated at a later stage than the passage of food through the mouth. It should make us leery, however, of assuming that all drives necessarily operate in the same way. Instead they may have evolved different mechanisms on the basis of adaptation. It would be interesting to study hunger comparatively in different animals, for example. Is eating terminated in the same way in a dog and in a herbivore? An animal which makes an occasional kill and must eat as much of it as possible to maintain itself until the next one might well have a different mechanism for controlling eating than an animal in which intake of food was more gradual and steady. In terms of our present knowledge, it is thus quite possible that some motivated behavior may conform to the model proposed by Tinbergen and Lorenz rather than that proposed by Deutsch.

Deutsch's model is illustrated in Figure 4–3. It functions as follows: The basic unit of the system is a *link*, which is connected with an analyzer and with the motor system. Each *analyzer* is sensitive to one environmental cue which sometimes precedes reinforcement. At the end of the chain of links there is a primary link which is activated by some physiological factor, such as dehydration or testosterone, and which has its activity terminated by some specific message such as that we have considered for thirst.

When the primary link is activated by a motive, the excitation travels down the *motivational pathway* to the links connected with it. At each link, if the link is not being activated by its own analyzer, the impulse simply continues on to other links. If, however, the analyzer is responding to its environmental cue, then the link causes the nerve impulse to travel into the motor system connected with that link. That will usually cause the analyzer connected with the next link in sequence to become activated by its environmental cue, and the motor activities will continue in order until the analyzer of the primary link is activated, causing reinforcement.

Let us apply the model to a thirsty rat which is dropped into a maze with which it is familiar. The maze has ten turns, with turn 1 closest to the starting point and turn 10 closest to the goal box, and the rat is dropped in at turn 4. The rat will have developed, through past running of the maze, analyzers corresponding to the turns in sequence. The analyzer corresponding to turn 4 will be activated by

Figure 4–3 *Deutsch's model of motivation.*

the rat's recognition of its location in the maze. That will cause it to move forward in the maze until it sees turn 5, which will activate the analyzer corresponding to turn 5, and so on until the rat reaches the end of the maze and drinks.

Obviously, the system is dependent for its operation on the links being connected in the sequence in which their analyzers are likely to become activated on the route to reinforcement. Deutsch assumes that (1) the stimulus for terminating activity of the primary analyzer for each drive is innate, (2) all links are connected by potential pathways at birth, and (3) pathways between links become functional on the basis of the links becoming activated in turn. (The *reinforcement pathway* serves to communicate from one link to another when one is being activated and thus makes this third type of learning possible.) The system is able to account for phenomena such as place learning and latent learning because links may be built up into chains (of knowledge about the environment) before any primary link fires (reinforcement).[41]

In the introduction we looked at research by James Olds on pleasure centers in the brain.[42] Olds found that if electrodes were implanted in the septal region of a rat's brain, the rat would press a lever almost indefinitely in order to receive the electrical stimulation. What do these results imply about a theory of motivation? At first glance, they would seem to eliminate a homeostatic theory and argue for a hedonistic one. According to the most widely accepted homeostatic model, it was reduction in drive stimuli which was reinforcing, while hedonism has always assumed that it was some sort of positive stimulation which was pleasurable, and thus sought out by the organism. Because it was this sort of positive stimulation which was found to be reinforcing in Olds's research, it seemed to argue for a hedonistic model.

On further consideration, the interpretation of the experiment becomes less clear. The same information may be carried by either a positive or a negative message. It is quite common for neurons to inhibit the activity of other neurons. Olds's results thus do not necessarily rule out a homeostatic model. It could be that drive stimuli inhibited the action of the pleasure centers, which were otherwise active. In that case, pleasure would correspond to a lack of homeostatic imbalance.

While almost any theory of motivation is compatible with the existence of some sort of center for reinforcement, there are more specific properties of these centers which most theories have difficulty in accounting for. One of these properties of the pleasure centers was shown in an experiment by Wyrwicka, Dobrzecka, and Tarnecki.[43] They found that animals which had been trained to perform a habit for food began to perform it if they were given intracranial stimulation. Animals which had not been trained on the habit did not perform it when they were given the electrical stimulation. In this case, as is pointed out by Deutsch and Howarth,[44] the stimulation seems to be activating a motive rather than merely reinforcing behavior. The result makes sense in terms of Deutsch's model, which assumes that reinforcement involves both arousal through the motivation pathway and reinforcement through the reinforcement pathway. In the naïve animals, there are no functional connections between the various links involved in the learned behavior. The motivational and reinforcement pathways connecting the links are developed as a result of the training the animals receive. The electrical stimulation is assumed to activate both the motivational pathway and the reinforcement pathway. It therefore not only acts as a reinforcer but also activates the links involved in the learned behavior and calls it out in the trained animals. It does not call out the behavior in the naïve animals, of course, because they lack the functional pathways necessary to performing the behavior in response to the motivation.

The results of the Wyrwicka, Dobrzecka, and Tarnecki experiment are especially interesting because they hint at how endocrines could have some of the results they do have. While the current-activation role of endocrines is built into Deutsch's model in the form of activation of primary links, which he explicitly states to be due to such physiological factors as increases in testosterone level, it is more difficult at first to see how early hormone levels could have permanent effects on adult behavior. (This phenomenon was pointed out earlier in the chapter, where it was noted that there are differences in the behavior of animals castrated before and after maturity.) In Deutsch's model, the presence or absence of hormones would determine whether the primary link became activated, and activity of the primary link would be necessary to chains of secondary links becoming connected with it. This model thus seems able to account for hormone influence on the development of structures involved in response patterns.

While Deutsch and his coworker Howarth have done a number or experiments applying Deutsch's theory to intracranial electrical stimulation of pleasure centers,[45] perhaps one of the simplest will best illustrate why it seems necessary to postulate separate motivational and reinforcement pathways. Habits learned and performed for intracranial stimulation differ from other motivated behavior in at least two ways. One of these is that the animal does not become satiated. An animal pressing a lever for food pellets will stop when its hunger drive has been satisfied; one pressing it for electrical reinforcers never seems to become satisfied. This result would make sense if, as Deutsch proposes, the electrical stimulation stimulated a motivational pathway and aroused the motive each time it was received. The second unusual characteristic of the habit performed for intracranial stimulation was demonstrated by Deutsch and Howarth. The extinction of the habit depends on the mere passage of time rather than on unreinforced trials.

Normally, an animal which has learned to press a lever for a reinforcement will need to press it many times without receiving the reinforcement before it will extinguish the habit. If it does not have extinction trials but is merely removed from the situation, it will show little diminution of the habit with the passage of years. As soon as it is returned to the box with the lever, it will, if hungry, begin to press the lever.

Deutsch and Howarth tried the simple experiment of training a rat to press a lever for intracranial stimulation and then removing the lever for 7 seconds. The lever was then returned, but pressing it no longer brought about brain stimulation. (That is, the animal was then given normal extinction trials.) Under these circumstances, the animal only pressed the lever the number of times it would have pressed it if it had also been pressing it during the 7 seconds. The animals stopped pressing the lever, not because the habit had extinguished from unreinforced trials, but simply through the passage of time. How could behavior which is insatiable also be forgotten in less than a minute? It probably could not be forgotten, but it could temporarily disappear if the motive on which it was based was inactivated. Apparently the electrical stimulation not only serves as a reinforcer but also arouses the motive which the reinforcer satisfies, as proposed by Deutsch's model. Many other more complicated experiments by Deutsch and Howarth support the same conclusion.

That the same electrical stimulation should both arouse and satisfy a motive seems paradoxical. The paradox, however, is not new to us. In the discussion of Hull's concept of secondary reinforcement, it was noted that according to his theory the same conditions aroused motives and reinforced them. Except that it does not propose that all motives are homeostatic, Deutsch's model illustrates how the paradoxical nature of secondary reinforcement could be brought about.

PHYSIOLOGY AND EMOTION

In looking at physiological mechanisms of motivation, which are essentially the same for all people, we have perhaps raised as important questions as we have answered. Different cultures, and even different individuals, are notoriously different in the motives on which they act. If their motives are based on the same physiological mechanisms, how can people be driven to such different ends? Ernest Hemingway, for example, used to amuse himself by putting the lions in someone else's lion act through their paces. Since lions are probably less easily managed by a stranger than by their usual trainer, it is perhaps not surprising that most novelists manage to find other ways of amusing themselves. How are we to account for the differences?

One way in which people come to be motivated differently has already been pointed out. They learn preferences for different incentives on the basis of experience, or, in the terms of Deutsch's model, secondary links connected to analyzers recognizing different environmental cues become connected to their primary links. Thus it is possible to learn to want to eat such diverse foods as roots and berries, uncooked meat, and raw mollusks. As well as the carrots, blueberries, steak tartare, and oysters eaten in our own culture, people have come to like eating a surprising number of things.

A second basic way in which motives can differ although based on the same physiological mechanisms was demonstrated in a study by Schachter and Singer.[16] Essentially, their findings show that physiological arousal is an ambiguous stimulus which may be perceived differently. The same physiological state may be interpreted as different emotions, depending on the social context in which it occurs.

What Schacter and Singer did was to have a physician inject subjects with either *epinephrine* or a *placebo,* a dilute saline solution having no physiological effects. The placebo treatment acted as a control and enabled the experimenters to be sure that the effects they were observing were not just due to the subjects knowing that they had been given a drug and feeling that it should have some effect. Some subjects who were given the epinephrine were correctly told what its physical effects would be—shaking hands, a flushed face, and a pounding heart. Others were misinformed as to its effects and told that it might make their feet feel numb. The prediction was that subjects who were misinformed about the effects of the epinephrine would ascribe their physiological arousal to an emotion aroused by the social situation they were in, while those who knew that the epinephrine caused their arousal would not experience any strong emotion.

An essential part of the experiment, then, was to create different social situations which the physiological arousal could be ascribed to. Two such situations were created, one in which the subject might reasonably expect to feel euphoric and one in which he might feel angry. Each involved the use of a confederate who was supposedly also a subject in the experiment. In one situation the confederate acted in a wild and silly manner, playing a game of basketball with scraps of paper and a wastebasket, making a slingshot, and playing with a hula hoop. In the anger situation, on the other hand, the confederate objected to a questionnaire which he and the real subject were filling out, eventually tearing it up and leaving the room. It was predicted that where the subject was misinformed about the effects of the epinephrine, he would report feeling the same as the confederate —happy or angry depending on the behavior of the confederate— but that he would not report these emotional reactions when he realized that his physiological arousal was due to the drug.

In general the results supported the hypothesis very strongly. In the euphoria treatment, the subjects who had been misinformed about the effects of the hormone not only reported more happy emotion than those who knew what the hormone did, they even behaved differently. The misinformed subjects significantly more often started playing the wild games with the confederate! Thus the subjects in the different treatments, although they were experiencing the same physiological arousal, attributed it to happiness or anger depending on the social context in which it occurred. Having interpreted the ambiguous stimulus of their physiological state as due to an emotion, they then behaved in a way appropriate to the emotion. The person who fights and the one who runs away, for example, may differ, not in physiological state, but in whether the physiological state is attributed to fear or anger. By interpreting individuals' emotions for them, cultures may call out radically different behavior from the same physiological base.

Summary

Some animal species show behavior which is complex, unlearned, and properly described as instinctive. Earlier in the history of psychology a futile attempt was made to describe most human behavior in instinctive terms. Later human behavior was viewed as virtually entirely learned, perhaps overlooking some innate features.

Research by ethologists has added several important concepts to our attempt to understand the interrelations of heredity and environment. These are the fixed motor pattern, the innate releasing mechanism, and imprinting. The meanings of these concepts were illustrated in studies of the behavior of rats, polecats, geese, monkeys, and small fish called sticklebacks. The ethological approach of not asking whether a behavior pattern is innate, but instead asking whether portions of it are innate, seems to lead to a clearer understanding of much animal behavior.

Following Lashley and Beach, four effects of hormones may be distinguished. They may influence the general excitability of the organism, the development of structures involved in behavior, the sensitivity of the sense organs, or the functioning of specific portions of the central nervous system. That the interrelationships among hormones, learning, and behavior are complex has been illustrated by studies of sexual behavior, the effects of stress, and psychiatric patients.

A model of physiological motivation developed by Deutsch seems to be more compatible with the ethological data than most. Two distinctive features of this model are that behavior is initiated and terminated in different ways and that separate pathways are involved in motivation and reinforcement. Consistent with Deutsch's model and especially significant in understanding human motivation is research by Schachter and Singer on emotional states.

Notes and Acknowledgments

1. Teale, Edwin Way (Ed.). *The Fascinating Insect World of J. Henri Fabre.* Greenwich, Conn.: Fawcett Publications, Inc., 1956.
2. Additional material on McDougall and instinct theories in psychology may be found in Edwin Boring, *A History of Experimental Psychology,* and C. N. Cofer and M. H. Appley, *Motivation: Theory and Research.*

3. Bernard, L. L. *Instinct: A Study in Social Psychology.* New York: Henry Holt and Company, Inc., 1924.

4. Cannon, W. B. *The Wisdom of the Body.* (2d ed.) New York: W. W. Norton & Company, Inc., 1939.

5. Richter, C. P. "Total self-regulatory functions in animals and human beings." *Harvey Lectures, 1942–1943* (38), pp. 63–103.

   This is summarized in Cofer, C. N., and M. H. Appley. *Motivation: Theory and Research.* New York: John Wiley & Sons, Inc., 1966, pp. 306–313.

6. Davis, D. M. "Self-selection of diet by newly weaned infants." *American Journal of Diseases of Children,* 1928 (36), pp. 651–679.

7. Harlow, Harry F. "Love in infant monkeys." *Scientific American,* June, 1959, and "The heterosexual affectional system in monkeys." *American Psychologist,* 1962 (17), pp. 1–10.

8. Spitz, R. A. "Hospitalism: An inquiry into the genesis of psychiatric conditions in early childhood" in Anna Freud et al. (Eds.), *The Psychoanalytic Study of the Child.* Vol. I. New York: International Universities Press, 1945, pp. 53–74.

   Spitz, R. A. "Hospitalism: A follow-up report on investigations described in vol. I" in Anna Freud et al. (Eds.), *The Psychoanalytic Study of the Child.* Vol. II. New York: International Universities Press, Inc., 1946, pp. 113–117.

9. Bowlby, J. *Maternal Care and Mental Health* and *Deprivation of Maternal Care.* New York: Schocken, 1966.

10. Tinbergen, Nicholas. Preface to Claire H. Schiller (Ed.), *Instinctive Behavior.* New York: International Universities Press, Inc., 1957, p. xvi. By permission of the publisher.

11. Eibl-Eibesfeldt, Irenaeus. "The interactions of unlearned behavior patterns and learning in mammals" in the symposium, *Brain Mechanisms and Learning.* Springfield, Ill.: Charles C Thomas, Publisher, 1961, pp. 53–73.

12. Tinbergen, N. *The Study of Instinct.* Fair Lawn, N.J.: Oxford University Press, 1958, p. 78.

13. *Ibid.,* p. 39.

14. Lorenz, Konrad. "Companionship in bird life" in Claire H. Schiller (Ed.), *op. cit.*

15. Tinbergen. *The Study of Instinct,* pp. 58–60.

16. *Ibid.,* p. 61.

17. *Ibid.,* pp. 61–62.

18. McGraw, Myrtle. "Maturation of behavior" in Leonard Carmichael (Ed.), *Manual of Child Psychology.* New York: John Wiley & Sons, Inc., 1949, chap. 7.

19. *Ibid.*

20. Katz, David. *Animals and Men.* Baltimore: Penguin Books, 1953, figs. 19 and 20. Photographs by kind permission of Dr. Rosa Katz.

21. Lashley, K. S. "Experimental analysis of instinctive behavior." *Psychological Review,* 1938 (45), pp. 445–471.

22. Beach, F. A. *Hormones and Behavior*. New York: Paul B. Hoeber, Inc., 1948.
23. Wilkens, Lawson. "The thyroid gland." *Scientific American*, March, 1960.
24. Rowan, W. "Experiments in bird migration: III. The effects of artificial light, castration, and certain extracts on the autumn movements of the American crow." *Proceedings of the National Academy of Sciences*, 1932 (18), pp. 639–654.
25. Allee, W. C. "Social dominance and subordination among vertebrates." *Biological Symposia*, 1942 (8), pp. 139–162.
26. Carpenter, C. R. "Psychobiological studies of social behavior in Aves: II. The effect of complete and incomplete gonadectomy on secondary sexual activity, with histological studies." *Journal of Comparative Psychology*, 1933 (16), pp. 59–98.
27. Tinbergen. *The Study of Instinct*, p. 65.
28. Selye, Hans. *The Physiology and Pathology of Exposure to Stress*. Montreal: Acta, 1950.

   Selye, Hans. *The Stress of Life*. New York: McGraw-Hill Book Company, 1956.
29. *Ibid.*, pp. 88–89.
30. Bliss, E. L., et al. "Reaction of the adrenal cortex to emotional stress." *Psychosomatic Medicine*, 1956 (18), p. 56.

   Hamburg, D. A. "Plasma and urinary cortico-steroid levels in naturally occurring psychological stresses." Ultrastructure and Metabolism of the Nervous System, *Proceedings of the Association for Research in Nervous and Mental Diseases*, 1962 (25), p. 426.

   Sachar, E., et. al. "Psychoendocrine aspects of acute schizophrenic reactions." *Psychosomatic Medicine*, 1963 (25), pp. 510–537.

   Sachar, E., et al. "Psychoendocrinology of ego disruption and reintegration in schizophrenia." To be published.

   Bunney, W. E., and J. A. Fawcett. "Possibility of a biochemical test for suicidal potential." *Archives of General Psychiatry*, 1965 (12), p. 232.
31. Bunney, W. E., John W. Mason, John F. Roatch, and David A. Hamburg. "A psychoendocrine study of severe psychotic depressive crisis." *American Journal of Psychiatry*, July, 1965, pp. 72–80.
32. Sachar, Edward J., John M. Mackenzie, William A. Binstock, and John E. Mack. "Corticosteroid responses to psychotherapy of depression: I. Evaluations during confrontation of loss." *Archives of General Psychiatry*, April, 1967 (16), pp. 461–470.
33. Klopfer, Peter H., aud Jack P. Hailman. *An Introduction to Animal Behavior: Ethology's First Century*. Englewood Cliffs, N.J.: Prentice-Hall, Inc., 1967, pp. 120–121.
34. Deutsch, J. A. *The Structural Basis of Behavior*. Chicago: The University of Chicago Press, 1960.
35. Tinbergen, *The Study of Instinct*.
36. Bellows, R. T. "Time factors in water drinking in dogs." *American Journal of Physiology*, 1939 (125), pp. 87–97.
37. Adolph, E. F. "The internal environment and behavior: III. Water content." *American Journal of Psychiatry*, 1941 (97), pp. 1367–1373.

38. Deutsch, J. A., and A. D. Jones. "Diluted water: An explanation of the rat's peference for saline." *Journal of Comparative and Physiological Psychology*, 1960 (53), pp. 122–127.

39. *Ibid*.

40. Hull, C. L., F. R. Livingston, R. O. Rouse, and O. N. Barker. "True, sham, and esophageal feeding as reinforcements." *Journal of Comparative and Physiological Psychology*, 1951 (44), pp 236–245.

41. Deutsch, J. A. *Op. cit.*

42. Olds, James. "Pleasure centers in the brain." *Scientific American*, October, 1956.

43. Wyrwicka, W., C. Dobrzecka, and R. Tarnecki. "On the instrumental conditioned reaction evoked by electrical stimulation of the hypothalamus." *Science*, 1959 (130), pp. 336–337.

44. Deutsch, J. A., and C. I. Howarth. "Some tests of a theory of intracranial self-stimulation." *Psychological Review*, 1963 (70), pp. 461–470.

45. *Ibid*.

46. Schachter, Stanley, and Jerome Singer. "Cognitive, social, and physiological determinants of emotional state" in R. J. C. Harper et al. (Eds.), *The Cognitive Processes: Readings*. Englewood Cliffs, N.J.: Prentice-Hall, Inc., 1964, pp. 426–449.

David Gahr

FIVE

PERSONALITY

In the last two chapters we have looked at the areas of learning and motivation. Personality is often approached as an adjunct to these areas. To attempt to account for the complex phenomena of personality in terms of inadequately established principles from other areas, however, leads to a neglect of some of the major phenomena of personal and social behavior. While principles of learning, motivation, and personal and social adjustment must someday become consistent with each other, it is by no means clear which theories will need to change for this rapprochement to come about. Recent studies by learning theorists of learning through observing others seem to be bringing learning theory closer to psychoanalytic theory in its point of view.[1] In this chapter personality will therefore be approached primarily from the point of view of psychoanalytic theory. It is felt by the author that this theoretical approach, not guided by theories drawn from other areas of study, has most clearly concentrated on the major attributes of personality as such.

There are, however, difficulties in presenting psychoanalytic theory in an introductory text. The most important of these difficulties is one which is common to the presentation of any highly descriptive approach. It is that the raw data upon which the theory is based are not easily summarized. Just as it is probably true that it is impossible to understand an ethological approach without observing animals in the wild, it is also difficult to understand a psychoanalytic approach without observation of analytically oriented psychotherapy. It will not be possible to do this. Instead it will only be possible to present a few experiments providing evidence on psychoanalytic hypotheses and some anecdotes to illustrate how the theory might be applied.[2] The reader will have to judge the usefulness of the theory largely on the basis of whether it gives him additional insight into himself. Let us look, then, at the three basic assumptions of psychoanalytic theory and a somewhat oversimplified account of the theory itself.

1   The first and most basic assumption of Freudian theory is that experience and behavior are *caused*, by the interaction of the individual's motives and the environmental forces on him. If this point of view is accepted, then even such apparently accidental occurrences as a slip of the tongue, inability to remember a name, and a nocturnal dream represent actions that are in some way and on some level motivated. As motivated behavior they are facts which a theory of behavior must account for and just as important as whether Lashley's rats chose the triangle or Harlow's monkeys preferred the cloth "mother."

2   The second of Freud's assumptions arose from the first. If all mental phenomena are motivated yet we are unaware of the motives for some of them, then some of our mental processes must be unconscious. Furthermore, this unconsciousness must be of a peculiar type. It is not the unconsciousness which results from not being provided with sensory receptors to make us able to be aware of something, as in our unconsciousness of the activities of the pace setter in

our heart. Instead it is an unconsciousness of something which yet influences our mental life and which, under the right circumstances, we can become conscious of. It is thus, in light of the first assumption, a motivated unconscious—a keeping something from awareness because we do not want to be aware of it.

A number of phenomena vividly demonstrate the operation of unconscious processes. While most people are familiar with some of these in the area of hypnotism, such as the carrying out of post-hypnotic suggestions without remembering that they have been suggested during a trance, the clearest evidence from hypnotism is less well known. It has recently been discovered that under hypnosis surgical patients will remember their experiences while they were under a general anesthetic.[3] There can be no doubt that such memories are unconscious under normal circumstances.

Another dramatic illustration of unconscious processes is the spontaneous occurrence of states of amnesia, sometimes with development of a new life and new personality during the amnesic period. One of the cases summarized by William James in 1890 provides a good example:

> The Rev. Ansel Bourne, of Green, R.I., was brought up to the trade of a carpenter; but, in consequence of a sudden temporary loss of sight and hearing under very peculiar circumstances, he became converted from Atheism to Christianity just before his thirtieth year, and has since that time for the most part lived the life of an itinerant preacher. He has been subject to headaches and temporary fits of depression of spirits during most of his life, and has had a few fits of unconsciousness lasting an hour or less. . . .

> On January 17, 1887, he drew 551 dollars from a bank in Providence with which to pay for a certain lot of land in Greene, paid certain bills, and got into a Pawtucket horse-car. This is the last incident which he remembers. He did not return home that day, and nothing was heard from him for two months. He was published in the papers as missing, and foul play being suspected, the police sought in vain for his whereabouts. On the morning of March 14th, however, at Norristown, Pennsylvania, a man calling himself A. J. Brown, who had rented a small shop six weeks previously, stocked it with stationery, confectionary, fruit and small articles, and carried on his quiet trade without seeming to anyone unnatural or eccentric, woke up in a fright and called in the people of the house to tell him where he was. He said that his name was Ansel Bourne, that he was entirely ignorant of Norristown, that he knew nothing of shop-keeping, and that the last thing he remembered—it seemed only yesterday—was drawing the money from the bank, etc., in Providence. . . .

*This was all that was known of the case up to June 1890, when I
induced Mr. Bourne to submit to hypnotism, so as to see whether, in
the hypnotic trance, his "Brown" memory would not come back. It
did so with surprising readiness. . . .*[4]

3   The third basic Freudian assumption is also illustrated in the
example just cited, for it is that the self is not unitary, but instead
composed of conflicting parts. This is quite clear in the case of Mr.
Bourne, but what is meant by saying that the normal person is made
up of conflicting parts? Another example, this one hypothetical, may
help make the point clear.

Imagine that you have just come home, late in the evening, from
a large dinner at a Chinese restaurant. Tired, and well filled with
shrimp curry and other exotic dishes, you go to bed. Just as you are
about to go to sleep, however, it becomes clear to you that you have
overindulged in curry powder, soy sauce, or both, for you find yourself consumed by a raging thirst. If you were not so nearly asleep,
you would get up and get something to drink. If you were not thirsty,
you would go to sleep. As it is, you lie there in a conflict situation,
with part of you wanting to get up and get a drink and part of you
not wanting to bother. As you lie there almost asleep, you are likely
to imagine mountain brooks, luscious watermelons, and frosty bottles
of beer. These dreams, unfortunately, do not do much to satisfy the
thirst.

This example is chosen to illustrate that not all psychological
conflicts are the life-and-death struggles between unreconciled parts
of a personality that may be found in highly disturbed individuals.
Instead, psychological conflict is something which we all experience
every day but which we may not pay attention to or recognize as
such. The division of the personality into conflicting parts by Freudian theory is simply a generalization about what impulses are most
frequently in opposition to each other when this conflict is experienced. Let us look, then, at what these parts of the personality are
and how they develop from each other according to the theory.

The infant, according to Freud, is all id. What does this mean?
Id is the name Freud gave to the basic, innate drives or impulses of
the individual. It would include not only those of known physiological basis, such as hunger and thirst, but also those such as the
contact-comfort drive of Harlow's monkeys that we do not know the
basis of. By saying that the infant is all id, Freud meant that the
infant is not aware of anything except his own biological drives.

Having no experience with the world, the infant is not aware of the nature of reality or, in fact, of the difference between himself and the rest of the world. It is only later that the child learns that he can move his fingers by willing it but cannot move the dresser by doing so.

At this earliest stage the infant thinks in what is called—because it comes first in development—*primary process thinking*. Because he is unacquainted with the real world, he cannot distinguish between real and imagined satisfaction of his desires. He thus attempts to satisfy his desires by imagining the object he desires. His fantasy gratification has the advantage of being immediate but has the grave disadvantage that it does not actually reduce the physiological drive the desire is based on. In this sense it is like the thirsty person's imaginary watermelon, which would be, in fact, an example of primary process thinking. This type of thinking thus characterizes all the thinking of the infant, while it is only found in some of the thinking of the adult—in dreams, and in humor.

It is the failure of the imagined gratification to provide long-term satisfaction that accounts, in Freudian theory, for the origin of the second major subdivision of the personality—the ego. It is only by learning about the nature of the world and by postponing gratification in order to work for real rewards that the child is able to obtain objects that will really reduce his drives. *Ego* is thus a name for those of our thought processes that show awareness of the nature of the world and make decisions accordingly, a type of process called *secondary process thinking*. To return a final time to our hypothetical example, it is the ego which knows that you must get out of bed to get the drink of water.

The ego thus corresponds approximately to the self we are consciously aware of, that sensible fellow who knows that you cannot get something simply by wishing for it. While the ego provides real objects for the impulses of the id, these drives are satisfied only in a modified form, modified so that the things that are consciously desired are things that are realistically possible. The unrealistic and irrational desires of the id are kept from consciousness. Besides being censored by the ego, these impulses of the id are being modified in another way by the process of development. What it is that is desired is being influenced by what objects have proved satisfying. One person comes to prefer eating potatoes, a second rice, and a third poi because of cultural differences in diet. The object choices, or objects desired by the young child for gratification of drives, may thus influence the desires of the adult in ways that the adult will not be consciously aware of, although this influence may be shown in behavior, as in the case of the man who marries a woman who has striking similarities to his mother which he himself does not recognize. In a sense, then, all motives are social motives from a psychoanalytic point of view, for the motives we act on as adults have been transformed by our social experiences in development.

Besides being influenced by what he wants to do and what he realistically thinks he can get away with doing, an adult is also influenced by considerations of what he has learned he ought to do. These considerations make up the third major component of the personality, the *superego*, and its origin is somewhat more complex according to Freudian theory.

According to the theory, the child at about the age of three or four falls in love with the parent of the opposite sex and develops a rivalry with the parent of the same sex, a phenomenon which Freud called the *Oedipus complex* (or *Electra complex* in the case of girls). While the highly Victorian culture in which Freud worked was scandalized at this imputation of sexuality to children, we should not be so easily shocked now that anthropological investigations have revealed that young children do engage in quite a bit of open sexual play in cultures where it is not forbidden. In fact, the observant parent can easily observe the Oedipus complex in his own children. When my eldest girl was four and my son was two, for example, they would only ride in the back seat of the automobile if the girl could sit on the side of the car closest to me and the boy on the side closest to his mother. As they grew older, this preference reversed, as indeed it should according to the theory.

The boy who has fantasies of winning his mother from his father's embraces, however, is up against apparently insuperable odds, even if his fantasies are not as complete or blood-chilling as the Oedipus myth. His father is simply too large and powerful a rival for him, so that the Oedipus complex is normally resolved by the child *identifying* with the parent of the same sex and getting vicarious satisfaction from the affection which his mother bears his father. (That this may not be the resolution in certain cases where the parent is a weak figure and does not enjoy the affection of the spouse need not concern us here, crucial as it may be for the child.) This process of identification is much more than a copying of the parent of the same sex, although this is one of its important results. It is a breakdown of the newly learned distinction between self and other, so that the boy actually feels himself to be his father and his father to be him. A much more superficial example can be found in an audience watching a boxing match. The man who ducks "his" opponent's blows and throws punches in the air from his seat in the audience has experienced a similar, if momentary, identification.

With the identification of the boy with his father, or girl with her mother, comes a transformation of the child to become the parent. The boy then becomes to the best of his ability what the father is, at least as he perceives the father, and incorporates his image of the father into his personality as his standard of right and wrong—the superego. This third major component of personality has two parts which are nicely distinguished in the service of the Episcopal Church: "We have done those things which we ought not to have done, and left undone those things which we ought to have done, and there is no health in us. . . ." The image of the things which ought to be done was called by Freud the *ego ideal*; the rules of what ought not to be done he called the *conscience.*

While the major significance of a Freudian theory of personality for social psychology is in the theory of conflict and ego defense, one interesting study may be cited at this point to show the usefulness of an identification theory of learning in accounting for social behavior. Sears, Maccoby, and Levin[5] interviewed almost four hundred mothers of five-year-old children to investigate the relationships between child-rearing practices of the mother and aggressive behavior on the part of the child. Two aspects of the mother's behavior were rated separately—the extent to which she tolerated aggression by the child and the amount of physical punishment she used to prevent aggression by the child. (While it might be thought these two indices measured the same thing, this was only true to a limited extent. Some mothers would not tolerate aggression by the child and used physical punishment to deter it, others would not tolerate it but used other means to avoid it, and so on.) Let us look at how the index of amount of punishment should be related to aggression by the child.

According to the usual learning theory, the more children are punished for aggressive behavior, the less they should engage in it. While there is some indication that punishment is not as effective as reward in learning, still it should exercise a deterrent effect which would enable the child to practice and learn other behavior instead.

A straightforward learning-theory approach would thus predict that the mothers who used more punishment for aggressive behavior by their children would have children who acted less aggressively. The opposite prediction, however, is made by a theory of identification. When the mother uses physical punishment on the child, she is serving as a model for aggressive behavior. If the child identifies with her and takes over her patterns of behavior, then the more the child is punished for being aggressive, the more aggressive he should become!

This latter possibility is exactly what the data showed. The mothers who had the fewest aggressive children were those who would not tolerate aggression but who managed to avoid it without showing aggression themselves. Those who had the highest proportion of aggressive children were those who were quite tolerant of aggression on the part of the child and who also used physical punishment on the child for aggressive behavior. The results thus support a theory of role learning and directly contradict a theory of learning based upon the learning of rewarded rather than punished responses. While the results of this, as of any single study, must be interpreted with caution, other studies using other methods again provide supporting results.[6]

The Measurement of Motives

By now the reader may have obtained the impression that it really is quite easy to understand the motives of the adult, reasoning that they would simply mirror the motives of the parent of the same sex, taken over through identification. It must thus be confessed at this point that this is by no means the case and that the account so far has been greatly oversimplified by the neglect of three complicating factors. The first of these factors is that the child develops over a considerable period of time and learns different modes of adjustment to the world at different stages. According to a psychoanalytic point of view, earlier modes of adjustment are never forgotten, but are instead simply denied expression as newer contradictory adjustments are learned. The young child, for example, who has learned to adjust to the world by complete dependency on his mother, does not forget this mode of adjustment as he grows older and learns a more independent role. As an adult he may relapse into it when later

learned modes of adjustment do not work, a phenomenon known as
✱ _regression._ The adult is thus viewed as a series of personalities laid
one on top of the other, stemming from different developmental
periods and with only some of the layers apparent from the surface.
While intensive study of the single individual may bring the various
layers to light, the almost infinite variety of possible patterns makes
it difficult to draw generalizations about all individuals or even all
that on the surface seem similar.

The second complicating factor is that in presenting a strictly
Freudian description of identification with the parent of the same sex
as the source of the superego, more recent developments in psychoanalytic theory have been overlooked. The discerning reader may
have noticed that while the Sears et al. study cited provides evidence
in favor of a theory of social-role learning, it does not provide evidence unambiguously supporting the rather simplified Freudian position which has been described. In the first place, it is questionable
that the Oedipus complex would be resolved by the age of five, so the
positive results are in a sense surprising. Furthermore, even if we
assume that the Oedipus complex has been resolved, classical Freudian theory would lead us to expect different results for the boys and
the girls in the sample. After the resolution of the Oedipus complex,
the girls should have internalized the behavior of the mother, and the
results obtained would have been predicted. The boys, however,
should have identified with their fathers, and their aggressive behavior should have been unrelated to the behavior of their mothers.

In fact, observations such as those cited, and especially studies
in cultural settings other than the one in which Freud worked, have
led psychoanalytic theorists to change and expand on Freudian theory.
For example, Freud's emphasis on the early development of the
child should not make us overlook the fact that socialization continues throughout the lifetime of the individual. From a sociological
point of view, society can only continue to exist if it manages to fill
the essential positions in the society and motivate individuals to carry
out the roles associated with those positions. All the necessary learning for the performance of adult roles cannot take place in childhood,
and the internal voice of conscience is supplemented by the external
voice of authority in ensuring compliance with the demands of
society.

Social control may be viewed as made up of two different mechanisms, although they usually work together. One mechanism for

ensuring compliance with social standards is that emphasized by the phrase "man in society." The individual member of a society usually belongs to a family, a work group, a neighborhood, a church, an occupation, a class, and a nation. If he attempts to violate the strongly held sanctions of his society, he can expect to be berated by his wife, shunned by his work group, rejected by the neighbors, lectured to by his minister, sanctioned by his union or profession, told that he is letting down the members of his class, and arrested on criminal charges by the representatives of his nation.

The other basic method of ensuring compliance to the norms of society is that implied in the phrase "society in man." Despite the ubiquitous forces waiting to punish the man who deviates from the dictates of his society, man has the illusion of being free, for he usually does not want to violate the norms. His socialization has been successful to the point of building into him the desire to act in the ways demanded by his society, and he is unaware of the various mechanisms waiting to punish him for deviation because it would never occur to him to deviate. This is the aspect of social control which is more emphasized by psychoanalytic theory. The other aspect, dealing with the effects of immediate pressures on the individual, will be considered at length in the chapters on small group processes.

The ways in which psychoanalytic theory has been changed to become more consistent with the results of cross-cultural studies are well exemplified in the work of Henry Murray,[7] who has been deeply involved in such studies himself. Murray differs from Freud in his views of both what makes up the superego and how it is formed. While parents, and most especially the parent of the same sex, are still viewed as especially important to its formation, it is recognized that children may identify with other important figures in their lives—not only teachers and other parent substitutes but also friends and even fictional characters—and that these other individuals also shape the values which children develop. Furthermore, the developing individual does not just internalize absolute oughts and ought nots, the ego ideal and conscience, but conditional prohibitions reflecting the norms of the culture. According to Murray, these deal with the time, place, mode, and object appropriate for the expression of an impulse. For example, while eating is an acceptable activity in our culture, there are prohibitions against eating human flesh (the wrong object), with the fingers of both hands (the wrong mode), or in church (the wrong place).

Because of the complexity of the development of social motives in any one individual, social psychologists have to a great extent left the study of the origins of these motives to psychotherapists, who can go into individual cases in great detail, and instead concentrated on measuring the motives after they have developed and relating them to social behavior. One of the first major steps in this direction was also taken by Murray with his development of the well-known *Thematic Apperception Test (TAT)*. Let us look at this test and at a typical experiment applying the measurement of social motives to the prediction of social behavior.

The Thematic Apperception Test is based on the idea, which was discussed in Chapter 2, that individuals will interpret ambiguous situations in terms of their own beliefs, values, and interests. This is especially true of strictly fantasy material, so that the interpretation of dreams is for the psychoanalyst one of the most important sources of information about the individual. Dreams have serious disadvantages for the systematic measurement of social motives, however. First, many people have difficulty in remembering them, which is not surprising since they reveal motives which are kept from consciousness. Equally important, the incident stimulating each dream differs, and is by no means always easily discoverable. Related to this is the final point that the dreams from any one period tend to depend upon the conflicts which the person is wrestling with at that period, and a considerable time may elapse before even a person's major motives appear in his dreams.

These factors argue for the advantages of using some type of known stimulus to trigger fantasy production. By the use of stimuli related to the more important social motives and conflicts, the fantasies can be led into areas that will provide a more systematic and complete picture of social motivation in a shorter period of time than completely unguided fantasy. Also, by knowing the stimulus which started the fantasy, changes and omissions may be more easily noted than where the stimulus must be recreated by inference. Just as it was easier in Allport and Postman's rumor-transmission study to identify distortions because the initial stimuli were known than it would have been if the initial stimuli had had to be inferred from the diverse end products of the rumor-transmission process, social motives are easier to measure from interpretations of known rather than unknown stimuli. Murray thus constructed the TAT as a series of pictures that the subject is to tell stories about. Twenty pictures are used, and they differ depending upon the sex and age of the subject so that situations likely to arouse emotional conflicts can be used.

The interpretation of the TAT is too complex to be discussed in a brief introduction such as this, and is not always equally rewarding, since the telling of brief conventional stories may enable the subject to reveal not very much about himself. At other times, however, a story will touch on central problems and adjustments of the individual. One such example is given by Holt, who uses it to outline the basic ideas in interpretation of the test. Let us look briefly at the story and refer to Holt[8] for a more detailed discussion of it.

In the card to which the story was told, "An adolescent boy looks straight out of the picture. The barrel of a rifle is visible at one side, and in the background is the dim scene of a surgical operation, like a reverie-image." The story told to it by a young college man, here called Nailson, was as follows: "Gee, it looks like a young fellow, (pause.) Oh, fellow is about fifteen, I guess. It's (pause). He's either seen or read about some operation in which the patient has gone through all kinds of tortures, and he decided he's going to become a doctor. He's going to fix things, they're not going to happen like that any more. These are old doctors, very old, long time ago, I guess. They're going to town, probably no ether or anything else. The kid was probably just a young baby at the time, maybe. Looks like he had a nightmare or two. And (pause) that determined his life for him. He's going to spend his whole time trying to be a doctor and not have any more operations like this. He's going to (pause). Well, it could be that he's something like Bliss or some one of the great doctors that invented anaesthetics, something to bring ease to the patient during the operation. Probably spend his whole life trying to develop something like that. Anyway, he's going to be a doctor, he's not going to have anything like this happen again."[9]

While there are a number of things that could be noted in the story, such as not mentioning the rifle, the confusion about the boy's age, and even that the boy is going to spend his time trying to be a doctor, let us look at just a portion of the story. The subject says, "He's either seen or read about some operation in which the patient has gone through all kinds of tortures," and immediately follows this with "and he decided he's going to become a doctor." What he appears to have said at this point is that the boy is going to become a doctor so that he can torture people! The rapidity with which this is denied, by saying, "He's going to fix things, they're not going to happen like that any more," suggests that this same thought is going through the mind of the subject and supports rather than denies the interpretation.

Most stories are not as revealing as this one. Nailson had gone through a period of overt sadism, during which he tortured the animals on his father's farm. After that, he had become very concerned over the welfare of the animals and had taken over all the slaughtering on the farm so that it would be done as humanely as possible. This particular mode of handling a motive, appearing to act on just the opposite motive (humaneness) while giving covert expression to the denied motive (sadism) by taking pleasure in the slaughtering, is called _reaction formation_. It is the same mechanism as that shown by the hero of the story.

Can behavior in social situations actually be predicted by tests such as the TAT? Yes, though certainly not perfectly. Let us look at an experiment by Birney, Burdick, Caylor, O'Connor, and Veroff[10] as an illustration, first describing it as it appeared to the subjects and then as it appeared to the experimenters. Subjects arrived at the laboratory in pairs, each having been told to bring one friend as a fellow subject. It was explained that one of each pair (the encoder) would have the task of putting messages into a code and that the other (the decoder) would have the task of translating the code messages back into English. The encoder would be scored on how many of the messages he managed to put into code within a limited period of time, and the decoder would be scored on what proportion of the code messages he received he managed to decode within a limited period of time.

For each coder, the task proceeded smoothly for the first few trials. After the second and third trials he was shown scores which indicated that his partner was not keeping up with him very well, and after the fourth trial he received a message from his partner asking him to "please slow down." At this point he had to decide whether to make the best score he could by continuing to work fast or to help his partner by slowing down. (Since the partner was being scored on the proportion of code messages decoded, the fewer code messages there were for him to decode, the easier it was for him to make a high score.) Finally, on the last trial, the coder was told that his partner would not have to decode the messages coded on that trial.

The reader may have guessed by now that the experiment was

rigged, for otherwise how could we know what messages the coder's partner would send him? In fact, there were no decoders. Each person was told that he was the coder and his partner was the decoder, and the message to slow down came from the experimenter. The purpose of this deception was to place each subject in the same rather common conflict situation—a situation where the person must decide between achieving the most that he can himself or helping a friend. (For the good student, the conflict is likely to occur whenever there is a course examination. Should you review for the exam with a friend who has less good notes although this will help him more than it helps you, or should you leave him to founder and study on your own?)

 The experiment thus presented the subject with a conflict between an *achievement* motive and a motive of *affiliation*, or maintaining close relations with others. Predictions were made on the basis of measures of these motives which had been taken before the experiment began, using a technique which is similar in principle to the TAT. It was predicted that subjects who were high in need for affiliation but not high in need for achievement would slow down and that those who were high in need for achievement but not high in need for affiliation would continue working rapidly. No predictions were made for subjects who were high in both needs or not high in either.

At this point the complicating factor of sex must be mentioned. The norms in our culture generally develop more achievement motivation in men, and less achievement motivation but more affiliation motivation in women. Because of this, situations must arouse stronger affiliation motivation to make men resolve conflicts in terms of affiliation than to make women do so. (This difference is reflected in the results of experiments on conformity, which invariably show women as conforming more than men.) In the present experiment, the affiliation motives were not sufficient to make the men deviate from their desires for achievement—they did not slow down to help their partners. The women, however, often did so. Three-quarters of the women with strong affiliation motives and weak achievement motives slowed down. Only a quarter of those with strong achievement motives and weak affiliation motives did so. These results are highly significant, although prediction of course is still not perfect—the wrong prediction was made for a quarter of the women. This should not surprise us, for our measures of motives are not perfect and there are other complicating factors. Prediction might have been better, for example, if we had known how close friends individual pairs of subjects were.

Conflict and Ego Defense

The third reason why the motives of the adult do not simply mirror those of the parent identified with leads us into a new and extended area. According to the theory, the internalized image of the parent only makes up one part of the personality, the superego. To understand social motivation, it is necessary to look at how conflicts among all three components of the personality are resolved, the subject matter of the theory of ego defense.

Freudian defense mechanisms have long ago found their way into popular terminology, and it is common to hear a person say that someone else is "repressing" or "projecting." In this everyday use of the terms, it is recognized that defense mechanisms involve a distortion of perception, that the person who is repressing or projecting is somehow not viewing the world as it really is. Other than this, however, it is often unclear just what a defense mechanism is and what function it serves for the individual. Since defense mechanisms play a central role in a psychoanalytic view of personality, it is well to try to be more precise about these matters.

Defense mechanisms exist, according to Freudian theory, to protect the ego from *anxiety*. Anxiety is a state that may be recognized introspectively. Everyone is familiar with the nervous reactions which precede trying and important situations, such as an employment interview. The pulse races, clothes become damp with perspiration, and there may be feelings of nausea and need to urinate. The feelings are those associated with fear, and in this case the cause of the fear is quite plain, just as it is in the more extreme situation of being exposed to combat in wartime. In other situations, however, the cause of the fear is less clear to an outside observer. Even after he was widely acclaimed as a great playwright, for example, Moss Hart spent the opening night of each of his plays in the men's room being sick. Finally, at the other end of the continuum, comes the case where the individual experiences the physical symptoms without either himself or anyone else being able to see anything fear-inspiring in the situation. This is a clear example of anxiety, for anxiety is simply the experience of fear without a conscious admission of what it is that

<u>one is afraid of</u>. Fear and anxiety may thus be mixed in any particular situation, for the person may be aware of what the threat is in the environment, but not completely aware of what the forces are in himself that make him react so violently to it. This was probably the case with Hart. Most established playwrights do not react so violently to the possible failure of one new play.

Initially, according to Freudian theory, anxiety was caused by the helplessness of the child. Totally dependent upon the mother for satisfaction of basic needs and knowing nothing about the real world, the infant would have no way of knowing when a drive such as hunger arose whether it would ever be reduced. The inability to cope with his own needs without the parent was thus the source of the original, or *traumatic, anxiety*. Extreme anxiety in the adult is thus viewed as a recapitulation of this early anxiety, an unconscious reacting to the situation as the child had reacted to his apparently hopeless state of powerless frustration. The source of anxiety in the adult is viewed as being similar to its source in the child—a fear of loss of love of the parent on whom the child was dependent. For the adult, however, it is not loss of love of the real parent that is feared, but loss of love of the parent image internalized in the superego. Anxiety is thus caused by indications that we have violated, or are liable to violate, our superego. It is classified according to the way impulses are being handled and the consequent nature of the threat into moral anxiety, reality anxiety, and neurotic anxiety.

Impulses which may be openly expressed without violating the superego do not, of course, give rise to anxiety. Since Freud emphasized the importance of sexual and aggressive impulses as those most likely to be denied direct outlet by society, let us take as a hypothetical example an aggressive impulse. Suppose that for some reason I had strong hostile impulses toward one of my colleagues, with whom I had to associate regularly in the course of my work. If I adjusted to this by deciding to act on the basis of the impulses, I would fear the feelings of guilt which I knew would follow my actions. This fear of punishment by the superego is called *moral* anxiety. If the impulses were sufficiently antisocial, I might well also fear the punishment which society would inflict on me for my behavior, a fear known as *reality* anxiety.

On the other hand, it is more likely that I would not plan to either murder my colleague or commit mayhem on him, but instead plan to check my impulses and behave in a socially acceptable manner toward him. In choosing this course of action, however, I would be running a risk that my impulses would prove too strong for me and that on some future occasion they might get out of hand and cause me to act in the way that I had decided not to. Fear of this possibility would be called *neurotic* anxiety.

Hypothetical examples in the area of defense mechanisms, like dreams and TAT stories, may well reveal the hidden motives of authors. At the risk of my perhaps revealing antisocial impulses of which I am only partially aware, let us continue the example to illustrate one of the defense mechanisms. Of the three types of anxiety, reality anxiety, or fear of the real world, would seem to be the easiest to cope with. If I suffer from uncontrollable hostile impulses, I must admit that I have a problem, for no matter where I go or what I do, there is always the danger that they will get out of hand. If, on the other hand, I can convince myself that it is not I but a part of my environment which is at fault, then the problem seems easier—I have to avoid only that part of my environment to keep out of trouble. Thus if I did have hostile impulses toward someone, I could conceal my unacceptable impulses from myself if I could convince myself that it was he who was aggressive. If he said "Good morning" to me when I arrived at work, I could question the way in which he was saying it and see his statement as sarcastic and provocative. I could thus convince myself that I was not hostile, but that my colleague behaved in such a manner that he would cause a saint to lose his temper. By seeing my own unacceptable impulses in others rather than myself, I would not only be able to conceal them from myself but also be able to convince myself that I only had to avoid contact with Dr. X in order to lead a happy and well-adjusted life. This mechanism of seeing one's own unacceptable impulses in others is called *projection*, and like all the defense mechanisms it serves to protect the self from anxiety.

Among the defense mechanisms a central role is played by *repression*—the forcing and keeping of perceptions out of awareness. This is true because all defense mechanisms involve distortion of reality, so repression must be used with other defense mechanisms. In the example of projection just given, the mechanism can only work if the individual manages to keep his own hostile impulses from his awareness. In reaction formation, discussed in the case of Nailson, anxiety over the unacceptable nature of the impulses being given covert expression can only be avoided by repressing the existence of the impulses from consciousness. The same is true in the case of *rationalization,* the giving of reasons other than the real ones to account for behavior of the self because the real motives are not consciously admitted—rationalization works with repression to try to avoid anxiety.

Many defense mechanisms could be listed, and any list involves problems of classification, for individual examples often show a mixture of mechanisms. When Nailson took over the slaughtering of animals on the farm, for example, he saw other people who might do the slaughtering as not being sufficiently concerned with avoiding unnecessary pain in the animals. This could be viewed as projection, although we have considered his general adjustment in this situation to be reaction formation. Thus only one more defense will be considered here, and readers will be referred to Anna Freud's[11] work for a more complete discussion of defense. James Joyce, in *Dubliners,* has a short story about a father who spends an unsatisfactory day at the office and comes home to beat his child. As any welfare worker knows, such cases are not as uncommon in the world as we would like to think. They illustrate the mechanism of *displacement,* the turning of a drive toward a substitute object because its expression on the original object is effectively prevented by society. When we turn to the topic of prejudice, we will see the importance of displacement in that social phenomenon.

It is indicative of the increase of interest in psychoanalytic theory as a source of experimental hypotheses that there are now too many good studies to be summarized in an introductory text. That was not the case only a few years ago, and the chapter on psychoanalytic theory in the *Handbook of Social Psychology,* published in 1954,[12] is almost completely devoted to a presentation of the theory with very few supporting studies cited. Current research using psychoanalytic theory as a source of hypotheses deals with such diverse areas as conformity, creativity, the expression of aggression, the experimental production of dreams, and the childhood origins of various defense mechanisms. Some of these areas will be discussed in later chapters of this book. For the present, because of its centrality to the theory, let us look at a study on repression. Then, only touching lightly on developmental research, which is so complex as to need an entire book to deal with it adequately, we can proceed to consider the research on *cognitive dissonance,* which was done to test a different theory but is largely applicable to psychoanalytic theory as well.

As Sears[13] has pointed out, many of the early studies of repression were "completely irrelevant to the problem," for they dealt with whether pleasant or unpleasant experiences are better remembered. According to Freudian theory, it is not whether an experience is pleasant or not that determines whether it will be subject to repression, but whether it is anxiety-arousing. If two college students spent the weekend quite differently—one studying for an exam, the other getting drunk and seducing the wife of a friend—it is quite possible that the second might have a more pleasant weekend than the first, but it is the second rather than the first who might be anxious to forget what he had done. An experiment on repression must thus compare memory under anxiety-arousing and non-anxiety-arousing conditions. A more extended theoretical treatment of this idea and relevant experimental data are presented by Rosenzweig.[14] (That it was necessary to do the study without either getting the subjects drunk or involving them in amorous intrigues points out one of the difficulties in doing research on defense mechanisms.) Rosenzweig's study was similar to one done by a student of Lewin's named Zeigarnik. According to Lewinian theory, the forming of an intention to carry out some action involves setting up a force within the personality directed to that end. Zeigarnik[15] had reasoned that if that were the case, uncompleted tasks should be better remembered than completed ones, and did a series of experiments to demonstrate such differential memory. Giving children a series of tasks to work on, she did indeed find that those they were forced to leave before completion were better remembered than those they were given enough time to complete. (The design was of course counterbalanced so that we know that it was not that the tasks they were not allowed to complete just happened to be more interesting or noteworthy.) One thing which Zeigarnik had observed was that subjects who saw the experimental task as a memory test and thus as a test of their personal merit tended to remember better the tasks which they had successfully completed. This is what would be expected on the basis of repression. Since under these circumstances failure to complete the task would be anxiety-inducing, memory for the uncompleted tasks should be forced out of consciousness. This psychoanalytic hypothesis was directly tested in experiments by Rosenzweig.[16] Using tasks similar to those used by Zeigarnik, he ran different groups of subjects under threatening and nonthreatening instructions. Sometimes subjects were told that the experimenter merely wanted to learn how long the tasks took so that he could use the tasks in later experiments. These subjects were not threatened and showed the *Zeigarnik effect*—they remembered the uncompleted tasks better than the completed ones. The other subjects were given instructions which implied that failure to complete the tasks was evidence of low intelligence. Since it is part of the ego ideal of most people that they have at least average intelligence, these instructions make failure to complete the tasks subject to repression. Rosenzweig found that under these conditions the subjects remembered more of the completed than of the uncompleted tasks.

There are, of course, individual differences in how easily people are threatened and the extent to which they resort to repression as a defense. One interesting recent study[17] not only reproduced Rosenzweig's results on the effect of instructions on repression but also showed that volunteers for experiments showed less repression than subjects who had to participate as a part of a course requirement. People who lack confidence in their own abilities and are easily threatened are less likely to volunteer.

Especially interesting is the question of why a person chooses one defense mechanism rather than another. That the reasons are linked to social variables is shown by studies such as those of Faris and Dunham,[18] which show that the incidence of schizophrenia is high among children raised in the slum areas of cities, while in the high-rent districts the incidence of schizophrenia is low and that of manic-depressive psychosis is high. From the point of view of psychoanalytic theory, this is a very suggestive relationship. Schizophrenia involves a breakdown of the discrimination between fantasy and reality, and would be expected to be related to threat to the individual at the very early stage of the differentiation of the ego from the id, leading to a continued dependence on fantasy as a source of gratification. Manic-depressive psychosis, on the other hand, seems to be most closely related to the development of an especially demanding superego, a development which cannot take place if the young child has already taken refuge in fantasy. That children in working-class homes and especially in slum areas may be exposed earlier to a threatening world while those in middle-class homes are more likely to be taught unrealistically high standards corresponds quite closely with commonsense observations on social-class differences in child rearing.

Unfortunately, there are complex problems involved in relating social class or urban residence to type of mental illness. There is still controversy, for example, over whether the high prevalence of schizophrenia in the core of the city could be partly or entirely due to migration of adult schizophrenics to that area. Furthermore, child-rearing practices vary not only with social class but also by ethnic group, and have changed considerably over time—partly because of the impact of changing psychological theories! Stronger evidence of the relationship between child socialization and adult personality comes from studies comparing different cultures, which frequently vary dramatically from each other and have remained quite stable for considerable periods of time. One of the best of these studies was carried out by Whiting and Child,[19] who found strong evidence of the effects of child rearing on adult personality.

A psychoanalytic theory of motivation may now be briefly summarized as follows: Children experience ways of gratifying their impulses in playing social roles and, in doing so, modify what their impulses will be as adults. They also identify with important figures in their lives and internalize standards of behavior. As adults they act in ways which will gratify their impulses while also trying to satisfy their internalized moral standards. To the extent that their impulses and moral standards are incompatible, they will try to work out ways of surreptitiously gratifying the impulses while denying the true nature of the impulses to themselves, again depending, in doing so, on the socially acceptable roles which they have learned. While defense mechanisms may distort perception in the attempt to defend the self from anxiety, they can never be completely successful where the demands of the id and the superego are sufficiently incompatible.

Cognitive Dissonance

As an introduction to another theory which is closely related to psychoanalytic theory, Festinger's theory of cognitive dissonance,[20] let us look at a strange but fairly common human institution, the initiation ceremony. In many cultures, individuals are only admitted to full adult status in the society when they have gone through an extensive and often quite painful initiation ceremony. Perhaps the most severe of these ceremonies is that practiced by the Thonga, which involves circumcision with a flint knife.[21] (This ceremony is so traumatic that anthropological films of the ceremony have been used to arouse physiological symptoms of stress in studies in the United States.) While not all cultures have initiation ceremonies at puberty, many have milder forms of initiation practiced on more limited groups. In the United States, pledges may have to be beaten with paddles or have to eat nauseating mixtures to be admitted to a fraternity, despite the efforts of university administrations to end such ceremonies. The new recruit in the armed forces, and especially the first-year man at one of the armed forces academies, is put through a regime which is so strenuous as to constitute an ordeal.[22]

If you talk to a person who has been to a school or joined a fraternity where initiation ceremonies are practiced, it is very rare to find that he regrets having been put through the ordeal. He is most likely to think that the experience "molds character" and that it made him more, rather than less, attracted to the group he was joining. Two interesting questions about initiation ceremonies are whether they do in fact increase group solidarity and, if so, why. An experimental study of this subject was done by Aronson and Mills.

In the Aronson and Mills study,[23] a girl comes to the laboratory to participate in a psychological experiment. She is told that the experiment consists of a frank discussion of sexual matters and that only people who are not easily embarrassed by such discussions can participate. In order to qualify, she must demonstrate that she can talk frankly about sexual matters by reading sexual materials aloud to a male research assistant. The materials she is required to read are a list of highly taboo Anglo-Saxon words and a passage from an author widely regarded as obscene. After going through this ordeal, she joins the discussion group only to find that they are having a very dull discussion of the sexual behavior of the rat and that she is not allowed to say anything anyway. Nevertheless, she rates the group as well worth joining and the discussion as highly interesting.

In other experimental treatments, girls either went through a milder initiation or none at all. The milder the initiation, the less attracted to the group they were, and the girls who went through no initiation at all rated the whole experience as a dull waste of time. The experiment thus clearly supports the commonsense belief that going through an initiation ceremony to join a group increases the attractiveness of the group for us. Why should this be the case?

From the point of view of psychoanalytic theory, somewhat different processes are involved, depending upon whether we are considering the relatively mild initiation rites of voluntary organizations or the more severe trials to which individuals may be subjected without any choice on their part. The latter case would include such extreme cases as the initiation rites of the Thonga and the treatment received by Jews in Nazi concentration camps. Let us consider the more severe rites first and then return to the milder initiations of our own society. In the extreme situation, the individual is in a situation where he is completely powerless with respect to his tormentors. All the social supports to the normal functioning of the personality have been removed, and all actions by which the person might maintain feelings of personal worth and identity have been blocked. This leads to anxiety because the most elementary demands of the superego cannot be met, and the individual is reduced to a state of passive dependency upon others which is similar to the condition of the young child. The situation is similar to that of the child in another respect, for the only source of gratification which is left open is the vicarious pleasure which may be obtained by identifying with the aggressor and turning hostile impulses inward. Through this disintegration of the existing personality and identification with the aggressor, a new superego is created incorporating the standards of the aggressor. The most dramatic support for this view comes from Bruno Bettelheim's observations on his fellow prisoners in a Nazi concentration camp during the Second World War.[24] Even some Jewish prisoners eventually came to identify with their SS guards. Those who reacted this way remade their prison uniforms to make them similar to those of the guards, took pride in their ability to withstand punishment, and administered severe beatings to each other as a game.

In the milder hazing practiced by voluntary organizations in our own society the individual is not reduced to such a state of helpless dependency, although the tendency to identify with the aggressor may exist to some extent. More important is the fact that the organization is voluntary—the individual has submitted himself to illtreatment by his own choice. Any indications that the organization was not worth having gone through the ordeal for would thus be anxiety-arousing, since they would indicate that the individual had not lived up to his ego ideal of being a sensible and rational person. In order to avoid this anxiety, the individual should find ways of justifying his choice by discovering attractive characteristics of membership in the organization. The finding of reasons for having joined the organization would then be considered as rationalization, the giving of reasons other than the real one for having done something because the real reason is anxiety-inducing. The results of the Aronson and Mills experiment would thus be predicted from psychoanalytic theory from considerations of anxiety and ego defense. The same prediction was made by the experimenters, but from a different theory, Festinger's theory of cognitive dissonance. Let us look at this theory and see in what ways it is similar to, and different from, psychoanalytic theory.

The theory is called a cognitive theory because it deals with cognitions, the ideas and relationships among ideas which exist in the mind of an individual. Unlike the balance theories, where a person or thing is an element for the purpose of the theory, dissonance theory is constructed so that an element is a belief about something. Thus "I like chocolates" would be a single element in dissonance theory, while in balance theory it would be a relationship between two elements, the self and chocolates. Each idea in the mind of the person being considered is an element, and each element has one of three relationships to each other element—they are either consonant, dissonant, or irrelevant to each other. Take, for example, the elements "I like chocolates" and "Alan always wears his Oxford tie." It is difficult to see any relationship of any kind between these two ideas. My liking for chocolate is not influenced in any way by my friend's sartorial habits, and the two elements are simply irrelevant to each other.

Elements are dissonant if, given the assumptions of the individual, one belief is inconsistent with the other. To use one of Festinger's favorite examples, consider the person whose mind contains the elements "I smoke" and "Smoking is bad for health." For most people these elements would be dissonant, because most people would also believe that they should avoid doing things which are bad for their health. For a person whose goal in life was to end it as rapidly as possible, the elements would be consonant rather than dissonant, for it would then be perfectly consistent for the person to smoke because it was bad for his health.

While dissonance may be aroused by any inconsistent perceptions, it is generally only aroused in sufficient amounts to be important in situations where one of the elements is a perception of the person's own behavior. If I believe that women usually hang clothes out to dry during fair weather and yet I perceive a woman doing so just as it starts to pour down rain, this would theoretically arouse a slight amount of dissonance. This dissonance, however, could be resolved very easily. I could decide that not all women pick fair weather to hang out their washing, that maybe the weather will clear up later, or that she may be hanging them out to get wet rather than to dry. The amount of dissonance would be slight because the matter was unimportant to me and because there were few other elements keeping me from changing my beliefs in the area. In perceptions of my own behavior, on the other hand, dissonance may be high and difficult to reduce. What I do is important to me, behavior is often hard to change, and perceptions have a stubborn resistance to change. It would be difficult for me to believe, for example, that I did not smoke while I was smoking.

Dissonance is thus most often aroused in situations that involve an individual's perception of his own decisions and behavior. When aroused, it acts as a drive which can cause an individual to change not only his perceptions of the world but also his actions in order to reduce the dissonance. To see how this may be done, it is necessary to look at what determines how strong the dissonance is. Festinger has proposed that the amount of dissonance is a function of the number of dissonant elements, the proportion of the elements in a given area that are dissonant, and their importance. Again some examples should help to make the theory clear. For most people, the perception that they had just badly burned their hands by picking up a red-hot piece of metal would be dissonant with their beliefs that they avoided unnecessary pain. For a soldier in combat, the amount of dissonance would be negligible if he also perceived that he had just saved his own life by the action. In this case, the consonant element would be considerably more important than the dissonant one. Similarly, a large number of consonant elements will reduce the dissonance resulting from a few dissonant elements. While I might suffer some dissonance if I perceived that a used car I had just bought needed the valves reground, the dissonance would certainly be less if I also noted that I had bought it for a very low price and it was satisfactory in other ways.

The factors which influence how great dissonance is also imply the ways in which it may be reduced. There are widely various ways, including changing behavior, changing the evaluation of the environment, and adding new consonant elements. Widely diverse experiments have been done demonstrating these various methods, and we will look at some of them as soon as we have returned to the Aronson and Mills experiment. In the Aronson and Mills experiment, the perception on the part of the subjects that they have gone through an unpleasant initiation in order to join a group is dissonant with their perception that the group is not worth joining. How can this dissonance be reduced? It can't be done by changing behavior, for the person has already been through both the initiation and the group discussion. For a girl to try to change her perception of the world by thinking that she had not participated in the experiment when she actually had would border on the psychotic. It is possible, however, to add consonant elements, by deciding that some things said in the group discussion were really very interesting and informative. In this way the evaluation of the group discussion can be changed, so that the discussion seems worthwhile and the people participating in it seem nice. This is the change which Aronson and Mills predicted and found for the girls who had gone through the severe initiation, while the girls who went through less initiation had less dissonance and thus less reason to perceive the experiment as interesting.

Besides changing your own evaluation of something in order to reduce dissonance, as the girls did in this experiment, it is possible to reduce it by changing social reality. The person who has doubts about how good his expensive new car is may reassure himself by reading the glowing advertisements for it put out by its maker, as a study by Ehrlich and others indicates.[25] Another strategy would be to try to convince all his friends that it is the best car in the world and that they were very unfortunate not to own one. Then how could he doubt the wisdom of his choice, when it was universally acknowledged that he had bought the best car there is? This mechanism of dissonance reduction may lie behind the glowing accounts of married life which newlyweds give to unmarried friends and those of parenthood which new parents give to childless couples.

Festinger and his colleagues have done one fascinating, if highly controversial, study of the operation of this means of dissonance reduction. Their account was published in a book, *When Prophecy Fails*.[26] History abounds in examples of new religious movements springing into being, often millenial movements—movements which believe that the day of judgment is at hand. Occasionally one of these sects will survive and undergo a transformation into a more bureaucratic and less evangelical church, a process described by Max Weber as the *routinization of charisma*. The majority, however, do not survive the death of their founder. From a study of the history of such movements, Festinger theorized that dissonance reduction played an important part in their evolution. In essence, his theory was that it was doubt about the validity of one's religious beliefs which first led religious groups to try to convert others to their views. He thus predicted that in a millenial movement, the attempt to convert others to the views of the sect would first occur when the prophecy was not fulfilled and the world did not come to an end on the appointed day.

He and his colleagues tested this idea by joining such a movement. A small item appeared in many newspapers in the United States telling of a woman in "Lake City" who believed that the world would soon come to an end and that she and a few other true believers would be picked up by craft from outer space while all others would be destroyed. When Festinger and his colleagues heard of this prediction, they went to "Lake City" and joined the movement, professing to share the woman's faith, a bit of deception for which they have been much criticized and which would have been especially troublesome for them had the prophecies of the sect proved accurate. (In Festinger's defense it should be noted that his description of the movement was much more sympathetic than any other published, after the appointed day passed without anything out of the ordinary happening.)

When the appointed hour approached, the members of the sect were divided. Some, in "Lake City," were met together in the house of their chief prophet. The others, largely students at a university where a faculty member had been converted, were home for Christmas vacation. Festinger's prediction was that the members who were gathered together would get social support from each other and would thus find some way to maintain their faith in the face of the disconfirmation of their chief prophecy. This group he predicted would then begin to try actively to convert others to the faith. On the other hand, he predicted that the isolated student believers would not be able to get any support for their beliefs when the prophecy failed and would thus give up their faith. This was, in fact, just what happened. The members of the sect meeting together decided that the world had been saved because of their faith and that they had a duty to tell others of this miraculous happening. They called the press and set out to convert others. The other members, however, returned to school rather shamefaced with no desire to discuss the matter further.

Dramatic as the support is which this study gave to dissonance theory, two postscripts should be added to it. One is the observation that the husband of the chief prophet did not share his wife's faith and spent the period when the visitors from outer space were expected soundly asleep. A consideration of how much dissonance would be involved in having married a woman who believed that you faced certain and immediate damnation would suggest that there must be large differences in tolerance for dissonance. The other postscript is more serious. A replication of the study by Hardyck and Braden[27] on a religious group whose members moved into fallout shelters because they expected a nuclear attack failed to obtain the results predicted from dissonance theory. While the group members did not give up their faith when the attack did not occur, they also did not set out to convert others to it. The authors of the study point out that there were differences between the group they studied and the group Festinger studied and conclude that dissonance theory needs to be further elaborated to be able to explain when proselytizing will or will not be the means used to reduce dissonance.

In the few years since dissonance theory was first described it has generated a vast wealth of experimental investigation which cannot be surveyed in an introductory text. Not all the studies have been well controlled, and the theory does in fact have sufficient ambiguity that precise predictions are sometimes difficult to make. The methodological problems of some of the studies supporting dissonance theory are reviewed in an article by Chapanis and Chapanis, who are led to the following: "In conclusion, all of the considerations detailed above lead us to concur with Asch's (1958) evaluation of the evidence for cognitive dissonance theory, and return once more a verdict of NOT PROVEN."[28] The conclusion of Chapanis and Chapanis, however, seems overly harsh on dissonance theory. While there are weaknesses in some of the studies supporting dissonance theory, that fact does not invalidate the positive results of the studies which are without such weaknesses. Even Chapanis and Chapanis concede that some methodologically sound studies do provide support for the theory, saying, "To test a theory like this, it is up to the experimenter to create various degrees of dissonance by introducing various discrepant cognitions within an individual. Whenever contradictory statements or syllogisms or opinions are used, there is not likely to be much controversy about the fact that they must lead to discrepant internal cognitions, and so, by definition, to dissonance. Indeed, studies on cognitive dissonance of this type have yielded results which are well-established, clear-cut, and consistent."[29] If it is the case, as it does seem to be, that clear support for the theory is provided by those studies which *are* well designed, then it would seem unreasonable to reject the theory because some poorly designed studies have also obtained results supporting it.

While dissonance theory is somewhat ambiguous, it is considerably less ambiguous than the psychoanalytic theory of defense mechanisms; yet the two theories make very similar predictions in a wide variety of social situations. In psychoanalytic theory, anxiety is aroused by an indication that a person has violated or is liable to violate the dictates of his superego. In dissonance theory, dissonance is aroused by indications that this behavior is inconsistent with his beliefs. There seems to be little difference between these two causes of disquietude other than the words used to describe them. The defense mechanisms and the means of reducing dissonance are also largely equivalent. Let us see if we can make a rough mapping of the mechanisms of one theory into those of the other.

The three basic ways of reducing dissonance are to change an element of behavior; to change the environment, or at least the perception of it; and to add new consonant elements. What are the psychoanalytic equivalents of these strategies? Bringing beliefs and behavior into agreement by changing the behavior would seem to be the most rational way of reducing dissonance, but even this alternative is likely to involve irrational elements. Even though the new source of action is less dissonant than the old one, some beliefs will undoubtedly support the old rather than the new behavior. The person who quits smoking because of the dissonance involved in its being bad for his health does not become free of all dissonance because of making the change, for memories of how much he enjoyed smoking will be dissonant with his new behavior. He is thus likely to try to cope with this new dissonance by using the other means of dissonance reduction at his disposal. He is likely, for example, to add consonant elements by assiduously studying literature indicating how bad smoking is for people. He might also try to gain social support by telling all his friends how much better he feels since quitting and trying to convince all his friends that they should quit also. This type of fervor from the new convert to an idea is easily observed in everyday life, not only in former smokers but also in people who have changed their political party, their religious beliefs, or their citizenship. *Hansen's law*, for example, points to the ways in which second-generation Americans renounce the cultural ties and characteristics of their national origins, although the third generation may again become interested in these ties to its cultural past. This method of dissonance reduction is quite equivalent to reaction formation, in which a person especially strongly condemns certain ways of obtaining pleasure precisely because of his difficulty in renouncing these impulses in himself.

Because the world is difficult to change, changing the environment is usually not a satisfactory way of reducing dissonance. Festinger gives the example of a person who has a compulsion to avoid stepping on a particular part of the floor although he can perceive that it is just as solid as any other part. This person could reduce his dissonance by taking an ax and chopping a hole in the floor at that point. Usually, however, the world is not so easily changed to make it consistent with our behavior. For that reason it is usually more practical to change our perception of the world without changing the world itself. This can be done by changing our evaluation of aspects of the world and by getting social support for our views. The first of these alternatives is illustrated in the Aronson and Mills study, the second in *When Prophecy Fails*. While there is no precise equivalent to these strategies in psychoanalytic defense mechanisms, a similar mechanism of a more limited sort is involved in projection. In this mechanism we manage to conceal the nature of our own motives by changing our evaluation of the meaning of the behavior of others.

The third major way of reducing dissonance is by adding new cognitive elements. This may involve reconciling apparent inconsistencies in our beliefs by adding new elements about the differences in the situations in which they are involved. A person who believed in American nationalism but not Chinese nationalism, for example, might add the element that he believed in national movements when they represented the will of the people as expressed in democratic institutions but not when they represented the actions of an arbitrary government. There seems to be no precise equivalent of this mechanism in psychoanalytic theory, although it is very close to the concept of differentiation in balance theory. Adding new elements may also involve coming to view the consonant beliefs as more important and the dissonant ones as less so, a mechanism which seems to be especially important in the creation of new political movements. As shown in studies such as *The People's Choice*,[30] political parties do not differ so much in the stands they take on issues as they do in what issues they consider important.

The cognitive changes which dissonance theory considers under the heading of adding new elements would be considered as repression and rationalization by psychoanalytic theory. Dissonance theory stresses that the force is taken out of some dissonant ideas by coming to consider them as relatively unimportant, while psychoanalytic theory stresses that they are actively forced out of consciousness. The two mechanisms differ only in degree, and the reinterpretation of the personality which takes place in psychotherapy involves changing ideas about what is important, as well as uncovering completely repressed material. The adding of completely new elements in dissonance theory is more similar to rationalization, in which new reasons are invented to support a course of action because the actual reasons are too anxiety-inducing.

While there is not a complete correspondence of the mechanisms of personality defense set out in psychoanalytic and dissonance theory, there is enough similarity to argue that they are in general talking about the same phenomena. Festinger has differentiated dissonance theory from conflict theory by arguing that conflict theory is describing the cognitive processes preceding commitment to a course of action, while dissonance theory is describing the cognitive changes which follow making a decision and becoming committed to it. While this distinction differentiates dissonance theory from experimentally based conflict theory, which is based upon isolated decisions, it will not serve to distinguish the domain of dissonance theory from that of the defense mechanisms, for these are based on observation of ongoing lives in which previous commitments to courses of action already exist. People do not generally seek psychotherapy because they are facing a difficult new decision and cannot make up their minds, but because of the problems arising from the decisions they have already made. This observation does not decrease the importance of the work of Festinger and his colleagues. In describing the same phenomena which psychotherapists have previously observed in more precise and testable terms and in providing a wealth of experimental evidence on them, they have contributed to clinical as well as social psychology.

Summary

Psychoanalytic theory makes three fundamental assumptions about personality. It is assumed that human experience and behavior are not accidental, but caused by the interaction of the individual with his environment. If this is the case, then many of the determinants of human behavior must be unconscious. Finally, personality is viewed as made up of conflicting processes rather than as being unitary.

Approaching individual development in terms of these assumptions can reveal much about social motivation. However, because of the difficulty in tracing the development of the motives of even one individual, it is often more practical to approach motivation from the point of view of current functioning than from a developmental perspective. The Thematic Apperception Test, developed by Henry Murray, illustrates this approach to social motivation. To understand the forces acting on an individual at a given time, it is necessary to consider the situation in which he is found as well as his motives.

Defense mechanisms develop to protect the individual from anxiety. The most basic of these is repression, the active keeping of material out of consciousness. Other defense mechanisms involve the use of repression as well. In displacement, for example, in which a motive is expressed against a substitute object, the individual is not aware that the object toward which the motive is being expressed is not the one which aroused the motive.

While a number of research studies bearing on psychoanalytic hypotheses have been carried out, the theory has not been as productive of research as some simpler and more clearly stated theories have been. Closely related to a theory of ego defense and more productive of experimental research is cognitive-dissonance theory. Studies of initiation and of disconfirmation provide typical examples of the research on this theory.

Notes and Acknowledgments

1. Bandura, Albert, Dorothea Ross, and Sheila A. Ross. "A comparative test of the status envy, social power, and secondary reinforcement theories of identificatory learning." *Journal of Abnormal and Social Psychology*, 1963 (67), pp. 527–534.
   Bandura, Albert. "Vicarious processes: A case of no-trial learning" in Leonard Berkowitz (Ed.), *Advances in Experimental Social Psychology*. Vol. 2. New York: Academic Press, Inc., 1965, pp. 1–55.
2. Useful and readable books for obtaining an elementary knowledge of psychoanalytic theory are:
   Brenner, Charles. *An Elementary Textbook of Psychoanalysis*. Garden City, N.Y.: Anchor Books, Doubleday & Company, Inc., 1955.
   Thompson, Clara. *Psychoanalysis: Evolution and Development*. New York: Grove Press, Inc., 1957.
   Freud, Sigmund. *An Outline of Psychoanalysis*. New York: W. W. Norton & Company, Inc., 1949.
   Freud, Anna. *The Ego and the Mechanisms of Defense*. New York: International Universities Press, Inc., 1961.
   Good, brief accounts are also given in:
   Hall, Calvin, and Gardner Lindzey. *Theories of Personality*. New York: John Wiley & Sons, Inc., 1957.
   Cofer, C. N., and M. H. Appley. *Motivation: Theory and Research*. New York: John Wiley & Sons, Inc., 1966.
3. Cheek, D. B. "Can surgical patients react to what they hear under anesthesia?" *Journal of the American Association of Nurse Anesthetists*, February, 1965 (33), pp. 30–38.
4. James, William. *The Principles of Psychology*. Vol. I. Dover Publications, 1950. Copyright 1890 by Henry Holt and Company, copyright 1918 by Alice H. James, pp. 391–392. By permission of the publisher.
5. Sears, R. R., Eleanor Maccoby, and Harry Levin. *Patterns of Child Rearing*. New York: Harper & Row, Publishers, Incorporated, 1957.
6. Sears, R. R., J. W. M. Whiting, V. Nowlis, and P. S. Sears. "Some child-rearing antecedents of aggression and dependency in young children." *Genetic Psychology Monographs*, 1953 (47), pp 135–236.
   Berkowitz, Leonard. "The effects of observing violence." *Scientific American*, February, 1964.
7. A good brief account of Murray's theoretical position is given in Hall and Lindzey. *Op. cit.*
8. Holt, Robert R. "The thematic apperception test" in Harold H. Anderson and Gladys L. Anderson (Eds.), *An Introduction to Projective Techniques*. Englewood Cliffs, N.J.: Prentice-Hall, Inc., 1951.
9. *Ibid.*, p. 184. By permission of the author.
10. Birney, R., H. Burdick, J. Caylor, P. O'Connor, and J. Veroff. Research summarized as chap. 6 of Edward L. Walker and Roger Heyns, *An Anatomy for Conformity*. Englewood Cliffs, N.J.: Prentice-Hall, Inc., 1962, pp. 54–68.

11. Freud, Anna. *Op. cit.*

12. Hall, Calvin S., and Gardner Lindzey. "Psychoanalytic theory and its applications in the social sciences" in Gardner Lindzey (Ed.), *Handbook of Social Psychology*. Reading, Mass.: Addison-Wesley Publishing Company, Inc., 1954.

13. Sears, R. R. "Functional abnormalities of memory with special reference to amnesia." *Psychological Bulletin*, 1936 (33), pp. 229–274.

14. Rosenzweig, S. "An experimental study of 'repression' with special reference to need-persistive and ego-defensive reactions to frustration." *Journal of Experimental Psychology*, 1943 (32), pp. 64–76.

    Rosenzweig, S. "The investigation of repression as an instance of experimental idiodynamics." *Psychological Review*, 1952 (59), pp. 339–345.

    Rosenzweig, S. "The experimental study of repression" in Henry A. Murray (Ed.), *Explorations in Personality*. New York: Science Editions, Inc., 1962, pp. 472–490.

15. Zeigarnik, Bluma. "Über das behalten von erledigten und unerledigten Handlungen." *Psychologische Forschungen*, 1927 (9), pp. 1–85. An English description may be found in Dorwin Cartwright (Ed.), *Field Theory in Social Science*. New York: Harper & Row, Publishers, Incorporated, 1951, pp. 6–20.

16. Rosenzweig, S. "An experimental study of 'repression'. . . ."

17. Green, Donald Ross. "Volunteering and the recall of interrupted tasks." *Journal of Abnormal and Social Psychology*, 1963 (66), pp. 397–401.

18. Faris, R. E. L., and H. W. Dunham. *Mental Disorders in Urban Areas*. Chicago: The University of Chicago Press, 1939.

    Faris, R. E. L. "Demography of urban psychotics with special reference to schizophrenia." *American Sociological Review*, 1938 (3), pp. 203–209.

19. Whiting, J. W. M., and I. L. Child. *Child Training and Personality*. New Haven, Conn: Yale University Press, 1953.

20. A very readable description of Festinger's cognitive-dissonance theory may be found in his article by that title in *Scientific American*, October, 1962.

    For a fuller account see Festinger, Leon. *A Theory of Cognitive Dissonance*. New York: Harper & Row, Publishers, Incorporated, 1957.

    For recent experimental studies utilizing the theory, see Brehm, J. W., and A. R. Cohen. *Explorations in Cognitive Dissonance*. New York: John Wiley & Sons, Inc., 1962.

21. Whiting, John, Richard Kluckhohn, and Albert Anthony. "The function of male initiation ceremonies at puberty" in Harold Proshansky and Bernard Seidenberg (Eds.), *Basic Studies in Social Psychology*. New York: Holt, Rinehart and Winston, Inc., 1965.

22. Dornbush, S. "The military academy as an assimilating institution." *Social Forces*, May, 1955 (33), no. 4.

23. Aronson, Elliot, and Judson Mills. "The effect of severity of initiation on liking for a group." *Journal of Abnormal and Social Psychology*, 1959 (59), pp. 177–181.

24. Bettelheim, Bruno. "Individual and mass behavior in extreme situations."

Journal of Abnormal and Social Psychology, 1943 (38), pp. 417–452.

25. Ehrlich, D., I. Guttman, P. Schönbach, and J. Mills. "Post-decision exposure to relevant information." *Journal of Abnormal and Social Psychology,* 1957 (54), pp. 98–102.

26. Festinger, Leon, Henry W. Riecken, and Stanley Schachter. *When Prophecy Fails.* Minneapolis: The University of Minnesota Press, 1956.

27. Hardyck, J. A., and M. Braden. "Prophecy fails again." *Journal of Abnormal and Social Psychology,* 1962 (65), pp. 136–141.

28. Chapanis, N. P., and A. Chapanis. "Cognitive dissonance: Five years later." *Psychological Bulletin,* 1964 (61), pp. 1–22.

29. *Ibid.,* p. 3. By permission of the publisher.

30. Lazarsfeld, Paul F., Bernard Berelson, and Hazel Gaudet. *The People's Choice.* New York: Columbia University Press, 1948.

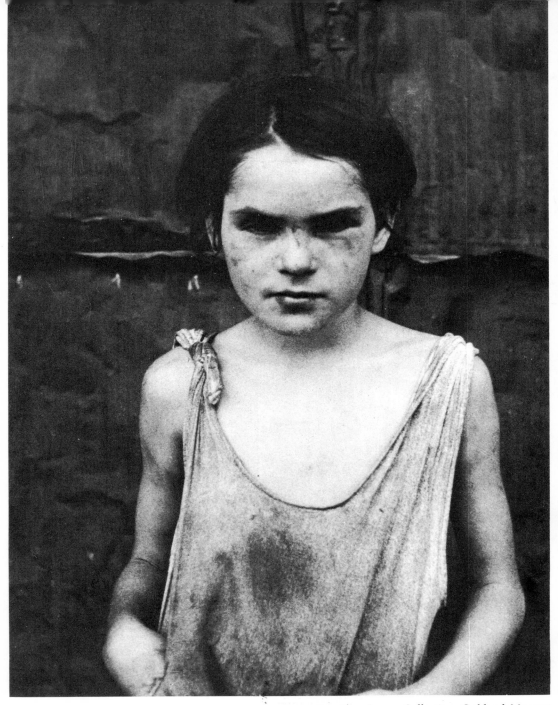

SIX

STRATEGIES & SYMPTOMS

Strategies of Happiness

Although he may not always be conscious of making a choice, each person selects to some extent his own strategy in seeking after happiness. To what extent, for example, should a person permit himself to care about another person? On the one hand, the person who remains indifferent to others guards himself against pain and disappointment. Enduring loneliness by isolating oneself from others, as Freud observed, is the surest safeguard against the unhappiness that may arise from human relations.[1] On the other hand, the gratification which loneliness brings is merely the negative one of absence of disappointment. To achieve the more positive satisfactions which come from having close relations with another person, one must take the risk of letting oneself care. It is a risk, because the person upon whom one becomes dependent may prove undependable. The lover who has just been rejected experiences more anguish than the person who has not yet loved at all. In the song, Frankie wouldn't have shot Johnny if he hadn't been "her man."

The problem of dependency is most clearly seen in courtship, and an excellent discussion of it is provided by Thibaut and Kelley.[2] As a couple become more and more deeply involved with each other, they neglect alternate relationships with others which they could fall back on; in short, they become dependent on each other. Each conceals his or her dependency from the other, however, because of what has been called the *principle of least interest*. This principle states that the person who cares least about maintaining the relationship is able to exploit the other. Consider a simple example. A boy with a car and a boy without a car are going to a restaurant together. Probably the boy with the car will have the most say about which restaurant they go to, for he is least dependent on the relationship. He could always get someone else to go out in his car to eat with him, while his friend could not always get someone with a car to take him out to eat. Similarly, in a courtship situation, the partner who cares the least about the other can use the threat of terminating the relationship to obtain what he or she wants, while the one who cannot get along without the other is more likely to give in. The emotionally detached and manipulative person, however, pays the price of not obtaining the rewards which only emotional involvement can bring.

While only involvement with the real world can bring gratification of our impulses, there are many ways of trying to deaden the pains of life. Some of the major ways are the use of drugs and intoxicants, developing forms of gratification which cannot be easily frustrated by the outside world, and escape into fantasy. Under stress, each way of adjusting may develop into well-developed symptoms. The occasional use of alcohol may become alcoholism. The person who takes pleasure in music may so completely escape into this world as to neglect all else. The person who daydreams may come to spend the greater part of his life in a world of fantasy.

In a sense, then, mental disorders develop as unsuccessful attempts to cope with life. The symptoms people develop, unpleasant as they may be, develop as the person's attempt to protect himself against something he sees as being worse. Although they may not be adaptive, symptoms are an attempt to adapt.

Let us look at a strategy which at first glance seems completely improbable—that of seeking failure. It can be observed in many situations. One example is cited by John Holt in *How Children Fail*:

> Can a child have a vested interest in failure? What on earth could it be? Martha, playing the number game, often acts the same way. She does not understand, does not want to understand, does not listen when you are explaining, and then says, "I'm all mixed up."[3]

To a person who fears failure, not trying and taking failure for granted can be less threatening than investing effort and perhaps failing anyway. More than that, being punished can help to relieve guilt. Without punishment, the person must face that he feels bad because of his own guilt about what he feels are his shortcomings. If he is punished, however, it is possible for him to convince himself that he feels bad because of the punishment rather than his own guilt. Externalization of the guilt relieves some of the anxiety, and it may even be possible for the person to convince himself that the punishment was undeserved. "I hate myself" can thus become "My wife does not understand me."

This particular mechanism seems to be a central one in alcoholism, and it is thus important to the alcoholic that he find someone to play the role of "persecutor." A good example of this is given by Eric Berne in *Games People Play*:

> In one case a female alcoholic in a therapy group participated very little until she thought she knew enough about the other members to go ahead with her game. She then asked them to tell her what they thought of her. Since she had behaved pleasantly enough, various members said nice things about her, but she protested: "That's not what I want. I want to know what you really think." She made it clear that she was seeking derogatory comments. The other women refused to persecute her, whereupon she went home and told her husband that if she took another drink, he must either divorce her or send her to a hospital. He promised to do this, and that evening she became intoxicated and he sent her to a sanitarium. Here the other members refused to play the persecutory roles White assigned to them; she was unable to tolerate this antithetical behavior, in spite of everyone's efforts to reinforce whatever insight she had already obtained. At home she found someone who was willing to play the role she demanded.[4]

Some of the mechanisms which an individual may use to defend himself against anxiety were presented in the last chapter. All people make some use of such defenses, but most people do not need to use them a great deal. As we pass from occasional anxiety routinely handled by mild defenses to debilitating anxiety and well-developed symptoms, we pass over the hazy boundary between mental health and *neurosis*.

Neurotic symptoms all seem to be effects of anxiety, ways of acting out impulses that cause anxiety, or attempts to cope with anxiety. Still there is much variety in the particular symptoms developed. One individual may experience anxiety directly, with feelings of panic and dread and physical symptoms such as heart palpitation and muscular tremor. Another may not complain of anxiety, but instead show selective memory loss and physical symptoms which mimic those of a physical illness. Each person has his own idiosyncratic pattern of symptoms, and even the classification of the patterns is a matter of some doubt. While there is thus no such thing as a typical neurotic pattern, a psychiatric case study[5] may give some impression of the way in which neurotic symptoms may represent an attempt to adapt: Following a minor accident a twenty-eight-year-old married man was admitted to a hospital claiming that the accident had made him blind. Since physical examination could reveal no injury which would have caused blindness, he was referred to the psychiatric department for an interview, where it was discovered that he had suffered the accident while on the way to the hospital to see his wife and newborn first child. He explained to the psychiatrist that since he was now blind, his first duty would have to be to divorce his wife as he could not keep her tied down to a blind man. Further interviews indicated that the man's symptoms made sense in terms of both his childhood and his current situation. His mother had been extremely domineering and his father submissive. The son had thus strongly resisted his own dependency longings, for giving in to them would symbolize unwilling submission to his mother's domination. He left home and resolved never to marry. Eventually he became so involved with a woman that he did marry her, but with the agreement that they would never have children. When she became pregnant and was unwilling to have an abortion, he saw his escape closed. Psychosomatic blindness was a last-ditch fight to escape, although he was not consciously aware that that was what it was. (Discussions with the psychiatrist about this background and its implications for his marital situation resulted in a cure of his blindness, and continued therapy with both the patient and his wife resulted in a much-improved marriage. It is unfortunate that not all patterns of symptoms are as easily understood.)

That the development of symptoms may serve a real function for the individual is most clearly shown in a study by Wolff et al.[6] This study differs from most studies of psychological disturbance in that it was predictive, and the individuals were studied while they developed the symptoms rather than after they had become disturbed. Wolff studied the parents of children who were dying of leukemia, an experience which often has very serious consequences for the mental health of the parent, as we shall see in looking into the causes of psychosis. Wolff predicted that those parents who actively faced the reality of the child's dying and dealt with the psychological stresses involved as they presented themselves would show the physiological general adaptation syndrome as measured by higher levels of excreted corticosteroid hormones. Those parents who developed psychological (reality-denying) defenses against this threatening perception of their child's dying were expected to have lower stress-corticosteroid symptoms. By assessing, by psychological methods, the degree to which each parent was facing the reality of the impending death, he estimated their level of corticosteroid excretion. His predictions were upheld by the evidence. The student will remember from the chapter dealing with endocrines that the general adaptation syndrome puts a severe physiological strain on the organism.

Neurotic symptoms have been variously classified. A typical categorization is that of Lazarus,[7] who lists *anxiety states, hysteria, obsessive-compulsive reactions, neurotic depression,* and *psychosomatic disorders.* Under anxiety states are included not only simple anxiety but also *asthenic reaction,* characterized by feelings of fatigue which the person assumes to have an organic basis; *hypochondriacal reaction,* with anxiety focused on particular physical symptoms; and *phobic reaction,* with fear of some particular type of situation or object. Each of these types of reaction represents an attempt to explain the anxiety that the person feels. Of course a person would feel upset if he had some physical basis for being so fatigued that he could not work, had a serious illness, or was exposed to a dangerous threat from outside. By ascribing his anxiety to one of these causes, the individual explains it to himself and makes it less threatening.

Under hysteria are classed *conversion reactions,* in which anxiety is transformed into a physical symptom such as paralysis or blindness, and *dissociative reactions*, in which some of the individual's memories are split off from consciousness. The young man in the motor accident mentioned at the beginning of this section is an example of the former of these reactions, while the Rev. Ansel Bourne discussed in the last chapter is an example of the latter. While the dissociative reaction is not common and the alternation of separate well-developed personalities is actually quite rare, the disorder is still especially interesting because of the light it throws on the role of unconscious processes in neurosis. Two cases which have been described at length are that of Christine Beauchamp, studied by Morton Prince[8] before the publication of Freud's first major work and thus uninfluenced by psychoanalytic theory, and the more recent case of Eve.[9]

A CASE STUDY

Prince's study is a psychological classic, and even today is perhaps as interesting a book as the introductory student may find to read. Who could resist a book which begins:

> Miss Christine L. Beauchamp, the subject of this study, is a person in whom several personalities have become developed; that is to say, she may change her personality from time to time, often from hour to hour, and with each change her character becomes transformed and her memories altered.[10]

The book is not only exciting, however; it is also the work of a patient and skeptical investigator. Over the years that he treated Miss Beauchamp, Prince conducted many small experiments to test his hypotheses about her case. It was only reluctantly that he came to believe that it was a true case of alternating. The skepticism of the author adds to the convincingness of the description.

The Miss Beauchamp who came to Prince for treatment was a proud, sensitive, diligent, and self-sacrificing young lady—a model in many ways of what society applauds. If she had not suffered from headaches, insomnia, bodily pains, and fatigue, she might have been thought highly successful. As it was, she remained an outstanding student despite her difficulties and avoided imposing them on her friends. One appreciates Prince's difficulty in trying to do psychotherapy with a woman whose attitude was:

> "I have never been in the habit of talking about my private affairs."[11]

Prince treated Miss Beauchamp for her physical symptoms by using hypnotic suggestion, with the usual amount of success. Each symptom could be temporarily cured in this manner, but either it or a similar one would recur. Miss Beauchamp's personality under hypnosis was no different from her waking personality.

Then one day another personality appeared under hypnosis. At first, Prince considered it merely another hypnotic state, but eventually it became clear that this particular state differed in mood, interests, abilities, and memories from the Miss Beauchamp Prince knew. The alternating personality, who eventually took the name Sally, sometimes controlled the activities of Miss Beauchamp, and at the end of these periods Miss Beauchamp had amnesia for what had happened during them. Sally, however, did not have amnesia for the periods when Miss Beauchamp was the dominant personality.

The first clue that Sally represented a different portion of the personality from Miss Beauchamp was that Sally referred to the conscious Miss Beauchamp as "She." Miss Beauchamp referred to the conscious Miss Beauchamp as "I." Here is an exchange between Prince and Sally on the subject of "She":

> "You are 'She'," I said.
> "No, I am not."
> "I say you are. . . ."
> "Why are you not 'She'?"
> "Because 'She' does not know the same things that I do."
> "But you both have the same arms and legs, haven't you?"
> "Yes, but arms and legs do not make us the same."[12]

Miss Beauchamp did not know who "She" was:

> "Well, you know who you are?"
> "Yes, Miss Beauchamp."
> "Exactly. You have got over the idea of being different from other persons—that there is a 'She'?"
> (Surprised and puzzled) "What 'She'? I do not know what you mean. . . ."
> "You used to tell me that you were not Miss Beauchamp."
> "I did not."
> "That when you were awake you were a different person."
> (Remonstrating and astounded) "Dr. Prince, I did not say so."[13]

Sally differed from Miss Beauchamp in many ways. She was impulsive, childish, and enthusiastic. She spent the last of Miss Beauchamp's money on candy and gorged herself, regularly made dates with a man who did not at first know of the existence of the staid personality of Miss Beauchamp, played practical jokes on her friends, smoked and drank. She then left Miss Beauchamp to awake with a hangover and amnesia for the previous day! Sally also differed from Miss Beauchamp in one way which was instantly apparent. Sally spoke with a bad stutter, while Miss Beauchamp was completely free of it.

The relationships of the various personalities shown by Dr. Prince's patient are not easy to describe. Any person may be reminded by some sensation of something he has not thought about for years, and memories and feelings may come back which had been in a sense unconscious. Under the influence of these memories he may show insights which he would not normally show, remembering, for example, what it is like to be a four-year-old. The process might strongly influence both his feelings and his behavior. Miss Beauchamp seems to have differed from this normal type of alternation of consciousness by (1) having kept many aspects of herself from expression because they did not live up to the high ideals she had for herself and (2) allowing these aspects to become sufficiently organized and autonomous, partly through experiences with hypnotism, to come to the fore. In a sense, the development of Sally was a stage in the cure of Miss Beauchamp, for the unconscious aspects of her personality first found expression as secondary personalities and were then integrated into a new and more complete self.

That the processes involved in the formation of secondary personalities such as Sally are essentially similar in kind to processes taking place in all people does not mean that all people have submerged secondary personalities. In most people unconscious processes are simply that—isolated processes. They are not organized into a secondary personality. From the rare case such as that of Miss Beauchamp where they are organized, we may gain interesting insights into the nature of the self. Sally was not only able to produce various neurotic symptoms in Miss Beauchamp, such as obsessive thoughts which Miss Beauchamp did not know the origin of. She was also able to give much more complete accounts of her dreams and experiences than most people can give. The following is Sally's account of how Miss Beauchamp lost some money. Miss Beauchamp did not yet know that it was lost at the time Sally told about it:

> "She yesterday received a letter from a photographer. She had it in her hand while walking down Washington street, and then put it into her pocket (side pocket of coat) where She kept her watch and

money (banknotes). As She walked along She took out the money and tore it into pieces, thinking it was the letter from the photographer. She threw the money into the street. As She tore up the money, She thought to herself, I wish they would not write on this bond paper."[14]

The case of Miss Beauchamp also illustrates the rather artificial nature of the distinctions made among different types of neurosis, for she showed all the different types at one time or another. She had attacks of anxiety, obsessive thoughts, compulsions to act in bizarre ways, and physical symptoms with psychological causes. She suffered from depression to such an extent that she almost succeeded in killing herself. Clearly we should not think of patterns of symptoms as discrete disease entities, but varying mechanisms which may be shown by the same person. Rather than classifying types of neurosis, we need to study the dynamics of the individual case.

A Psychosis: Schizophrenia

Besides neurosis there are a number of other varieties of mental disorder. Some are clearly the result of organic deterioration or damage of the brain. Others are as poorly defined as "character disorder," a category which includes alcoholism, drug addiction, and an apparent ability to not live up to the expectations of society without feeling guilt. Also familiar to most people are psychosomatic disorders, with symptoms such as ulcers and high blood pressure, which are real organic illnesses even though they result from psychological stress.

Within this broad range of types of disorder, *schizophrenia* is especially important to understand. It is one of the *psychoses*, serious disorders which involve major disturbances in the perception of reality, in speech and thought, and in mood and social relations. It is also quite a common disorder in our culture, accounting for approximately half the hospital beds which are occupied by psychiatric patients.

Psychoses are generally divided into schizophrenia, in which the disturbance involves thought processes, and *manic-depressive psychosis*, in which the emotions are more disordered. While there does seem to be some tendency for symptoms to cluster into syndromes, we have seen that the categories also represent a good deal of oversimplification. Some individuals have patterns of symptoms which have some of the characteristics of schizophrenia and some of those of manic-depressive psychosis. There is probably about as much oversimplification in summing up a person's pattern of symptoms by calling him a schizophrenic as there is in summing up all his attitudes by calling him a Democrat. Any particular description of symptoms is thus an idealized model which no particular case would fit.

Perhaps the most striking symptom of schizophrenia, and one which is shown very frequently, is a basic disturbance of the use of language. Rather than words being selected which will make communication possible, they are combined on the basis of idiosyncratic and illogical associations or common associations that are out of place in that particular communication. This may lead to varying amounts of language disturbance, from slightly idiosyncratic use of language to a *word salad* which is completely incomprehensible. An example of the former would be the sentence, "I like coffee, cream, cows, Elizabeth Taylor."[15] While each association is clear enough, the overall direction of the sentence is not.

Concept-formation tasks show similar disturbances of the thinking of schizophrenics. If asked to classify objects, they will do so in idiosyncratic ways which are difficult to describe. A knife might be classed with an apple, an orange, and a banana because it could be used to peel the apple. Similarly, the experimenter and furniture in the room may be classified along with the experimental objects. These and similar types of distortion have led some investigators to conclude that the basic problem in schizophrenia is a failure of attention processes and consequent inability to exclude irrelevant material from consciousness.[16]

Loss of contact with reality is shown in a variety of ways. Delusions, unshakable beliefs that are clearly mistaken, are held by many schizophrenics. These may take many forms, with feelings of being persecuted, delusions of grandeur, and sexual delusions the most common. Disordered perceptions are shown in responses to projective tests such as the Rorschach, and sometimes in distorted perceptions of one's own body. One study found that a majority of schizophrenics were unable to recognize photographs of their own bodies.[17]

Besides showing disturbance of langauge and thought, schizophrenics also show changes in their emotions and behavior. Their emotions often seem inappropriate, with the person showing great anxiety or rage for no apparent reason. Certain other emotions seem to be blunted, so that joy and sadness are absent even when they would be appropriate. An experience of great emotional meaning, such as the death of a parent or child, will be described with no apparent feeling. This emotional withdrawal mirrors a social withdrawal from the world. One common early symptom of schizophrenia is a withdrawal from normal social contact with others.

The wide variety of symptoms described do not all develop at the same time, and the course of symptom development differs from one person to another. In some cases the onset of symptoms is fairly sudden, they are clearly related to extraordinary stresses on the individual, and the individual is depressed and confused. These individuals are unlikely to have well-developed delusions. Their illness is clearly a reaction to specific stresses, and the chances of their recovering are relatively good. Because their symptoms are clearly related to a reaction to particular stresses of life, these individuals are frequently described as having *reactive* schizophrenia. On the other hand, other individuals develop their symptoms more gradually over a longer period of time and without the symptoms being as clearly related to extraordinary stress. Perhaps because they have a longer period of time in which to develop secondary symptoms in the attempt to understand the effects of the primary symptoms, they are more liable to develop systematic delusions. These individuals generally were less well adjusted before the onset of their symptoms, and have a poorer chance of recovering. Because their symptoms reflect processes which have continued for a considerable period of time, they are sometimes described as showing *process* schizophrenia.

Rogler and Hollingshead, in a study which throws much light on the origins of schizophrenia, provide a good example of its onset. Although the woman, whom they gave the pseudonym of Mrs. Padilla, was expecting another child, her husband was keeping a mistress:

> "When the birth pangs began my husband could not be found. He had put on his guayabera (fancy shirt) and gone out into the street. The midwife had to be rounded up. (The midwife delivered twins to Mrs. Padilla in their one-room shack.) Two days after the birth my husband went out into the street again. He was not concerned at all about my condition. In addition to having to care for four children, I was not feeling well at all."

> Mr. Padilla rejected the twins, which hurt Mrs. Padilla; to complicate the situation, one of the twins was not healthy; he vomited black and green fluid. Mrs. Padilla became so distraught she took the baby

to the municipal hospital. The doctor recommended that the baby be left there, and although Mrs. Padilla wanted to stay with the infant she was told that she could visit the child only twice a week.

One day she went to visit the infant and left a sister to care for the other children and to look after the house. She related:

"When I returned from the hospital I found the house in a turmoil. My sister was sitting in the middle of the mess reading a cheap novel. I became very angry. I grabbed a broom and began to hit her. I threw her out of the house. Then I became very sleepy and I went to bed and I woke up late at night. It was only then I realized what I had done."

(Mrs. Padilla had knocked her sister unconscious and thrown her out of the house. The unconscious girl was lying in the muddy street when a neighbor revived her.)

After ten days the baby was brought home from the hospital in a city-owned ambulance, but Mrs. Padilla worried still more because he had diarrhea and continued to vomit. When ten more days passed and the child did not appear to be improving, Mr. Padilla insisted that they consult a curandera *(folk healer) who prescribed castor oil. . . .*[18]

The parents gave the child castor oil, and the child died. At that time Mrs. Padilla became psychotic.

A THEORY OF SCHIZOPHRENIA

The evidence on what causes schizophrenia is still so unclear that it is possible for intelligent and well-informed people to see the disorder as being due to a wide variety of different factors. Different theorists have viewed it as entirely due to hereditary factors, as a failure of motivation resulting from inadequate childhood training, as a breakdown of the ego resulting from a disturbed relationship to the parents in early childhood, as a result of social disorganization in modern industrial society, and as a disorder of thinking resulting from inconsistencies between verbal and nonverbal communication. Even this list does not exhaust all the theories which have been proposed, and various combinations are possible, so that it is possible to see the disturbance as, for example, having a genetic basis but being aggravated by certain environmental conditions. Each theoretical approach has some evidence to support it, and no theory is able to account for all the evidence. The theory to be presented here should thus be viewed as incomplete and speculative even though it is consistent with a number of research findings. Even an incomplete explanation, however, represents a good deal of progress over what was known about the disorder a decade or two ago. Since a great deal of research is now being done on schizophrenia, it is quite possible that in a few years we shall have a much more comprehensive explanation of it.

It would seem that any explanation of schizophrenia would need to account for at least three things: which people develop the disorder, when they develop it, and the particular symptoms they develop. Although we shall see that the situation a person is in at the time he develops schizophrenia has a good deal to do with his becoming psychotic, yet there are people who come through adverse circumstances without becoming psychotic. The difference needs to be explained. Similarly, the person who does become schizophrenic does so at a particular time, often after many years of an apparently normal adjustment to life. Why did it happen at that time? Finally, some people become so severely disturbed as to be classed as psychotic, but their symptoms are not those of schizophrenia. Why do some people develop one disorder and other people another? Until we can answer these questions, we cannot say that we really know the causes of schizophrenia.

In some ways, the immediate reasons for becoming psychotic at a particular time are the easiest to study. When a person develops schizophrenia, there are many people around who are easily located and can report on what happened to him at the time. It is much more difficult at that time to get adequate reports on childhood events which occurred many years before. Let us thus start with the easiest question to answer, the events which push a person over the brink into schizophrenia. These may help to give us insight into the nature of the disorder and hint at the answers to the other questions.

An especially informative study is the one by Rogler and Hollingshead from which the example of Mrs. Padilla was taken. By studying schizophrenics who were still living with their families, they could be certain that the symptoms they were studying were characteristic of the illness and not reactions to having lived in a mental hospital. Furthermore, they were able to match a control group to the sample of schizophrenics, so that they could discover the ways in which the psychotics differed from other individuals living under the same conditions.

The study was carried out in the slums and public housing

projects of Puerto Rico, an environment in which schizophrenics generally continue living with their families. The first step was to locate a sample of schizophrenics, a step which involved visiting 300 families and obtaining psychiatric diagnoses on fifty-five individuals. The extremely good cooperation the researchers obtained is indicated by the fact that no person who was asked to undergo a psychiatric examination refused to do so! In this way twenty families were located in which at least one spouse was schizophrenic. Another twenty families were chosen from adjacent residential areas, similar to the first group except that there was no psychosis. The two groups of families were then intensively studied and compared.

The results were striking. The study revealed few differences in the childhood experiences of the sick and well individuals and virtually no differences in their adjustment to life prior to the crises which culminated in the illness. Up until about a year before becoming ill, schizophrenics did not show social withdrawal, difficulty in earning a living, or interpersonal conflicts with others. They were normal, insofar as individuals living a marginal existence in a slum can be normal.

What did distinguish the schizophrenics from the nonschizophrenics was a series of crises which threatened the schizophrenic's conception of himself and with which he could not cope. This was most clearly demonstrated in the relationship between schizophrenia in women and the death of a child. As the authors put it:

> The death of children is linked significantly to the mental status of the mother. Twelve children died in seven families. Ten of the twelve deaths were in families in which the mother is suffering from schizophrenia. Six of the seven families who have faced the death of a child are in the sick group. All deaths preceded the onset of mental symptoms in the parents.[19]

The self-conception of a woman who is a mother probably depends more upon her ability to care for her children than upon any other factor. The death of one of the children represents a failure which destroys the purpose of life. A massive denial of reality is one of the few alternatives left open. Similarly, a man's ability to support his family is probably the role most necessary to his preserving his good opinion of himself. It is thus not surprising that difficulty in earning a living is one of the factors associated with the onset of schizophrenia in men. In that case, however, it is more difficult to say whether the symptoms of schizophrenia or the economic difficulties come first, for they augment each other. A person who is out of work for reasons not associated with personal symptoms may develop symptoms, and the symptoms may make it more difficult for him to find work.

In many ways the observations of Rogler and Hollingshead suggest that a vicious cycle is involved in the development of schizophrenia. Continued stresses, such as illness and unemployment, reduce the person's ability to cope with the world. Reactions to the stress, such as Mrs. Padilla's beating her sister, estrange others and cut the person off from normal sources of consolation and social support. Finally some especially threatening event pushes the person over the brink of being able to face reality. From that point on, symptoms develop in an attempt to understand the effect of other symptoms. A person who was unable to remember things because of repression, for example, might imagine a physical explanation of the symptom.

The interaction of stress and the disturbance of interpersonal relations is reflected in the variety of factors which Rogler and Hollingshead found to be associated with the onset of schizophrenia:

> *Systematic comparisons of the six types of perceived personal problems reported by the sick persons (and families) with those of the well persons (and families) demonstrate that each of the diagnostic family types in the sick group encountered many more problems than the well families during the problematic year. There are more economic difficulties and more severe physical deprivation in the sick than in the well families. There are far more interspouse conflicts among the sick families than the control families; difficulties with members of the extended family are more frequent and more severe. The sick families report more quarrels and fights with the neighbors. There are more physical illnesses in the schizophrenic families. Finally, more sick persons than well persons, male as well as female, note a disparity between their own perception of the difficulties they encountered and the ways they think their spouses viewed these same problems. Stated otherwise, the schizophrenic men and women think their spouses do not understand the personal difficulties they face, as well as the men and women in the control group do. In general, the person who is diagnosed as suffering from schizophrenia perceives himself as bombarded by a multiplicity of personal and family problems he is not able to handle. The behavioral evidence shows, however, that he struggles to solve them by every means available to him.[20]*

The final and precipitating cause of schizophrenia thus seems to be a threat to a person's conception of himself which is so pervasive and overpowering that he must escape from it into fantasy. This does not, however, solve the problem of why some people seem to break down more easily under stress than others. The underlying causes leading to these individual differences still need to be investigated.

It has been widely accepted that individuals inherit a susceptibility to schizophrenia. Because of methodological errors in the studies which led to that conclusion, many of them pointed out in an excellent review of the literature by Jackson,[21] it is by no means clearly established that there is a genetic factor. Some of the methodological errors which were made are instructive. In one study, which concluded that there was a genetic factor because schizophrenia ran in families, a family history of schizophrenia was one of the bases for classifying an individual as schizophrenic! A great deal of confusion also stemmed from the study of identical twins. One study referred to twins who were "separated," and many people thought that the investigator meant that they had been separated early in life. Since there was a very strong tendency for both the twins to have schizophrenia if one of them did, this seemed to point to a genetic factor. Actually, the investigator merely meant that the twins had been separated for at least five years before becoming schizophrenic. Since they averaged thirty-three years of age at that time, that clearly did not mean that they had not been raised together.

It is quite possible that a tendency to schizophrenia may be inherited. The observations, however, are in some ways more compatible with a social-learning explanation of individual differences in susceptibility. Let us look at two pieces of evidence which have been used to support a genetic explanation. One is that *identical* twins are more likely to be similar to each other in whether they are schizophrenic than are *fraternal* twins. Since identical twins have exactly the same heredity while fraternal twins are no more similar to each other genetically than are any other siblings, this seemed consistent with a genetic explanation. However, similarity between twins who have been raised together could be partly due to similarity of social environment. This would be greatest for identical twins and fraternal twins of the same sex, and less for fraternal twins of opposite sex. Where sex of fraternal twins has been reported, the same-sexed fraternal twins are almost as similar to each other in whether or not they have schizophrenia as the identical twins.[22] This is clearly not consistent with a genetic explanation.

Sex also is a factor in the relationship of schizophrenia in parents and schizophrenia in children. A child is approximately three times as likely to become schizophrenic if his mother is schizophrenic as he is if his father is schizophrenic. As this is true regardless of the sex of the child, it is not consistent with any known mechanism of genetic inheritance. It is consistent with the fact that the mother has much more social influence on the child than the father.

The evidence on schizophrenia in parents and children thus seems to be at least as consistent with a social explanation of schizophrenia as with a hereditary explanation. If, as our discussion so far has indicated, schizophrenia results from a threat to the self, then it may well be that the very earliest years when the child is first forming an impression of himself as an autonomous being are especially important in making him more or less resistant to threats to the self later. A relationship to a disturbed mother in early childhood seems to make the child more likely to develop schizophrenia later, regardless of whether it is schizophrenia or some other pattern of symptoms which the mother shows. Again the observations are more consistent with a social explanation than a biological one.

If the precipitating cause of schizophrenia is an overwhelming threat to the self, what alternative does the person have besides becoming schizophrenic? Not everyone who becomes psychotic does become schizophrenic, even though schizophrenia is the most common psychosis in our culture. Let us look briefly at the other major psychotic reaction, manic-depressive psychosis, and consider what makes some people show one set of symptoms and other people show another. Manic-depressive psychosis involves two syndromes which seem, at first glance, to be exact opposites of each other.

The manic is bubbling over with energy and good humor. His mood is one of boundless optimism and enthusiasm, and he throws his energy into one ambitious project after another, although he never finishes any of them. His behavior is characterized by wild silliness, with an inability to sit still. His clowning and joking would be enjoyable if he did not carry them so far, but he is liable to have more sexual and aggressive content to his humor than society will tolerate. Thinking is not disordered as in schizophrenia, although thoughts jump rapidly from one topic to another and there may be a good deal of grandiosity in both thought and behavior. An example of manic behavior which illustrates both its wildness and its sexual and aggressive content is a university professor who began to punctuate the points in his lecture by throwing articles of clothing at his students.

Psychotic depression, on the other hand, involves the opposite of many of these characteristics. Movements are slow and occur rarely. The individual's mood is one of black despair. Rather than the self-pity which may characterize neurotic depression, the depressed psychotic has a pitiless hatred of himself which may lead to suicide. In some ways, however, the depressive is similar to the manic. He has a similar inability to concentrate, and may have similar delusions. The two disorders are classed together because there are some individuals who alternate between the two states, lending support to the view that mania is a way of trying to ward off depression by throwing oneself into other activities.

Manic-depressive psychosis differs from schizophrenia in both the cultural circumstances and family situations in which it occurs. Schizophrenia occurs in conditions of cultural disorganization. It is seldom found in nonindustrial cultures unless they are undergoing rapid change after contact with industrial cultures. It has an especially high incidence in the center of the city in American cities where that area is a melting pot for different ethnic groups, but does not have an especially high incidence in the central areas of older European cities which are not trying to assimilate new minority groups. Similarly, schizophrenia occurs in disorganized families, as we have seen. Manic-depressive psychosis, on the other hand, occurs in cultures and families which are, in some senses at least, well integrated.

Schizophrenia seems to involve an identity crisis which may be brought about by threats to the self in maturity, which may also reflect doubts about the self stemming from living in cultural anomie, and which may even go back to problems of the initial formation of the self in infancy. The blotting out of reality and escape into fantasy shown in schizophrenia constitute the crudest and most primitive defense, and may be learned in response to threats occurring at such an early age that no more adequate methods of coping with anxiety have yet been learned.

The following example of childhood schizophrenia, taken from Erik Erikson, gives an idea of the extreme inadequacy of early socialization which has more often been observed in schizophrenia than in manic-depressive psychosis. In this case the family disorganization was due to the mother being quarantined but remaining within the home, and she was able to observe and describe with unusual clarity the situation that preceded the baby girl's illness:

Her mother told me that Jean's extreme disorientation had begun after the mother had become bedridden with tuberculosis. She was permitted to stay at home in her own room, but the child could speak to her only through the doorway of her bedroom, from the arms of a good-natured but "tough" nurse. During this period the mother had the impression that there were things which the child urgently wanted to tell her. The mother regretted at the time that, shortly before her illness, she had let Jean's original nurse, a gentle Mexican girl, leave them. Hedwig, so the mother anxiously noticed from her bed, was always in a hurry, moved the baby about with great energy, and was very emphatic in her disapprovals and warnings. Her favorite remark was, "Ah, baby, you stink!" and her holy war was her effort to keep the creeping infant off the floor so that she would not be contaminated by dirt. If the child were slightly soiled, she scrubbed her "as if she were scrubbing a deck."

When after four months of separation Jean (now thirteen months old) was permitted to re-enter the mother's room, she spoke only in a whisper. "She shrank back from the pattern of the chintz on the armchair and cried. She tried to crawl off the flowered rug and cried all the time, looking very fearful. She was terrified by a large, soft ball rolling on the floor and terrified of paper crackling."[23]

In babyhood the manic-depressive, on the other hand, appears to have an adequate socialization up to the time when he begins to find independent movement getting him into trouble. Then he learns that he is rejected or accepted by the adults of the family according to extremely forceful standards which have little or nothing to do with him as an individual. The manic-depressive patient tends in childhood to have been successful in living up to the stereotyped patterns of behavior visualized by the strongest of the adults who raised him, and it is only when he reaches the quite different and more complex demands of adulthood and society at large that he has the catastrophic reaction of manic-depressive psychosis. This is illustrated in a study by Gibson[24] comparing manic-depressives' family backgrounds with those of schizophrenics which concludes that families of manic-depressive patients make stronger efforts to raise or maintain their social prestige, have stronger aspirations that the patient will raise the family prestige, and are more concerned about what various social groups think of them. Similarly, the families of manic-depressives were characterized by strong envy among the children, which the future manic-depressive responded to by failing to utilize his individual and personal abilities to the utmost. The pressure on the child to both maintain a traditional way of life and succeed in terms of it was great.

These observations on the families of manic-depressives fit in well with cross-cultural indications of the incidence of the disorder. It is common in well-integrated traditional societies which would be expected to be successful in transmitting their beliefs and values to the new generation. Among the Hutterites, for example, a religious group with highly integrated communal living arrangements, it is more than four times as frequent as schizophrenia.[25]

This is just about the opposite proportion from that generally found in the United States. Manic-depressive psychosis thus does seem to occur more in well-integrated cultures and families, while schizophrenia characterizes disorganized cultures and families.

We have thus arrived at first approximations of the answers to our three questions of which people develop schizophrenia, when they develop it, and why they develop the symptoms they do. The answers suggest that the people who are most likely to develop it are those who were least well integrated into a family and homogeneous culture during early childhood, that they develop it as a result of repeated threats to the self with which they are unable to cope, and that the symptoms represent both the immediate effects of escape into fantasy and the development of explanations of what is happening to the individual. As research on schizophrenia continues, these answers will undoubtedly be modified in many ways.

The Effects of Psychotherapy

Individuals who are mentally disturbed have open to them a wide variety of different methods of therapy, although their choice is limited by their socioeconomic status. As Hollingshead and Redlich demonstrated in *Social Class and Mental Illness*,[26] psychotherapies such as psychoanalytic treatment tend to be more available to wealthier patients, while organic methods of treatment tend to be more employed on those who cannot afford to pay. Excluding such organic treatments as the use of drugs and electric shock, there is still a wide variety of types of psychotherapy. Psychoanalytically oriented therapy has as its goal making the unconscious conscious. In Rogerian client-centered therapy, the therapist's expressing unconditional positive regard for the patient is felt to be essential. According to learning-theory approaches, the symptom is the disease—a concept strongly in disagreement with the psychoanalytic view that it is a superficial indication of a much deeper problem. Despite these very differing views of psychotherapy, however, different therapists may proceed in much the same manner. Is what they do effective?

Every field of knowledge seems to have myths which grow up around its history. The history of the field is not of great interest to most people, yet everyone knows something about it. The result is that, through a process similar to rumor transmission, there grows up a history of the field as it should have happened. Psychology, too, has a history similar to the history of England presented in the humorous book *1066 and All That*.

One of the tenets of this fictitious history of psychology is that Freud was the first person who was interested in unconscious processes. From the case studies done by William James and Morton Prince before they were familiar with Freud's work, we have been able to see that that was not the case. Here we must turn our attention to a second item of pseudo history which asserts that "Eysenck demonstrated in the 1950s that psychotherapy does not work."

What Dr. H. J. Eysenck did, in an article in 1952 and a popular paperback book in 1953,[27] was to compare four groups of patients. Two of these groups received various forms of psychotherapy; one was a "control" group consisting of neurotics admitted to state mental hospitals; and the fourth was another "control" group consisting of individuals receiving disability payments for neurosis treated by general practitioners. Eysenck found that within each of these groups about two-thirds of the patients were "cured." From this he concluded, not that it had been demonstrated that psychotherapy was worthless, but that it had *not* been demonstrated that psychotherapy was of value. This was an understatement, for if we look at the methodology of the comparison we may easily see that *no conclusions of any kind* may be drawn from the figures presented.

In an excellent review of the literature on learning-theory approaches to psychotherapy,[28] Breger and McGaugh break down the common methodological errors in evaluations of psychotherapy into (1) *sampling biases*, (2) *observer biases*, and (3) lack of *experimental controls*. Let us look at these three general types of research weakness, for the figures presented by Eysenck exemplify all three types.

On the matter of sampling, the four different groups are so different from each other that it is very difficult to compare them. Eysenck assumes that the patients at state mental hospitals must be the most disturbed initially, as no one in his right mind would allow himself to become a patient in such an institution. The argument does have some force. Equally likely, however, is the possibility that individuals become patients in state mental hospitals if their behavior shows a sudden and radical change—in other words, if their illness would be classed as reactive rather than process. Such individuals have a higher probability of rapid recovery than individuals whose disturbance is longer in developing and less clearly a reaction to specific circumstances. The main thing is that we just do not know what types of patients the four groups represent and thus cannot make meaningful comparisons among them.

A more important difficulty is that of observer biases. Instead of concluding that two-thirds of neurotics will be cured no matter what type of treatment they receive, perhaps we should conclude that the people treating others will assume that they have cured two-thirds of them regardless of the amount of improvement shown. State mental hospitals do not like to spend money on custodial care. If they can get a patient back into the community, they will do so. As an indication of this, let us look at the control group in an experimental study of therapy done by Fairweather. The control group represented psychiatric patients who were discharged by a veterans' hospital after receiving the usual therapy offered by that institution. They are probably roughly comparable to the discharged patients in Eysenck's comparison, and were carefully studied 6 months after discharge. At that time it was found that 46 percent had been rehospitalized some of the time, 62 percent were unemployed, and 14 percent were living with their wives.[29] These few figures should help in the interpretation of what it means to be "cured" if the criterion of cure is being discharged from a mental hospital.

Psychoanalytically oriented psychiatrists have generally set much higher standards of mental health. Some of those discussed by Jahoda in *Current Concepts of Positive Mental Health* are "resistance to stress," capacity for "independent behavior," "perception free from need distortion," and "adequacy in love, work, and play."[30] The "cured" group above could hardly be considered cured by these standards.

Perhaps the least meaningful Eysenck figures were those from the medical practitioners who had no special training in psychiatric diagnosis or therapy. They considered that they had helped two-thirds of their patients. It is to be hoped that they had.

The greatest problem in the comparison Eysenck makes, however, is the problem of experimental control. A commonly held ideal of experimental psychology, a field which Eysenck would like to see clinical psychology emulate, is that experimental and control groups should only differ from each other in a limited number of known ways. It is adherence to this ideal which makes it possible to draw some conclusions about the differences found between the groups. We have seen that the four groups compared by Eysenck differed in the populations they were drawn from and in the criteria of being cured. They also differed in a variety of ways in the therapy which they had received. Neither the patients at the state mental hospitals nor those going to general medical practitioners were allowed to continue without help of any sort. The therapies which were used were almost as various as the practitioners: drugs, occupational therapy, control of the environment, electric shock, stern lectures, and sympathetic listening were probably all employed—in what proportion no one can tell. It may well be that if widely various procedures are tried on neurotic patients, many of the patients will improve. Without better experimental control it is impossible to tell why.

Eysenck's comparison obviously did not demonstrate that psychotherapy is not effective. It is true, however, that there is still only incomplete evidence that therapy is effective. There seem to be several reasons for this. One, which has already been hinted at in discussing Eysenck's work, is that the evaluation of its effectiveness is an extremely complex and difficult research problem. Many of the studies in the area, whether purporting to show that therapy is effective or that it is worthless, suffer from the kinds of methodological problems that have been discussed.

A second problem is that "people receiving psychotherapy" is probably much too crude a category to be amenable to research, for it covers such a wide variety of different types of problems. What would be improvement for a psychopath who seemed to feel no guilt in violating any of the laws and customs of his society would be the opposite of improvement for a person who was suffering from guilt and depression. To look for general criteria of improvement which would apply equally to all is probably as futile as to look for criteria of improvement which would apply equally well to a person with measles, one with a broken leg, and one with a toothache.

A third reason, however, seems to be that some therapists make their patients improve more than they would without therapy, and some make them improve less than they would without therapy![31] Psychologists will have to take what comfort they can from the related finding that it seems to be the more experienced therapists who make their patients better and the less experienced ones who make them worse.

An extremely interesting study which may help to clarify why some therapists may actually interfere with the recovery of their patients was done by Richard Cutler. Ideally, therapists should be able to perceive accurately the problems of their patients and respond to them in ways that are motivated by the needs of the patient rather than the needs of the therapist. Cutler[32] studied the possibility that unresolved conflicts on the part of the therapist led to inaccurate perception of the patient and inappropriate action by the therapist. While only two therapists were intensively studied, the results are extremely suggestive.

Areas where the therapist had unresolved conflicts were identified by comparing the therapist's own ratings of the extent to which he showed various characteristics with the ratings made of him by nine judges who knew him well. Large discrepancies were taken as an indication of unresolved conflict. If, for example, the therapist saw himself as very low in submissiveness while others saw him as high in this characteristic, this discrepancy would be considered an indication of unresolved conflict in that general area. It was predicted that in areas where the therapist had unresolved conflicts he would (1) consistently misperceive how much his own behavior showed those characteristics he had conflict about, (2) misperceive the extent to which the patient's behavior showed those characteristics, and (3) act in ways which were more motivated by his own need to defend his ego than by the therapeutic task. These predictions were strongly supported by the data. To the extent that therapists misperceive their patients and act toward them in ways that are motivated by their own problems, it is not surprising that some "therapy" is found to have negative effects.

"Psychotherapy" is thus a word which covers a multitude of conditions. Rather than ask, "Is psychotherapy effective?" we need to ask, "Is this type of treatment effective with this type of person?" Even though all methods of treatment have not been shown effective under all circumstances, there is unambiguous evidence that some forms of treatment are effective under some circumstances. Let us look at two studies, one dealing with severely disturbed hospitalized patients and the other dealing with individuals who are normally well adjusted. While they differ in other ways, the studies are similar in that both use group processes as a change technique and both employ more adequate criteria of change than most studies.

The first study, by Fairweather and his colleagues, explored the effects on hospitalized patients of participating in task-oriented problem-solving groups. Life in a hospital usually requires the patient to play a dependent role which may ill prepare him for life outside the hospital. The experimental treatment program which Fairweather and his colleagues introduced rewarded the patients for playing a more normal adult social role. As they put it:

> In the traditional program, all problems regarding the patient are taken up with him as an individual matter. His role is very clearly a subordinate one in which he relies upon the staff for their final decisions without any voice about possible courses of action. On the other hand, the social system of the small-group treatment program clearly delineates the patient's role as that of participant in group discussion and recommendations. Although the final decision regarding such recommendations rests with the staff, each patient's task group has the responsibility and is rewarded for recommending realistic and meaningful courses of action for each of its members, with particular emphasis on daily living and future plans.[33]

Conditions were carefully controlled so that differences between the treatment and control groups could be clearly attributed to the experimental treatment program, and the two groups were studied in a variety of different ways. Two general findings clearly emerged: (1) The experimental treatment program led to better adjustment on the part of the patients after they left the hospital. Those who had participated in the small-group program were significantly more likely to be employed, to talk with other people, and to have friends after leaving the hospital than those who had not. (2) Adjustment after leaving the hospital had very little relationship to other measures taken while the patient was in the hospital. Most importantly, it had almost no relationship to whether the patient's attitudes toward the treatment program were positive or negative. If the treatment program had been evaluated in terms of the attitudes of the patients rather than their adjustment to community life, its effectiveness would not have been discovered. Since some studies of the effectiveness of therapy have relied on patients' statements about how much they have been helped, this is important to note.

Miles's study[34] differs from Fairweather's in dealing with a group of individuals with normal psychological adjustment rather than a severely disturbed population. It is similar, however, in the careful attention to providing relevant control groups and adequate criteria of change. The experimental group was composed of thirty-four elementary school principals who attended a two-week training laboratory in human relations. Their change was evaluated not just through self-report techniques and ratings by the laboratory staff but also by their associates on the job. In follow-ups after 3 and 8 months, they were found to have become more sensitive to the needs of others, more egalitarian in their ways of doing things, and more skillful leaders as a result of the laboratory experience. While this is impressive evidence of the effectiveness of the human relations laboratory, it is even more interesting to note what did and did not correlate with change. Long-term change was unrelated to personality factors. However, individuals who were more secure in their jobs changed more. Most important, there was no relationship between how much an individual perceived himself as having changed and how much he had changed according to external judges. *Those who expected to change the most through taking the program actually changed the least.* These results underline the importance of developing objective criteria in evaluating psychological change rather than relying on the individual's own report. As such criteria are developed, psychotherapy may for the first time be intensively and adequately evaluated.

Summary

While they are not usually adaptive, psychological symptoms frequently are *attempts* to adapt. This adaptation may be necessary because of a situation which is untenable for the individual, sometimes not for obvious, external reasons, but because of an interaction between an idiosyncratic combination of personal developmental experiences and the situation. In attempting to adapt, individuals must cope in some way with anxiety. Neurotic symptoms represent effects of anxiety, ways of acting out anxiety-arousing impulses, or attempts to cope with anxiety. All individuals show some neurotic symptoms, and the lines separating neurosis from complete mental health on the one hand and from psychosis on the other cannot be perfectly drawn. Similarly, different patterns of symptoms have been described, but these are abstractions which are not perfectly descriptive of actual individual human beings.

Among psychotic patterns, the manic-depressive and schizophrenic were discussed. Schizophrenia is especially important to understand because of the large numbers of people it disables. It is characterized by inappropriate emotional responses and disturbances of language and thought. The manic-depressive psychoses are characterized more by deep emotional changes and less by disordered thinking and language than schizophrenia.

Any explanation of a psychosis should be able to explain which people develop the disorder, when they develop it, and why they develop that pattern of symptoms rather than a different one. While a certain amount is known about the origins of psychoses, no explanations exist which would meet all these criteria. The work of Rogler and Hollingshead on schizophrenia seems to be an especially promising lead in the understanding of this disorder.

Until very recently there has been no well-controlled research on psychotherapy. While it is not true, as is commonly believed, that it has been proved that psychotherapy does not work, it is also true that there has been little well-controlled research which demonstrates that it does. Exceptions to this generalization are recent studies by Miles dealing with normally well-adjusted individuals and Fairweather dealing with severely disturbed individuals. Both studies point out the importance of the social environment in individual change.

Notes and Acknowledgments

1. An excellent discussion of strategies in adaptation to life makes up the second chapter of Freud, Sigmund. *Civilization and Its Discontents.* Garden City, N.Y.: Doubleday & Company, Inc., 1958.
2. Thibaut, John W., and Harold H. Kelley. *The Social Psychology of Groups.* New York: John Wiley & Sons, Inc., 1959.
3. Holt, John. *How Children Fail.* New York: Pitman Publishing Corporation, 1964, p. 3. Used by permission of the publisher.
4. Berne, Eric. *Games People Play.* New York: Grove Press, 1964, p. 78. Used by permission of the publisher.
5. White, Robert W. *The Abnormal Personality.* New York: The Ronald Press Company, 1956, pp. 263–264.
6. Wolff, C., et al. "Relationship between psychological defenses and mean urinary 17-hydroxycorticosteroid excretion rates: I. A predictive study

of parents of fatally ill children. II. Methodological and theoretical considerations." *Psychosomatic Medicine*, 1964 (26), pp. 576–609.

7. Lazarus, Richard S. *Adjustment and Personality.* New York: McGraw-Hill Book Company, 1961, pp. 337–347.

8. Prince, Morton. *The Dissociation of a Personality.* New York: Longmans, Green & Co., Inc., 1913.

9. Thigpen, C. H., and H. M. Cleckley. *The Three Faces of Eve.* New York: McGraw-Hill Book Company, 1957.

10. Prince, Morton. *Op. cit.*, p. 1. Used by permission of David McKay Company, Inc.

11. *Ibid.*, p. 9.

12. *Ibid.*, p. 27.

13. *Ibid.*, pp. 28–29.

14. *Ibid.*, p. 80.

15. Maher, B. A., K. O. McKean, and B. McLaughlin. "Studies in psychotic language" in P. J. Stone, D. C. Dunphy, M. S. Smith, and D. M. Ogilvie (Eds.), *The General Inquirer.* Cambridge, Mass.: The M.I.T. Press, 1966, p. 489.

16. McGhie, A., J. Chapman, and J. S. Lawson. "Effect of distraction on schizophrenic performance." *British Journal of Psychiatry*, 1965 (111), pp. 383–398.

17. Arnhoff, F. N., and E. N. Damianopoulos. "Self-body recognition and schizophrenia." *Journal of General Psychology*, 1964 (70), pp. 353–361.

18. Rogler, Lloyd H., and August B. Hollingshead. *Trapped: Families and Schizophrenia.* New York: John Wiley & Sons, Inc., 1965, pp. 194–195. Used by permission of the publisher.

19. *Ibid.*, pp. 171–172.

20. *Ibid.*, pp. 409–410.

21. Jackson, Don D. (Ed.). *The Etiology of Schizophrenia.* New York: Basic Books, Inc., Publishers, 1960.

22. *Ibid.*, p. 60.

23. Erikson, Erik. *Childhood and Society.* New York: Copyright 1950 © 1963 by W. W. Norton & Company, Inc., 1963, pp. 196–197. Used by permission of the publisher.

24. Gibson, R. W. "The family background and early life experience of the manic-depressive patient." *Psychiatry*, 1958 (21), pp. 71–91.

25. Eaton, J. W., and R. S. Weil. *Culture and Mental Disorders.* New York: The Free Press of Glencoe, 1955.

26. Hollingshead, A. B., and F. C. Redlich. *Social Class and Mental Illness.* New York: John Wiley & Sons, Inc., 1958.

27. Eysenck, H. J. *Uses and Abuses of Psychology.* Baltimore: Penguin Books, Inc., 1953.
Eysenck, H. J. "The effects of psychotherapy: An evaluation." *Journal of Consulting Psychology*, 1952 (16), pp. 319–324.

28. Breger, L., and J. McGaugh. "Critique and reformulation of 'learning-theory' approaches to psychotherapy and neurosis." *Psychological Bulletin*, 1965 (63), no. 5, pp. 338–358.

29. Fairweather, George (Ed.). *Social Psychology in Treating Mental Illness.* New York: John Wiley & Sons, Inc., 1964, p. 164.
30. Jahoda, M. *Current Concepts of Positive Mental Health.* New York: Basic Books, Inc., Publishers, 1958, pp. 41, 47, 49, and 55.
31. Cartwright, R. D., and J. L. Vogel. "A comparison of changes in psychoneurotic patients during matched periods of therapy and no-therapy." *Journal of Consulting Psychology,* 1960 (24), pp. 121–127.
32. Cutler, Richard. "Countertransference effects in psychotherapy." *Journal of Consulting Psychology.* 1958 (22), pp. 349–356.
33. Fairweather, George. *Op. cit.,* p. 31. Used by permission of publisher.
34. Miles, Matthew B. "Changes during and following laboratory training: A clinical-experimental study." *Journal of Applied Behavioral Science,* July, 1965 (1), no. 3, pp. 215–242.

SEVEN

EFFECTIVE LEARNING & REMEMBERING

For almost a century psychologists have been studying learning, and their results have done much to clarify the processes involved in this complex activity. Some of the results, having to do with rather technical questions of learning theory, are primarily of interest to other psychologists. Other results, which can be applied in everyday life, are of interest to all. In the latter category come questions of how to learn and remember most efficiently. Interestingly, many of the most important discoveries about learning and remembering efficiently were made in the first extensive study of learning, that of Hermann

Ebbinghaus.[1] Using himself as his only subject, Ebbinghaus spent some time each day for over 2 years memorizing, remembering, and testing himself on lessons. The monograph in which he described his results was such an important contribution to our understanding that an English translation of it is still in print, although the original work was published in 1885.

Because learning had not been studied experimentally, Ebbinghaus had to devise his own methods for studying it. He needed, for example, some way of measuring how much he had learned. There are a number of ways in which we show the effects of past learning which he might have used. If I look at a face and say to myself, "Oh, yes, I have met this person before," then it is an example of *recognition*. Exemplifying a type of memory less frequently studied in experimental investigations of learning, I may remember the circumstances under which I met the person before and reexperience in memory the events of that time. This type of memory is called *reintegration*. If I can call the person's face to mind when the person is not present, it is an example of *recall*. These various types of memory differ in how sensitive they are in showing the effects of learning. It is easier to recognize something than to recall it, and a multiple-choice exam may thus show more evidence of past study than an essay test.

More sensitive than any of the other measures of learning is the one which Ebbinghaus devised, *relearning*. Even after you have forgotten something so completely that you no longer recognize it, you can still learn it a second time more rapidly than you learned it the first. The saving of time on relearning is such a sensitive measure of the effects of learning, in fact, that it can even show the effects of hearing Greek before the age of three on testing at the age of fourteen![2]

Ebbinghaus thus measured the effects of previous learning by means of *a saving score*. This score was calculated to show what percent of the time it took to learn the material a first time was saved when it was being learned for the second time. If, for example, it took 30 minutes to learn the material the first time and only 20 minutes the second time, then the person would have saved ten-thirtieths of the time, or 33⅓ percent. This measure gave Ebbinghaus an indication of the effects of practice which was comparable for learning tasks which differed somewhat in difficulty.

As well as a way of measuring learning, Ebbinghaus needed material to learn which would meet two requirements: different lessons should be approximately equal in difficulty, and learning one lesson should not be any help in learning a different lesson. To provide such material, he invented the *nonsense syllable*—two consonants with a vowel between, such as "gub," "xil," etc. Not all such syllables are exactly equal in difficulty, for some remind us of words more than others. They are close enough, however, so that averaged out over a number of lists they soon approximate equality. More important, they are not interconnected with each other the way words in a sentence are. A person who reads "The name of the killer . . ." can predict with almost complete confidence that the next word will be "is." The person who reads one nonsense syllable knows no more than he did before about what the next one will be.

Using these methods, Ebbinghaus discovered many interesting things about learning and remembering. What, for example, is the course of forgetting? Do you forget at a steady rate, or do you forget more or less in the first hour after learning than you do in an hour a week later?

Ebbinghaus found that much forgetting takes place immediately after learning and then there is less and less forgetting as time proceeds. If he rememorized a lesson after only an hour, it still took him half as long as the original learning had. If this rate of forgetting were to continue, we would remember nothing by the end of 2 hours! How much Ebbinghaus had forgotten after varying periods of time is illustrated in Table 7–1.

While other studies of learning have supported Ebbinghaus's finding that forgetting is most rapid immediately after learning, there

Table 7–1 *The course of forgetting over time*

TIME BETWEEN LEARNING AND RELEARNING	PERCENT OF ORIGINAL TIME SAVED	PERCENT OF MATERIAL FORGOTTEN IN TERMS OF TIME TO LEARN
20 minutes	58.2	41.8
1 hour	44.2	55.8
8.8 hours	35.8	64.2
1 day	33.7	66.3
2 days	27.8	72.2
6 days	25.4	74.6
31 days	21.1	78.9

SOURCE: Ebbinghaus[3]

were two reasons why his data showed this phenomenon in a more extreme form than some studies. The first of these has to do with his use of nonsense syllables as material to be learned. Although the forgetting curve has the same general shape with more meaningful material, it does not fall off as rapidly. If Ebbinghaus had learned poems instead of nonsense syllables, he would not have lost half the effects of his learning within the first hour. He would, however, still have forgotten quite a bit during that time.

The second reason why Ebbinghaus forgot the nonsense syllables so rapidly has to do with how he spent his time while waiting to test himself. He spent it learning other lists of nonsense syllables. Imagine that you were to spend 2 hours studying foreign languages—the first hour learning Italian vocabulary, the second learning French vocabulary. As you can imagine, you would probably get the two languages thoroughly confused with each other, and in doing so you would illustrate two basic phenomena of learning, retroactive inhibition and proactive inhibition. *Retroactive inhibition* refers to the way in which new learning makes us forget old learning which preceded it in time. At the end of the first hour you might know the Italian vocabulary, but then studying French might confuse you and make you forget the Italian. This would be an example of retroactive inhibition. In general, the more similar the activity following learning is to the learning itself, the more the learned material will be forgotten. A person forgets least if he sleeps immediately after learning, somewhat more if he thinks about a subject quite different from the one he has just studied, and most if he studies a similar type of material. By studying more nonsense syllables, Ebbinghaus engaged in the one activity which would make him most rapidly forget the nonsense syllables he had already learned.

Ebbinghaus also suffered from *proactive inhibition*, but this showed up in difficulty learning nonsense syllables rather than difficulty remembering them once learned. Returning to the example of learning the foreign-language vocabulary, we can see that you would not only forget the Italian through studying the French; you also would find it more difficult to learn the French through having already studied Italian. The material you had already learned, being similar to the new material you were trying to learn, would intrude and cause difficulty in learning the new material. This is the phenomenon of proactive inhibition.

Another interesting result of Ebbinghaus's research had to do with the effects of *overlearning*. The question which he answered may be put as follows: "Does it do any good to continue studying material even when you have already learned it well enough to recite it?" Such learning is called overlearning because it is additional study even after the material seems to have been mastered. Ebbinghaus studied its effects by comparing learning to a criterion of one errorless repetition with learning to a criterion of two errorless repetitions. A *criterion* of learning is the level of performance which must be reached before we say that the material has been learned. The criterion of one errorless repetition (being able to recite something once without making an error) is what we usually take as evidence of having learned something. In setting a criterion of two errorless repetitions, Ebbinghaus was requiring overlearning, or additional study after he seemed to have learned the material. He found that the additional study did pay off. He remembered the material better if he continued to study it beyond the point where he could recite it correctly.

His memory for the material was improved even more by repeated learning of it on different days. The first time he learned a list of twelve nonsense syllables, for example, he had to repeat it on the average 16½ times. Relearning it the next day took 14 repetitions. The day after that took on the average only 10½. Each time that he learned the material it took less work to do so, until eventually he reached the point where he forgot very little of the material in a 24-hour interval. While much of what we learn is forgotten in the first hour after learning it, this is only true the first time that we learn it. If we are learning it for the third time, we will forget very little in an hour—or even in a day.

While most of his research used nonsense syllables, Ebbinghaus also tried memorizing stanzas of Byron's poem *Don Juan*. He found that this material, being meaningful, required much less work to memorize. This result also is important in understanding how to study effectively, for it implies that anything which can make material more meaningful to the learner can make it easier to learn. Later in the chapter we shall look at some of the ways in which material can be made more meaningful, but for now let us look at just one of these ways—by actively anticipating the material rather than passively reading it.

How can active recitation make material more meaningful? If we look at our own experiences while we read something or try to recite it, we may see a marked difference. Imagine, for example, that you are trying to learn where you are not supposed to park a car in

Britain. The highway code, which you will need to know to obtain a driving license, reads as follows:

54. *Do not park or let your vehicle stand*
    (a) *at or near a road junction, a bend, the brow of a hill or a humpback bridge;*
    (b) *on a footpath;*
    (c) *near traffic lights or a pedestrian crossing;*
    (d) *in a main road or one carrying fast traffic;*
    (e) *opposite or nearly opposite another standing vehicle, a refuge, or other obstruction (e.g. road repairs);*
    (f) *alongside a standing vehicle;*
    (g) *where there is a continuous white line, whether it is accompanied by a broken line or not;*
    (h) *at or near a bus stop, school or hospital entrance, or where it will obscure a traffic sign;*
    (i) *on the "wrong" side of the road at night.*[4]

Now, if you try to learn this material by reading it over and over again, your mind will be filled with the things you are reading, and each of them will seem perfectly reasonable at the time. Of course you should not park on a footpath! If you cover up the example and try to recite the material, however, you will make an interesting discovery. There are many other places where you would not dream of parking a car that are not mentioned in the code, and you will start naming them as well as the places listed. What did the rules say about parking in front of a police station, fire station, railway station, or hospital? Only the hospital was mentioned. What about parking on footpaths, bicycle paths, sidewalks, or in a minor street carrying only slow traffic? Only the footpath is explicitly excluded, although the sidewalk would probably be counted as a footpath. By now you can see that the difference between reading and reciting is that in reciting you have in your mind not only those things which you have just read but also similar things with which you were familiar before. Confusing the old material with the new is one of the major problems in memorizing. By trying to recite early in the learning process, you can relate the material you are trying to learn to what you know already and specifically notice how the new material is similar to, or different from, what you expected. It is in this sense, then, that the material becomes more meaningful. Rather than just trying to memorize "hospital" and remembering library, police station, and ferryboat landing as well, you can make the material more meaningful by noticing that hospitals and schools are mentioned and no other institutions are.

If making material more meaningful makes it easier to learn and if attempted recitation is one way of making the material more meaningful, then we would expect that it would be useful to spend quite a bit of study time reciting. An experiment by Gates[5] compared the efficiency of spending varying proportions of study time on reading and on reciting. He found that it was most efficient to spend four-fifths of the time reciting and only one-fifth of the time reading!

From these few research results, we may draw a number of conclusions about how to study most efficiently. It is possible to learn much more in the same amount of time if the usual practice of reading and underlining is abandoned. Instead, it is more efficient to:

1. Avoid retroactive and proactive inhibition by varying the type of studying being done. Rather than do all studying in a solid block of several hours, intersperse study periods with other activities throughout the day. Avoid studying similar materials one right after the other.
2. Take advantage of less rapid forgetting of material which is being learned for the second time. Rather than try to learn everything in the last few days before the test, try to have learned it once before and to relearn it just before the test.
3. Last-minute cramming can be both helpful and harmful. The material which is studied at the last minute is better remembered. Because of retroactive inhibition, material which is not included in the last-minute review is forgotten through the effects of studying the material which is reviewed. In other words, last-minute review is an unmixed blessing only if everything can be reviewed at the last minute. If the material is being learned for the second time and an entire evening is available for studying, this may well be possible. In that case, last-minute cramming should be quite efficient and should also have the advantage of being followed by sleep, so that new learning will not interfere with it. On the other hand, studying during an hour or two before an exam is generally harmful, as this is not a long enough period of time to cover all the material. (An exception to this is where only a very short lesson is being learned.) A good general principle is thus to review on the night before an exam, but not on the day of the exam.
4. Perhaps the most important point is that material is learned most efficiently if the majority of the time is spent on active self-quiz. Imagine, for example, that you are trying to learn the material in this book and that you have neglected all the other principles of

efficient study which have been given. It is the night before the final exam, and you are just picking up the book for the first time. How should you approach your task?

If you spend the night reading, you will probably have just about enough time to read the book through once. After one reading, however, you would not remember much of the material. If time were so short that you could not both read the book and quiz yourself on the material, you would probably learn more by not reading the book. Instead, you could skim it and quiz yourself on it in the same length of time. The procedure is to ask questions and look for the answers, working from general to specific points: What is the title of the book? If you were writing a book of that title, how would you break the material down into chapters? How do the chapter titles in this book compare with those you would have used?

After learning the chapter titles, you would then work on each chapter. Using this chapter as an example, what are its main sections? Again, how do those sections differ from those you would have used if you had been writing on "Effective learning and remembering"? By relating the material which you are trying to learn to what you know already, it is easier to learn it. You can also find cues to what is important in section headings, italics, names and dates, numbered points, tables and diagrams, and the first and last sentence in each paragraph. Using these cues, you would in this chapter learn such things as four types of memory and how Ebbinghaus tested his memory, the course of forgetting over time, what retroactive and proactive inhibition are, and four principles of efficient study, of which this is the fourth.

By active self-testing, then, one may learn much more material in the same amount of time than one could by simply reading it over and over again. While it is not recommended, at least by the author, that you avoid reading this book, it is recommended that you actively ask yourself questions about the material as you read.

The Nature of Memory

One of the most interesting research endeavors of the present time is the attempt to discover the biological basis of memory, and it is quite likely that within a few years we shall have a good idea how information is stored in the brain. Biologists and psychologists are equally involved in this endeavor. As one researcher put it privately, the biologists know what is there but do not know what they are looking for, while the psychologists know what they are looking for but do not know what is there! He expressed confidence that the psychologists would be more likely to find the seat of memory than the biologists, for he felt that a person has a better chance of finding something if he knows what he is looking for even if he does not know where to look.

In this section we are going to consider what it is that the psychologists and biologists are looking for, that is, the basic characteristics of memory which would need to be accounted for by any biological mechanism of memory. These include limited central processing capacity and differences between long- and short-term memory.

Let us try an experiment. As soon as you finish reading this sentence, close your book and try to recite as much as you can of the Gettysburg Address before reading on. How much of Lincoln's famous address were you able to remember? Or didn't you ever learn it? Now that you have thought about it for a while, are you still able to remember the two basic characteristics of memory listed in the last paragraph? This sentence is here to confuse you if you looked ahead to the end of the paragraph for a moment before trying to remember the Gettysburg Address.

Have you ever looked up a telephone number, such as 9637597, and then had someone speak to you just as you were about to start dialing it? If so, the interruption of your attention probably made you forget the number. Similarly, if our little experiment was successful, trying to remember the Gettysburg Address will have made you forget that limited central processing capacity and differences between long- and short-term memory are what this section will deal with. These two examples illustrate the first difference between long- and short-term memory: short-term memory is easily disrupted by anything that takes your attention from it for a moment, while long-term memory is not dependent on continuous attention. You probably managed to remember some of the Gettysburg Address, although it may have been years since you last paid any attention to it. It is stored in long-term memory.

The way we remember a telephone number for just a moment before dialing it is quite unusual, for it represents an ongoing process rather than storing the information in any permanent way. We may even recite it over and over again quite consciously. In all other types of memory, where material is remembered over a longer period of time, it is organized in ways to make it more meaningful. The telephone number given above, for example, may be remembered quite easily if it is viewed as three numbers decreasing by threes, followed by two sets of two numbers decreasing by twos. The initial set of three numbers starts with three times three: 963. The first set of two numbers starts with two less than the first series started with: 75. The last set of two numbers starts with nine again: 97. The number is thus 9637597. Ways of organizing material in order to remember it more easily will be the subject of the last section in this chapter.

Because long-term memory involves coding the material in some way, that is, changing the material in order to store it, there is one quite clear distinction between long- and short-term memory. In long-term memory, the more slowly the material is presented, the better it is remembered, for this gives the most time for coding. In short-term memory, the faster the material is presented, the better it is remembered, for otherwise the material presented first is forgotten while the last material is being presented. The rapidity with which material which has been noticed is forgotten is well illustrated in experiments by Sperling.[6] Twelve symbols are flashed on a screen for a fraction of a second. If the subject is asked to remember any one row of four symbols, he generally manages to remember three of the symbols in that row. He would seem to be able to remember nine of the twelve symbols all together. But if he is asked to remember as many of the twelve as he can, he forgets some while he is giving the others, so that he can only remember four or five. In other words, forgetting seems to be even more rapid than Ebbinghaus thought—we may forget half of what we notice within the first second!

This is true because we must pay attention to the material and work on it in order to store it in long-term memory, and the amount which our central nervous system can process in this way at any one time is very limited. This is illustrated in a study by Posner.[7] Posner's subjects tried to remember a series of numbers while at the same time carrying out certain arithmetic operations on them. The operations were viewed by the researcher in terms of how many *bits* of information reduction took place, so we must now digress for a moment to consider what a bit is: *A bit is the amount of information required to divide the number of alternatives in half.* Suppose, for example, that you were trying to guess a number between 1 and 100 inclusive. You might ask, "Is it 50 or less?" Whether the answer to this question was "Yes" or "No," it would reduce the number of possible answers in half. You would have obtained one bit of information. You may thus see that the number of bits of information contained in choosing, for example, one number from eight possibilities is three bits. Eight divided by two three times gives only one remaining alternative. The bit is thus a relatively precise measure even though it does not sound as if it were. The amount of information in any given message may be measured in terms of it.

To return to Posner's research, the importance of the bit in his study is that it enabled a precise measurement of the amount of calculation which the subjects needed to carry out while remembering the numbers. A very orderly relationship was found between that measure and how many numbers the subjects forgot. The more their attention was taken up in carrying out the operations on the numbers, the more numbers they forgot.

The overall picture we get of memory is thus of two different ways of storing information. Material is initially remembered for short periods of time by means of some sort of ongoing process. The amount of material which can be held in attention in this way is very limited, and any distraction will cause it to be forgotten. While the material is being remembered in this way, it is also being transformed in some way in order to store it for longer periods of time. The transformation takes time and work, but when it is complete, the material is stored in a different way. Now it can be allowed to drop out of consciousness for long periods of time and yet can be called back again. Forgetting takes place only very slowly once the long-term storage has taken place. Information at this stage is probably no longer stored by means of an ongoing process, but instead by means of structural changes in the nervous system.

THEORIES OF FORGETTING

There have been four popular theories of how forgetting takes place, and at various points so far in the book we have considered three of them. Let us look at them again, for there would seem to be evidence that they all take place. The three which have been considered, either directly or indirectly, are the repression, interference, and consolidation theories. (The consolidation theory has not been introduced by name, but is essentially the idea that information is forgotten while it is being changed from short-term to long-term storage.) The theory which has not yet been considered is the passive-decay theory, which holds that memories simply deteriorate with age.

As we have seen in an earlier chapter, there is considerable evidence that material which is threatening to the self is actively forced out of consciousness. Even if this is true, however, it would be a mistake to believe that if it were not for repression, we would be able to remember everything which had ever happened to us. The vast majority of things which a person forgets, such as what he ate for dinner a week ago last Wednesday, are probably forgotten by processes other than repression. It is even doubtful that repression is responsible for one effect which is commonly explained in terms of it, the loss of memory following an accident. An individual who has been knocked unconscious by a blow to the head commonly loses all memory for the period just before the blow as a result of the concussion. It is tempting to assume that this is a case of repression and that it is the anxiety associated with the experience which causes forgetting. As I. M. L. Hunter points out in his very interesting paperback book *Memory*,[8] however, there are at least two reasons to doubt that this is the explanation. The first is that the memory cannot be brought back under hypnosis or drugs the way a repressed experience usually can. The second is that equally painful injuries of a different type, such as gunshot wounds to the head, generally do not cause amnesia. Rather than repression causing momentary retrograde amnesia, it seems to be caused by a disruption of short-term memory before that memory has been consolidated in long-term memory. We shall thus return to it again when we consider consolidation theory.

The interference theory of forgetting holds that it is learning new things which makes us forget those we had learned before. In looking at the phenomenon of retroactive inhibition, we have seen some of the evidence that this is, in fact, the basis of much forgetting. But how could learning one thing cause a person to forget another? A look at the area of concept learning may provide some clues to the answer.

When psychologists began to study learning, it seemed that learning to give a response to a stimulus was about the simplest form of learning possible. Yet when you stop to think about it, a conditioned response is really quite a complex thing. Before any other learning can take place, the organism must pay attention to certain aspects of the environment and recognize these aspects as being different from other aspects. Perhaps learning to recognize a stimulus is really a simpler form of learning than learning to respond to it. Recent interest in the area of perceptual recognition is at least partly based on the belief that it is.

Most learning, however, does not involve just learning to recognize one stimulus, but instead involves responding to classes of stimuli. This is especially true of human beings because language identifies classes. A person classifies an object as a chair and responds to it as one of a class made up of all chairs, rather than simply learning to recognize that particular object. People learn *concepts*, that is, classes into which dissimilar objects are placed. "Mammal" is an example of such a concept. Even though it includes such diverse animals as mice, orangutans, and whales, it is still not an arbitrary collection of organisms. There are general principles which will enable a person to tell whether a new example of an organism should be classed as a mammal or not.

What is learned in learning a concept? As current theory conceives it, the learning is partly the developing of a series of questions. Is it alive? Is it an animal? Warm-blooded? And so on. Such a series of questions is called a *decision tree,* and each of the end points of the tree is a concept. Two simple examples of such trees taken from Earl Hunt's *Concept Learning*[9] are presented as Figure 7–1.

Looking at concept learning as involving, among other things, the development of decision trees will help us to see how new learning may cause apparent forgetting of things which were known before. Consider the fragment of a decision tree shown in Figure 7–2.

At one time, MGs were the only sports cars commonly seen in the United States, and the simple decision tree above would enable a person to recognize them. If asked, "What kind of car is that?" he would be able to give a correct response every time the car was an MG. Other cars were being built, however, and sooner or later the person was bound to be exposed to a Morgan. At that time he learned something new—that not all squarish sports cars were MGs. However, his performance at naming sports cars probably deteriorated, for it would take time to learn what new questions would have to be added to the decision tree to reliably distinguish the MG from the Morgan. For a while his decision tree would look like that in Figure 7–3.

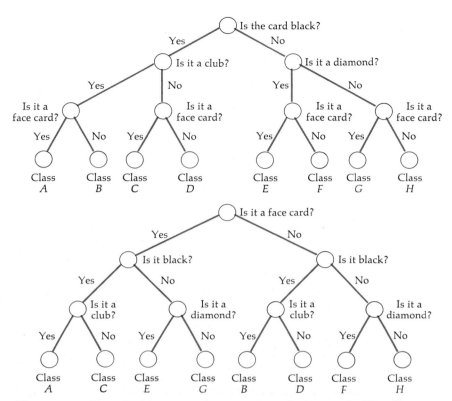

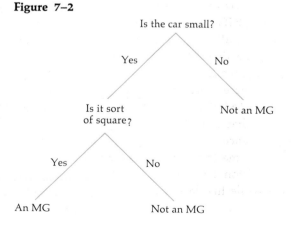

Figure 7–1 *Two decision trees for grouping playing cards (Hunt⁹)*

Figure 7–2

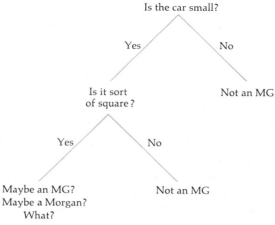

Figure 7-3

Through further learning, then, his performance would have deteriorated. In fact, we would say that he had forgotten something he had once known, for he would no longer be able to identify MGs reliably. Much forgetting is probably of this type.

Another cause of forgetting has become apparent in recent years as a body of research has developed supporting the *consolidation hypothesis.* This hypothesis proposes that it takes some time after something is learned for the memory of it to consolidate and become permanent. A crude analogy is given by saying that the hypothesis proposes that memory is like concrete—learning gives it form but it takes time to set. This hypothesis was apparently first stated by Burnham,[10] but modern interest in it stems largely from a review of the literature by Glickman in 1961.[11]

The consolidation hypothesis has two important implications for forgetting. The first is that anything which disrupts the newly established memory before it has consolidated will lead to permanent forgetting. The memory will not be simply repressed or unavailable; it will be gone completely. The second implication is more exciting than the first, for it is that anything which improves the consolidation process can improve memory. Let us look at studies of these two phenomena in turn.

As was mentioned earlier, retrograde amnesia was the first phenomenon which hinted at the necessity of consolidation of the memory trace. Events immediately preceding unconsciousness resulting from a blow to the head seem to be permanently forgotten, although memories for earlier events which are forgotten right after the blow gradually come back. It is the permanent loss of the most recent memories which seems to argue that the process of storing the information in memory was interrupted before the material had been adequately stored.

While observations of this type had been made on amnesia, it was the development of *electroconvulsive shock* (*ECS*) as a technique of treating mental disorder which led to more extensive study of consolidation. In this form of treatment, which is becoming less used as drugs with psychological effects are developed, a seizure is induced in the patient by means of electric shock. Like a blow to the head, the shock induces amnesia for immediately preceding events. The amnesia again does not seem to be due to repression, and strangely enough a single shock treatment is not remembered as a painful experience, although repeated treatments may cause an experience of unpleasant anxiety. The use of this type of treatment with people led to an interest in studying its effects with animals.

By now, a considerable body of literature has developed on the effects of electroconvulsive shock. The studies taken together indicate that (1) ECS does cause permanent loss of some memories, (2) there is not one period during which all memory will be lost and another during which no memory loss will occur, but instead a gradient of amount of loss with time, (3) ECS also has punishing effects when administered repeatedly, and (4) the period of consolidation depends on a number of factors, not all of which are yet understood.

Because the data on consolidation have been criticized on the basis that the effects could be due to punishing effects of ECS, let us look at the data on that issue first. Some of the earliest studies on consolidation were studies in which the animal was rewarded for performing some act and then for various groups ECS followed after varying lengths of time. The poor performance which was found in those animals who received the shock shortly after learning could, in these experiments, have been due to the shock being a punishment. The animals would not be as likely to repeat the rewarded response if it was also severely punished.

This criticism, however, would not apply to experiments in which the animals were learning *not* to do something instead of learning to do it. Many of the more recent experiments have been of that type. Consider, for example, the following experiment by Madsen and McGaugh.[12] A rat is placed on a platform above a metal floor. When the rat steps off the platform, a mild shock is delivered to its feet. After this happening only once, it is much less likely to step off the platform within 10 seconds of being placed on it in a second test. It has shown one-trial learning.

Now another rat is placed on the platform. It too receives a foot shock when it steps off. It is then removed from the apparatus and given an electroconvulsive shock. What behavior do we expect from it? If the effect of the ECS is due to punishment, the second rat should be even less likely to step off the platform the next time than the first rat was, for it has received more punishment. If, on the other hand, the ECS interferes with consolidation of memory for immediately preceding events, the second rat should be more likely to step off the platform the next time than the first rat was, for it would have less memory of the foot shock. This latter effect is what Madsen and McGaugh found. Over half of the rats in the first condition stayed on the platform in the second test, while less than one-fifth of the rats in the second condition did so. In this case, the ECS has interfered with consolidation rather than simply serving as a punishment.

Repeated ECS, however, does act as a punishment or negative reinforcer, and animals learn to avoid it. This is perhaps best illustrated by another study by McGaugh and Madsen.[13] The procedure of this study was as follows: A T-maze was used, with the goal boxes at the two ends of the T distinctively different from each other. Thirsty rats were given a number of trials in the maze, with water in each of the goal boxes. Following that, the rats were divided into two groups. Each rat in one group was placed in one of the goal boxes and given a painful but not convulsive shock. The next day the animal was allowed to run through the maze, and it was noted what percentage of the rats avoided the side of the maze where they had been shocked. The next day the rat was again shocked in the same goal box, the following day it was tested again, and so on.

This procedure provides quite a sensitive test of the aversive effects of the shock. After being shocked only once, over three-quarters of the animals avoided the side of the maze where they had been shocked. After being shocked twice, all of them did.

What about the other group of rats? They were given the same treatment, but electroconvulsive shock was used instead of nonconvulsive shock. If the ECS is punishing, they too should learn to avoid the goal box where they were shocked. In time they do, but there is little evidence of any learning for the first few trials. After one shock, half the rats run to each side. After a second shock, only 40 percent run to the side where the shock was. After a third shock, however, over half the rats again run to the shock side. Apparently the punishing effects of a small number of electroconvulsive shocks are not great enough to be readily apparent in behavior. After a large number of ECSs, however, the punishing effects are sufficient to cause the rats to avoid the shock side of the maze. These results are shown in Figure 7–4.[14] That it takes a series of electroconvulsive shocks to be sufficiently punishing to have observable effects on behavior may at first seem surprising, since the shock is obviously painful when it is received. The result makes sense, however, in terms of the other effect of ECS in preventing consolidation. Most of the memories of ECS are probably obliterated before they are stored, and only memories of discomfort at the moment of its cessation retained.

The processes of memory would seem much simpler and easier to understand if a fixed period of time were necessary for information to be placed in long-term memory storage. If, for example, consolidation took 5 minutes, then ECS less than 5 minutes after learning would cause complete forgetting of the material learned, and shock

Figure 7–4 *Percent of rats avoiding one of two goal boxes in which ECS (solid line, closed circles) or subconvulsive (2 ma) shock (dashed line, open circles) was received. Median running times are shown in parentheses. Treatments and test trials were given on alternate days. (McGaugh and Madsen[14])*

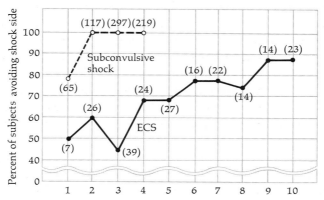

more than 5 minutes after learning would have no effect. Unfortunately, the world is not that simple. The closer in time the ECS is to the learning, the more forgetting it causes. In a study by Hudspeth, McGaugh, and Thomson,[15] for example, an almost negligible amount was remembered if ECS came immediately after learning. A good deal more was remembered if the shock came 20 seconds later, but consolidation was still not complete after half an hour—ECS at that time still caused some loss of the learned material. Apparently some information is stored in permanent memory almost immediately, and some takes a great deal of time to be stored there. Just how that could come about may be part of a more general question that we do not yet know the answer to: just what is learned when something is partially learned, or remembered when something is partially forgotten?

Imagine, for example, that you are trying to remember the name of Hansen's law, which was discussed in Chapter 5. You remember that it was a law or a principle or a theory or a generalization or something like that. Also it was named for some Scandinavian. Was it Svensen, Olson, or what? This process of hunting in memory for something which is partially remembered gives some hint as to the nature of the process. To return to the concept of the tree structure which was discussed earlier, the person who is searching in memory seems to remember which way to go at some of the junctions in the tree structure but not at others. The name is classed as being Scandinavian and ending in either "sen" or "son," but the actual name is forgotten.

Even this type of anecdotal evidence, however, gives us no clues as to what is happening when forgetting is more complete. Consider Ebbinghaus relearning a list of nonsense syllables. He has forgotten them so completely that he cannot recall when he looks at the list that he has ever seen it before. Yet he learns it more rapidly than he did the first time. Obviously, introspective evidence is of no use here, for in terms of introspection there is no effect of previous learning. What is remembered that results in a saving of time in relearning remains a mystery. It also remains one of the important phenomena of memory which must someday be accounted for.

That certain insults to the central nervous system will cause amnesia is interesting evidence in favor of the consolidation hypothesis but is not particularly striking. Amnesia has, after all, been known for a long time. The really exciting evidence on consolidation comes from studies showing facilitation of consolidation rather than interference with it. Suppose an animal is injected with a central-nervous-system stimulant and then given learning trials. It will, not too surprisingly, learn the material faster. Now consider a different type of study. The animal first carries out the learning trials. After the learning trials are over, it is injected with the stimulant. Finally, after the effects of the stimulant have worn off, it is tested on the learning. Now if the animal shows better performance than a control animal that did not receive the drug, this result cannot be due to either more efficient learning in the first place or more efficient performance due to effects of the drug at the time of testing. It is difficult to see any explanation other than a facilitation of consolidation.

A number of studies of this type have been done, and the results strongly support the consolidation hypothesis. Data from one of these studies, done by McGaugh and his colleagues, are shown as Figure 7–5. Note that injection of strychnine sulfate (which is a stimulant in nonconvulsive doses) improved performance just as much if it took place shortly after learning as it did if it took place before the learning.

We have thus seen at least three bases of forgetting. Repression is the most important in understanding personal conflicts and psychological disturbance but probably does not account for the majority of forgetting. Interference from other learned material is probably the most important in terms of the amount of forgetting due to it, but consolidation is undoubtedly more significant in helping us to understand the biological basis of memory. We may even see, in the near future, some disorders of memory effectively treated with drugs.

One question, however, still remains. Does memory deteriorate simply through the passage of time? We may never have a complete answer to that question. Some processes which can take place with the passage of time, such as the damage of tissue resulting from rupture of blood vessels, can undoubtedly cause forgetting. Whether there is any passive decay of the memory trace in the absence of this type of accident cannot be determined simply because of the effects of the types of forgetting we have already considered. New learning causes too much old material to be forgotten for us to be able to tell whether any old material would have been lost without the new learning. We thus know of three types of forgetting—or perhaps four.

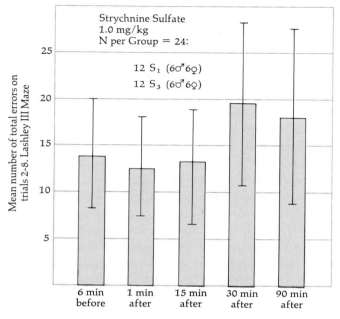

Figure 7–5 *Effect of strychnine sulfate on maze learning as a function of time of injection (either before or after each daily trial). Vertical lines indicate plus and minus one standard deviation from the mean of each group. (Kimble[16] based on data from McGaugh, J. L., C. W. Thomson, W. H. Westbrook, and W. J. Hudspeth. "A further study of learning facilitation with strychnine sulfate." Psychopharmacologia, 1962 (3), pp. 352–360).*

Meaning and Memory

Is there more than one way to learn the same thing? Pioneer work on this question was done by George Katona and discussed in his book *Organizing and Memorizing.*[17] Organizing was not, for Katona, a step in memorizing. Instead he conceived of the two processes as being quite different, a matter of looking for patterns in the case of organizing or of simply repeating the material over and over again in the case of memorizing. He did a series of experiments to compare the results of these different types of process.

So that the two processes could be compared, it was necessary that (1) the same material be learned by each process, and that (2) it be learned equally well. If this is the case, how could the results of the processes differ at all? Katona considered two different ways. It is possible that the material learned in one way might be remembered longer than the material learned in the other, even though learning seemed to be equal in an immediate test. Also it is possible that there might be differences in the extent to which the material learned could be applied in a new situation. Let us look at two of Katona's experiments which demonstrated differences of these types.

The difference in retention of principles and memorized material is beautifully demonstrated in the first of these experiments, dealing with learning a table illustrating an economic principle called the *acceleration principle*. It may be briefly stated as follows: slight changes in demand for consumer goods will cause great changes in demand for the machinery to make these goods. The principle was illustrated with a hypothetical example of demand for shoes and for machinery to make the shoes. Imagine that you had a stable demand for 1,000,000 pairs of shoes each year and that the shoes were made on machines that could make 2,000 pairs of shoes each per year. You would thus need always to have 500 shoemaking machines. Assume further that each machine lasted 10 years. To replace the machines which became worn out, you would need to produce just 50 shoe-making machines each year.

Now imagine that the demand increased from 1,000,000 pairs of shoes each year to 1,100,000 pairs. This is an increase in demand of only 10 percent. Yet look at the effect this would have on demand for the shoemaking machines. You would now need 550 machines instead of 500, so you would have to make not only 50 new machines to replace ones which had worn out but also an additional 50 to meet the additional demand for shoes. An increase of only 10 percent in demand for shoes thus leads to an increase of 100 percent in demand for shoemaking machines.

In Katona's experiment, one group of subjects was given an explanation of the above principle and a table illustrating it. These subjects were not asked to learn the table, but merely to understand the economic principle. (The table is presented as Table 7–2.) The other group of subjects was given the table but not the explanation. These subjects were asked to memorize the table, and repeated it until they could reproduce it without error.

Table 7–2 *Katona's example*

YEAR	NUMBER OF SHOES PRODUCED (PAIRS)	NUMBER OF MACHINES REQUIRED	PRODUCED
I	1,000,000	500	50
II	1,100,000	550	100*
III	1,150,000	575	80†

* 50 + 50.
† 55 + 25.
SOURCE: Katona[18]

After a month, subjects from both experimental treatments were asked to reproduce the table. Not one of the subjects who had memorized the table was able to reproduce it accurately enough for it to illustrate any principle. A typical reproduction, for example, had the columns of the table standing for how many shoes were produced and how many were sold and the rows standing for the quarters of the year. (This incidentally, is a good example of assimilation. The table became more similar to a company's annual financial report.) On the other hand, half the subjects who had tried to understand the principle reproduced the table well enough to illustrate it, even though they had not been asked to learn the table and certainly did not expect to be tested on it a month later. This is an excellent illustration of what may be the most important principle of effective learning, that material is most efficiently learned by understanding it.

Often, of course, finding general principles in material to be learned greatly reduces the amount of material there is to be learned. An old rule of spelling, for example, states that a word ending in a single consonant following a single vowel must double the consonant before adding a suffix beginning with a vowel. Learning the principle involves storing much less information than learning the hundreds of thousands of cases which follow the rule. Even where there is no apparent information reduction through organizing, however, it still seems to make material easier to learn. Especially interesting in the results of the preceding experiment is that the subjects who studied the general principle even remembered specific details better than the memorizers. Such words as "shoes" and "machines" were remembered much more frequently by those who had learned the material in an organized way.

Another of Katona's series of experiments dealt with the extent to which material learned in different ways could be transferred to a new situation. For these experiments he used what he called match tasks, as the tasks required moving matchsticks to form various patterns. For example, how could you transform the five squares shown below into four squares by moving only three matches? (Note that each match must be used to form a side of a square and that sides cannot be formed of double matches lying side by side.)

Some of the subjects memorized rules for solving each task, while others were taught in various ways that emphasized general principles. These principles may be conceptualized in different ways. The same number of matches will make the most squares if the squares are bunched together so that one match can serve as a side of two squares at the same time. Or, to view it differently, a minimum number of squares constructed from a maximum number of matches will present an appearance of being full of holes and having a very long perimeter.

By now, you may have been able to solve the example. If not, try removing the two matches making up the lower right-hand corner square and the match making up the bottom of the second square from the left. Use these three matches to form a square on top of what used to be the second square from the left. Can you see how this solution exemplifies the general principles? You have made four matches which formerly served double functions come to serve only single functions.

In a series of experiments using problems of this type, Katona reached two main conclusions. One is similar to the one we have already discussed: the subjects who learned with understanding retained their knowledge longer. The other should not be surprising either: the more the subjects learned general principles rather than specific solutions, the better they were able to transfer their knowledge to a new task.

Figure 7–6 (Katona[19])

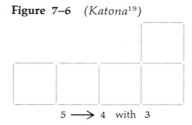

5 ⟶ 4 with 3

MNEMONIC DEVICES

Besides general approaches to learning material of the types which we have been considering, individuals have also devised various specific systems of memorizing. To what extent are these systems effective? Are there various tricks by means of which we can greatly improve our ability to learn? The evidence so far seems to be that memory systems, or *mnemonic devices,* do work but have only limited usefulness in most real-life situations.

The demonstrations of memory systems by performers are often very impressive. The man who can stand on a stage and learn, for example, the names of a large number of strangers seems to have a memory far superior to that of the rest of us. How many strangers can you meet at a party and not get their names mixed up? The memory expert, however, has at least one advantage. He is not expected to do anything else while he is learning the names. He stands on the stage, the center of attention. The names are presented to him, and he learns them. What do you do at the party? As your hostess takes you around the room introducing you to the strangers, you are careful not to trip over tables, dogs, loose rugs, other people, and so on. Your hostess addresses a stream of irrelevant comments to you, and the people to whom you are introduced say various things to which you are expected to respond. A number of interesting conversations continue throughout the process, and you probably do not hear a quarter of the names at all. In other words, the memory expert has the advantage that he can give undivided attention to the material he is learning, while much of your attention is on your own behavior and other irrelevant matters. Attention is the first requirement for learning, and part of learning to have a better memory is probably a matter of learning to manipulate the situation so that you can pay attention to what you are supposed to be learning. People such as politicians who must meet many people and remember the names of at least some of them probably learn to program their behavior to a great extent. By learning to run off the required social responses automatically, they free their attention for learning names.

The memory systems themselves, although they differ in details, usually seem to operate on two bases, through the use of visual imagery and through learning a code which reduces the amount of information which must be learned. Of these, the visual imagery is the more puzzling. The more striking and bizarre the way in which the information is visualized, the more easily it is remembered. It may thus be that the process is effective for two reasons: associating the material with the image may make it more meaningful and thus easier to learn, and the improbable nature of the image may make the material less subject to interference from similar material. This latter phenomenon has been observed in studies with nonsense syllables and is known as the *von Restorff effect*. If some syllables are made to stand out in the list by printing them in red ink or a different typeface, they will be better remembered than the rest of the list.

One of the simplest mnemonic systems, called the *successive-comparison system*, relies solely on the use of visual images. In learning a list of objects by means of it, each one is visualized in combination with the one following it. Suppose, for example, that you were to learn the list "tree, hat, barn, faucet." You would first try to form a visual image in which "tree" and "hat" were combined, making it striking and unusual. You would not want to simply visualize a hat in a tree, for that would be too commonplace. Instead you would want to imagine something unusual, such as the hat inverted and used as a pot with the tree growing out of it, or a tree which had hats growing all over it as fruit. Next you would form an image combining "hat" and "barn," then one combining "barn" and "faucet." Note that each item takes part in two images, one with the item before it and one with the item after it. If you simply learned an image combining "tree" and "hat" and then another combining "barn" and "faucet," you would have no way of knowing that "barn" followed "hat."

Even this very simple system is apparently quite effective. Wallace, Turner, and Perkins had subjects employ it in learning, not a list, but paired associates.[20] The subjects were first instructed in the use of the system, then given a list of 500 pairs of words. In each case, they were to learn to give the second word in response to the first. After going through the list only once, they were able to remember 99 percent of the words! This performance is far superior to what is usually found in paired-associates learning.

More complex mnemonic systems involve learning a code and using it to reduce the amount of information which must be learned or at least put it in a more meaningful form. In some ways the most interesting of these systems is one devised by an English school-master named Brayshaw and discussed in I. M. L. Hunter's interesting paperback book entitled *Memory*.[21] Brayshaw's system was used for translating dates and other numerical facts into words, and the students in the school of which Brayshaw was headmaster attempted to learn over two thousand numbers by means of it. The code which needed to be learned is given in Table 7–3.

Once the student had learned the code, he learned a verse for each date. The word in which the date was coded was accented in the verse, and the content of the verse described what happened on that date. (In learning dates, the initial 1000 was not coded, so 1000 had to be added to each number.) Some examples are given below:

> 1066 *By* men, *near Hastings, William gains the crown:*
> 1087 *A rap in forest New brings Rufus down.*
> 1100 *Gaul's coast first Henry hates, whose son is drowned:*
> 1135 *Like beagle, Stephen fights with Maude renoun'd.*[22]

The code could only work because vowels, which appeared very frequently, did not stand for any numbers. With long practice, the student could learn to translate the word back into the date quite easily. "Coast" stands for 1100, for example, because the "c" stands for 1 and the "st" for 00. This 100 is added to the already assumed base of 1000, making 1100. Because few people want to learn very many dates these days, Brayshaw's system has fallen into disuse. It is, however, a well-thought-out system, and uses rhyme and meter to make the material easier to learn.

For learning certain things, then, mnemonic systems do seem to work. Another study illustrating this was done by S. Smith, and is discussed by George Miller in a provocative article entitled "The magical number 7, plus or minus 2."[23] The study also illustrated some effects of the limit on human information-processing capacity which has already been mentioned.

Smith's study involved the memorizing of binary digits. In our normal base ten number system we have ten symbols to stand for numbers from zero through nine. After nine, we have run out of symbols, so we must use position combined with the various symbols to stand for larger numbers. Ten is the first number for which we

Table 7–3 *Brayshaw's code*

1	2	3	4	5	6	7	8	9	0	00
B	D	G	J	L	M	P	R	T	W	St.
C	F	H	K		N	Q		V	X	
			S			Z				

must employ a new position, one place to the left of that symbolizing single units. Every grade school child learns about the ones column, the tens column, the hundreds column, and so on. Binary digits differ from base ten numbers in that only two symbols are employed, a symbol standing for zero and a symbol standing for one. Position must thus be used to symbolize any number larger than one. Rather than a ones column and a tens column, binary notation has a ones column, a twos column, a fours column, an eights column, and so on by multiples of two. In binary notation the number "10011001" stands for one times 128, plus no times 64, plus no times 32, plus one times 16, plus one times 8, plus no times 4, plus no times 2, plus one times 1. In base ten numbers, this is $128 + 16 + 8 + 1 = 153$. Awkward as binary notation seems at first glance, it is useful in working with computers because numbers may be symbolized simply by the presence or absence of electrical charges.

Smith's experiment involved transforming binary digits back into base ten digits to make them easier to learn. He first tried learning lists of binary digits and found that he could remember twelve of them with a single repetition. He then tried grouping the digits by twos, so that instead of learning "11" he learned "3," and so on. This doubled the number of digits he could remember, for he still had to learn only twelve of the new digits to stand for twenty-four of the old digits. Next he tried coding the information by transforming the digits three at a time. That is, he translated "111" into "7," "110" into "6," and so on. Again he could remember twelve of the transformed digits, and now they enabled him to reconstruct thirty-six of the original binary digits. Is there no end to the process?

There is. When he coded the digits four at a time, he could only reproduce forty digits, rather than the forty-eight which might be expected. When he coded them five at a time, he could still only recreate a list of forty. The reason is obvious if one imagines himself in Smith's position. Five digits must be kept in mind and translated. While this translation is going on, new digits are being read which must be stored in short-term memory until they are translated. A person can only pay attention to just so much at any one time. The improvement of Smith's digit span from twelve digits to forty, however, shows the effectiveness of the recoding of information which he did.

The studies which have been cited to show the effectiveness of mnemonic systems, however, also show their limitations. Most of them are only good for quite specialized purposes. How many people want to remember for a short time long lists of binary digits? Even systems which do have some generality, such as Brayshaw's, are only useful for rote memorization. As we have seen in looking at Katona's research, material is remembered most efficiently when it is organized in a meaningful way. It is only when no meaningful organization is possible and there is no alternative to rote memorization that mnemonic systems are really useful.

A second limitation is related to the first. The material can only be reproduced in exactly the form in which it is learned. Imagine, for example, that you devised some system to enable you to learn the names of the members of some organization in alphabetical order. The system would enable you to recite "Aitken, Allen, Anderson," etc. It would not enable you to remember that Aitkin tended to drink too much at meetings, that Allen flirted with the secretary, and that Anderson was a karate champion.

Another interesting thing to note is that while mnemonic systems do work, they probably do not work quite as well as the research on them seems to indicate. Experiments on them generally involve teaching the subjects new methods of memorizing and then testing them with these new methods before they have used them to learn very much. This procedure minimizes the effects of proactive inhibition. The material learned by means of the memory system is unlike any other material which has been previously learned, so old learning does not get confused with the new material learned. Perhaps if the subjects regularly used the mnemonic system in their daily lives for a few years prior to the experiment, the system would be found to be much less effective.

Despite these limitations, however, mnemonic systems illustrate two more general principles of effective study which may now be added to our list. (Can you remember the first four?) They are as follows:

5. Use visual imagery to make the material to be learned more vivid. The more unusual the image, the more helpful it will be in remembering the material.
6. Look for ways of recoding information to reduce the amount which must be learned. A general principle involves less information to learn than a series of examples. Whether the information to be learned is reduced by the use of a code, as in Brayshaw's system, or by finding general principles, as in Katona's research, it is easier to learn a small amount of information than a great amount.

Summary

Memory may be tested in a number of ways. Sometimes when a person says that he remembers something, he means that he recognizes it when he encounters it again, while at other times he means that he can recall it when it is not present. In his pioneering work on remembering, Ebbinghaus used the method of relearning to test his memory. The results of his study and similar more recent studies enable us to draw generalizations about effective memorizing. Some of these principles deal with the avoidance of interference, the rate of forgetting at different lengths of time after learning, the advantages of relearning, and the value of active self-quiz.

Of the four major theories of forgetting, there is one which is extremely difficult to obtain evidence on. This is the passive-decay theory, which proposes that material is forgotten simply through the passage of time. The other three theories, dealing with forgetting through interference, repression, and the loss of material as it is transferred from short-term to long-term memory, are all supported by considerable research evidence. Rather than there being one cause of forgetting, there are apparently several different ways in which material is forgotten.

While Ebbinghaus's research dealt with the memorizing of nonsense syllables, material is more easily learned if it can be made more meaningful. Sometimes this may be done simply by becoming aware of an internal structure which is actually in the material, a process which Katona described in his book *Organizing and Memorizing*. Some other material which lacks intrinsic structure may be artificially organized through the use of mnemonic devices, or artificial aids to memory. Two important ways in which such devices aid memory seem to be through the reduction of the amount of information which needs to be learned and through the use of visual imagery.

Notes and Acknowledgments

1. Ebbinghaus, Hermann. *Memory: A Contribution to Experimental Psychology.* New York: Dover Publications, Inc., 1964.
2. Burtt, H. E. "An experimental study of early childhood memory." *Journal of Genetic Psychology,* 1941 (58), pp. 435–439.
3. Ebbinghaus. *Op. cit.,* p. 76.

4. *The Highway Code.* Issued by the Ministry of Transport, Great Britain. Published by Her Majesty's Stationery Office, 1964. By permission of Director of Publications, Her Majesty's Stationery Office.

5. Gates, A. I. "Recitation as a factor in memorizing." *Archives of Psychology,* 1917, no. 40.

6. Sperling, G. "The information available in brief visual presentations." *Psychological Monographs.* 1960, whole no. 498.

7. Posner, Michael I. "Immediate memory in sequential tasks." *Psychological Bulletin,* 1963 (60), pp. 333–349.

8. Hunter, I. M. L. *Memory.* Baltimore: Penguin Books, Inc., 1966.

9. Hunt, Earl B. *Concept Learning: An Information Processing Problem.* New York: John Wiley & Sons, Inc., 1962, p. 226. By permission of the publisher.

10. Burnham, W. H. "Retroactive amnesia: Illustrative cases and a tentative explanation." *American Journal of Psychology,* 1903 (14), pp. 382–396.

11. Glickman, S. E. "Perseverative neural processes and consolidation of the memory trace." *Psychological Bulletin,* 1961 (58), no. 3, pp. 218–233.

12. Madsen, M. C., and J. L. McGaugh. "The effect of ECS on one-trial avoidance learning." *Journal of Comparative and Physiological Psychology,* 1961 (54), pp. 522–523.

13. McGaugh, J. L., and M. C. Madsen. "Amnesic and punishing effects of electroconvulsive shock." *Science,* 1964 (144), pp. 182–183.

14. McGaugh, J. L., and M. C. Madsen. "Amnesic and punishing effects of electroconvulsive shock." *Science,* Apr. 10, 1964 (144), Fig. 1., p. 182. Copyright 1964 by the American Association for the Advancement of Science. By permission of the American Association for the Advancement of Science.

15. Hudspeth, W. J., J. L. McGaugh, and C. W. Thomson. "Aversive amnesic effects of electroconvulsive shock." *Journal of Comparative and Physiological Psychology,* 1964 (57), pp. 61–64.

16. Kimble, Daniel P. (Ed.). *The Anatomy of Memory.* Palo Alto, Calif.: Science and Behavior Books, 1965, p. 276 (based on data from McGaugh et al.). By permission of the publisher.

17. Katona, George. *Organizing and Memorizing.* New York: Columbia University Press, 1940.

18. *Ibid.,* p. 210. By permission of the publisher.

19. *Ibid.,* p. 58. By permission of the publisher.

20. Wallace, Wallace H., Stanley H. Turner, and Cornelius C. Perkins. *Preliminary Studies of Human Information Storage.* Signal Corps Project 132c. Institute for Cooperative Research, University of Pennsylvania, 1957.

21. Hunter. *Op. cit.,* pp. 298–299.

22. *Ibid.,* p. 299. By permission of the publisher.

23. Miller, George. "The magical number 7, plus or minus 2: Some limits on our capacity for processing information." *Psychological Review,* 1956 (60), pp. 81–97.

EIGHT

VALUES, ATTITUDES & OPINIONS

Social psychology, along with the other social sciences, has been concerned with the nature and causes of social problems. In attempting to explain matters of such urgency, it is perhaps not surprising that social psychologists have turned to a theoretical concept which combines both motivational and perceptual aspects. This concept is that of *attitude*, a relatively enduring tendency to respond to an object in some way. Attitudes, like learning, cannot be observed directly, but must instead be inferred. They are usually, but not always, inferred primarily on the basis of verbal statements.

It is interesting that while people often do not tell the truth, and in fact where their own impulses are concerned may not know it, we can learn a great deal about them by what they say. This is true partly because individuals may share views of the world to such an extent that they are not aware of holding them. What "everybody knows" differs from group to group and class to class and reflects underlying characteristics which the respondent may not be aware of. A simple example should help make this point clear.

One of the things which "everyone knows," but is not always willing to talk honestly about, is the nature of the social-class distinctions made in his community. That we do not discuss these distinctions openly is not surprising, for we have an underlying suspicion that it is wrong of us to make them. While the American public is becoming more sophisticated, it is still widely believed that, as Warner and his associates have written:

> *In the bright glow and warm presence of the American Dream all men are born free and equal. Everyone in the American Dream has the right, and often the duty, to try to succeed and to do his best to reach the top. Its two fundamental themes and propositions, that all of us are equal and that each of us has the right to the chance of reaching the top, are mutually contradictory, for if all men are equal, there can be no top level to aim for, no bottom one to get away from; there can be no superior or inferior positions, but only one common level into which all Americans are born and in which all of them will spend their lives. We all know that such perfect equality of position and opportunity does not exist.*[1]

While everyone knows that social-class distinctions are made, not everyone knows how the distinctions he makes are influenced by his own social position. The entire hierarchical social structure is not equally visible from all positions in it. In general, we have the clearest view of social levels close to our own and a better view of those below us than those above. Only the systematic investigator succeeds in learning what everyone knows—the variety of different class distinctions made by people in different castes, classes, and ethnic groups. These principles are well illustrated by Figure 8–1, taken from *Deep South*, a study of the social structure of a Southern city in the 1930s done by Allison Davis and Burleigh and Mary Gardner. Only the upper-upper and lower-upper classes agree in the distinctions which they make, and the person they see as "nobody" is "way-high-up" from another point of view. Nor is it surprising, in terms of what we know about the importance of self-esteem, that

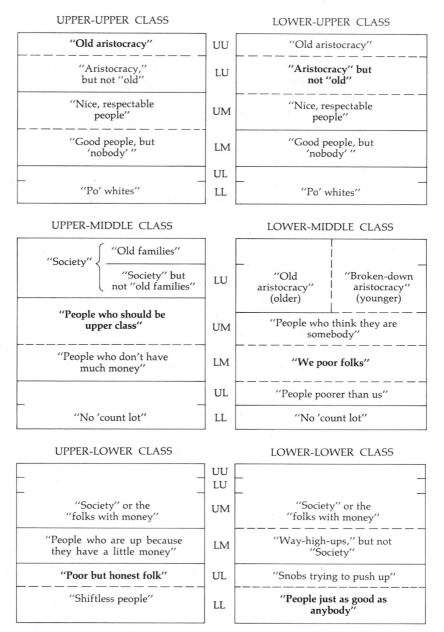

Figure 8–1 *The social perspectives of social classes. (Davis, Gardner, and Gardner[2])*

each person's view of the social structure assigns his own class a position equal in dignity to that of any other. Although members of the upper-lower class (regularly employed laborers) were a "no 'count lot" to the upper-middle class and "snobs trying to push up" to those below them, they viewed themselves as "poor but honest folk." Thus the individual, in giving his own perception of the social-class structure, also reveals where he fits into it.

From the point of view of a psychoanalytic approach to personality, attitudes represent ego functioning, a distinction which may help to clarify both their usefulness and their weaknesses in predicting behavior. While the more punitive restrictions of the superego may be represented only in a disguised form and some of the more ego-alien impulses of the id may not be apparent at all in attitudes, attitudes still represent views about the nature of reality which play an important role in structuring behavior. They cannot be unrelated to moral standards and impulse, for they serve to justify the individual's behavior to himself. They are not the only determiners of behavior, and they decrease in usefulness as predictors when strong forces in either the environment or unconscious portions of the personality are brought into play.

An example of strong environmental factors combining with unrecognized impulses is found in many cases of religious conversion. The desire to be able to be dependent upon an all-good and all-powerful authority, just as once we were dependent upon our parents, is an impulse which is present to some extent in even the most irreligious. The person in whom this impulse is weak may remain relatively indifferent to religion; the one in whom it is stronger may need to fight against it by the reaction formation of openly belittling and defying authority. Powerful preachers have thus frequently had the experience of converting their hecklers more easily than those who were listening to them in respectful silence. J. A. C. Brown, who has an interesting discussion of this topic in his *Techniques of Persuasion*, gives, among others, the following example from the career of John Wesley:

> *A few weeks later another woman who had come to scoff remained to pray; she had been "remarkably zealous against those who had cried out and made noise, being sure that any one of them might help it if they would. And the same opinion she was in still, till the moment she was struck through, as with a sword, and fell trembling to the ground. She then cried aloud, although not articulately, her words being swallowed up. In this pain she continued twelve or fourteen hours, and then her soul was set at liberty."*[3]

Under most circumstances, however, unconscious impulses do not cause this much distortion of one's perceptions of his own attitudes.

Definitions of Terms

For the purpose of analysis, it is possible to consider the ideas which people have as composed of beliefs and sentiments. A *belief* is a prediction about the nature of the real world. If I believe that pi is approximately 3.1416, this does not say anything about whether I would like it to be this large or not. It simply means that whether I like it or not, I will expect the circumference of a circle to be about 3.1416 times its diameter. A *sentiment*, on the other hand, is a positive or negative feeling toward something. If I dislike solving problems of solid geometry, this says nothing about the nature of the world. It simply tells of one of my emotional reactions to something.

Although we can distinguish between beliefs and sentiments in this way, in reality most of our ideas are composed of a mixture of the two. I would not have a sentiment toward solid geometry problems unless I had beliefs about their nature, for example. We thus react to the world, not in terms of pure beliefs and sentiments, but in terms of *opinions*, *attitudes*, and *values*—in which our beliefs and sentiments are inextricably bound up together. Nor do opinions, attitudes, and values differ from each other in kind. All are evaluative statements, differing only in how general is the significance they have for the individual. If I say that I like ice cream, this is probably a statement of opinion, for my ideas about ice cream probably do not influence my ideas about anything else. An opinion, then, is an evaluative statement without much significance for the organization of the cognitive structure of the individual.

At the other end of the continuum of significance is the value. A value is a positive or negative sentiment toward something which is broad enough to serve as a criterion for evaluating attitudes and courses of action in a wide variety of areas. If democracy is a value for me, then my ideas about democracy are not isolated from most of my other ideas, as my opinion about ice cream is. Instead, this value will influence what I think about a very wide range of things, from poll taxes in Mississippi to communism in Romania and from the Athenian city-state to Castroism in Latin America.

Between the opinion and the value in generality lies the attitude. Attitudes do not have the general significance for evaluating most situations that values do, nor do they represent isolated reactions to things the way opinions do. Instead they are evaluations of things broad enough to structure important areas of an individual's cognitive structure. Examples would be attitudes toward the role of women, organized religion, and war. Of course, individuals differ in how their cognitive systems are organized. Some people may have only isolated opinions on the role of women, seldom think about the matter, and ascribe little importance to it. Others may have an attitude in this area, influencing how they view dating and marriage customs, women working outside the home, and female political candidates. For an early suffragette, on the other hand, equality for women might be a value which influenced how she reacted to most other things.

The way in which attitudes are organized around values is well illustrated in a study by Milton Rosenberg.[1] In the first stage of the study, he measured the attitude positions of a large sample of undergraduate students on the question of whether members of the Communist party should be allowed to address the public. He also measured the importance of a wide range of values for these individuals and the extent to which allowing members of the Communist party to address the public would serve to attain or block the achievement of these values. His prediction was that there would be a strong relationship between seeing a course of action as furthering an important value and endorsing that course of action. This prediction was strongly borne out by the data. The students who saw their values as furthered by allowing Communists to speak favored doing so, while those who saw their values as hindered by this policy generally did not.

Even more interesting was the second part of the study. Using individuals who could be deeply hypnotized as subjects, Rosenberg looked at the effects of experimentally changing an individual's attitude toward some topic of importance to him. The first part of the study had shown that we endorse attitudes which we see as furthering our values and disagree with those we see as blocking our values. What will happen if our attitudes are changed under hypnosis so that we now endorse an attitude which we see as being in opposition to our basic values? Two ways of resolving the inconsistency are possible. We could change the value, or we could change our beliefs about the relationship between the attitude and the value. Both these types of reactions were found. Some subjects changed their values to make them more consistent with the attitudes they had acquired under hypnosis, while others maintained their previous values but no longer saw their attitude as being related to their more general value position. Rosenberg's study is one of the more striking demonstrations that our attitudes are organized around our values and that a change in our cognitive structure necessitates other changes to restore consistency.

The Measurement of Values

While the majority of our research techniques have been devised to measure attitudes, we should not thus forget about the more general cognitive structuring which takes place around values. It may well be that the measurement of values lags behind that of attitudes because of the paradox that while values are vitally important to an individual, he often is not aware of them. One reason for this is that many of an individual's most important values are shared by virtually all members of his culture. Because they are shared, they are not questioned, and the individual is likely to assume that they are shared by all people and are a part of human nature. Only by a comparison of different cultures can the basic values of any one become clear. To the Zuni Indians, for example, the preservation of human life was such an important value that murder was virtually unknown and suicide inconceivable. If you look at things from their point of view, it certainly seems obvious that the desire to live is such a basic part of human nature that it is inconceivable that a person should take his own life. Yet from a different value position, such as that in traditional Japanese culture, it is just as inconceivable that a person should choose to continue his life in dishonor. Neither view is a part of any universal human nature; each represents the value position of a culture.

People, then, can generally not say what their basic values are simply because they are so basic that they cannot conceive of anyone not holding them. How, then, can we identify what the values of a culture are? One way is implied in the example just given. Even though people may not be able to state their values, the values which they leave unstated because they seem self-evident may be very informative. In other words, in a cross-cultural study an informant may be able to give a number of reasons why a particular custom is practiced. It is only when the reason seems so self-evident that no further reason is possible that a statement of a basic value may have been reached.

Another way in which verbal materials can be used to infer values is through the analysis of the characteristics shown by the heroes of the myths, legends, and stories of a culture. This is a technique which is essentially similar to the clinical analysis of projective tests except that it is applied at the cultural rather than the individual level. In either case, the desires and values of the individual or the culture are reflected in the problems, characteristics, and behavior of the characters described. The characteristics of the hero of a myth are often so stressed as to impress even the casual reader, and it is probably not possible to read *The Odyssey*, for example, without seeing that cunning is more highly valued in it than honesty.

While a casual reading may reveal much, however, *content analysis*, or the systematic categorization of verbal materials, may reveal much more. This is nicely illustrated by a study by Leo Lowenthal[5] which represents one of the earliest uses of content analysis to infer values. Lowenthal studied American culture at the start of the Second World War, using as his materials the 125 popular biographies appearing in *The Saturday Evening Post* and *Collier's* at the end of 1941 and start of 1942. The values he found reflected in these stories strikingly anticipated the characteristics which Riesman was later to describe in *The Lonely Crowd* and *Individualism Reconsidered*. In contrast to the self-made men and captains of industry who had been the heroes of an earlier period of biographical literature, an overwhelming proportion of the individuals described were important in the sphere of consumption rather than that of production. Even more striking was the uniformity of the characteristics which were approved and disapproved in the individuals portrayed, a uniformity which is succinctly described by the author:

> When we turn to a study of the approval and disapproval our authors attach to the various character traits they describe, we find a striking and simple pattern.
>
> In tone the catalogue of these traits, like the mythology of success, resembles a digest of military orders of the day; brusque laudations and reprimands. There is no room for nuances or ambiguity. In content it is on a very simple level and the criterion of approval or disapproval is also very simple. The yardstick is social adjustment. Once we realize the subconscious and conscious opinions of present-day society on what an adjusted person should or should not be, we are

thoroughly familiar with the evaluation of character traits and their owners. The yardstick has three scales: behavior toward material tasks; behavior toward fellow men; and behavior in relation to one's own emotions. The one who is efficient scores in the first sphere; the one who is sociable, in the second; the one who is always restrained, in the third.

In a separate study of all passages mentioning character traits, we found that of a total of seventy-six quotations referring to a hero's commendable behavior toward "things to be done" not fewer than seventy, or over 90 per cent, mentioned competence, efficiency, and energy; the remaining six referred to ambition. . . .

Out of a total of forty-eight quotations mentioning commendable behavior in relation to people all forty-eight quote "cooperation," "sociability," and "good sportsmanship.". . .

The number of quotations pertaining to disapproved character traits is very small, but conspicuous among them are criticisms of the unrestrained expression of emotion. It is virtually horrible that one of our baseball heroes "is no man for a jest when losing a game. . . ."[6]

While the characteristics of our heroes have changed somewhat since the period Lowenthal studied, his characterization has the ring of truth to anyone who can remember reading American magazines during the Second World War.

Values may be inferred not only from verbal statements but also from behavior itself. The difficulty in doing so is that the same item of behavior may serve many different values. Consider, for example, a person who spends a good deal of money to build a new house. He may be trying to make life easier for his wife, provide better study and play areas for his children, provide space for entertaining which will impress his friends, get himself accepted by a higher social class, bolster his view of himself as a creative person, or provide himself with a large mortgage in order to reduce his income tax!

Since the same bit of behavior can be used in the service of many different values, what is necessary is to find different behaviors which are *functional equivalents*. Different items of behavior are functional equivalents if one will serve as a substitute for another. Let us look at a simple example. Suppose that Andrew takes Mary Jane out and necks with her every weekend, but then Mary Jane goes on a trip lasting for several weeks. What does Andrew do? We will draw very different conclusions about what it is that he values depending on whether he now spends his weekends writing letters to

Mary Jane or spends them necking with her room-mate. In other words, the behaviors that are equivalent from the point of view of the person who is being studied indicate what it is that the person values.

Values are especially clearly revealed when a person has an urgent and difficult choice to make. To a large extent we manage to organize our lives in order to avoid difficult choices. A man's job and his family both have claims on his time, but these claims are usually kept from seriously conflicting by devoting certain hours of every day to each. The ways in which roles and schedules are worked out may keep a man from even being aware of the great potential for conflict which exists until his boss schedules an important meeting for the evening of his wife's birthday. In crisis situations, however, the norms of society may break down and the individual may feel the full conflict of his different value commitments, and it is at these times that a person's values are especially clearly revealed. The norms of the Comanche Indians specified that if the camp was attacked by a hostile tribe, it was the warrior's duty to save his mother-in-law first. This cultural prescription argues for a very different relative valuing of human relationships from that existing in our own society.

That men may not be aware of their values until they are threatened and that crisis situations may call them to make choices which reveal these values, sometimes to their own surprise, are points which are well illustrated in a journalist's account of something which has been quite rare in American political life, a revolution. The account, "The battle of Athens, Tennessee," was written by T. H. White before he became famous for writing *The Making of the President 1960*, and is reprinted in *Outside Readings in Sociology*.[7]

Most Americans probably seldom think about the fact that they do not believe armed force should be used to resolve political differences. Although assassinations have taken place, they cause shock and bewilderment. The willingness to accept the legitimacy of the government in power, whether or not one happens to have voted for it, is a fairly recent development in human political institutions, and a belief in the *rule of law* is one of the more important American values (although a value which is seriously threatened by the discriminatory treatment of black Americans). In describing this value as held by the British, A. C. Dicey considers it to have three characteristics, of which the first two more obviously apply to the United States than the third:

That "rule of law," then, which forms a fundamental principle of the constitution, has three meanings, or may be regarded from three different points of view.

It means, in the first place, the absolute supremacy of predominance of regular law as opposed to the influence of arbitrary power, and excludes the existence of arbitrariness, of prerogative, or even of wide discretionary authority on the part of the government. Englishmen are ruled by the law, and by the law alone; a man may with us be punished for a breach of the law, but he can be punished for nothing else.

It means, again, equality before the law, or the equal subjection of all classes to the ordinary law of the land administered by the ordinary law courts; the "rule of law" in this sense excludes the idea of any exemption of officials or others from the duty of obedience to the law which governs other citizens or from the jurisdiction of the ordinary tribunals. . . .

The "rule of law," lastly, may be used as a formula for expressing the fact that with us the law of the constitution, the rules which in foreign countries naturally form part of the constitutional code, are not the source but the consequence of the rights of individuals, as defined and enforced by the courts. . . .[8]

In 1946, Athens, Tennessee, was not ruled by the rule of law. Instead it had a splendid example of arbitrary authority, a political machine which could not be voted out of office simply because the members of the machine always counted the votes to show themselves reelected! There are safeguards against this simple expedient in American political institutions. Poll watchers from both parties must be present when votes are cast and counted, and irregularities are investigated by the courts. In Athens, however, the officials were important members of a statewide political machine, and the courts always decided in favor of the machine. White described the county machine as follows:

Paul Cantrell, state senator from the McMinn area and boss of the county, was a medium-sized, bespectacled man of sallow complexion, a big head, and little neck. Cantrell loved two things: money and power. He had a nervous fidgety way about him; he rarely looked directly at a man when he talked to him; towards the end, an armed deputy accompanied Cantrell as guard when he strolled through Athens, the county seat. Pat Mansfield, his sheriff, was a tall, handsome man from Georgia. Pat was kind to his family and gave money to his church. He might have been popular but many people resented the sour troop of plug-uglies he had recruited to be his deputy sheriffs. Pat did Cantrell's bidding. . . .

The machine bossed the county with a rough hand. The sheriff had sixteen regular deputies and about twenty or thirty other men he would deputize in "emergencies." Three of the deputies had served penitentiary terms. One of them had been convicted of taking a little girl out and violating the age of consent. It wasn't rape, but then it wasn't good, either; and God-fearing people like those who farmed and worked in McMinn didn't like it. When the deputies arrested a man they often slugged him until he was sensible. Nobody talked back much in public because it wasn't safe. The deputies threatened to kill people they didn't like. . . . One GI who was home on leave during the war was shot and killed by a deputy at a public entertainment house near Athens; a sailor home on leave was killed at the other end of the county.[9]

When the veterans came home from the Second World War, they formed a nonpartisan opposition group to oppose the machine in the 1946 elections. The state of politics in the county at that time is perhaps best shown by their campaign slogan, "Your vote will be counted as cast." When it came to making good this promise, however, the GI party had difficulty:

Election day saw Athens an armed camp. As the voters came to the polls, they found the Cantrell machine in ominous demonstration of force. Almost two hundred armed deputies strutted about, pistols and blackjacks dangling from their belts, badges gleaming. The deputies were strangers. . . .

Bob Hairell, another GI watcher at the twelfth precinct, was in trouble. The machine wanted to vote a nineteen-year-old girl; Hairell objected. One of the deputies settled the argument by pulling his blackjack and laying Hairell's head open. Hairell was off to the hospital. The Daily Post-Athenian sent a reporter to get the story on Hairell. He, too, was slugged and told not to ask questions. At four, the polls closed. In the eleventh precinct, the two GI watchers, Charles Scott, Jr. and Ed Vestal, were thrust to one side as the machine prepared to count the vote. Through the plate glass door of the polling place, the people could see the two boys penned in their corner of the large room. By this time, Jim Buttram, the campaign manager, had decided that the vote of the eleventh precinct wasn't worth trading off against the lives of two of his men. . . .[10]

When the armed deputies took the ballot boxes away to the security of the jail to count the machine back into power, the GIs knew that they were in trouble. While the precincts that had been fairly counted gave them a three-to-one lead, the ballot boxes in the jailhouse would be sufficient to put the machine back in power. Then none of them would be safe, especially as some of their men had gotten a bit carried away and had disarmed some of the deputies. There was only one thing to be done and they did it—they took arms from a National Guard armory and laid seige to the jailhouse. Their rifles and tommy guns weren't much use against the brick jailhouse, but dynamite was, and the jail fell at 3:30 A.M. Four deputies and ten GIs had been wounded during the day. The courts threw out all the votes except those that had been counted with watchers of both parties present, putting the GI slate into office. Armed force had been necessary to restore Athens to the rule of law, and so ordinary law-abiding citizens had used armed force.

Attitude and Opinion Measurement

While the technicalities of attitude-scale construction are beyond the scope of this book, a brief look at some of the problems which any scaling technique must overcome should help develop sophistication in interpreting the results of studies using these techniques. Not only poorly constructed attitude scales but also poorly understood ones can be quite misleading. Consider, for example, the apparently simple matter of finding out whether a person is for or against something. Surely this is something which we may find out simply by asking him one question, the approach of *opinion polling*. But what question should we ask? Let us take for example an area of considerable controversy at the moment of writing, American involvement in Vietnam. A few of the questions which might be asked about this topic are as follows:

1. Do you favor continuation of the war in Vietnam?
2. Do you support the policies of the Johnson administration in Vietnam?
3. Do you favor U.S. intervention in Vietnam?
4. Do you favor meeting our treaty obligations to the government of South Vietnam?
5. Do you favor resisting communist aggression in Vietnam?
6. Do you favor dropping napalm bombs on the people of Vietnam?

The proportion of the population found to support existing policy will obviously differ a great deal depending on which of these or many other possible questions is asked. At first glance it would seem that we could reject a number of the questions as biased and misleading and agree on one as being unbiased. People holding different attitudes, however, will feel that different questions are unbiased. A strong supporter of the war might well feel that the central question is whether or not to resist communist aggression and that question 5 is thus the least biased. A strong opponent of the war would point out that napalm bombs are being dropped and that the controversy is over whether this should continue. Each might well conduct an opinion poll, using his own preferred question, and find strong public support for his position. The supporter of the war would find that most people favor resisting communist aggression, while its opponent would find that most people disapproved of dropping bombs on other people.

Ruling out these obviously biased questions, can we find one which is not biased? Probably not. Whatever is happening in Vietnam, it is not technically a war, since war has not, at the time of this writing, been declared by Congress. The word "intervention" in the third item implies an outside power interfering in the internal affairs of another country—an implication which is either true or untrue depending on your attitude toward the Vietnam conflict. Finally there is the question of whether the policies should be linked to the Johnson administration. On the one hand, they are the policies of that administration; on the other, mentioning Johnson's name makes the response to the question influenced by attitudes toward Johnson as well as toward the conflict. In short, there does not seem to be such a thing as an unbiased question. The question we ask depends on what we really want to know. If it is the amount of support that President Johnson is getting for his policy, we should mention him by name. If it is the extent to which a policy is supported, we should not. While public-opinion polls may tell us much of value, their results are quite misleading unless the effects of emotionally loaded terms, group norms, and forces toward cognitive balance are taken into account in interpreting their results.

Because of the difficulty in writing an unbiased question in opinion polling, *attitude scaling* is often used even if the research problem is to decide how many people are in favor of something and how many are opposed to it. Attitude measurement does not attempt to find one unbiased item, but depends upon assigning numerical values to various items and then interpreting the pattern of the individual's agreements and disagreements. The zero point on the scale (dividing the people who are for from those who are against) may then be decided upon in various ways and without being dependent on writing any item which falls exactly at it. A comparison of two common methods of attitude-scale construction, Thurstone's *equal-appearing intervals* and Guttman's *scalogram analysis*, should help to clarify the strengths and weaknesses of this approach.

Equal-appearing-intervals scaling depends upon judges to assign numerical values to items and to decide upon the zero point. A very large number of attitude statements are collected from a variety of sources, and a number of judges sort them into categories ranging from most favorable toward the object of the attitude to most unfavorable toward it. The categories are not named; instead the judge defines them for himself so that they seem to him to be equally spaced along the favorable-unfavorable continuum, with the center category representing neutral items.

Items are eliminated on which the judges are in great disagreement. Thus if a scale were being constructed on attitudes toward the war in Vietnam, it is quite possible that judges would place the item "We should resist communism aggression" in different categories. Some might see agreement with this item as constituting endorsement of the war and sort it toward the pro end of the scale, while others might see it as essentially measuring a different attitude from support of this particular war and thus place it in the middle category. If this were the case, this item would be eliminated in constructing the scale.

In equal-appearing-intervals scaling, then, the neutral point on the scale is represented by items which the judges agree represent a neutral attitude. Two questions may be raised about the meaningfulness of this as a criterion. The first is that since irrelevant items are generally sorted into the neutral category, it is difficult to know that any particular item which the judges place in that category is really neutral rather than irrelevant. The second is equally serious. Will judges who hold different attitudes themselves be in agreement on what a neutral attitude is?

This second question has been the subject of some interesting research. Early studies, such as that of Hinckley, seemed to indicate that judges sorted items in the same way regardless of their own views. Hinckley, however, had screened his judges for "carelessness," excluding any who placed a large proportion of the items in any one category.[11] Hovland and Sherif later investigated the possibility that it might well be that these judges were not careless, but that it was the holding of strong attitudes in the area which led judges to displace the items. Using judges with strong attitudes, Hovland and Sherif found that they markedly displaced neutral items away from their own position and only judged a few items as being toward the end of the scale where they themselves fell.[12] Thus a person who is himself black, for example, is likely to judge most of the items on Hinckley's scale of attitudes toward Negroes as being anti-Negro.

While there are more refined methods of scaling such as successive-intervals and paired-comparisons techniques which can assign scale scores which are independent of the attitudes of the judges, these methods do not solve the problem of finding the neutral point. However, if the results of Hovland and Sherif's study are taken seriously, then perhaps we would be misguided to say that the problem is that we cannot identify the neutral point. What an individual understands us to mean when we tell him that 54 percent of a population are in favor of something is that 54 percent are on the pro side of what *he* considers to be a neutral attitude. Perhaps, then, there is no such thing as a neutral attitude, but only various points along a continuum which different groups consider to be neutral. If this is the case, then we can only communicate with an individual by using his own frame of reference. We would then need to use different neutral points to communicate our results to different groups in language they would understand. We might well have to tell segregationists that the vast majority of some population were pro-Negro, in terms of what they considered to be pro-Negro, while telling civil rights workers that the majority of the same population were anti-Negro, as they understood that term.

Guttman's scalogram analysis uses quite a different approach to attitude scaling and even uses a different type of item. The equal-appearing-intervals scales we have been discussing use items such as "I think we should call a temporary halt to bombing North Vietnam." The person who favors increasing the scope of the war would obviously not agree with this item; but then neither would the one who wanted to withdraw from Vietnam completely. In other words, each item represents a point on the attitude continuum, and people will be more likely to endorse the item the closer that point is to their own view. The approach is analogous to asking individuals a series of questions such as "Are you about 5½ feet tall?" The person who is either much taller or much shorter will answer "No."

Guttman's approach uses questions which are much more like asking "Are you over 5 feet tall?" No matter how much over 5 feet tall the person is, he will answer the question "Yes." By using items of this type, Guttman has managed to develop a method of attitude scaling which does not require any judges. Let us look at how this is done.

Consider the following set of items, which illustrates an imperfect Guttman scale:

1. Are you over 4 feet tall?
2. Are you over 4½ feet tall?
3. Do you wear shoes larger than size 9?
4. Are you over 5 feet tall?
5. Are you over 5½ feet tall?
6. Are you over 6 feet tall?
7. Are you over 6½ feet tall?

It is obvious that if it were not for item 3, individuals would agree with all items up to a certain point and disagree with all from then on. When an extraneous item is introduced, such as item 3, this ceases to be true. While there is some relationship between height and shoe size, some people less than 6 feet tall wear size 10 shoes and some people over that height do not. Thus when we use the type of items used in a Guttman scale, we should be able to tell whether the items are all measuring the same thing by whether or not we can arrange them in an order such that agreement will change to disagreement at one point and not change back again. If this is not the case, we have extraneous items such as 3 above.

In using this approach, then, it is not necessary to use judges to eliminate extraneous items. The investigator selects items which he thinks all measure the same thing. If he is right, the answers which the individuals in his sample give to the questions should come very close to fitting into the pattern we have described. Individuals can then be scored by the point at which they stop answering "Yes" and start answering "No."

Two points are worth mentioning about this approach. One is that you never get an absolutely perfect scale pattern. Consider, for example, a Bogardus social-distance scale. In the scale, individuals are asked how close relations they are willing to have with members of a minority group—will they accept the minority-group member as a fellow citizen, as a neighbor, as a friend, and as a relative by marriage? While there are few people who would, for example, admit a Negro as a friend but not as a neighbor, it is possible that a person who defined friendship as very casual acquaintance and who was very concerned with property values in his neighborhood might give this answer. A small proportion of answers deviating from the expected pattern is thus not enough to make the scale considered invalid.

The other point is that it is an important question whether the attitude items get at a good sample of all the important attitudes in an area. Guttman's view here was that if the investigator understood the structure of the attitude area, the items which he selected would scale on the first try. If it were necessary to eliminate some items to make the rest scale, such as our item 3 above, this was an indication that the investigator did not know what he was trying to measure. In this case, he was advised to throw his data away and study the area further before trying to construct a scale! Understandably, few investigators have been willing to abide by this injunction, and there are serious questions about scales constructed by eliminating large numbers of items. If many have been thrown out, what do the rest measure? (Thurstone methods try to deal with this problem by using a large sample of items to begin with, but again it is unclear whether the items which scale may not represent a subset which differs in important ways from those which do not.)

To return to the question with which we started, how does scalogram analysis define the neutral point of the scale? In this case a neutral attitude is considered to be represented by the person who just doesn't care one way or the other. The neutral point is thus defined as the attitude held by people who have the weakest feelings about the issue. It is likely that this approach also would show different attitudes as being neutral in different groups.

From this brief discussion we may see that many useful techniques have been devised in the area of opinion and attitude measurement but that a number of cautions should be observed in interpreting their results. In the case of opinion polling, special attention should be paid to the wording of the question. What social forces influence what answer will be given, and how might these forces be changed by slight changes in wording? In the case of attitude measurement, the methods by which the scale was constructed should be examined: Does the scale contain a good sample of the important attitudes in the area it purports to measure? What items were eliminated, and are they different in some important way from those that were included? How well do the remaining items scale? How is the neutral point defined, and for what groups is this a valid definition? In the case of either attitude or opinion measurement, of course, it is also necessary to consider the sample of people upon whom conclusions are based. For the individual who intends to actually do attitude measurement himself, useful treatments of the topic (in increasing order of difficulty) may be found in Edwards, *Techniques of Attitude*

Scale Construction;[13] Green, "Attitude Measurement" in Lindzey's *Handbook of Social Psychology;*[14] and Torgerson, *Theory and Methods of Scaling.*[15]

The Transmission of Social Class

The factors which influence an individual's attitudes and values will form a large portion of the remainder of this book. As a preliminary introduction to this area, let us look at one specific question—how social-class differences are transmitted from one generation to another.

As indicated by the quotation from Warner given earlier, the United States has strong norms of social equality, and it is considered un-American to make distinctions among people based upon wealth, family background, education, and style of life. In fact, such distinctions are harder to make than in some societies, yet people make them all the time. Thus Vidich and Bensman in *Small Town in Mass Society* describe the public norm that specifies that:

> With the exception of a few "old cranks" and "no goods," it is unthinkable for anyone to pass a person on the street without exchanging greetings. . . . The pattern of everyone talking to everyone is especially characteristic when people congregate in groups. Meetings and social gatherings do not begin until greetings have been exchanged all around. The person who feels he is above associating with everyone, as is the case with some newcomers from the city, runs the risk of being regarded a snob, for the taint of snobbishness is most easily acquired by failing to be friendly to everyone.[16]

Yet even in this egalitarian community, distinctions are made in private, and in fact make up a major topic of conversation, as shown by a few of the comments made about others when they are not present:

> "I'd say that he's worth at least $30,000. Why the cows and buildings are worth that alone."
> "You'd think a man with his money would give more than $50 to the church. . . ."
> "There's a guy making $2,800 and he's got a new Pontiac. . . ."
> "Lend him a cent and you'll never see it again."
> "He cleaned up during the war. . . ."
> "He could be doing well if he stopped drinking."[17]

These comments imply more than simply distinctions based upon wealth, although that is one important part of the assessment of social class. Judgments are also made on how the wealth was acquired and how it is used. As a first approximation, social-class distinction may be considered to be the awarding of prestige to individuals on the basis of the role they play in society.

The reality of social-class distinctions is perhaps best shown by the great correspondence between the social-class distinctions made by the residents of a community and those made by research workers on the basis of quite different criteria. In his monumental study of a Midwestern community, *Elmtown's Youth*,[18] A. B. Hollingshead assigned families to social-class levels by a laborious but thorough procedure. First he asked twenty-five members of his sample of the community to assign thirty families to their classes, without giving any indication of how many classes should be used. After eliminating families about which there was great disagreement and checking the class assignment of the remaining twenty on a second sample of townspeople, he was able to assign the remaining families to five classes. He used this list to find out the class position of the 535 families in his sample by having thirty-one new raters compare each of the families with other families on the list of twenty of known class position. In short, he found out the distinctions which residents of the town actually made in assigning prestige to their fellow residents.

Elmtown was also studied by Lloyd Warner,[19] whose six-class system is perhaps the most widely used in studying social class. (It was Warner's classification scheme which was used in *Deep South*, from which Figure 8–1 is drawn.) While Warner uses a six-class system, the highest, or upper-upper, class is only found in old cities with long-established wealth, so Warner was in agreement with Hollingshead in finding five classes in Elmtown. Of the 134 families rated by both methods, approximately 80 percent were placed in the same social class by both,[20] which is really quite high agreement when different procedures are used to assess anything as subjective as social class.

Social class, as measured by sociological techniques, thus seems to agree quite well with social class as used by individuals in assessing their fellow townspeople. What are the characteristics which the sociologists or the townspeople use in making their judgments? Hollingshead found that the things mentioned by his informants could be grouped into five categories:

> *(1) The way a family lived—this included place of residence, type of dwelling, and furnishings; (2) income and material possessions; (3)*

participation in community affairs, politics, religion—"civic minded,"
"radical," "conservative," "good community man," "don't give a
damn about education"; (4) family background, including ancestry,
kin, and national origin; (5) reputation or prestige.[21]

Warner found that he could predict most of the variation in social-class level from the four factors of occupation, house type, source of income, and dwelling area.

Much could be written about social class, for it influences most aspects of our lives, from dating patterns[22] through the chances of being admitted to a college fraternity[23] to income after graduation,[24] the exertion of political influence,[25] whom we go to see if our children have difficulties at school,[26] and even the type of disorder we are liable to develop if we become mentally disturbed.[27] What is most interesting about it, however, is that the perceptions, attitudes, and behavior characteristics of social-class position are passed on from generation to generation. In a society with strong ideals of equality, where the very existence of class distinctions is often denied, how is it possible for this to happen? In this section we shall look briefly at two characteristics of society which help to make it possible—the support of social-class distinctions by restrictions in who associates with whom and differential treatment of individuals from different class backgrounds by social institutions.

As has been seen, both Warner and Hollingshead point to dwelling area as one of the more important indicators of social-class status. Since young children usually play with others who live very close to them, early relationships outside the family are drawn largely from individuals of similar social class. These neighborhood differences are reflected in the differences existing among neighborhood elementary schools. As James Conant wrote:

> *The contrast in money available to the schools in a wealthy suburb*
> *and to the schools in a large city jolts one's notions of the meaning*
> *of equality of opportunity. The pedagogic tasks which confront the*
> *teachers in the slum schools are far more difficult than those which*
> *their colleagues in the wealthy suburbs face. Yet the expenditure per*
> *pupil in the wealthy suburban schoo¹ is as high as $1,000 per year.*
> *The expenditure in a big city school is less than half that amount. An*
> *even more significant contrast is provided by looking at the school*
> *facilities and noting the size of the professional staff. In the suburb*
> *there is likely to be a spacious modern school staffed by as many as*
> *70 professionals per 1,000 pupils; in the slum one finds a crowded*
> *often dilapidated and unattractive school staffed by 40 or fewer pro-*
> *fessionals per 1,000 pupils.[28]*

There is thus ample opportunity for children to learn the class-linked attitudes of their parents during the years when they associate largely with others of similar class position. What happens, though, when they move on to the high school where, especially in a small town with only one high school, they are brought into contact with youths from all class levels? Do they associate freely with all, or have they already learned to choose their friends on bases that are related to their class background?

Hollingshead investigated this question in his extensive study of high-school-age youth in Elmtown. He found that the distinctions made by high school students did not perfectly correspond with those made by adults, for they used only three categories—"the elite," "the good kids," and "the grubby gang." As shown in Table 8–1, there was nevertheless a very strong relationship between placement in these categories and social-class position of parents using Hollingshead's five-class system.

A more crucial question is whom the boys and girls actually associated with. Hollingshead looked at the leisure-time association of the students in groups. The results for boys are shown in Table 8–2.

It is important to note, in reading the table, that there are more boys in classes III and IV than in I, II, or V. Thus it was possible for the relatively small number of boys in classes I and II combined to have 38 percent of their clique associates in class III, while the larger number of boys in class III only drew 11 percent of their associates from classes I and II. The influence of social class on leisure-time association is very clear, so clear in fact that no boy from classes I and II associated with any boy from class V. The association between class and friendship was even more marked for the girls, but less marked in the case of boys dating girls. In general, boys sometimes dated girls from social classes lower than their own, who were re-

Table 8–1   *Peer rating of students from five different social classes*

PEER RATING	I AND II NO.	%	III NO.	%	IV NO.	%	V NO.	%
The elite	27	77	30	21	9	5	0	0
The good kids	8	23	114	78	133	73	4	15
The grubby gang	0	0	2	1	41	22	22	85
Total	35	100	146	100	183	100	26	100

SOURCE: Hollingshead[29]

Table 8–2 *Percentage of clique relations observed within and between classes for males*

BOYS FROM CLASS	DREW THIS PERCENTAGE OF THEIR ASSOCIATES FROM CLASS			
	I AND II	III	IV	V
I and II	49	38	13	0
III	11	61	27	1
IV	5	33	60	2
V	0	13	31	56

SOURCE: Hollingshead[30]

puted to be "fast." Girls did not date boys from classes lower than their own. Thus we see one way in which social class is perpetuated. Even in the high school of a small town, individuals associate with others from social classes near their own, who hold attitudes similar to their own in those areas where class predicts attitude.

Besides associating with people who hold attitudes similar to their own, individuals born into different social classes carry on class differences because they have different experiences with the world which give them attitudes characteristic of their class position. The upper-class individual learns to give commands and have them obeyed; he learns that situations can be changed for the better by taking an active part in changing them. The lower-class individual learns that he has no power and that it is best to be inconspicuous.

Again *Elmtown's Youth* provides good examples, in accounts of what happened when a class I and a class IV boy were late for school:

> *The following Wednesday morning, Frank Stone, Jr. (class I), parked his father's Cadillac in front of the high school at a quarter after eight, climbed out leisurely, picked up his notebook, and walked into the office and casually remarked, "I guess I'm late again."*
>
> *The principal looked hard at him and spoke firmly, "What's the story this time?"*
>
> *. . ."I didn't wake up, I guess."*
>
> *"This time you are going to detention like everyone else." He wrote young Frank an excuse, placed his name on the detention list, and, as he handed him the excuse said, "This means one hour in detention. I want to see you there at three-fifteen tonight."*

Frank Stone did not go to detention, however, and the principal called his father. The principal told the superintendent what he had done and left for a choir rehearsal. When Mr. Stone brought his son in, the superintendent met Frank and asked:

> "Haven't you gone home yet?" Young Frank, burning with rage, retorted, "Mr. [Principal] made me come back for detention. Dad is really sore."

The superintendent talked with Frank and had him wait for a while in his outer office (not the detention room). Some days later he explained to the researchers:

> "I did not want to put young Frank in the detention room with the rest of the kids; so I sat him there in the outer office, and I deliberately worked around in my office until about five-thirty. Then I came out and said, 'Frank, I guess you have been here long enough. You go on home and let's not have any hard feelings.' I talked to his father later about the whole thing, and I think we have come to an understanding."

Following this incident, many class I and class II students managed to avoid being sent to detention when they were late. "Boney" Johnson, a class IV boy, did not fare so well. His English teacher refused to admit him late to class, so he went to the principal's office for an excuse:

> Before "Boney" could say a word, he barked, in a sarcastic tone: "So my pretty boy is late again! I suppose it took you half an hour to put on that clean shirt and green tie! [The principal arose from his desk, walked around, and looked at Boney's trousers and shoes and went on.] Ha, you have your pants pressed today! I suppose you took a bath last night, too. New shoes, and they're shined."

Like Frank Stone, "Boney" tried to skip detention. He, however, did not succeed in getting out of the building:

> The Superintendent rushed out of his office and stood at the head of the stairs. The principal pushed and shoved "Boney" up the stairs as he repeated, "You can't get away with that stuff." As they neared the top, "Boney" broke from his grasp and started down the hall toward the side door. The Superintendent blocked his path, and "Boney" ran upstairs. The principal leaped and grabbed him by the coat collar with his left hand. "Boney" turned and started to fight. The principal spun him around, seized the visor of his cap with his right hand and yanked it down over his eyes. While "Boney" was fighting to get the cap off his face, the principal hit him three times with the heel of his hand on the back of the neck near the base of the skull. "Boney" cursed, struggled, and hit in all directions. Soon he broke free and ran towards the Superintendent, who shook and slapped him three or four times. Both men then grabbed him by the arms and shook him

vigorously. The Superintendent angrily screeched, "You're going out of this building. You're never coming back until you bring your father and we talk this over."[31]

"Boney" Johnson did not come back—he dropped out of school. The example does not illustrate what is best in American education, or even, it is to be hoped, what is typical. There have been too few studies to indicate yet what is typical, and that the incidents described are not unique to Elmtown is made clear by Jonathan Kozol's observations on teaching in the Boston public school system. The case of "Boney" Johnson and those reported in more detail by Kozol in his book[32] illustrate how social institutions teach different attitudes to individuals from observably different backgrounds.

Because political attitudes are closely related to social class, a study of political socialization by Edgar Litt[33] is particularly interesting. Although class is related to neighborhood, it is rare to find an entire community which is uniform in its social-class composition. Where communities are not independent, but actually parts of a major metropolis, however, they often do represent very restricted samples on the spectrum of class, status, and power. Litt studied three such communities in the Boston metropolitan area to see whether schoolchildren in the different communities were taught different things about politics. The upper-middle-class community he called Alpha, the lower-middle-class community Beta, and the working-class community Gamma. Some of their characteristics are shown in Table 8–3, where it will be noted that one of their most striking differences is in voter turnout.[34] This difference is in line with national trends. The higher an individual's socioeconomic status, the more likely it is that he will vote.

To find out whether the nature of the community influenced

Table 8–3 *Socioeconomic and political characteristics of Alpha, Beta, and Gamma*

CHARACTERISTIC	ALPHA	BETA	GAMMA
Percent of working force in professions	38	15	7
Median family income	$5,900	$4,250	$3,620
Median voting turnout (percent) for five gubernatorial elections	67.8	43.8	32.1

SOURCE: Litt[34]; from U.S. Bureau of the Census, *General Characteristics of the Population: Massachusetts, 1960,* and Secretary of State, *Compilation of Massachusetts Election Statistics: Public Document 43,* Boston: Commonwealth of Massachusetts, 1950–1960.

what children were taught about politics in its schools, Litt looked at three things—the attitudes of community leaders in the three communities, the contents of the textbooks used in civic education courses in the three school systems, and the attitude changes shown by students who took the courses in the three communities. Let us look first at the textbooks.

Litt content-analyzed all the civic education textbooks from each of the three communities for the preceding 5 years, using the following categories:

1. Emphasis on citizen political participation—*references to voting, norms of civic duty, political activity, and the effectiveness of citizen action in influencing the behavior of public officials.*
2. Political chauvinism—*references to the unique and nationalistic character of "democracy" or "good government" as an American monopoly, and glorified treatment of American political institutions, procedures, and public figures.*
3. The democratic creed—*references to the rights of citizens and minorities to attempt to influence governmental policy through non-tyrannical procedures.*
4. Emphasis on political process—*references to politics as an arena involving the actions of politicians, public officials, and the use of power and influence contrasted with references to government as a mechanistic set of institutions allocating services to citizens with a minimum of intervention by political actors.*
5. Emphasis on politics as the resolution of group conflict—*references to political conflicts among economic, social, and ethno-religious groupings resolved within an agreed-upon framework of political rules of the game.*[35]

The results of the content analysis are shown in Table 8–4.

From the content analysis we may see that all the textbooks emphasized the democratic creed, and none of them had any significant amount of chauvinistic material. However, only in Alpha and Beta is activity emphasized. Only in Alpha is there any significant emphasis on the political process or conflict resolution, the two types of material which probably best serve to give a realistic picture of how politics really works. Also noteworthy is the increase in unclassified material as we go down the socioeconomic scale. This material may perhaps best be described as a recitation of historical facts which do not illustrate any principles but which can be memorized.

The differences in the textbooks were partially, but not completely, in line with differences in what the leaders of the communities thought should be taught in civic education courses. Only in

Table 8–4 *References on salient political dimensions in civics textbooks (in percent)*

POLITICAL DIMENSION	ALPHA	BETA	GAMMA
Emphasis on democratic creed	56	52	47
Chauvinistic references to Americal political institutions	3	6	2
Emphasis on political activity, citizen's duty, efficacy	17	13	5
Emphasis on political process, politicians, and power	11	2	1
Emphasis on group conflict-resolving political function	10	1	2
Other	3	26	43
Totals	100	100	100
Number of paragraphs	(501)	(367)	(467)

SOURCE: Litt[36]

Alpha did a majority of the leaders feel there should be emphasis on the process of politics or its conflict-resolution function, so this important difference in the textbooks did reflect the attitudes of community leaders. However, leaders in all the communities thought there should be an emphasis on participation (they would probably not be leaders if they did not believe in participation), and this emphasis was lacking in Gamma texts. Also, a number of leaders in both Beta and Gamma felt that chauvinistic material should be included.

The differences in the textbooks thus reasonably well reflect the differences in the communities. Did they have any effect on the students? With one exception, students in the three communities changed in the directions we would expect from the textbooks they were exposed to. The exception is belief in political participation, which was not significantly changed in any community. The students in all communities, however, increased in their belief in the democratic creed and decreased in their political chauvinism. Reflecting the differences in the textbooks, only the students in Alpha came to see politics as involving people and power and as resolving group conflict. Different attitudes were in fact taught to students from different social-class backgrounds. As Litt concludes:

In sum, then, students in the three communities are being trained to play different political roles, and to respond to political phenomena in different ways. In the working-class community, where political involvement is low, the arena of civic education offers training in the basic democratic procedures without stressing political participation or the citizen's view of conflict and disagreement as indigenous to the political system. Politics is conducted by formal governmental institutions working in harmony for the benefit of citizens.

In the lower middle-class school system of Beta—a community with moderately active political life—training in the elements of democratic government is supplemented by an emphasis on the responsibilities of citizenship, not on the dynamics of public decision making. Only in the affluent and politically vibrant community (Alpha) are insights into political processes and functions of politics passed on to those who, judging from their socio-economic and political environment, will likely man those positions that involve them in influencing or making political decisions.[37]

Alexander Hamilton would have been delighted.

Summary

Although individuals do not always tell the truth and sometimes do not know it, what they are willing and able to say still reveals a great deal about them. Their verbal statements reveal their values, attitudes, and opinions. These are similar in that they are all composed of mixtures of beliefs and sentiments, but differ in how general they are. Values are the most general and opinions the most specific.

Because most of our values are shared by most of the people with whom we associate, we are often not aware of holding them, for we cannot conceive of anyone being different. On the rare occasions when our basic values are challenged, we may behave in ways that surprise ourselves, as was illustrated in "The battle of Athens, Tennessee." There are not as well-standardized ways of measuring values as there are of measuring attitudes, but values may be inferred in a number of ways, the most important of which is content analysis of verbal materials. An early study by Leo Lowenthal illustrates the technique.

Two of the problems which must be solved by any method of attitude scaling are the assigning of numerical scores to items and defining the point which separates a favorable from an unfavorable attitude. These two problems are approached differently by the Thurstone methods and Guttman's scalogram analysis. An understanding of the difficulties which the various methods have in solving these two problems will enable the reader to better evaluate published attitude surveys. If adequate methodological safeguards are not employed, attitude surveys and opinion polls may produce extremely misleading results.

Attitudes are highly related to the positions which the individual occupies in the social structure, and the transmission of social-class differences in attitude from generation to generation is one of the basic processes of society. Two studies centering on public education investigated the role the school system plays in this transmission of attitudes from generation to generation. There has not yet been enough research to indicate the extent to which the findings of the two studies are typical or atypical of American education in general.

Notes and Acknowledgments

1. Warner, W. Lloyd, Marchia Meeker, and Kenneth Eells (Eds.). *Social Class in America*. Chicago: Science Research Associates, Inc., 1949, p. 3.
2. Davis, Allison, B. B. Gardner, and M. R. Gardner. *Deep South: A Social Anthropological Study of Caste and Class*. Chicago: The University of Chicago Press, 1941, p. 65. Copyright © 1941 by The University of Chicago. By permission of the publisher.
3. Brown, J. A. C. *Techniques of Persuasion*. Baltimore: Penguin Books, 1963, p. 234. By permission of the publisher.
4. Rosenberg, Milton. "An analysis of affective-cognitive consistency" in M. Rosenberg et al., *Attitude Organization and Change*. New Haven, Conn.: Yale University Press, 1960, chap. 2.
5. Lowenthal, Leo. "Biographies in popular magazines" in William Petersen (Ed.), *American Social Patterns*. Garden City, N.Y.: Doubleday & Company, Inc., 1956, pp. 63–118.
6. *Ibid.*, pp. 96–97. Copyright 1944 by Paul F. Lazarsfeld and Frank Stanton. Reprinted by permission.
7. White, Theodore H. "The battle of Athens, Tennessee" in Edgar A. Schuler et al. (Eds.), *Outside Readings in Sociology*. New York: Thomas Y. Crowell Company, 1952, pp. 737–749. Copyright by Theodore H. White. First printed in *Harper's Magazine*, January, 1947, pp. 54–61.
8. Dicey, A. V. *Introduction to the Study of the Law of the Constitution*. London: Macmillan, 1939, pp. 202–203, 9th ed., by permission of Thorold, Brodie, Bonham-Carter, and Mason, Solicitors.
9. White, Theodore H. *Op. cit.*, p. 739. Reprinted by permission of the author.
10. *Ibid.*, pp. 742–743. By permission of the author.

11. Hinckley, E. D. "The influence of individual opinion on construction of an attitude scale." *Journal of Social Psychology*, 1932 (3), pp. 283–296.
12. Hovland, C. I., and M. Sherif. "Judgmental phenomena and scales of attitude measurement: Item displacement in Thurstone scales." *Journal of Abnormal and Social Psychology*, 1952 (47), pp. 822–832.
13. Edwards, Allen. *Techniques of Attitude Scale Construction*. New York: Appleton-Century-Crofts, Inc., 1957.
14. Green, Bert F. "Attitude measurement" in Gardner Lindzey (Ed.), *Handbook of Social Psychology*. Vol. 1. Reading, Mass.: Addison-Wesley Publishing Company, Inc., 1954.
15. Torgerson, Warren S. *Theory and Methods of Scaling*. New York: John Wiley & Sons, Inc., 1958.
16. Vidich, Arthur J., and Joseph Bensman. *Small Town in Mass Society: Class, Power, and Religion in a Rural Community*. Copyright © 1958 by Princeton University Press, published by Anchor Books, Doubleday & Company, Inc., Garden City, N.Y., 1960, p. 40. By permission of Princeton University Press.
17. *Ibid.*, p. 44. By permission of Princeton University Press.
18. Hollingshead, A. B. *Elmtown's Youth*. New York: John Wiley & Sons, Inc., 1949.
19. A good comparison of Hollingshead's and Warner's research may be found in: Kahl, Joseph A. *The American Class Structure*. New York: Holt, Rinehart and Winston, Inc., 1960, pp. 33–40.
20. Warner, W. Lloyd, et al. *Democracy in Jonesville*. New York: Harper & Row, Publishers, Incorporated, 1949.
21. Hollingshead, A. B. *Elmtown's Youth*. New York: John Wiley & Sons, Inc., 1949, p. 29. By permission of the publisher.
22. *Ibid.*, p. 231.
23. Levine, G. N., and L. Sussman. "Social class and sociability in fraternity pledging." *American Journal of Sociology*, January, 1960, pp. 391–399.
24. West, Patricia Salter. "Social mobility among college graduates" in Reinhard Bendix and Seymour Martin Lipset (Eds.), *Class, Status and Power*. New York: The Free Press of Glencoe, 1960, pp. 465–480.
25. Vidich, Arthur J., and Joseph Bensman. *Op. cit.*, pp. 211–227.
26. Charters, W. W., Jr. "The social psychology of educational administration" in *Perspectives on Educational Administration and the Behavioral Sciences*. Eugene, Oreg.: The Center for the Advanced Study of Educational Administration, 1965, p. 75.
27. Hollingshead, A. B., and F. C. Redlich. "Social stratification and psychiatric disorders" in N. J. Smelser and W. T. Smelser (Eds.), *Personality and Social Systems*. New York: John Wiley & Sons, Inc., 1963, pp. 314–322.
28. Conant, James. *Slums and Suburbs*. New York: McGraw-Hill Book Company, 1961, p. 10. By permission of Conant Studies, Educational Testing Service.

29. Hollingshead, A. B. *Elmtown's Youth*. New York: John Wiley & Sons, Inc., 1949, p. 222, table XIV. By permission of the publisher.
30. *Ibid.,* modified from table XI on p. 214. By permission of the publisher.
31. *Ibid.,* pp. 188–191. By permission of the publisher.
32. Kozol, Jonathan. *Death at an Early Age: The Destruction of the Hearts and Minds of Negro Children in the Boston Public Schools.* Boston: Houghton Mifflin Company, 1967.
33. Litt, Edgar. "Civic education, community norms, and political indoctrination." *American Sociological Review,* February, 1963 (28), pp. 69–75.
34. *Ibid.,* p. 70. By permission of the publisher and the author.
35. *Ibid.,* p. 70. By permission of the publisher and the author.
36. *Ibid.,* p. 72. By permission of the publisher and the author.
37. *Ibid.,* p. 74. By permission of the publisher and the author.

TO BE SOLD & LET

BY PUBLIC AUCTION,

On MONDAY the 18th of MAY, 1829,

UNDER THE TREES.

FOR SALE,

THE THREE FOLLOWING

SLAVES,

VIZ.

HANNIBAL, about 30 Years old, an excellent House Servant, of Good Character.
WILLIAM, about 35 Years old, a Labourer.
NANCY, an excellent House Servant and Nurse.

The MEN belonging to "LEECH'S" Estate, and the WOMAN to Mrs. D. SMIT

TO BE LET,

On the usual conditions of the Hirer finding them in Food, Clothing and Medical Assistance.

THE FOLLOWING

MALE and FEMALE

SLAVES,

OF GOOD CHARACTERS.

ROBERT BAGLEY, about 20 Years old, a good House Servant.
WILLIAM BAGLEY, about 18 Years old, a Labourer
JOHN ARMS, about 18 Years old.
JACK ANTONIA, about 40 Years old, a Labourer.
PHILIP, an Excellent Fisherman.
HARRY, about 27 Years old, a good House Servant.
LUCY, a Young Woman of good Character, used to House Work and the Nursery.
ELIZA, an Excellent Washerwoman.
CLARA, an Excellent Washerwoman.
FANNY, about 14 Years old, House Servant.
SARAH, about 14 Years old, House Servant.

Also for Sale, at Eleven o'Clock,

Fine Rice, Gram, Paddy, Books, Muslins, Needles, Pins, Ribbons, &c, &c.

AT ONE O'CLOCK, THAT CELEBRATED ENGLISH HORSE,

BLUCHER,

NINE

PREJUDICE

Ideology

In the vast majority of situations an individual confronts in living, his culture prescribes the general outline of how he shall behave. Although an individual may decide for himself what he shall eat for breakfast, his culture has already decided the tools he may eat it with. Although he may choose what he wants to say, the language he may say it in has been provided to him. As Berger[1] points out, it is this circumstance which gives truth to the statement, "The dead are more powerful than the living." Although individuals have learned the values and behaviors of their culture, however, the way in which the lessons of the past should be applied to the new situations of the present is not always clear, and one of the major functions of leaders is to define situations in such a way that courses of action are justified in terms of the traditions and values of the past. The leader succeeds largely through defining situations in a way that will be satisfying to his followers. To be satisfying, the definition must not only provide a potentially rewarding course of action but also justify this course of action. In other words, the leader defines ambiguous situations in a way that provides a course of action satisfactory to his followers and justifiable in terms of past cultural values.

This function of leaders of justifying new courses of action in terms of old and accepted values is perhaps most clearly seen in the area of political leadership. Consider the following three statements of political philosophy:[2]

> *When in the Course of human events it becomes necessary for one people to dissolve the political bands which have connected them with another, and to assume among the powers of the earth, the separate and equal station to which the Laws of Nature and of Nature's God entitle them, a decent respect to the opinions of mankind requires that they should declare the causes which impel them to the separation.*[3]

> *The history of all hitherto existing society is the history of class struggles.*
> *Freeman and slave, patrician and plebian, lord and serf, guildmaster and journeyman, in a word, oppressor and oppressed, stood in constant opposition to one another, carried on an uninterrupted, now hidden, now open fight, a fight that each time ended, either in a revolutionary reconstitution of society at large, or in the common ruin of the contending classes.*[4]

> *If men wish to live, then they are forced to kill others. The entire struggle for survival is a conquest of the means of existence which in turn results in the elimination of others from these same sources of subsistence. As long as there are peoples on this earth, there will be nations against nations and they will be forced to protect their vital rights in the same way as the individual is forced to protect his rights. There is in reality no distinction between peace and war. Life, no matter in what form, is a process which always leads to the same result. Self-preservation will always be the goal of every individual. Struggle is ever-present and will remain.*[5]

In the first statement, from the Declaration of Independence, that independence is seen as being sanctioned by the laws of God and nature. The second statement, from the Communist Manifesto, sees revolutionary class struggle as having the sanction of all previous human history. The third, from a speech of Adolf Hitler on March 15, 1929, justifies German military conquest in terms of a Darwinian struggle for survival. Yet we would never imagine that the Declaration of Independence was inspired primarily by the religious beliefs of its signers, that Marx became a revolutionary because he felt so strongly about historical issues, or that it was Hitler's interest in Darwinism which inspired his political career.

These comprehensive views of the world, composed of beliefs and values and serving to justify the actions of those holding them, are known as *ideologies*. Less comprehensive examples are easily found. Morticians tend to believe that the quality of the funeral arrangements paid for by the bereaved indicates the amount of affection he had for the deceased; most medical doctors in the United States believe that adequate medical treatment can only be provided if it is financed primarily by the payments of individual patients; teachers such as myself believe that the whole quality of human existence would be improved by providing more money for education.

Since ideological positions prescribe how situations shall be viewed and what values applied to them, the greatest human conflicts involve opposing ideologies. Again the views which Americans have of the war in Vietnam will serve as an example. The "hawks" and the "doves" define the situation quite differently. Those who favor the war point to the aggressive expansionism in statements of communist ideology, the infiltration of South Vietnam by North Vietnamese Communists, the history of aggression of China against India, and the support which China is giving to the Vietcong, and argue that the situation is one of the United States defending South Vietnam against external aggression. Those who oppose the war point to the intention of the Geneva Conference that elections should be held in a unified Vietnam, the role of the United States in establishing and maintaining a separate government in South Vietnam, the probability that Ho Chi Minh would have won elections held in a unified Vietnam, and the large number of South Vietnamese fighting on the side of the Vietcong, and argue that the United States is intervening in the internal affairs of another country. The differences between the two points of view are partly differences about facts and partly differences about what should be valued. The differences about fact can be resolved by appeal to evidence; those about value cannot.

Most importantly, the ideologies do not necessarily state the things which make individuals support them. Their function is to justify a position, and this may frequently be done more effectively by appeal to reasons other than those for which the position is actually held. For example, I might support the war because I was employed by a weapons supplier and feared that I would lose my job if it were concluded. I might oppose it because I feared that I might be drafted and killed in combat. It is unlikely that I would publicly give either of these reasons for my position.

In looking at prejudice, then, it might be a mistake to seek the source of prejudiced behavior in stereotyped views of other groups or the ideology of White supremacy. While ideologies serve a useful function for the individual in justifying his behavior to himself and others, they are probably not the most important source of that behavior. To find that, we must look at those impulses which he does not completely admit to himself but which are covertly gratified by his behavior.

The Gratifications of Prejudice

For individuals defined as White, the maintenance of a system of domination over those defined as Negro has served three main ends—economic exploitation, sexual exploitation, and the expression of aggressive impulses. These three goals have interacted in such complex ways that at the present time fear may be a major motive impelling the maintenance of the inequality. Slavery was first and foremost a system of economic subjugation, and the complex barriers of unequal employment opportunities, unequal pay for equal work, and residential segregation have served to maintain this economic subjugation. The economic gains to be had from such a system have been declining, however, with the spread of industrialization and automation. Exploiting a group as unskilled laborers led to large economic gains for the exploiting group with a system of plantation agriculture which had need of a vast army of unskilled laborers. It has become less and less profitable as even in agriculture unskilled labor has become unable to compete with rational mechanized farming. Tenant farmers, whether White or colored, no longer make substantial profits for the man who owns the land.

While societies have complex institutions to permit the gratification of sexual impulses, not all impulses may be gratified within the bounds of these institutions. That slavery as an institution allowed the White man wide latitude in gratifying these impulses and did not maintain "racial purity" is attested to by the 348,847 mulattoes living in the slave states in 1850.[6] The continuation of sexual exploitation beyond the end of slavery has been one of the main factors shaping the development of the ideology of White supremacy and has had complex psychological consequences for those defined as White and those defined as Negro alike. A classic study of these consequences was carried out by John Dollard in 1937.[7]

For the White man, access to colored women was provided by his greater wealth and his control of the legal system. He justified it to himself by the strong component of the White-supremacist ideology which portrays Negroes, whether male or female, as "primitive" and sexually insatiable. It would seem at first glance that whether he had a long-term liaison with a mistress or casual affairs with prostitutes and others, he at least stood only to gain as far as impulse gratification went. This, however, was not the case, for his ideology had consequences for his sexual relations with White women. One common sexual problem which is intensified by such an arrangement is to divide women into two classes—those who are "good" but therefore must be sexually pure, and those who are "bad" but sexually desirable—a split which lies behind the popularity in fiction of the heroine who appears to be sexually loose and thus has the attractiveness of the "bad" girl but who turns out to be pure after all.[8] In attaching sexuality primarily to colored women, the White supremacist lost the capacity to enjoy marriage fully, to have a relationship which combined intellectual and emotional closeness with sexual gratification.

Beyond this, he was liable to suffer from guilt over his sexuality and from fear of Negro men. The stereotypes he developed of the Negro as oversexed led him to fear their approaches to White women, whom he feared would find them as irresistible as he found colored women. Also he feared, not without some justification, the retribution which Negro men might seek for past insults should they ever be in a position to inflict it. To a great extent, the elaborately subservient role which Whites have demanded from Negroes has been demanded to reassure the Whites that the Negroes do not intend to attack them. This fear is undoubtedly a major factor in the resistance to complete equality today.

The easy access of White men to colored women is becoming

more and more a thing of the past. Even in 1937 Dollard reported that:

> An upper-class woman reported on old-time concubinage as it existed in her town. The white man, a judge of the supreme court of the state, had a Negro mistress living in a cabin in his back yard. He had three daughters by her whom he treated well. . . . The white wife of the judge lived in seclusion at their home. Informant added that this was antebellum practice and does not happen often in these times. She repeated the assurance that respectable people condemn such things strongly now and that only low-grade white people have sexual traffic with Negroes.[9]

The White man who dreams of having a Negro mistress is more and more likely only to dream of it. The major significance of such dreams today may well be in the fear they give him of complete equality.

The Expression of Aggression

While both economic and sexual interests may be involved in prejudice, there is mounting evidence that aggressive impulses are more important. Let us look at an experiment[10] and then consider its results from a psychoanalytic point of view.

An individual comes to a laboratory in response to a newspaper advertisement for subjects to participate in a study of learning. He is greeted by a thirty-one-year-old man dressed in a gray technician's coat, who introduces himself as the experimenter, and is introduced to a fellow subject. Both subjects are paid in advance, and then the experiment is explained to them. It is on the effects of punishment on learning. One subject is to serve as the teacher, reading pairs of words to the other, who is to learn them. Slips of paper are drawn, and the individual finds that he has been assigned the role of teacher.

The experiment is then explained in more detail. The second subject is strapped into a chair in the adjacent room, and electrodes are attached to him. The teacher is taken back into the main room, where he is shown the shock generator with which the learner is to be punished for incorrect responses. This instrument bears an engraved panel reading "Shock Generator, Type ZLB, Dyson Instrument Company, Waltham, Mass. Output 15 Volts–450 Volts." It has thirty lever switches set in a horizontal line, ranging from 15 volts to

450 volts by 15-volt increments. In addition, each group of four switches has a verbal designation. These designations are "Slight Shock, Moderate Shock, Strong Shock, Very Strong Shock, Intense Shock, Extreme Intensity Shock, Danger: Severe Shock."[11] The last two switches are simply labeled "XXX."

The teacher is given a 45-volt shock to demonstrate how the shock generator works, and is instructed to shock the learner each time he makes an error. He is also instructed that with each error, the shock level should be raised by 15 volts. He is reassured that although the shocks can be extremely painful, they will not cause permanent tissue damage. After a few preliminary trials to make sure that the instructions have been properly understood, the experiment begins.

If the teacher continues to carry out his instructions, he will administer increasingly strong shocks to the learner, who makes quite a few errors. If this happens, the learner will pound on the wall and then stop answering the questions after receiving the 300-volt shock. The experimenter will instruct the teacher to consider the absence of response incorrect and to continue raising the shock level. After 315 volts the learner will again pound the wall, and then will not be heard from again, nor will he answer any further questions.

As you may have guessed by now, although none of the subjects did so, the "learner" is a confederate of the experimenter and is not receiving any shocks. The experiment was designed to see what level of shock the "teacher" would administer before refusing to obey the instructions of the experimenter.

Clearly the subject has been placed in a conflict situation. On the one hand, he has been told that he should continue administering greater and greater shocks right up to the maximum on the scale. On the other, there are very strong cultural prohibitions against causing great pain to an unwilling victim, even in the interests of science. How would the subject be expected to react to this conflict? Judging from the replies of other individuals who had the experiment described to them and were asked how they would expect it to come out, most people would expect the majority of subjects to refuse to give any higher shock at a relatively low level. No one in this sample expected more than 3 percent of the subjects to go to the maximum shock level.

As may be seen from Table 9–1, the results were very different from these expectations.[12] Out of forty subjects, five refused to give

Table 9–1 *Distribution of break-off points*

VERBAL DESIGNATION AND VOLTAGE INDICATION	NUMBER OF SUBJECTS FOR WHOM THIS WAS MAXIMUM SHOCK
Slight shock	
15	0
30	0
45	0
60	0
Moderate shock	
75	0
90	0
105	0
120	0
Strong shock	
135	0
150	0
165	0
180	0
Very strong shock	
195	0
210	0
225	0
240	0
Intense shock	
255	0
270	0
285	0
300	5
Extreme intensity shock	
315	4
330	2
345	1
360	1
Danger: severe shock	
375	1
390	0
405	0
420	0
XXX	
435	0
450	26

SOURCE: Milgram[12]

further shock after the learner pounded on the wall and stopped answering questions after 300 volts. Another nine became defiant somewhere between this point and the maximum shock level. Over half the subjects, twenty-six in all, continued to the maximum shock on the scale.

This continuation did not come easily for them, and there were marked signs of internal conflict. As the experimenter, Stanley Milgram, reports:

> *In a large number of cases the degree of tension reached extremes that are rarely seen in socio-psychological laboratory studies. Subjects were observed to sweat, tremble, stutter, bite their lips, groan, and dig their fingernails into their flesh. These were characteristic rather than exceptional responses to the experiment.*
>
> *One sign of tension was the regular occurrence of nervous laughing fits. Fourteen of the 40 subjects showed definite signs of nervous laughter and smiling. The laughter seemed entirely out of place, even bizarre. Full-blown, uncontrollable seizures were observed for 3 subjects. On one occasion we observed a seizure so violently convulsive that it was necessary to call a halt to the experiment.[13]*

Three facts are significant about this experiment. The first is that individuals are quite inaccurate in predicting how they will react to some situations. Although everyone is confident that *he* would defy the experimenter, few of the individuals actually in the situation did so. Second, the experiment is interesting in giving evidence on the signs of internal conflict. Most important, however, the experiment gives frightening evidence on the extent to which individuals may follow the commands of authority even when those commands require them to violate their own moral standards. To understand these findings, we must digress for a moment and consider a psychoanalytic view of aggression.

Freud's view of aggression was that it is a drive second in importance only to sex in explaining human behavior. Like sex, it is denied free expression by the demands of society as internalized in the superego, and thus may be repressed and expressed in an indirect manner. As the question of repression is central to the question of aggressiveness, let us consider how a repressed drive may be distinguished from the absence of a drive. If John does not behave in an aggressive manner, is there any way to know whether he is repressing aggressive impulses or simply does not have them?

The first way of making this distinction is in terms of reactions to forces toward change. To draw an analogy, imagine that you are looking at a tall fir tree which has been cut almost through at the base. Attached high up on the trunk are a number of ropes, and a controversy has arisen as to whether these are very weak ropes with no force being exerted on them or are all under a great deal of tension, attempting to pull the trunk in opposite directions. If the tree is left alone, there may be no way to decide between these views. It is easy to decide the controversy, however, by attaching a strong cable and attempting to pull the tree over. If the ropes are having no effect on it, it will fall easily. If they are exerting strong forces, you will not be able to pull it over.

Similarly, if a force induced on a personality does not have an effect, it may safely be assumed that there are other forces holding the personality constant, a point which Lewin[14] developed in analyzing social norms. Let us take a social example. Imagine that for some unknown reason you are trying to start a quarrel with a stranger in a bar. First you bump his elbow and spill his beer. Then you criticize him for being so clumsy as to spill the beer on you. Next you complain loudly that he smells so bad that you must move to another seat. In getting up, you grind your heel into his foot. These stimuli represent increasingly strong instigations to an aggressive response on his part, and it would be normal to expect increasingly hostile responses by him to each of your actions. If, on the other hand, you obtained no normal aggressive response from him—if he apologized for spilling the beer, for being clumsy, for smelling bad, and for having large feet—you could safely assume that he had strong forces within him holding any aggressive impulses in check. The individual with strong defenses against the expression of an impulse, then, will not express the impulse even when we can be certain from the stimulating conditions that it is present, while the person who does not employ these repressive defenses will express the impulse freely when circumstances call it out. This difference is illustrated in Figure 9–1.

Figure 9–1 illustrates the possibility of another more dramatic demonstration of the existence of repression. Even strong restraining forces may break down under sufficient instigation. Consider another example. You want to discriminate between a man who does not drink alcoholic beverages because he does not care for them and one who does not drink them because he is a reformed alcoholic who keeps himself away from alcohol with great difficulty. Each may re-

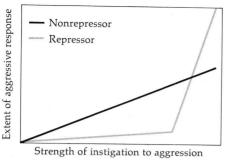

Figure 9–1

fuse a drink if it is offered to him. What will happen, however, if circumstances exert such strong pressures on the two men that each takes a drink? (To choose a farfetched example, it might be imagined that they are in a lifeboat on the North Atlantic in midwinter with nothing to drink but Scotch.) The man who actually dislikes alcohol should have little difficulty in taking one drink and stopping. The former alcoholic, if he once starts, may well find it impossible to stop.

In other words, repression may be broken down by strong instigation. If it is, the person who has strong defenses to hold his impulses in check will find the impulses he was holding in check added to those arising from the situation, and thus express the impulses to a much greater extent than the individual who had neither the strong impulses nor the strong defenses. It is for this reason that Figure 9–1 shows the person who represses aggressive impulses as behaving in a more aggressive manner under very strong instigation than the person without such defenses. The defenses would not be employed if there were not impulses to be controlled.

Next, the same result might be obtained if it were possible to remove the controls of the superego. In the case of the ropes attached to the tree, it would be possible to see if one was exerting any force by cutting the one opposite it. In the case of the individual, large quantities of alcohol may cause an individual to do things that he not only would normally not do but would not normally be aware of wanting to do.

Finally, impulses which are denied direct expression may make themselves apparent in other ways. They may be expressed in a disguised manner or against a substitute object. The man who apologized when you provoked him in the bar may have incorporated a good deal of sarcasm in his replies, perhaps even without awareness: "I'm *so* sorry." (Like ——— I am.) "I always spill my beer." (When some clumsy oaf jostles me.) The provoked man may also go out and express his aggression against someone who is less able to retaliate than you are. Both these tendencies may be apparent in response to a projective test such as the TAT. It is the latter which is of the greatest significance in understanding racial prejudice.

We are now in a position to better understand two of the results of Milgram's experiment. If people do have strong aggressive impulses which they keep from awareness, we should not be surprised that they cannot correctly anticipate how they will act in a situation designed to give free expression to these impulses. Similarly, it should not surprise us that since these impulses are forbidden, much conflict and anxiety should be experienced when they are expressed. Why, however, should this particular situation cause people to act on the basis of motives which are usually kept well under control?

Authority figures play an especially important role in a psychoanalytic theory of personality, for the restraining forces of the superego are seen as the internalized voice of authority. While later theorists have stressed more than Freud that it is not solely parents but also peers, teachers, and other significant figures who contribute to the formation of the superego, parents are still generally regarded as its most important source in most cases. This has two especially important consequences. The first is that the way in which an individual copes with his impulses may be at least partially understood from knowledge of his childhood relationships with his parents, a point which we shall return to when we consider personality factors in prejudice. The second consequence, which has received less attention, is the role which authority can play in freeing the individual from the dictates of his conscience.

Let us return to viewing the individual in Milgram's experiment as subject to conflicting forces. On the one hand, he has aggressive tendencies which are repugnant to him and which he denies from his own consciousness. On the other hand, he has a well-developed moral code which keeps these tendencies constantly in check. Finally, he has the remains of a childlike fear of violating the dictates of authority figures and his peers, the elements which initially shaped that moral code. Under most circumstances his peers and nearly all authority figures will be acting in support of his conscience, restraining him from actions condemned by society. An additional voice of authority added to what he carries inside himself—for example, his employer urging him to greater effort in his work—may do little to make him abide even more closely by the dictates of his conscience, for this force is opposing the strong forces of his impulse. But a voice of authority telling him to do what his conscience considers it wrong to do—say, a superior telling him not to bother working hard—may have dramatic effects on his behavior, for this voice of authority undermines the force of the superego, which is founded on authority, and encourages him in doing what his impulse wants him to do. Similarly, an authority giving tacit acquiescence to inhuman acts against minority groups calls out those acts.

This explanation of Milgram's experiment manages to explain the result while also explaining the obvious fact that people do not do everything that authority figures tell them to do. It does so, however, at the cost of assuming that people have strong aggressive impulses which are gratified by inflicting pain upon others. Evidence for this view will be provided in the section on situational factors in prejudice. Let us briefly consider one piece of evidence from Milgram's research at this point, however. One of the variations which Milgram ran on his basic experiment was a control group in which the "teacher" chose the level of shock to be given with no suggestion from the experimenter.[15] As would be expected, the level of shock given was considerably lower on the average than in the experimental condition. Two out of forty control subjects, however, gave the maximum possible shock!

Personality Factors in Prejudice

The relationship between personality factors and prejudice has been extensively studied by Adorno and his colleagues in their monumental work *The Authoritarian Personality*.[16] While a number of difficult methodological questions are involved in the interpretation of their study,[17] it also has a number of strong points and is probably the single most informative work in this area. Furthermore, some of its main findings have been supported by more recent research using different techniques. Epstein,[18] for example, studied the relationships among authoritarianism as a personality characteristic, the amount of displaced aggression a person has toward others, and the social status of the victim of the aggression. Using an experimental situation in which aggression was expressed by the subject's administration of an electric shock to someone instead of merely verbal expression of attitudes, he obtained results which supported two of the findings of the original study of the authoritarian personality. (1) Individuals high in authoritarianism expressed more aggression toward the experimental victim, and (2) turned their aggression toward victims lower in social status than themselves.

In the 990 pages of *The Authoritarian Personality* there is much more material than can be summarized in an introductory text. In this section we shall look at just a portion of the study, the intensive-interview study of forty highly prejudiced and forty relatively unprejudiced individuals drawn from a broad cross section of American society and roughly matched on demographic characteristics. The individuals were rated by persons with a variety of theoretical orientations, and without the raters' knowing whether a particular individual was high or low in prejudice.

The overall theoretical view of the authors, which was highly influenced by psychoanalytic theory, was that prejudice, like other attitudes, develops partly through direct learning and partly as an expression of personality needs. That the former of these two ways is not the only way of acquiring prejudiced attitudes is nicely demonstrated in a study by Hartley.[19] If people are prejudiced against minority groups simply through having learned to be prejudiced against them, then they should have no prejudice against a group which does not exist and which they have thus never heard of. In Hartley's research, subjects were asked social-distance questions about both real and imaginary groups. While some subjects refused to express opinions about "Danerians," "Wallonians," and "Pirenians," most of them did so without hesitation. Considerable prejudice against the nonexistent groups was found, and in general the people who rejected them most strongly were the same people who rejected real-life groups.

To the extent that prejudiced attitudes are not the result of social learning, but an expression of personality needs, they should be found in individuals who have strong aggressive needs but also strong superego controls on the direct expression of aggression, for it is in this predicament that an individual would be likely to turn his aggression against a more socially approved object. Who would we expect these people to be?

In the Sears, Maccoby, and Levin[20] study of the socialization of aggression, which was referred to in Chapter 5, we saw evidence that aggressiveness may result from identification with an aggressive parent. A boy with a strict, aggressive, and punitive father would be expected to develop the type of conflict about the expression of aggression which may result in the expression of his aggression against a substitute object. He would develop strong aggressive impulses partly through the resentment he might feel at the punishment which was inflicted on him and partly through the model of successful aggression which was constantly before him. The punishment would not result in his not identifying with his father, however; through the mechanism of identification with the aggressor, it would result in his idealizing him. To the extent that the superego represents an internalization of the parent, the child would develop a moral code which was as harsh and punitive as the parent.

In contrast to the child with milder and more lenient parents, then, the child with harsh and punitive parents should develop both stronger aggressive impulses and stricter internal controls on the direct expression of those impulses. He should consciously idealize his parents, while unconsciously being resentful of them. His aggressive impulses should be anxiety-inducing to him because of his strict moral code, and various defenses would need to be employed in dealing with them. These defenses would make him less in contact with his own emotional reactions, and raise the possibility of his expressing the resentment he was not consciously aware of against substitute objects which were not as strictly outlawed by his moral code as the initial source of the resentment.

Viewing the prejudiced individual as a person who is expressing aggressive impulses against a substitute object thus leads us to make several predictions about him. He should, first of all, have had aggressively punitive parents. He should consciously idealize these parents but unconsciously feel resentment against them which is expressed indirectly. Finally, he should be out of contact with his own emotional reactions. Evidence that all these characteristics are found in prejudiced individuals, and thus strong support for this view of the personal origin of prejudice, is found in *The Authoritarian Personality*.

Evidence on the first two of the expectations is provided in Else Frenkel-Brunswik's chapter, "Parents and childhood as seen through the interviews."[21] More prejudiced men, significantly more often than less prejudiced, described their fathers as distant and stern rather than relaxed and mild and described their homes as dominated by their fathers. Even more interesting are the questions of what the child was punished for and the type of punishment which was used. The first comparison was between punishment for violating rules and punishment for violating principles. As Frenkel-Brunswik puts it:

> In particular, discipline for violation of rules, primarily "moralistic," was contrasted with discipline for violation of principles, primarily "rationalized" (Category 10). As the first of two variables to be considered in this context, the choice between these two opposite alternatives on the part of the parents would seem to be crucial for the establishment of the child's attitude toward what is considered right or wrong: it probably decides the externalization vs. internalization of values. These two types of discipline further imply different resultant attitudes toward authority.

> In the first case, discipline is handled as "vis major," as a force outside of the child, to which at the same time he must submit. The values in question are primarily the values of adult society: conventions and rules helpful for social climbing but rather beyond the natural grasp of the child. At the same time this type of value lays the foundation for an attitude of judging people according to external criteria, and for the authoritarian condemnation of what is considered socially inferior.

> The second type of discipline invites the cooperation and understanding of the child and makes it possible for him to assimilate it.[22]

In somewhat simpler terms, demands that the child conform to arbitrary rules which he cannot understand are liable to lead to the child's developing a moral code which is similarly arbitrary and ego-alien. Unable to express his impulses directly because of his arbitrary conscience, the child would need to express aggression against substitute objects who could be moralistically condemned on the basis of these principles. This variable again significantly distinguished between the more and less prejudiced subjects, with more prejudiced men and women having been disciplined for the violation of rules, rather than of principles.

The most significant variable, however, was the type of punishment used. More and less prejudiced subjects were differentiated at the .01 level of statistical significance by whether the punishment used was traumatic or assimilable. The distinction is not simply a matter of the extent of physical punishment, although references to "whipping," "not sparing the rod," and "beating the life out of me" were common in the protocols of the more prejudiced subjects. Also considered in making the ratings was arbitrariness through not making clear to the child what he or she was being punished for as well as the use of threats and methods of punishment with which the child could not cope. Examples of the latter are the following:

> "But mother had a way of punishing me—lock me in a closet—or threaten to give me to a neighborhood woman who she said was a witch. . . . I think that's why I was afraid of the dark."

> "Father picked upon things and threatened to put me in an orphanage."[23]

> "I was kind of temperamental when I was little. I had temper tantrums if I didn't get my way. My mother cured them—she dunked me under the water faucet until I stopped screaming."[24]

We thus see considerable evidence that the use of harsh and arbitrary punishment is an important factor in the development of prejudice. Another possibility, however, must be considered. Is it possible that the more prejudiced subjects are simply prejudiced against their parents, as well as against minority groups, and thus describe them as distant, arbitrary, and cruel? This possibility must be ruled out, for the more prejudiced subjects actually idealized their parents *more* than the less prejudiced, a point which supports a theory of identification with the aggressor. On the variable of "Conventional idealization vs. objective appraisal of parents," the more prejudiced men and women idealized their parents more than the less prejudiced (significant at the .01 level in each case). The same individuals who described their parents as "beating the life out of me" could find nothing to say against those parents when asked to describe them. Although holding their parents up to admiration, however, these subjects often found it difficult to pick out specific characteristics to admire:

> One of the outstanding features in the above quotations . . . is the use of superlatives in the description of parents, such as "excellent man in every way," "best in the world," "most terrific person," etc. If more detailed and specific elaborations are made at all, they refer to material benefits or help given by the parents. Where there is no readiness to admit that one's parents have any weakness in them it is not surprising to find later an indication of repressed hostility and revengeful fantasies behind the mask of compliance.[25]

Some support for the view that the more prejudiced individuals had repressed aggression against their parents was also found in the

Thematic Apperception Test protocols of these individuals. An example of such feelings from the interview study is as follows:

> *F 32: Altogether she thinks her "father is a grand person." When asked whether, since no one is perfect, there were any little faults that she could name, she said that she couldn't think of any. He never drank; well, he swore a little bit. And he was argumentative. (However, in discussing her vocation, subject had mentioned that the father had been willing to finance the education of the boys, but that he expected the girls to stay home and be ladies, so what the girls got they got on their own. In another connection, subject remarked that she had got nothing out of her father. He provided them with the necessities of life, but would not give them anything extra. He never allowed the girls to entertain boys at home. Nevertheless, subject stated that she was closer to her father than to her mother.) When the interviewer broached the topic of her brothers and sisters, subject replied, "I'm right in the middle—don't they say middle children are forgotten children!" When asked if she thought that was so, subject closed up, merely remarking that her parents showed no partiality.*[26]

The evidence on the final question about more prejudiced people, whether they are less in contact with their emotional reactions, is less easily summarized, for it was not so much singled out for analysis by the authors as a constant theme running through a number of separate parts of the study. Perhaps it emerges most clearly in what more and less prejudiced women were looking for in a marriage partner.

> *The traits which the typical high-scoring woman tends to desire in men are likewise primarily instrumental in getting the things she wants. They are: hard-working, "go-getting," energetic, "a good personality," (conventionally) moral, "clean-cut," deferent toward women.*

> *By contrast, low-scoring subjects tend to emphasize as desired traits companionship, common interest, warmth, sociability, sexual love, understanding, presence of liberal values. Sometimes their quest for love is so intense and unrealistic that it becomes a source of disappointment to them.*[27]

This divorce of the individual from impulse also comes out, for the men, in the drawing of a dichotomy between "good" and "bad" women, which we considered in the discussion of how a White wife and Negro mistress may be cast in these different roles. "Dichotomy vs. fusion of sex and affection" discriminated between high- and low-scoring men at the .01 level.

While not all the predicted relationships were found in the work on *The Authoritarian Personality* and only a very small part of the evidence which was found can be summarized in a brief account, a clear picture does emerge from the work as a whole which is strongly supportive of a psychoanalytic view of prejudice. While more or less prejudiced behavior may be called out in the same person by different circumstances and while the object of his aggression may depend on cultural opportunities, prejudice seems to consist primarily of unrecognized aggressive impulses turned against a relatively powerless victim.

Situational Factors in Prejudice

While different childhood experiences may make a person more or less likely to express his aggressive impulses against a member of a minority group, it is a concrete social situation which calls out those impulses. Prejudice, like rumor, "serves the twin functions of explaining and relieving emotional tensions felt by individuals."[28] It is when social conditions provide a threat to the self that the emotional tensions are created which are expressed and explained through prejudice. Thus personality differences may help explain who will participate in a lynch mob and who will not, but it is social forces which primarily determine when and where lynch mobs will come into being.

Of the various sources of self-esteem available to American men, the occupational role is perhaps the most important. While the family is undoubtedly the most important group for most men, with occupational groups definitely secondary in importance (a point which was dramatically demonstrated by Killian's[29] research on disasters), it is the peculiarity of the man's occupational role that his relations with his family are also extremely dependent upon it. The husband and father who is not also the provider for the family not only has failed in his occupational role; he is unable to play a traditional masculine role in his family, a point which is illustrated by the matriarchal family structure which characterizes many underemployed segments of the population. A threat to a man's means of earning a living is thus one of the most important threats which may be made to his conception of himself and to his role in society.

If hostility to minority groups is displaced aggression in response to frustrating situations, then economic insecurity and threats to employment should be among the major factors calling it out. If a man loses his job, the anxiety which he feels through not living up to his self-conception could be both explained, by blaming his failure on a minority group, and also relieved, by venting his hostility against it. Evidence in favor of this view is presented by John Dollard et al.[30] For the years analyzed, from 1882 to 1930, there was a significant negative relationship (a correlation of $-.67$) between the number of lynchings per year and the price for cotton crops. Although individuals do not say that they have lynched another person because the price of cotton is low, the number of such incidents is certainly predictable from this index of economic insecurity.

Even stronger evidence of the role of occupational threats to the self as a factor in ethnic prejudice is provided by a study of Second World War veterans carried out by Bettelheim and Janowitz.[31] It is stronger evidence, since in considering a correlation between changes in two variables over time, we must keep in mind that rather than one causing the other, they might both be caused by other historical changes.

A correlation may be due not only to causation but also to the two factors which are correlated being related to a third factor. There is, for example, in the Netherlands, a correlation between the number of nesting storks in a given locality and the human birth rate. This correlation does not indicate that storks do bring babies after all, but simply reflects the relationship of both factors to urbanization. Rural families in the Netherlands, as in many other countries, tend to have more children than urban families. Since storks nest in rural areas rather than large cities, the correlation between stork nesting and birth rate results. But the Bettelheim and Janowitz study, through showing a relationship between personal economic frustration and prejudice for people in the same area at the same time, demonstrates that the relationship found by John Dollard et al. was not simply an artifact of other historical events during the period covered.

Bettelheim and Janowitz based their study on a sample of 150 veterans of the Second World War residing in Chicago. The sample was random except that former officers were not included, since they would have had quite different experiences in the armed forces, and members of discriminated-against minority groups were excluded, since they would be expected to have different prejudices from those of the dominant cultural group. Prejudice was measured in a way which is interesting because it comes closer to measuring prejudiced behavior than many attitude-measurement techniques.

A person who spontaneously tries to convince others that the rights of a particular group should be restricted, without the person he is trying to convince even having mentioned the subject of that group, is not only reflecting attitudes but also engaging in political behavior against the interests of the group. Bettelheim and Janowitz thus classified a person as intensely prejudiced against a particular group if he advocated such restrictive actions against the group when he was simply asked about his experiences in the armed forces. Next most hostile in his behavior toward the group is a person who comes out in favor of action against the group but only does so when he is questioned about it. This reaction was classified as outspoken prejudice. While it represents behavior which is politically hostile to the minority group, it does not represent the degree of hostility which spontaneous behavior does. Classed as less prejudiced than either of these individuals is the person who holds unfavorable views about the minority group but does not favor political action against it. His views were classified as stereotyped. Finally, a person was classed as tolerant of a particular group if he held only isolated stereotypes, not all of which were unfavorable. Subjects were classified into these four categories with respect to each minority group on the basis of an interview lasting between 4 and 7 hours.

No significant relationship was found between the degree of prejudice expressed against Negroes or Jews and a person's position in the social structure at the time he was interviewed. His age, salary, religious affiliation, socioeconomic status, and education had no consistent relationship to his views. Quite a strong relationship emerges, however, when his occupational mobility is examined, as will be seen from Table 9–2.

For 130 of the sample of 150 it was possible to find out about prior civilian employment. They were classified as upward mobile if their employment at the time of interview was one or more steps higher on the Alba Edwards socioeconomic scale than their previous employment, classified as downward mobile if their present job was one or more categories lower than their previous job, and of course considered to show no mobility if the two jobs fell at the same point on the scale. As would be expected from our previous consideration of the importance of a man's occupation to his conception of himself, the most prejudice was shown by those who were downward mobile,

Table 9–2 *Intolerance and mobility*

	DOWNWARD MOBILITY		NO MOBILITY		UPWARD MOBILITY		TOTAL	
	NO.	%	NO.	%	NO.	%	NO.	%
Anti-Semitic								
Tolerant	2	11	25	37	22	50	49	38
Stereotyped	3	17	26	38	8	18	37	28
Outspoken and intense	13	72	17	25	14	32	44	34
Anti-Negro								
Tolerant and stereotyped	5	28	18	26	22	50	45	34
Outspoken	5	28	40	59	17	39	62	48
Intense	8	44	10	15	5	11	23	18
Total	18	100	68	100	44	100	130	100

SOURCE: Bettelheim and Janowitz[32]

while the greatest tolerance was found among those who achieved upward mobility.

On one important point, however, Bettelheim and Janowitz obtained results which differed markedly from those of the research on *The Authoritarian Personality*. When they investigated the reactions of the more and less prejudiced men to the controlling institutions of society, they found that the *least* prejudiced men were *most* accepting of social authority. As they put the matter:

> When acceptance or rejection of the four representative institutions was compared with the degree of anti-Semitism . . ., it appeared that only an insignificant percentage of the tolerant men rejected them, while nearly half the out-spoken and intense anti-Semites did so. This is in marked contrast, for example, to studies of certain types of college students, in whom radical rejection of authority is combined with liberalism toward minority groups.[33]

It seems unlikely that the difference between the results of Bettelheim and Janowitz's study and the research on *The Authoritarian Personality* is actually due to differences in the samples used, for as has already been pointed out, the research on *The Authoritarian Personality* was not simply based upon college students. Instead the difference in results may be due to the type of questions asked. As Frenkel-Brunswik et al. put it, " 'Authoritarian submission' refers to an inability seriously to criticize, reject or actively rebel against one's main ingroup (particularly the family) figures and values."[34] The controlling institutions which Bettelheim and Janowitz obtained reactions to—the Veterans Administration, the political-party system, the federal government, and the economic system—probably did not represent the ingroup to their subjects. As those guys in Washington who run our lives, the controlling institutions which Bettelheim and Janowitz investigated are probably just as good candidates for the displacement of aggression as minority groups.

Sometimes an individual case will dramatically illustrate a general trend, and this has happened with respect to the relationship between threats to the self and the expression of aggression. While this chapter was being written, James Meredith was shot while making a protest march through Mississippi. According to his friends, the man who admits to having shot Meredith has never taken a strong stand on any political issue. What does distinguish him from most men is that his business failed a short time before the shooting. He states that he has no idea why he shot Meredith.

So far we have been considering the role of prejudice in expressing aggression. Does it also serve to explain anxiety-causing perceptions? It is easy to see how some stereotypes could do so. The most common stereotypes of Jews which Bettelheim and Janowitz found, for example, are as follows:

> They are clannish; they help one another. . . .
> They have the money. . . .
> They control everything (or have an urge to control everything); they are running the country. . . .
> They use underhanded or sharp business methods. . . .
> They do not work; they do not do manual labor.[35]

It is not difficult to see how holding such views could help a person to rationalize his own economic failure. It is more difficult, however, to see how the common stereotypes of Negroes could do so. These stereotypes seem to be related to deeper impulses than economic competitiveness, for the tendency here seems to be to see the minority group as dominated by those impulses which the prejudiced person has difficulty in controlling. This, then, would be a case of projection, with the individual explaining the anxiety which he feels by attributing threatening intentions to others. An excellent experimental demonstration of this method of coping with anxiety was carried out by Bramel, Bell, and Margulis.[36]

Subjects were shown either slides or a movie dealing with the Soviet Union. Half the subjects seeing each were led to believe that high readings on a dial indicated that they were showing physiological fear reactions to the stimuli dealing with the Soviet Union but not to other stimuli. Through necessarily elaborate deception, their atittudes toward the Soviet Union were measured both before and after exposure to the stimuli without their realizing that this was part of the same study. There were thus four groups of subjects. They were (1) those who were led to believe that they had shown marked fear responses to very innocuous and peaceful slides dealing with the Soviet Union, (2) those who believed that they had shown fear responses to a film portraying the Soviet Union in a very threatening manner, (3) those who saw the slides without being led to believe that the slides had frightened them, and (4) those who saw the film without being led to believe that the film had frightened them.

On the basis of dissonance theory the experimenters predicted that those subjects who thought they had been frightened by the innocuous slides would explain their fear to themselves by deciding that the Soviet Union was actually more dangerous to the United States than they had previously thought. Those who had seen the film were not expected to show this reaction, as they would be able to explain their fear reactions in terms of the threatening nature of the film itself. These predictions were supported by the results. The subjects who had been led to believe that they were frightened by the slides, in comparison with those who were told nothing about their physiological reactions to the slides, changed more in the direction of seeing the Soviet Union as dangerous on the postexperimental questionnaire. They also changed significantly more than the subjects who had seen the apparently more threatening film. This result shows quite clearly that views of the world may change to explain anxiety-inducing self-perceptions.

The predictions of the experimenters were drawn, however, not from psychoanalytic theory but from dissonance theory. In this as in many other situations the two theories seem to make identical predictions. As the authors of the study conclude:

> Let us consider one final potential alternative interpretation of the experimental results. Suppose that finding an explanation of one's anxiety is itself anxiety reducing. Not knowing the cause of one's emotional state is perhaps a source of discomfort (anxiety), and this discomfort is reduced when the person thinks he has found an explanation for his feelings. This hypothesis is so akin to the dissonance interpretation that it is very difficult to distinguish between the two. Both hypotheses focus upon the discrepancy between one's emotional state (or cognitions concerning it) and the surrounding situation. According to one point of view, this discrepancy produces an uncomfortable state called dissonance, which the person can reduce by believing there is danger in the environment. According to the

other hypothesis, the discrepancy produces an uncomfortable state called anxiety, which can be reduced in the same way. It is doubtful whether a profitable distinction can be made at this time between the two approaches.[37]

The Changing of Prejudice

In this chapter we have been considering prejudice as an example of the ways in which impulses, perceptions, and behavior interact in social behavior. At the risk of some oversimplification, we might generalize that the current social conditions influence the pressures brought to bear on individuals and are thus the main factor influencing the amount of prejudice present in the society at a given time and place, that individual differences in personality influence how different individuals are likely to react to the social pressures, and that cultural beliefs and values as expressed in ideologies influence the targets against whom impulses may be turned. In this type of analysis, then, behavior is not viewed simply as the expression of attitude, but to at least an equally great extent attitudes are seen as developing to justify behavior. If the ideology of White supremacy did not exist, man would have to invent it, as, in fact, he has.

If this point of view is correct, it has important implications for the changing of behavior, for it implies a secondary role for attitude. Rather than change attitudes and assume that behavior will then change also, it implies that it would be more effective to change the social forces which influence behavior and assume that attitudes would then change to justify the new behavior. Support for this point of view comes from the work of dissonance theorists on forced compliance.

Any behavior which is inconsistent with the beliefs of the person engaging in it should generate dissonance. As will be recalled from the discussion in Chapter 5, its amount is thought to be a function of the number, proportion, and importance of the dissonant elements. Even a frugal man would feel little dissonance in observing that he had just handed a ten-dollar bill to a stranger if he also observed the consonant element that the man was an armed robber. Behavior which is inconsistent with some of our beliefs thus arouses little dissonance if it is consistent with other, more important beliefs. This observation has important implications for the changing of beliefs. If a person can be induced to behave in a way inconsistent with his beliefs, the amount of dissonance aroused should depend upon his perception of how much choice he had in acting as he did. If he perceives himself as having been forced by circumstances to act in that way, there should be little cause for him to change his beliefs. If he perceives himself as having acted in that way of his own free will, then dissonance will be aroused which can be reduced by changing his beliefs to agree with his behavior.

One of the best-known studies of this point was carried out by Festinger and Carlsmith.[38] Each subject spent 1 hour in an extremely boring psychophysical experiment, making repeated judgments of weights. At the end of the hour, the experimenter told the subject that the purpose of the experiment was to see whether individuals would perform better if they were told beforehand that the experiment was interesting than if they were told nothing beforehand. The subject was then enlisted as a confederate and was asked to tell the next subject that the experiment was interesting and fun. For performing this service, the subject was paid one dollar in one experimental condition, twenty dollars in another. Control subjects were not asked to lie to the waiting subject. After the subject had carried out his instructions, he was asked by another experimenter to rate how interesting the experiment actually had been.

The prediction which was made was that the subjects who were paid only one dollar for lying would have little justification for having done so and that to justify their behavior to themselves, they would thus have to change their evaluation of how interesting the experiment was. (If the experiment really was interesting, of course, they would not have told a lie at all.) It was thought that the subjects who received twenty dollars for telling the next subject that the experiment was interesting would have less dissonance. It was a small matter, after all, and in the interests of science, and who wouldn't do it for twenty dollars? It was thus predicted that since they would not have to reduce dissonance by changing their evaluation of the experiment, they would continue to rate it as uninteresting. These predictions were supported. The control subjects and those who were paid twenty dollars for telling the next subject that the experiment was interesting both rated the experiment as unenjoyable. The subjects who were paid only one dollar rated it as significantly more enjoyable. By inducing these subjects to act in a way contrary to their beliefs, the experimenters had induced them to change their beliefs.[39]

This and similar studies by dissonance theorists thus provide a new point of view on the material from *The Authoritarian Personality* dealing with parental discipline. In that work the point was made that harsh and arbitrary discipline led to standards of behavior in the child remaining ego-alien and an important source of conflict, while milder discipline with a stress on principles led to a greater assimilation of standards into the self. From a dissonance point of view, changing behavior because of strong threats would not create dissonance and would not lead to attitude change, while a milder threat, if it was sufficient to produce behavioral compliance, would result in the child changing his attitudes to support his new behavior. Evidence in favor of this view is provided in an experiment by Aronson and Carlsmith.[40] Children who were prevented from playing with a toy for a period of time by a mild threat evaluated it as less desirable afterward. Those who were prevented from playing with it either by a strong threat or by having it removed from the room found it more desirable than they had before.

Applying these theoretical ideas to the area of prejudice, it would seem possible that prejudice may develop not so much because children of the dominant cultural group are told stereotypes about minority-group members as because they are required by their parents to act in certain ways toward them. Evidence in favor of this interpretation comes from the work of the Sherifs[41] on the production of intergroup conflict. When the activities at a boys' camp were structured so that the members of two clubs, created for the purpose, had to compete with each other for rewards, the boys in each club developed hostility toward, and stereotypes of, the members of the other. Since the clubs were set up so that each boy initially had as many friends in the other club as he had in his own, these stereotypes must have been created rather than learned.

Perhaps the most interesting demonstration of the effects of behavior on attitudes in the area of prejudice, however, is the work of Deutsch and Collins[42] on interracial housing. The study was a natural experiment—one in which the experimenters did not create the conditions they observed but did manage to find conditions such as they would have liked to create for the purposes of the study. They studied housing projects which were similar in the ratio of Negro to White families, the socioeconomic level of the inhabitants, the nature of the staff, and other relevant variables but which differed in the pattern of occupancy. Two projects were chosen in New Jersey in which all the Negro families were housed in one area and all the White families in another, and were compared with two similar projects in New York where families were assigned to housing units without regard to color.

Striking differences were found in the behavior and attitudes which developed in the two types of housing project. In the integrated projects, it was common for Negro and White women to associate with each other and choose each other as friends, while in the segregated projects this was virtually unheard of. More interesting, community norms developed such that in the integrated projects there were social pressures on the two groups to be friendly toward each other, while the norms in the segregated projects specified that they should have nothing to do with each other. As might be expected from this, over half the White women in the integrated projects reported having developed more favorable attitudes toward Negroes since moving to the project, while only a small percentage of the White women in the segregated projects did so.

These results might not have been found if hostility between the two groups had been so great that violence had erupted when they were brought together. Sherif tested the theory that more contact is the solution to intergroup conflict in his camp study by bringing the two clubs together. A free-for-all fight developed rather than more favorable attitudes. The difference between these two results is consistent with dissonance theory, which holds that it is not contact as such which changes attitudes, but behavior. In a situation such as that studied by Deutsch and Collins, where minimal social pressure is sufficient to bring about tolerant behavior between two groups, increased contact should bring about more favorable attitudes. In a situation where hostile attitudes are so strong that extreme coercion, such as armed intervention, is necessary to ensure behavioral compliance, no dissonance would be generated, and no attitude change would take place. So far the evidence would seem to indicate that in many places in the United States integration could be carried out peacefully and that stateways thus can change folkways.

Summary

While attitudes are the most easily measured aspect of prejudice, they probably are not the most important in causing prejudiced behavior. As suggested by dissonance theory, attitudes not only cause behavior but also develop to justify it. Many motives may be served by prejudiced behavior, including economic, sexual, and aggressive motives. In strong prejudice, aggression is perhaps the most important.

The study of aggression has been approached from the point of view of psychoanalytic theory, emphasizing the control of aggression by both conscience and external authority. Adorno and his coworkers found prejudice so intimately bound up with attitudes toward authority that they entitled their monumental study of prejudiced individuals *The Authoritarian Personality*. More recent research by Milgram has indicated that individuals will express a surprising amount of aggression toward a protesting victim at the command of an authority, a finding which may be interpreted in terms of authority as an external conscience.

The expression of aggression is influenced by both the individual's personality and the environmental forces acting on him at the time. Research on authoritarianism has shown relationships between identification with harshly punitive parents and prejudice, while Bettelheim and Janowitz found the threats to the self involved in downward social mobility to be especially important. Prejudiced attitudes help the individual explain to himself anxiety which actually comes from other sources, a phenomenon which was investigated in an ingenious experiment by Bramel, Bell, and Margulis.

Just as prejudice develops partly to justify aggressive behavior toward minority groups, tolerant attitudes may develop in order to justify acting in a friendly manner toward members of these groups. The influence of behavior on attitudes was investigated in the forced-compliance studies of dissonance theorists such as Festinger, Aronson, and Carlsmith. Dissonance theory was used in this chapter to explain the results of a field study by Deutsch and Collins. Their study indicated that under certain conditions, public policy can change private attitudes.

Notes and Acknowledgments

1. Berger, Peter L. *Invitation to Sociology: A Humanistic Perspective*. Garden City, N.Y.: Anchor Books, Doubleday & Company, Inc., 1963.
2. These three quotes and their complete sources may be found in Carl Cohen (Ed.), *Communism, Fascism, and Democracy*. New York: Random House, 1963. By permission of Carl Cohen.
3. The Declaration of Independence in *ibid.*, p. 481.

4. Marx, Karl, and Friedrich Engels. "The Manifesto of the Communist Party" in *ibid.,* p. 90.

5. Hitler, Adolf. "Man must kill" in *ibid.,* p. 410. Reprinted by permission of the Public Affairs Press, Washington, from G. W. Prange (Ed.), *Hitler's Words: The Speeches of Adolph Hitler from 1923–1943.*

6. Figures given by Abraham Lincoln in a speech made answering Douglas in 1857. From Carl Sandburg, *Abraham Lincoln.* Vol. I. *The Prairie Years.* New York: Dell Publishing Co., Inc., 1959, p. 227.

7. Dollard, John. *Caste and Class in a Southern Town.* Garden City, N.Y.: Anchor Books, Doubleday & Company, Inc., 1949.

8. Wolfenstein, M., and N. Leites. *Movies: A Psychological Study.* New York: The Free Press of Glencoe, 1950.

9. Dollard, John. *Op. cit.,* pp. 150–151. By permission of the author.

10. Milgram, Stanley. "Behavioral study of obedience." *Journal of Abnormal and Social Psychology,* 1963 (67), pp. 371–378.

11. *Ibid.,* p. 373. By permission of the author and the publisher.

12. *Ibid.,* p. 376. By permission of the author and the publisher.

13. *Ibid.,* p. 375. By permission of the author and the publisher.

14. Lewin, Kurt. "Group decision and social change" in E. Maccoby et al. (Eds.), *Readings in Social Psychology.* New York: Holt, Rinehart & Winston, Inc., 1958, pp. 197–211.

15. Milgram, Stanley. "Liberating effects of group pressure." *Journal of Personality and Social Psychology,* 1965 (1), pp. 127–134.

16. Adorno, T. W., Else Frenkel-Brunswik, Daniel J. Levinson, and Nevitt R. Sanford. *The Authoritarian Personality.* New York: Harper & Row, Publishers, Incorporated, 1950.

17. See Christie, Richard, and Marie Jahoda (Eds.) *Studies in the Scope and Method of "The Authoritarian Personality."* New York: The Free Press of Glencoe, 1954.

18. Epstein, Ralph. "Authoritarianism, displaced aggression, and social status of the target." *Journal of Personality and Social Psychology,* 1965 (2), no. 4, pp. 585–589.

19. Hartley, E. L. *Problems in Prejudice.* New York: King's Crown Press, 1946.

20. Sears, Robert R., Eleanor E. Maccoby, and Harry Levin. "The socialization of aggression" in Eleanor Maccoby et al. (Eds.), *Readings in Social Psychology.* New York: Holt, Rinehart and Winston, Inc., 1958, pp. 350–359.

21. Frenkel-Brunswik, Else. "Parents and childhood as seen through the interviews" in Adorno, Frenkel-Brunswik, Levinson, and Sanford, *op. cit.,* pp. 337–389.

22. *Ibid.,* p. 372. By permission of the publisher.

23. *Ibid.,* p. 373. By permission of the publisher.

24. *Ibid.,* p. 375. By permission of the publisher.

25. *Ibid.,* p. 343. By permission of the publisher.

26. *Ibid.,* p. 347. By permission of the publisher.

27. Frenkel-Brunswik, Else. "Sex, people, and self as seen through the interviews" in Adorno, Frenkel-Brunswik, Levinson, and Sanford, *op. cit.,* p. 401. By permission of the publisher.

28. Allport, Gordon, and Leo Postman. "The basic psychology of rumor" in E. Maccoby et al. (Eds.), *Readings in Social Psychology.* New York: Holt, Rinehart and Winston, Inc., 1958, p. 55.

29. Killian, Lewis M. "The significance of multiple-group membership in disaster." *American Journal of Sociology,* 1952 (57), pp. 309–314.

30. Dollard, John, et al. *Frustration and Aggression.* New Haven, Conn.: Yale University Press, 1939, p. 31.

31. Bettelheim, Bruno, and Morris Janowitz. "Ethnic tolerance: A function of social and personal control." *American Journal of Sociology,* 1949 (55), pp. 137–145.

32. *Ibid.* Copyright 1949 by *American Journal of Sociology.* p. 140. By permission of The University of Chicago Press.

33. *Ibid.* Copyright 1949 by *American Journal of Sociology.* pp. 142–143. By permission of The University of Chicago Press.

34. Frenkel-Brunswik, Else, Daniel J. Levinson, and Nevitt R. Sanford. "The antidemocratic personality" in *Readings in Social Psychology.* (3d ed.) Edited by Eleanor E. Maccoby, T. M. Newcomb, and E. L. Hartley. Copyright 1947, 1952, © 1958 by Holt, Rinehart and Winston, Inc., p. 641. By permission of the publisher.

35. Bettelheim, Bruno, and Morris Janowitz. "Ethnic tolerance: A function of social and personal control." *American Journal of Sociology,* 1949 (55), p. 145 (excerpts from Table VII). Copyright 1949 by *American Journal of Sociology.* By permission of The University of Chicago Press.

36. Bramel, Dana, J. E. Bell, and Stephen Margulis. "Attributing anger as a means of explaining one's fear." *Journal of Experimental Social Psychology,* 1965 (1), pp. 267–281.

37. *Ibid.,* p. 281. By permission of the authors and the publisher.

38. Festinger, Leon, and J. M. Carlsmith. "Cognitive consequences of forced compliance." *Journal of Abnormal and Social Psychology,* 1959 (58), pp. 203–210.

39. Dissonance reduction is not the only factor influencing how much attitude change will take place when a person espouses a position different from that he previously held. For a recent survey of this complex research area, see Carlsmith, J. M., B. E. Collins, and R. K. Helmreich. "Studies in forced compliance: I. The effect of pressure for compliance on attitude change produced by face-to-face role playing and anonymous essay writing." *Journal of Personality and Social Psychology,* 1966 (4), no. 1, pp. 1–13.

40. Aronson, E., and J. M. Carlsmith. "Effect of the severity of threat on the devaluation of forbidden behavior." *Journal of Abnormal and Social Psychology,* 1963 (66), pp. 584–588.

41. Sherif, Muzafer, and Carolyn Sherif. *An Outline of Social Psychology.* New York: Harper & Row, Publishers, Incorporated, 1956.

42. Deutsch, Morton, and Mary E. Collins. *Interracial Housing.* Minneapolis: The University of Minnesota Press, 1951. Also to be found in William Petersen (Ed.), *American Social Patterns.* Garden City, N.Y.: Anchor Books, Doubleday & Company, Inc., 1956.

TEN

GROUPS IN STABILITY & CHANGE

One striking thing about human beings is that they usually change so little. Although superficial preferences and behaviors change, there seems to be a hard core to the personality which is quite resistant to change. The boy scout who was always working for merit badges becomes a businessman striving for awards from service clubs. The trusting person remains trusting despite experiences similar to Candide's, while his friend remains suspicious of the world despite being treated well by it.

Such everyday observations of ourselves and others might well lead us to believe that all important characteristics of human beings were fixed early in life, if we did not know of exceptions. Some people do become radically different people. Not only cases of multiple personality but the more common events of religious and political conversion show that radical change in the beliefs, values, and behavior of an individual is possible. Why, then, is it so rare?

Some clues are given by cases of individuals who have changed drastically. Let us look at one case described by Zorbaugh in *The Gold Coast and the Slum*.[1] It is the case of a girl from a small town who moved to Chicago:

> "Emporia, Kansas, was my home until I was twenty-two. My father had a small business there. He was an upright, God-fearing man. . . . He taught us to obey the Ten Commandments, to go to church on Sunday, to do all the things the 'respectable' do in a small, gossiping place."[2]

She was highly thought of in Emporia, where she was regarded as something of a musical prodigy, playing Chopin and Bach in public recitals at the age of ten. Her father thus spent the money to send her to college, although this was difficult for him to manage as he had quite a number of children. When she finished college, she went to Chicago to continue her musical career. Her life there was not easy, for she had to earn all the money for her own support and her music lessons, as well as find a good deal of time to practice. A combination of this demanding program and the environment of the cheap rooming house soon cut her off from almost all human contact.

> "One gets to know few people in a rooming house, for there are constant comings and goings, and there is little chance to get acquainted if one wished. But one doesn't wish. . . . There were occasional little dramas—as when a baby was found in the alley, and when the woman in the 'third floor back' took poison after a quarrel with her husband, or when police came to arrest a man who had eloped from Pittsburg with his wife's sister, and a new trio of roomers robbed most of the 'guests' on the second floor; there were these occasional little dramas when the halls and bathrooms were the scenes of a few minutes' hurried and curious gossip. But the next day these same people would hurry past each other on the stairs without speaking."[3]

Although she had to get up at six to be at work by eight, work as a waitress until five, walk a mile to get home, and work on her music until eleven, she was kept going by her ambitions. She had nothing else—she had made no friends in Chicago, her mother had died, and she had broken off with the rest of her family, who disapproved of the way she was living. Then her music teacher told her that there was no hope of her ever realizing her ambitions.

> "What did I have? I had no clothes, no shows, no leisure—none of the things all girls are supposed to love. My health was breaking under the strain. I was in debt. The answer was Nothing—absolutely nothing! And there stretched ahead of me long years of nothing, until I married an honest but poor clerk or salesman and tried to make ends meet for a brood of hungry mouths, or until I became one of those broken-down, old working women I had patronizingly pitied that first week at the Y.W.C.A.

> "Of course, there were two ways out: I might slip into the lake, there, and end it all. But somehow I didn't think seriously of that. Or I might do as some of the girls in the house, become a 'gold digger,' play life for what there was in it, pay with what there was in me. . . ."[4]

She chose the latter alternative and became the mistress of a man who picked her up in the restaurant where she worked. Thus a very proper young lady, who had shortly before felt above even speaking to the other people in the rooming house where she lived, became changed into something which she could never conceive of being.

When we look at how little people usually change, we are liable to forget the very great extent to which they are maintained the same by the roles they play and the people they know. This may perhaps be most easily experienced by attending after a number of years a reunion of a high school or college graduating class. Now you may be a pillar of the community, the terror of your competitors and subordinates, or a distinguished artist. To them you may remain the unpleasant fat boy whom the girls didn't like or the daring prankster who set off the stink bomb in the chapel. This too is one of your selves, and what is disturbing about the reunion is the ease with which you slip into the role and become the old self again. This was very well described by William James in his description of *reference groups.*

> *Properly speaking,* a man has as many social selves as there are individuals who recognize him *and carry an image of him in their mind. To wound any of these his images is to wound him. But as the individuals who carry the images fall naturally into classes, we may practically say that he has as many different social selves as there are distinct* groups of persons about whose opinion he cares. He

generally shows a different side of himself to each of these different groups. Many a youth who is demure enough before his parents and teachers, swears and swaggers like a pirate among his "tough" young friends.[5]

In a sense, then, we exist only through the eyes of others. Reference groups are vitally important to the individual's self-esteem, for it is they that judge whether he is living up to his idealized picture of himself. By interpreting what moral standards are applicable to any given situation, they function as external parts of the individual's conscience and are important agencies of social control, as mentioned in Chapter 5. However, as can be seen in the case described by Zorbaugh, a person only cares about the opinions of others in regard to what he aspires to be. Again James put the matter well:

> *I, who for the time have staked my all on being a psychologist, am mortified if others know much more psychology than I. But I am contented to wallow in the grossest ignorance of Greek. My deficiencies there give me no sense of personal humiliation at all. Had I "pretensions" to be a linguist, it would have been just the reverse. . . .*

> *So our self-feeling in this world depends entirely on what we back ourselves to be and do. It is determined by the ratio of our actualities to our supposed potentialities; a fraction of which our pretensions are the denominator and the numerator our success: thus, self-esteem =*
> $$\text{self-esteem} = \frac{\text{Success}}{\text{Pretensions}}$$[6]

This description, which anticipates the work on level of aspiration cited in Chapter 2 even to the extent of pointing out how self-esteem may be protected by lowering aspirations, helps to understand the case of the woman described by Zorbaugh. She had staked her all on being a musician just as James had staked his all on being a psychologist. Cut off from all relevant sources of social support, she became completely dependent upon the evaluation of her teacher in maintaining her conception of herself. An indication that she could not succeed as a musician destroyed the self for which she had lived and made radical reorganization of her self necessary.

Acceptance and Rejection by Groups

Although not easily susceptible to experimental manipulation, the importance of groups in maintaining or changing the self is dramatically illustrated in a number of observational studies. Let us look at some of these studies now and then return again to the question when we consider social norms in the final chapter.

Shils and Janowitz[7] carried out an extensive interview study on Germans surrendering on the western front in the Second World War to try to determine why German resistance remained so effective in what was militarily a hopeless situation. They investigated such questions as who surrendered, when they surrendered, how they surrendered, and what they were concerned about after doing so. Essentially, what they found was that:

1. The men who surrendered were those who were not effectively integrated into their fighting unit, such as those from ethnic minority groups. Those who were accepted by their comrades tended to go on fighting even if they were strongly opposed to both National Socialism and the war.
2. If individuals did surrender, it was generally when they had been isolated, either physically or psychologically, from their groups. Thus surrendering took place not only when an individual was isolated from his comrades by the contingencies of battle but also when he had just returned from home leave. Contact with his family tended to loosen his ties to his army unit.
3. To a great extent, soldiers surrendered as groups rather than as individuals.
4. After surrendering, they expressed a good deal of guilt, not about having failed their country, leaders, or political beliefs, but about letting down their comrades in arms.

All these observations supported the view that the men fought, not primarily for ideological reasons as had been earlier imagined, but out of loyalty to the small group to which they belonged. We should not, perhaps, expect such strong group influences under all circumstances. An army group differs from most other social groups in being part of a *total institution,* one which meets all the needs and provides all the social contacts of its members. Under most circumstances the potential for conflict through belonging to different groups with different views is stronger.

Just as loyalty to a reference group may be an extremely important social motive, failure on the part of an individual to make members of his reference groups accept his perceptions of himself may be a devastating experience. Participants in social interaction cast each other in roles, while each endeavors to get the other to accept him as the person whom he believes himself to be, playing the role which he believes himself to be playing.[8] Trying to reach agreement on the identity of the interacting individuals and the roles they are playing may involve a good deal of bargaining. When a parent punishes a child, for example, the parent may perceive himself as "doing what is good for the child," while the child defines the interaction as "being mean." Similarly, in an interaction between two professional colleagues, the elder may define the situation as one in which he is an older and wiser individual giving sage advice to his less experienced junior. The younger may perceive the situation as one in which two equals are making idle conversation or even as one in which he is humoring an old bore. To the extent that the individual is forced to admit that he has failed to get important individuals to accept his views of himself, he is aware that he is not living up to his ego ideal and suffers anxiety.

Prisoners, hospitalized patients, armed forces recruits, and members of cultural minority groups share the predicament that those with whom they must associate do not acknowledge the qualities which they see in themselves. A Jewish immigrant who was revered as a Talmudic scholar in his village in Eastern Europe may be recognized only as another impoverished immigrant by many of the Americans he meets in his new home, and one of the main protests of black Americans is that "nobody knows my name." As an example of a similar problem arising from social-class differences, let us look at a long-term study of Stanford students carried out by Robert Ellis.[9]

As is well known, Stanford is an institution of high academic standing and high tuition charges. Schools in wealthier neighborhoods better prepare students to meet the high admission standards of such an institution and the high tuition keeps out those who might be qualified but cannot afford to go, and both these factors serve to ensure that the social-class distribution will be heavily weighted toward the upper end of the continuum. The social-class breakdown of the students in Ellis's sample is shown in Table 10–1.[10]

What happens to working-class students who attend such an institution on scholarships? First, let us look at what the scholarship students are like when they reach Stanford. They are an even more highly selected group than most Stanford students—not only outstanding in terms of aptitude scores and high school achievement but even more likely than normal Stanford students to have held important positions of leadership in high school. The average scholarship student at Stanford was not only near the top of his class in high school, he was also captain of the football team or president of the

Table 10–1 *Percentage distribution of undergraduate students at Stanford*

CLASS	PERCENT
Upper	12
Upper-middle	49
Middle	27
Lower-middle	10
Upper-lower	1
Lower-lower	0

SOURCE: Ellis[10]

student body. Furthermore, he was prepared for Stanford in another way, for he had taken over a pattern of values and aspirations more typical of the middle class than of his class of origin, a type of *anticipatory socialization* often observed among the socially mobile.

For the individual who finds his high school work so easy that obtaining outstanding grades still leaves him sufficient time to excel in extracurricular activities, success must seem a relatively easy matter, and it is not surprising that these boys had even higher expectations of success at Stanford than the students who won national scholarships which were simply based on academic achievement. The schools which they had attended, however, had not prepared them for the academic competition at Stanford, and for the scholarship students as a whole there was no relationship between how high grades they expected to get in college and how high grades they actually got.

The situation in which they found themselves is familiar to anyone who has been an adviser to students in a college with high academic standards. Coming from schools where they were clearly superior to the other students in academic performance, many students suddenly found themselves competing for the first time with others of equal ability. The point may perhaps be best illustrated by the case of one such student I have known. In his home town, Millstone, New Jersey, he was regarded as a prodigy—excelling scholastically and in extracurricular activities. When he won a scholarship to an outstanding liberal arts college, he arrived with expectations which were realistic in terms of his past experience. He expected to be at the top of his class without having to do much work, and to win a Rhodes scholarship without its interfering with his having a good time. In terms of the group he was now competing with, however, such aspirations were quite unrealistic. He did graduate quite high in his class, but he had to work unexpectedly hard to do so, and he did not win a Rhodes scholarship.

The self-disconfirmation of the scholarship students at Stanford, however, was made more severe by their reception by other students. While they had been popular student leaders before, they were not accepted by the upper-middle-class Stanford students. Significantly more of them than of the general student body were considered unpopular or social isolates by their dormitory counselors. By the time they graduated, more of them than of the general student body were diagnosed as being personally disturbed. Like the woman described by Zorbaugh, they had been unable to get the world to see them as they saw themselves, with serious consequences for their mental health.

While rejection by an important reference group has devastating effects upon the individual, acceptance into a group holding different beliefs and values from that of the individual may be an important source of attitude change. This is dramatically illustrated in a study carried out by Newcomb[11] at Bennington College from 1935 to 1939. Bennington was, at that time, a very atypical academic institution, for the faculty believed that "one of the foremost duties of the college was to acquaint its somewhat oversheltered students with the nature of their contemporary social world."[12] While the girls at Bennington, like the Stanford students in Ellis's study, came from prosperous and politically conservative homes, they encountered, unlike the Stanford students, a faculty who saw it as their social duty to communicate to them their own progressive political beliefs.

In performing this duty they were apparently very successful, for the political views of the girls changed a great deal while they were at Bennington. This is best illustrated by the way in which girls who had been at the school varying numbers of years voted in a mock presidential election in 1936. While 62 percent of the freshmen supported the Republican candidate, a proportion which reflects the political preferences of the families from which they had come, the percentage fell to only 14 percent for those girls who had been at the school more than 2 years. These results are illustrated in Table 10–2.[13]

The dramatic change shown by students at Bennington was probably largely due to its being a small, isolated, and cohesive community. The student body at that time only numbered about 250 girls, and the college community was so self-sufficient that there was no need for the students to go off the campus—it had its own store, post

Table 10–2 *Votes in the mock election (in percent)*

VOTED FOR	FRESHMEN	VOTE BY JUNIORS AND SENIORS
Republican	62	14
Democrat	29	54
Socialist or Communist	9	30

SOURCE: Newcomb[13]

office, beauty parlor, and recreational facilities. These conditions all favored the development of the college community as the major reference group for the students.

Nevertheless, not all the students accepted the college community as their major reference group, and not all of them changed their political preferences. Let us look at the characteristics of those who remained politically conservative and those who became or remained nonconservative in terms of balance theory.

Since Newcomb had not yet devised his A-B-X balance model at the time of doing this study, he did not describe his results in terms of it. The distinctions he did draw, however, can be reasonably well represented in terms of a balance model. He described the students in terms of the following: (1) Their community identification, the extent to which they accepted the college group. This will be represented in our analysis as having positive sentiments toward the college group. (2) Their awareness of their own radicalism or conservatism. This will be represented in balance terms by the accurate or inaccurate portrayal of the relationships between the political opinion of the college group and parents. (3) Their acceptance or nonacceptance of the college group as a reference point for political opinions. This will be represented as having positive or negative sentiments toward "college political views." (4) Their acceptance or nonacceptance of parents as positive reference points for political affairs. This will be represented as positive or negative sentiments toward "parents' political views."

Using this mapping, let us portray the cognitive structures of the girls who did and did not change in terms of Rosenberg and Abelson's balance model as described in Chapter 2. It will be immediately apparent that all students who have positive sentiments toward both their left-wing college group and their conservative parents will suffer from imbalance, as these two cognitive elements have

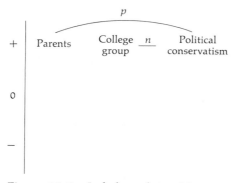

Figure 10–1 *Imbalanced cognitive structure of conservative student.*

different relationships with conservatism. The cognitive structures of a conservative girl and radical girl in this predicament are shown in Figures 10–1 and 10–2, respectively.

Rosenberg and Abelson propose that imbalance may be dealt with by attitude change, differentiation, or stopping thinking about the issue. Each of these methods could be useful to the Bennington girl in reducing her imbalance. By becoming radical and rejecting her parents or by remaining conservative and rejecting the college group, she could reduce imbalance, although not remove it completely if she retained a unit relation with each group. Differentiation provides a more elegant solution. By deciding that she liked the college group but that they had little experience with the world and had thus accepted some silly notions about politics, the conservative girl could reduce imbalance without dissociating herself from her friends. Similarly, the girl with progressive political views could reduce imbalance

Figure 10–2 *Imbalanced cognitive structure of nonconservative student.*

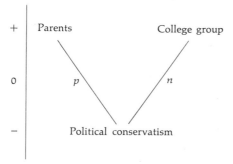

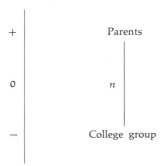

Figure 10-3 *Rejection of college group by conservative student.*

by deciding that she loved her parents but that they were out of touch with the contemporary world and too uninformed about politics for their views in this area to have much value. Finally, the girl who had little enough contact with the more radical students or who never talked politics with her parents might be able to keep herself in ignorance of the conflicting views of these two groups.

These various possibilities correspond reasonably well to the cognitive structures which Newcomb found, although not preserving all the richness of his descriptions of individual students. Let us look first at the views of the students who did not change their political views, but remained conservative. These are portrayed in Figures 10-3 to 10-6, corresponding to groups 1 to 4 in Newcomb's description. The girls represented in Figure 10-3 rejected the college group and were in turn rejected by it. They were aware of their relative conservatism in comparison with the other students. Those represented in Figure 10-4, on the other hand, had managed to remain ignorant of the views of the rest of the community by only associating with a few other conservative students, a type of stopping thinking reflected in behavior. The differentiation solution is represented by Figure 10-5, representing students who liked the other members of the college group but considered their political views not worth listening to. Finally, the girls represented in Figure 10-6 had so little to do with the college group that its political views simply were not a part of their cognitive structures.

The cognitive structures of the girls who did change toward the political left are similarly consistent with their attitudes. They are represented in Figures 10-7 to 10-10, corresponding to groups 5 to 8 in Newcomb's analysis. The girls portrayed in Figure 10-7 again used

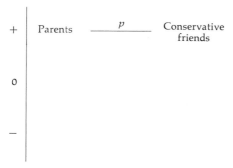

Figure 10–4 *Unawareness of views of college group on part of conservative student.*

a differentiation solution. In their own words, they "agreed to differ" with their parents on political matters. They differ from the next group, represented in Figure 10–8, in that the latter achieved independence of their parents earlier and with less conflict. Having been independent for some time, they are not aware of how much their parents' political views differ from their own.

The girls represented in Figure 10–9 represent a rather interesting case. Rebelling against conservative parents, they became so radical that they rejected the college group as being too conservative. They developed off-campus reference groups which were more radical than the dominant position at the college. Finally, Figure 10–10 portrays a group of students who were extremely dependent upon the college group for social support. They were unaware of how their nonconservative political views differed from those of their parents.

Figure 10–5 *Differentiation of college political views from college group by conservative student.*

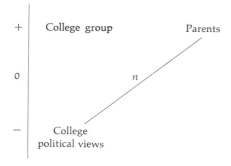

+   Parents

0

–

Figure 10–6 *Self-isolation from college group by conservative student.*

We may see, then, that political attitudes developed by the Bennington students were consistent with their relationships to important reference groups. While the analysis of these relationships in terms of balance theory has been somewhat simplified in that unit and sentiment relationships have not been analyzed separately, it may have been sufficient to demonstrate that reference-group phenomena may be portrayed in balance-theory terms and that this portrayal leads to predictions of attitudinal stability or change. A similar analysis could be carried out to predict what would happen to the political views of the girls after they left Bennington. After the consideration of small-group processes we shall return to them again, as Newcomb did after a period of 20 years, to see how their beliefs changed and developed.

Figure 10–7 *"Agreeing to differ" with parents on political matters by nonconservative student.*

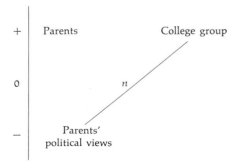

+   Parents   College group

0   *n*

–   Parents'
    political views

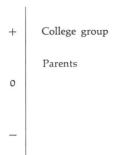

```
+      College group

       Parents

0


–
```

Figure 10–8 *Lack of awareness of parents' political views on part of non-conservative student.*

Conformity

As we can see from the discussion above, the extent to which a group can influence a person depends to a very great extent on its importance to him. Much socialization consists of teaching a person who he is, and thus what groups he must care about the opinions of. The elaborate ceremony which marks initiation into a fraternal organization, for example, teaches the initiate that he is now a member of a select group and has special obligations to its members. Even temporary groups, to which the individual has no important ties, may exert some influence, however. One answer to the question, "Who am I?" is the very general one, "A human being." The approval and disapproval even of a group of strangers thus serves, to some extent, to support or undermine the self. This importance of other people, sim-

Figure 10–9 *Rejection of college group as too conservative by radical student.*

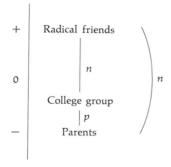

```
+      Radical friends
                          \
                    n      )
0                          )  n
       College group       )
            | p           /
–      Parents           /
```

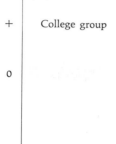

+ College group

0

Figure 10–10 *Conformity to college group by nonconservative student.*

ply as people, is illustrated in Killian's research on the effects of multiple reference groups in disaster. While loyalty to the family was the most important influence on behavior—so important that even firemen left their jobs to look after their families—feelings of responsibility for strangers were more important for many individuals than their occupational roles. As Killian reported:

> For people whose usual occupational roles bore little or no relationship to the needs created by the disaster, identification with the community as a whole and disregard of their occupational roles came still more easily. Many merchants and clerks rushed from their stores to aid in rescue work, leaving both goods and cash on the counters. The postmaster in one tornado town left the post office completely unguarded, even though the windows were shattered and mail was strewn about the floor.[14]

Similarly, laboratory studies of conformity have shown the great effects which even *ad hoc* groups, simply brought together for the purpose of the experiment, may have on individual behavior. Best known in this area is the classic research of Asch.

The subjects in Asch's experiments were brought together to participate in an experiment on perceptual judgment. On each trial one standard line and three comparison lines were presented, and the task of each subject was to tell which comparison line was of the same length as the standard. The perceptual task was easy, and subjects in a control group where there was no deception made almost no errors. In the experimental groups, however, all the subjects except one were confederates, instructed to give certain agreed-on incorrect answers on some of the trials. Since the one naïve subject was always seated so that he would give his judgments last, he was preceded on each of these critical trials by the unanimous choice of an incorrect alternative. The question to be investigated was the extent to which his judgments would be influenced by the group.

In a typical experiment,[15] which employed seven confederates, considerable conformity was found. While 26 percent of the subjects made no incorrect judgments despite the group pressure, the remainder ranged from one to eleven errors out of the twelve critical trials. In variations on the experiment two other interesting findings emerged. While the amount of conformity depended upon the number of individuals unanimously giving incorrect judgments up through three, a larger group had no more effect than the three confederates did. Even more interesting, the provision of even one other individual who gave correct judgments greatly reduced the effects even of a majority of seven. The unanimity of the judgments seems to be a critical factor in group pressure.

One question which might be raised about the early conformity experiments, such as those of Asch, is whether the results have been influenced by the triviality of the judgments being made. Thus it might be argued that it is not surprising that individuals will go along with the crowd in judging the length of lines, which they couldn't care less about, but that that is no reason to expect them to do so on an issue which is important to them. That conformity is not confined to trivial issues, however, is well demonstrated by Milgram's more recent research.[16] By slightly varying the experimental conditions in his experiment on obedience to authority which was described in the last chapter, Milgram transformed it into a conformity experiment. By further variations, he was able to create mutually supporting or mutually opposed authority and conformity pressures.

Conformity pressures were created by having not one "teacher" but three. The first was to read the stimulus words, the second to inform the subject whether he was correct or incorrect, and the third to administer the punishment. Instead of the experimenter suggesting the level of shock to be used as punishment, this decision was left to the three teachers. The instructions to the teachers were that the level of shock to be administered was to be the *lowest level suggested by any of the three teachers*. The real subject was always assigned the role of third teacher, while the first two teachers, like the "learner," were confederates. By the first and second teacher always suggesting raising the shock one level when the learner made an error, group pressure was put on the real subject which was comparable to the authority pressure in the first experiment. Nevertheless, he had effective control of the level of shock administered, for according to the instructions he had only to suggest a lower level for that to be the level administered.

Because of other variations in experimental procedure, the results are not strictly comparable to those obtained in the first experiment. In this experiment, the victim gave verbal feedback, including grunts, screams, and a protest that he suffered from a weak heart! Despite this, considerable conformity was found in comparison with a control group, and fifteen out of forty subjects in the conformity situation continued raising the shock level after the victim had stopped answering the questions.[17] Since the victim had stopped answering the questions at the 300-volt shock level, it is clear that conformity is not limited to trivial decisions.

The experiment was varied further.[18] Mutually supporting or conflicting authority and group pressures were created by combining the conditions in the two experiments already described. Three teachers were used, but the experimenter instructed them in the level of shock to be employed. By having the first two teachers go along with the experimenter's instructions, conformity pressures were added to authority pressure. By having them successively defy the experimenter and refuse to continue participating in the experiment, group pressures were made to conflict with authority pressure. The results of these variations support Asch's observations of the relatively small effect of increasing pressures by enlarging the group and the relatively great effect of destroying the unanimity of the group. Adding conformity pressure to authority pressure did little to increase the compliance of the subjects above that found with authority pressure alone. Defiance of the experimenter on the part of fellow subjects, on the other hand, greatly reduced the level of shock which the real subject was willing to administer. These results, like Asch's, suggest that it is the lack of *any* reference-group support which make it difficult for the individual to engage in an idiosyncratic course of action.

Research on conformity, like that on prejudice, illustrates how situational pressures and personality factors interact in the determination of behavior. Even though Milgram found striking differences between experimental and control groups in his simple conformity experiment, for example, there were three subjects in the experimental group who refused to give over 30 volts shock despite the group pressure, and there was one subject in the control condition who thought he was administering 450 volts to a man with a heart condition without any group pressure.

This finding of great individual differences in response to group pressure is in agreement with Asch's earlier findings which led to a good deal of research on the personality characteristics associated with yielding or not yielding to group pressure. The most important findings of one quite extensive research program of this type, carried out by Tuddenham and his colleagues at Berkeley, are summarized as follows:

> The most consistent and significant finding is that of a marked negative correlation between intelligence and measures of intellectual achievement and drive on the one hand, and yielding on the other. . . .
>
> A second group of variables negatively correlated with yielding seems to contain a common element of psychological sensitivity and perceptiveness, both of self and of others. Here are found ratings Perceptive, Imaginative, Trait-Introspection, and questionnaire scales with such titles as Psychological Mindedness, Self Acceptance, Tolerance, Flexibility, and Intraception. Crutchfield's finding of lack of rigid self-control or authoritarianism among his nonyielders, and Barron's belief that nonyielders are intraceptive and empathic, are congruent.
>
> However, these variables can not be taken to imply that the independent-minded subject is "well-adjusted" socially in the conventional sense as compared with the yielder. Correlations between yielding and ratings of adjustment are close to zero, a result also reported by Crutchfield and Barron.[19]

If we speculate a bit upon these findings, we can see that the first may represent different learning experiences of different individuals. A person of high intellectual potential and achievement is likely to find, in a number of situations, that he is more likely to be right than other individuals. Learning to trust his own judgment and to a great extent ignore the opinions of others would be for him an adaptive thing to do. For the less intelligent person, this would not be the case. He is much more likely to learn that things may not be what they seem to be to him and that it is safer to go along with the judgments of the crowd.

More interesting psychologically is the other group of variables. They seem to portray the nonconformer as being in more direct contact with his own impulses. This does not lead to his being better adjusted socially, for some of the impulses may be quite antisocial. It does lead to greater self-awareness and, by analogy from himself to others, to greater awareness of the emotional responses of others.

Support for this view of conformity as the result of certain types of ego defense is found in an interesting study by Breger. His theoretical approach was psychoanalytic:

> Conformity is conceptualized as stemming from a more pervasive ego-defensive process, centering around the repression of hostility, and consisting primarily of the ego defenses of repression, denial, reaction-formation, and turning against the self. . . . The assumption is made that individuals who conform when faced with group pressure do so because at some level of awareness they perceive opposition to the group as an act of defiance and aggression which arouses anxiety and calls into play one or more of the above defense mechanisms. . . . As is characteristic of all defense mechanisms, these involve an unwarranted overgeneralization on the part of the individual employing them such that situations not necessarily involving hostility (e.g., giving an accurate judgment in an Asch situation) are reacted to on the basis of this latent perception.[20]

Two predictions were made from this theoretical orientation, and both were supported by the results of the experiment. First, it was predicted that people who conformed more would express less hostility in a direct manner and more in an indirect manner on a Thematic Apperception Test. Just as the highly authoritarian subjects in the research on *The Authoritarian Personality* did not express their hostility directly against parent figures in the TAT cards, but did tend to tell stories in which these figures were injured, blinded, sick, and killed, it was predicted that the more conforming subjects would express their hostility in a similarly disguised manner. A "TAT total defended hostility" score was computed by scoring all responses which indicated indirect expression of hostility, against the self or others, and subtracting scores for responses indicating direct expression of hostility. This measure was correlated with conformity scores at the .01 level.

The second prediction was that the subjects who conformed more would express less aggression against an authority figure in a situation where aggression was a reasonable response. The subjects were given an impossible experimental task (placing pegs in holes which they fit tightly without the peg's touching the sides of the hole, while working against a stop watch) and were constantly criticized by the experimenter for their poor performance while they were working. At the end of this frustrating experience, a confederate tried to induce each subject to be critical of the experimenter. As was predicted, the subjects who were willing to criticize the experimenter were those who conformed less in the conformity task.

It is important to note that Breger's results do not indicate that high conformers are unable to express aggressive impulses at all, but that they do not express them as directly as low conformers or against a high-status experimenter. If high conformers were unable to express aggression at all, no conformity would be found in Milgram's situation where the subject must act in an aggressive manner in order to conform. Unrecognized aggressive impulses may not only be expressed in an indirect manner or turned against the self, they may also be turned against other low-status individuals. From the positive correlation of conformity with authoritarianism and its negative correlation with tolerance, it would be expected that more conforming individuals would actually express more hostility against low-status minority groups. More research on this topic would be useful in understanding the relationships of ways of handling impulses, conformity, and prejudice.

Role Conflict

Individuals occupy many different positions in society, as was indicated by the quotation from James contrasting the way a young man may act in the presence of his parents and the way he may act among his friends. For each of these positions—father, electrical engineer, Baptist, Democrat, South Carolinian, etc.—there is one or more reference groups holding expectations about how a person in that position will behave. As was illustrated in Newcomb's Bennington study, these expectations are enforced by *sanctions*—rewards for conforming to expectations and punishments for violating them. The Bennington girl who held to conservative political beliefs, or the Stanford boy who dressed and acted in accordance with his working-class origin, was not accepted to the rewards of friendship with fellow students. These expectations about the behavior of a person holding a given position are referred to as the *role* associated with that position.

It is thus clear that roles may easily be in conflict. As the daughter of a wealthy and conservative family, the Bennington girl is expected to support conservative political candidates. As a Bennington student, she is expected to support nonconservative candidates. This is a conflict between two different roles—the differing expectations come through her holding two different positions, daughter and Bennington student. Her plight is thus similar to that of a person of fundamentalist religious faith who was a biologist or an account executive for an advertising firm. As a fundamentalist, a man would be expected to believe in special creation. He would not be expected to believe in the widespread use of strong alcoholic beverages. If he were also a biologist, he would be expected to support those beliefs in evolution which have been supported by biological data. If he were an account executive, he would be expected to treat his clients to strong drink. This type of conflicting expectation, stemming from holding two different positions, is referred to as *interrole* conflict. It may be avoided to some extent by a judicious choice of positions, so that the individual does not join groups which have conflicting expectations about his behavior. Members of fundamentalist sects who are either biologists or account executives are relatively rare.

More difficult to avoid is *intrarole* conflict, conflicting expectations held by different groups about the occupant of the same position. A classical case of this is the foreman in industry. He is not clearly a part of either labor or management. The workers expect him to represent their interests to management, while management expects him to represent it in overseeing the workers. It is clearly impossible to do both at the same time. This type of conflict is very common. Anyone who represents a company in dealing with the public, a man who performs a job involving liaison between two departments of a company rather than being clearly assigned to one, or even a university professor divided between research and teaching is in a situation involving conflicting loyalties between the expectations of different groups.

In the extensive research on which their book *Organizational Stress* was based, Kahn et al. found that 48 percent of their national sample suffered from some role conflict in their occupational role. The greater the frequency of contacts outside the company in performing a job, the more stress was involved. Similarly, the greater an individual's contact with people outside his department in the company, the more stress was involved. Furthermore, for people occupying positions involving similar interdepartmental responsibilities, those who most restricted their contacts outside their own department experienced the least anxiety. These findings support the view that inability to meet conflicting expectations is an important source of anxiety for individuals. (The last one, incidentally, also illustrates the fallacy of the common view that all the problems of organizations can be solved by providing "better communications.") Let us thus look at two other research studies for further indications of how individuals react to role conflict.

The first of these studies is one of the classical investigations of voting behavior, published as *The People's Choice*, by Lazarsfeld, Berelson, and Gaudet.[21] It is based on a sample of one person from every fourth house in Erie County, Ohio, during the presidential election of 1940, and employed a *panel design*.

In all studies of changing attitudes, such as those of voters prior to an election, one basic problem is whether each person should be interviewed only once or more than once. If each person is interviewed only once, there is no way of knowing the extent to which individuals change their minds. A poll in June might show 45 percent in favor of the Republican candidate, 48 percent in favor of the Democratic candidate, and 7 percent undecided. If another poll the next month showed 47 percent in favor of the Republican, 48 percent in favor of the Democrat, and 5 percent undecided, this would not necessarily mean that 2 percent who had been undecided had made up their minds on the Republican. Instead, it might well be that some who had been in favor of the Democrat had switched preference to the Republican, a smaller number had made the opposite change, and some of the undecided individuals had come out in favor of each of the candidates. Only the repeated interviewing of the same individuals will clearly reveal such changes.

The use of a panel of respondents, who are interviewed repeatedly, also has disadvantages, however. If the only people interviewed are the members of the panel, there is no way of knowing whether the process of being repeatedly interviewed has sensitized them to political phenomena in a way which makes them atypical of other voters. This problem may, to a large extent, be avoided by the use of control groups. The procedure used by Lazarsfeld et al. provides a good example. The initial sample was divided into four groups matched on characteristics related to voting behavior. One of these groups served as the panel, and was repeatedly interviewed throughout the course of the campaign. The other groups were used to check on whether the panel had become atypical of the population of voters. One of these samples was interviewed each time the panel was reinterviewed. The lack of any significant difference in voting intention between the panel and the other sample at each of these times provided a strong argument that reinterviewing of the panel members had not made them differ from other voters in the election.

The result of applying this method clearly showed the importance of class and group affiliations of individuals in determining how they would vote. Interviewers' ratings of the socioeconomic status of the respondent were good predictors of voting, but statements by the respondents themselves of whether they felt they belonged more to "business" or "labor" were better. Similarly, religious affiliation and urban or rural residence were good predictors of voting. Catholics were found more likely than Protestants to favor the Democratic candidate even when socioeconomic status was held constant. Also, as might be expected, rural residents were more likely to favor the Republican candidate than were urban residents.

Great events were taking place during the election campaign of 1940, and the role which the United States was to play in these events was the major issue of the campaign. During the campaign France accepted Hitler's peace terms, the first 14 days of air raids on London were carried out, and Italy invaded Greece. During such a time as this, could voting actually be predicted from such variables as a person's socioeconomic status, religious affiliation, and place of residence?

Because the way an individual views events is influenced by the groups to which he belongs, perhaps it should not surprise us that it could. This is made most obvious by comparing individuals whose various affiliations reinforced each other. Of wealthy, Protestant farmers almost 75 percent voted for Willkie, while 90 percent of urban Catholic laborers voted for Roosevelt.

Even more interesting is the way in which voting intentions changed over the course of the campaign. For each member of the panel, the researchers constructed an "Index of political predisposition" based on the three factors mentioned above. By the end of the campaign, voting intention was in greater agreement with the predictions from this index than it was at the beginning. In other words, one major effect of discussing the issues was to make people vote more as other people like themselves voted. As the authors commented:

> Knowing a few of the respondents' personal characteristics, we could tell with fair certainty how they would finally vote: they would join the fold to which they belonged. . . . Thus about two thirds of the crystallizers with a Republican predisposition decided by October to vote Republican, and about three fourths of those with a Democratic predisposition decided for the Democrats. From a simple three-factor index we could predict with considerable accuracy the outcome of deliberations that the deciders themselves could not foresee. What the political campaign did in these cases was not to form new opinions

*but to raise old opinions over the thresholds of awareness and deci-
sion. Political campaigns are important primarily because they activate latent predispositions.*[22]

For the wealthy Protestant farmer or the Catholic laborer it is
easy to see how the reference groups with which he associated might
show him where his political interest lay over the course of the campaign. What happened, however, to the poor Protestant farm laborer
or the wealthy Catholic businessman? Such an individual would be
subject to interrole conflict. The Catholic businessman, for example,
would be expected to support the Republican candidate by his
wealthy business acquaintances but expected to support the Democratic candidate by his fellow Catholics. That these *cross pressures*
would be strong is illustrated in Figure 10–11, which shows that
while 76 percent of Protestants at the two highest socioeconomic
levels supported the Republican candidate, only 29 percent of com-
parably wealthy Catholics did so.[23]

The dilemma of the potential voter exposed to cross pressures
is similar to that of the Bennington girl in Newcomb's study, and
similar ways of resolving imbalance are possible. The Catholic businessman might differentiate, for example, by deciding that while his
business acquaintances were fine people with excellent judgment
about most things, they were biased about political matters through
all being wealthy, and that his Catholic reference group thus provided a better guide to political decisions. For most people, however,
avoidance of political affairs is easier than it was for students at
Bennington, and the stopping-thinking solution of avoiding political
commitment was the main effect of cross pressures observed in this
study. Voters who were subject to cross pressures showed less interest in the campaign, made up their minds whom to support at a
later date, and were less likely to vote than those who were not subject to cross pressures.

Besides showing the importance of reference groups and role
conflict in political affairs, *The People's Choice* thus somewhat modifies the idealized picture of the election process which is presented in
campaign oratory. Instead of elections being decided primarily by
independent voters, who decide whom to support on the basis of
issues presented in the campaign, they are largely decided by the
activities of people who are committed to one party at the time the
campaign starts. These individuals, not subject to cross pressures, are
the most active and influential throughout the campaign. While the
"independent voters" who are subject to cross pressures do have

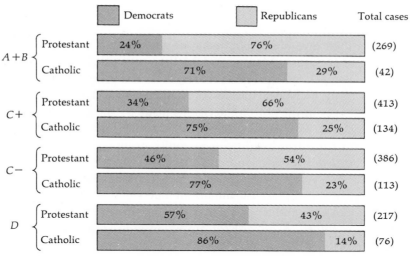

Figure 10–11 *Voting preference by socioeconomic level and religion. (Lazarsfeld, Berelson, and Gaudet[23])*

more apparent choice, as Milgram's work on the liberating effects of group pressures would indicate, these same cross pressures are liable to lead to a stopping-thinking resolution to their imbalance. The independent voter is typically uninterested in the campaign and unlikely to vote.

If political decisions may be avoided by voters, it is not so easy for the person who holds a politically relevant position to avoid them. The city manager, the chief of police, or the superintendent of schools is expected to make recommendations about issues as a part of his job. Each is, like the foreman in industry, a man in the middle between the conflicting interests of various organized groups. Consider the plight of a superintendent of schools about to make his annual recommendation about salaries for teachers in his district. The teachers expect him to press for as high salaries as possible—and because they believe in good education and obtaining highly qualified individuals to provide it, they feel that they are morally right in expecting him to do so. Members of the city council of a major city in the district, however, in viewing the various services competing for tax funds, are likely to feel equally morally justified in expecting him to keep salaries as low as possible. Labor unions, business organizations, the parent-teacher association, newspaper editors, veterans', church, farm, and fraternal organizations—all are likely to have similar expectations one way or the other. Whatever the superintendent recommends, he will have to face his friends and his wife, who have their own ideas about what he should do.

Gross, Mason, and McEachern[24] studied this type of intrarole conflict, using approximately half the school superintendents in the state of Massachusetts as their sample. They found that the differences in the real-life decisions made by these men were explainable in terms of a combination of the social pressures they perceived emanating from various community groups and the personality characteristics of the men.

When a group holds expectations about your behavior, there are two especially important questions which you may raise about the expectations—whether they are justified and whether they can be enforced. A request for aid by an injured person might seem morally justified to an individual, but it could not be enforced by sanctions. A request for money by a robber might not seem morally justified, but could perhaps be enforced by the ultimate sanction of death. Similarly, the expectations of community groups differ in whether the superintendent sees them as legitimate or not and whether he perceives a group as able to apply sanctions against him if he does not comply with it. The authors reasoned that superintendents differed in the extent to which they paid attention to these two different considerations. They classed superintendents as having a *moral* orientation if they felt that there were many things which they should always or never do, having an *expedient* orientation if they felt that whether they engaged in most behaviors should depend upon the circumstances, and having a *moral-expedient* orientation if they felt that there were quite a number of things which they should always or never do but many others which depended upon circumstances. To choose examples outside the range of professional behavior of school superintendents, a person would seem to have a moral orientation if he believed that he should never smoke, drink, dance, swear, or betray a confidence. On the other hand, we would not have much hesitation in classing a person as having an expedient orientation if he felt that whether or not he engaged in such activities as theft and murder should depend upon the circumstances. Use of such extreme examples, more extreme than those used by Gross et al., would result in classifying most people as moral-expedients.

It was thus expected that superintendents with a moral orientation would pay more attention to whether expectations were legitimate, those with an expedient orientation would pay more attention to whether they could be enforced, and those with a moral-expedient orientation would try to consider both. Specific predictions were made on this basis, although these are too complex to consider here. (A simplified example would be that a moralist might retain a teacher whom he personally thought to be good despite powerful community groups demanding that the teacher be fired, while an expedient would never do so.)

The predictions were strongly supported by the results. For the issue of teachers' salaries, for example, correct predictions were made for 88 percent of the moral-expedients, 91 percent of the expedients, and 95 percent of the moralists. The decisions superintendents had actually made were highly consistent with the researchers' expectations from the superintendents' personality characteristics and their perceptions of reference groups in their communities.

One important question remains unanswered by the research, however. Were the superintendents accurate in their perception of the community pressures? The superintendents' decisions were made before the community pressures were reported. From the work on dissonance theory, we might expect that they would distort their perceptions after making their decisions in order to justify the decisions they had made. An expedient superintendent might decide after he had asked that salaries be kept the same that the city council would have employed sanctions against him if he had not done so, for this would justify his behavior to himself and perhaps even to some extent to his staff. The question is whether he thought that the council would do so at the moment of making the decision.

While this question points to an interesting area for further research, it does not seriously detract from the value of the Gross et al. study. Whether groups only influence decisions or both influence and rationalize them, there can be no doubt about their vital importance to the decision maker.

Summary

Individuals usually show remarkable stability in their attitudes, behavior, and personality characteristics. That this stability is not due to personality being rigidly fixed in early childhood is shown by those cases where dramatic change does occur. Rather than personality being unchangeable, it usually remains the same because the individual's reference groups support him in continuing to act the way he has acted before. By interpreting what moral standards are applicable to a given situation, a reference group or authority figure may function as a part of an individual's conscience.

Because the individual sees himself through the eyes of his reference groups, rejection by the group amounts to self-rejection, raises anxiety to intolerable levels, and prepares the ground for dramatic personality change. The dynamics of this change were illustrated in a case study of a woman in Chicago and in a long-term study of scholarship students at Stanford. Similarly, by applying existing beliefs and values to new situations, the group which accepts the individual changes him. Balance theory is an aid in the analysis of the dramatic changes shown by Bennington College students in a study by Newcomb.

The dramatic effects which groups have on individuals can to some extent be reproduced in the psychological laboratory. While there are great individual differences in how much individuals conform to group pressure, some individuals will show considerable conformity even when they must violate important values in doing so. Similar dynamics seem to be involved in conformity to the pressures of a group or an authority figure, and the conformity pressures are greatly weakened by anyone refusing to go along with the authority or group.

Individuals cannot always conform to group pressures, for they belong to many groups which have conflicting expectations for them. Intrarole conflict is caused by different groups having differing expectations for the individual occupying some one position, while interrole conflicts result from holding different positions with different expected behaviors. Studies of voting and of decision making by school superintendents have shown the very great extent to which an individual's behavior may be predicted from an analysis of the role expectations of his reference groups.

Notes and Acknowledgments

1. Zorbaugh, Harvey W. *The Gold Coast and the Slum: A Sociological Study of Chicago's Near North Side.* Chicago: The University of Chicago Press, 1929.
2. *Ibid.,* Copyright 1929 by The University of Chicago. All rights reserved. p. 76. By permission of The University of Chicago Press.
3. *Ibid.,* pp. 78–79. By permission of the publisher.
4. *Ibid.,* p. 80. By permission of the publisher.

5. James, William. *Principles of Psychology.* New York: Dover Publications, Inc., 1950, p. 294.

6. *Ibid.,* p. 310.

7. Shils, Edward A., and Morris Janowitz. "Cohesion and disintegration in the Wehrmacht in World War II." *Public Opinion Quarterly,* 1948 (12), pp. 300–306 and 308–315.

8. An interesting book extending the theory of self and reference groups beyond what is possible in an introductory text is McCall, George J., and J. L. Simmons. *Identities and Interactions.* New York: The Free Press of Glencoe, 1966. Their analysis emphasizes the extent to which individuals improvise interaction within the broad latitude permitted by social roles.

9. Ellis, Robert A. "The cognitive failure of the upwardly mobile." Paper presented at the West Coast Conference for Small-Group Research, 1964.

10. *Ibid.,* from Table I. By permission of the author.

11. Newcomb, Theodore M. "Attitude development as a function of reference groups" in E. Maccoby et al. (Eds.), *Readings in Social Psychology.* New York: Holt, Rinehart and Winston, Inc., 1958, pp. 265–275.

12. *Ibid.,* p. 265. By permission of the publisher.

13. *Ibid.,* p. 266. By permission of the publisher.

14. Killian, Lewis M. "The significance of multiple-group membership in disaster." *American Journal of Sociology,* 1952 (57), p. 313. By permission of the publisher.

15. Asch, Solomon E. "Effects of group pressure upon the modification and distortion of judgments" in Maccoby et al. (Eds.), *op. cit.,* pp. 174–183.

16. Milgram, Stanley. "Group pressure and action against a person." *Journal of Abnormal and Social Psychology,* 1964 (69), pp. 137–143.
Milgram, Stanley. "Liberating effects of group pressure." *Journal of Personality and Social Psychology,* 1965 (1), pp. 127–134.

17. Milgram, Stanley. "Group pressure and action against a person," p. 141.

18. Milgram, Stanley. "Liberating effects of group pressure."

19. Tuddenham, Read D. "Correlates of yielding to a distorted group norm." *Journal of Personality,* 1959 (27), p. 281. By permission of the author and publisher.

20. Breger, Louis. "Conformity as a function of the ability to express hostility." *Journal of Personality,* 1963 (31), p. 248. By permission of the publisher.

21. Lazarsfeld, Paul F., Bernard Berelson, and Hazel Gaudet. *The People's Choice.* New York: Columbia University Press, 1948.

22. *Ibid.,* pp. 73–74. By permission of the publisher.

23. *Ibid.,* p. 22. By permission of the publisher.

24. Gross, Neal, W. S. Mason, and A. McEachern. *Explorations in Role Analysis: Studies of the School Superintendency Role.* New York: John Wiley & Sons, Inc., 1957.
Gross, Neal, A. McEachern, and W. S. Mason. "Role conflict and its resolution" in Maccoby et al. (Eds.), *op. cit.,* pp. 447–459.

By the author

ELEVEN

SMALL-GROUP PROCESSES

Although psychology is often defined as the study of the individual, roughly half the research in contemporary social psychology is concerned with the study of small groups rather than of individuals. There are two reasons for this. One, which has been touched on in the last chapter, is that it is largely through small groups that individuals interact with societies. From the young child, who is socialized not by his culture but by his family, through the adult, who does not have contact with religion, employment, and politics but with a church group, a work group, and a local political party, small groups mediate the contact of the individual with his society.

The second reason for studying small groups is that they are the smallest social units in which many social processes can be observed. Such basic social phenomena as communication channels, power relationships, differentiation of status and role, and the creation of norms simply do not exist in isolated individuals. While care must be exercised in applying the results of studying these phenomena at the group level to phenomena at the level of institutions or cultures, there is at least less discontinuity in doing so than there is in extrapolating from individuals to cultures. It is for this reason that even a general psychology text is not complete without some consideration of the processes in which an individual participates as a member of a group.

The present chapter, then, is intended as both a review and an extension of the principles developed in the earlier portions of the book. It is a review, because if the concepts which have been discussed are useful, they should help us to understand group processes also. It is also an extension, however, because some new concepts will have to be introduced to extend the theory to a new social level. Since an extended discussion of group processes would be the subject matter of another book, the discussion here will be limited to the one topic of the ways in which functioning groups differ from arbitrarily assembled conglomerations of individuals.

While many important things may be learned about individuals by studies such as those by Asch and Milgram where individuals are brought together only for the purpose of participating in the experiment, it is important to keep in mind that such a collection of people differs in many ways from a functioning social group. To avoid confusion, let us follow the precedent of Sherif and refer to the former situation as a *togetherness situation* and reserve the term *group situation* for the latter.[1] That togetherness situations and group situations may have strikingly different effects on behavior is nicely illustrated in a study by French.[2]

Subjects came to the laboratory five at a time. In order to create a group situation, members of fraternity basketball teams came to the laboratory together. For the togetherness situation, five strangers were used in each experimental session. In either case the subjects were set to work on a problem-solving task, and the experimenter left the room, locking the door behind him. Shortly after he left, sirens were sounded, "Fire!" was shouted in the hall, and smoke began to filter up between the floorboards of the laboratory. How did the subjects react to this novel stimulus situation?

To see if we can guess, let us try to place ourselves in the position of one of the quite sophisticated Harvard students who participated in the experiment. He would probably know that psychologists may try almost anything as an experiment and that in all probability the fire was a hoax. Why, otherwise, would he have been locked in the laboratory, and why would the experimenter have left? The problem, of course, is that he might be wrong in this analysis. Even if the chance were only one in a million that the fire was real, would he want to take this chance of being trapped in the laboratory? On the other hand, since the fire was probably not real, would he want to appear foolish by taking the hoax seriously?

As was indicated in the discussion of *The Acquaintance Process*, individuals on first acquaintance usually do not reveal deeply personal information about themselves. While a person might not mind revealing to a close friend that he was frightened or had been made a fool of by the experimenter, he would generally be more reluctant to reveal this to a fellow student whom he had just met but whom he might expect to meet again. These considerations enable us to predict the outcome of French's experiment—an outcome which differs from what common sense would lead most people to predict. In general, the groups of friends showed goal-directed activity designed to get them out of the laboratory. Some of this was quite effective. When, for example, they used the table as a battering ram to knock down the door, the experimenter had to intervene. The strangers, on the other hand, ignored the alarms. They continued working on the problem-solving task which they had been set.

Defining the Situation

One of the first things a group must do in coming together for the first time is to attempt to define an ambiguous situation. Social organizations do not operate simply on the basis of formal rules but also on the basis of innumerable shared conventions. Consider, for example, a work group in which management has attempted to define the situation by setting a piece-rate method of payment for production. This method of payment does not succeed in compelling the workers to accept the situation as a competitive one in which each person should maximize his economic gains by producing as much as possible. It is equally possible, as much industrial research has shown, for the group to set standards as to how much each man should produce. By punishing individuals who exceed the quota, it is possible to keep the production rate down to one which is easy for any member of the group to fulfill. Nor does this exhaust the possibilities. Each man might produce at a rate which he found comfortable, but each member of the group report an equal share of production.

The importance of group definitions of ambiguous situations is demonstrated in a study of an employment agency carried out by Peter Blau.[3] The rules of the employment agency were designed to select the best-qualified applicant for each available position. To achieve this end, the specified procedures called for obtaining detailed information from each applicant and selecting the best-qualified applicant from those for whom this information was on file. The department Blau studied, however, was primarily concerned with placing individuals in the clothing industry, in which slack periods alternated with periods of feverish activity. When a company was hiring, it did not want the best-qualified man the next day—it wanted any reasonably qualified person immediately. Employers not only called the employment agency to fill positions—they placed signs in front of their shops advertising them and often hired the first person who walked in off the street.

To meet these changed conditions, not foreseen in the general rules of the employment agency, the workers in the department adopted their own procedures. Applicants were reinterviewed frequently, so that a large pool of available manpower was always in the office. Interviews were kept short to deal with this flood of applicants, for it was not necessary to know much about a person in order to place him. By following these procedures, the interviewers were able to fill certain positions immediately with someone who was waiting in the office at the time the vacancy was reported. While the applicant who was sent might not be the best qualified, he at least had a good chance of arriving before a passerby was hired.

The importance of different definitions of the situation is shown in the same study by how two different work groups within the department reacted to a new evaluation procedure initiated by a new department head. While evaluation of interviewers had previously not been taken very seriously and had been based simply on the number of interviews carried out, the new department head instituted a complex method of evaluation based on eight different criteria, including such considerations as the proportion of interviews resulting in placements.

The interviewers in one group had been employed by the employment agency for a considerable period of time. During the earlier period of their employment they had developed an approach which stressed, as the overall policy of the employment agency did, the goals of recommending the best-qualified man for the job and of providing extensive counseling for applicants. They had become accustomed to working together toward those goals in a cooperative manner. Finally, since they had been employed for more than 1 year, they had tenure with the agency and could only be fired for cause. The new evaluation procedure did not have much impact on their methods of work.

The members of the other group, however, were almost all new employees. They had not had time to establish cooperative ways of doing things, and they were on probationary 1-year appointments. They were quite concerned to maximize their ratings and devised some ingenious ways of doing so.

Blau used as a measure of competitive practices the extent to which an individual was more likely than others to fill with his own applicants positions that he had been the first person to hear about. The noncompetitive interviewer might let other interviewers find out about the position so that the best man might be recommended for it. The competitive interviewer could raise his own rating by placing one of his own applicants in the position. Some of the ways of doing so were given by one of the interviewers:

> "When you take an order, instead of putting it in the box, you leave it on your desk. There was so much hiding of orders under the blotter that we used to ask, 'Do you have anything under your rug?' when we looked for an order.

> "You might leave an order you took on your desk, or you might leave one you pulled from a box on your desk, even though you made no referral. . . .

> "Or you might take an order only partially. You write the firm's name, and a few things; the others you remember. And you leave it on the pad of order blanks. You keep on doing this, and all these orders are not in the box.

> "You can do some wrong filling out. For instance, for a rather low-salary job, you fill out 'experience required.' Nobody is likely to make

a placement on that except you, because you know that experience isn't required.

"Or, if there are several openings on one order, you put the order into 'referrals' [file category for filled job openings] after you made one placement. So you have a better chance of making the next placement than somebody else. Time and again, you see four, five, openings on one order filled by the same person."[4]

In the more competitive group, the most competitive individuals were most productive, for they were best at the practices needed for success in that situation. In the less competitive group, on the other hand, competitive individuals were excluded by their colleagues from information which all the others shared. They were unable to compete effectively with an organized group, so they were less productive than the others. Because of its better organization, the noncompetitive group was more productive as a whole than the competitive group.

One of the major problems of the developing group, then, is to agree on how the situation should be defined. In doing so, members are likely to import definitions from similar situations with which they have been familiar in the past, just as the members of the noncompetitive group carried over the ideas they had developed in their early years with the agency into the period of the new department head. Another way of looking at the research on *The Authoritarian Personality* which has been discussed is to see it as showing individuals carrying over into adult relationships the relationships to authority figures which they learned in childhood. Nor is the group's task of defining the situation ever complete. As was indicated in the section on ideology, groups constantly encounter new situations, and one of the main functions of leaders is to help define the way in which they should be viewed.

Filling Positions

Division of labor is the most obvious characteristic of formal organization and, as was pointed out by Max Weber in his analysis of bureaucracy, enables ordinary people to perform extraordinary tasks. One man, no matter how gifted, could not produce a Chevrolet, nor could one man make the decisions which must be made to keep a Chevrolet plant running. Dividing up difficult tasks into manageable pieces is essential to large-scale organization and is what makes large-scale organization complex.

That a similar division of labor takes place in small informal groups is not so immediately apparent, for the positions in the structure are not named and delimited by a job description as they are in a formal structure. Careful analysis, however, reveals a similar structuring of groups. Consider, for example, what happens on a camping holiday where camp is broken each morning and established each evening. On the first day it may take 2 hours to pitch camp. First everyone tries to set up the tent, getting in each other's way and accomplishing very little. Then all realize that nobody has gathered wood for a fire. By the time the fire is finally started and dinner cooking, they are probably very tired and hungry.

As the holiday proceeds, the process becomes more and more efficient. Without anything being said, some people take over the responsibility of pitching the tent each evening, while others build a fire and do the cooking. Although individuals may not be designated as "chief supply officer," "head cook," and "billeting officer," division of labor has been established.

The positions which exist in a group going camping and the roles associated with them, however, are largely specific to the activities of the group. Are there any group roles which are general in the sense that they will be found in virtually any organized group regardless of its purpose? Psychiatric observations, such as Bion's,[5] on therapy groups would suggest the existence of at least a crude leadership role. Members of the group cast the therapist in roles with which they are familiar, such as "father" or "teacher." They seem to expect to be told in an authoritative way what they should do to improve their relationships with other people, and if the therapist refuses to play this type of role, they exert considerable pressure on him to induce him to do so. Bion's comments on what may be going on beneath the surface conventionalities of groups are a provocative source of hypotheses about group functioning. He considers, for example, the possibility that failure to attend some meetings and silence during others may be one way of asserting leadership over a group. The person who comes late to some meetings, fails to come to others at all, and sits back looking quietly disdainful of the proceedings of those which he does attend makes his sentiments quite clear to the other members of the group and acts out feelings which others may share. If the feelings are widely shared, he may become the emotional leader of the group. It is not only in formal elections that abstention may be a form of protest.

Using well-standardized observational procedures and both real-life and laboratory groups, Bales[6] and his associates have done extensive studies of both the stages of problem solving and the nature of leadership in small groups. While not showing identical leadership roles in all small groups, the results did show certain roles to occur quite frequently and others to be rather rare. The first possibility to be investigated was that the typical small group has one leader who fits our conception of what a "great man" should be—active, efficient in getting tasks accomplished, and also extremely popular with the members of the group. While early research gave some support to a belief in the existence of such individuals, further research revealed that they are quite rare. Despite the efforts of group members to cast the leader as the great man, revealed in group therapy, most groups do not succeed in maintaining such a structure over a period of time. While ratings of productivity and popularity are positively correlated during the first meeting of the group, the correlation disappears with time. It becomes increasingly difficult for the same man to be the severe taskmaster and the jolly good fellow as time goes on.

Dual leadership roles in groups were thus found to be extremely common, with one leader stimulating efficiency in dealing with tasks which the group had to perform and the other, socially the most popular, dealing with interpersonal conflicts which arose within the group. This type of division of labor is common enough that research on American families has shown strong tendencies for the father and mother to be cast respectively in these two roles. As in the family, productivity and satisfaction both tend to be higher in groups with this structure if the task leader and socioemotional leader are on good terms with each other than if they are in conflict.

Not all groups have a dual leadership structure, however, and not all are harmonious. Another common role identified by Bales is that of the *overactive deviant*, a person who is very active in interaction and attempts to dominate the group, but is rated by the group members as low on both task ability and likability. Another way of viewing such an individual is as a contending leader. While his ideas are deviant in the group in which he is participating, he might play a leadership role in a group in which they are shared.

Finally, individuals were identified who were unpopular, thought to have little task ability, and inactive. These individuals were frequently cast in the role of scapegoat by the group. Bales and his colleagues thus showed the generality of the development of role differentiation in groups, and found some similarity in the types of leadership roles which are usually developed.

In an interesting study using three confederates, Schachter[7] explored the relationships of agreement or disagreement with the majority, communication within a group, and acceptance or rejection by the group. One confederate, the *deviant*, took a position at variance with the group majority and maintained it throughout the group discussion. The second, the *slider*, started out by disagreeing but allowed himself to be convinced by the other group members. The third, the *mode*, always supported whatever position the majority were in favor of at that moment. The groups were also systematically varied on both how attractive they were to their members and whether the topic on which the confederates agreed or disagreed with the group was relevant to the main purpose of the group.

As might be expected, the majority of communications in the group were devoted to trying to persuade the deviant to agree with the rest of the group. Within the time limits of this study, most of the groups never gave up this effort, although in groups to which the members were highly attracted and in which the deviant was disagreeing about something vital to them, the group members frequently ended up ignoring him. Even more interesting is the relationship between agreement with the rest of the group and selection for a position of leadership.

At the end of the meeting, each group elected members to various committees, varying from the executive committee, which had much authority but little repetitive work to do, to the correspondence committee, which involved little power but a good deal of drudgery. Both the mode, who simply voted with the majority, and the slider, who allowed himself to be convinced, were frequently elected to the important leadership positions in the groups. The deviant was almost inevitably elected to a position which gave him a great deal of work to do but no authority to make decisions.

Without too much distortion, this result may be summarized in everyday language in the lyrics of *H. M. S. Pinafore*:

> *I always voted at my party's call*
> *And never thought of thinking for myself at all.*
> *I thought so little they rewarded me*
> *By making me the ruler of the Queen's Navy.*

There was one exception to assigning the most odious position to the deviant, however, and it supports Bion's observations on obstructionism as a path to leadership. In the groups where the members were not attracted to the group and where they had been tricked by the experimenter into discussing something which was irrelevant to the purpose of the group meeting, deviation would be a good way of expressing disgust with the whole proceedings which was probably quite generally felt by the group members. In these groups only, the deviant was generally elected to the executive committee.

Developing Interpersonal Relations

As a togetherness situation develops into a group, specific relationships develop among its members, a process involving at the start inaccurate perception of inadequate information. Thibaut and Kelley,[8] in an excellent analysis, have shown the importance of the production of behavior as well as its perception at the early stages of the relationship. According to their analysis, which explains a number of interesting research findings, individuals generally first produce behaviors which can be produced at relatively low costs to themselves and which do not reveal much about themselves to others. Cultural patterns often provide materials for such superficial interaction, as in discussion of the weather and the latest baseball results. Less stereotyped topics of conversation, while perhaps potentially more rewarding for the future relationship, have the danger of giving the other person power to hurt the individual by revealing material which he might not want generally known. To pick an extreme example, even the most confirmed masochist might be reluctant to tell a stranger about the collection of whips he had at home, even though by his silence he might pass up a possibility of finding out about his new acquaintance's sadistic tendencies.

One result of this initial caution in interaction is that the way in which two strangers perceive each other can be influenced by what they are told about each other before meeting. Individuals who are told that they will probably not like each other are not only inclined to see the undesirable characteristics in each other; they also behave in a fashion which makes them less attractive to each other. Individuals who are told, as part of an experiment, that they will like each other behave in ways which make them do so. These phenomena are closely related to the mechanism of projection, in which the attribution of one's own forbidden impulses to others is probably aided by behavior which calls out the expected response from the other.

Because of the biasing in the initial acquaintance which people have of each other, the long time it took the students in *The Acquaintance Process* to form accurate perceptions of each other is not surprising. On the other hand, as Newcomb's study showed, in a group where people will continue to interact with each other for a long period of time whether they like each other or not, there is the opportunity for perceptions to become more accurate. Initial impressions are thus probably less important in social groups than they are in social situations where the relationship may be terminated on the basis of the first inaccurate information.

As friendship patterns develop in the group, one important function they serve is to provide channels of communication. This was demonstrated in the negative relationship between competitiveness and productivity in the cooperative work group in Blau's study, which resulted from the competitive members of the group being excluded from information shared by the others. It is even more dramatically demonstrated on the community level in Vidich and Bensman's *Small Town in Mass Society: Class, Power and Religion in a Rural Community*.[9] In the community which they studied, a small group was able to dominate local politics simply through its members' being the only ones who knew when nominating petitions for the positions were due. (The local newspaper carried a statement of who had been nominated *after* nominations were closed.) Since their candidate was the only one nominated, he was regularly elected.

Besides serving as a communication channel, a friendship also gives one person power to influence another. Kurt Back,[10] for example, varied attraction to a two-person experimental group in each of three different ways. In one case, interpersonal attraction was varied by telling the subjects that they would like each other. In other treatments, the prestige of the group and the potential rewards of belonging were manipulated. Regardless of the basis of attraction to the group, it was found that individuals were more influenced by groups to which they were more attracted than by groups to which they were less attracted. These results support the balance studies and studies of reference groups we have considered, which show interpersonal attraction to be an important source of social power.

They also show that there are other sources of power besides personal attraction, however. Both the prestige offered by group membership and more mundane financial rewards give the group power to influence members. French and Raven[11] have discussed five bases of social power, while Thibaut and Kelley have provided a theoretically more elegant treatment in which all social power is reducible to changes in the costs and rewards to the person over whom power is being exerted. Of French and Raven's sources of power, *reward* power and *coercive* power are self-explanatory. *Legitimate* power stems from the holding of a position which is accepted as giving an individual the right to make decisions influencing others. It would seem to operate in terms of both internal and external rewards. As was seen in Milgram's study of obedience, the internal punishments of the superego may exert very powerful pressures on the individual to ensure his obedience to an authority regarded as legitimate. Supplementing these internal forces, however, are the sanctions which other people employ to enforce the unwritten laws of their culture. The operation of these sanctions was illustrated in the consideration of the rule of law.

As Thibaut and Kelley[12] have pointed out, *expert* power may operate largely in terms of the expert's ability to cut costs for others. An individual who has the ability to tell another how to manufacture a product at less cost, win an election, play the oboe, or catch trout clearly has the ability to increase the rewards or decrease the frustrations of others. Finally, *referent* power, which Raven and French assume to operate in terms of identification, would lead to reward or the lack of it through the operation of balance theory.

It is doubtful whether this or any other list of sources of power in social relationships is completely comprehensive. Control of channels of communication, for example, does not seem to clearly fit any of French and Raven's categories. The secretary who allows some people to see a decision maker on short notice and makes others wait may not have any special expertise and may not be using her position in a way regarded as legitimate, but there can be no doubt that she is exercising power.

In many of the studies which we have considered in this book we have seen the importance of social power. The effects of differences in social position have been considered in discussing *Elmtown's Youth* and the differential transmission of political indoctrination. Referent power has been the most extensively discussed, in considering the formation of the superego, dissonance and balance theory, and reference groups. The topic is an important one, and further study of the exercise of power in group and community settings is one of the more important tasks before the field of social psychology.

Developing Social Norms

Closely related to the definition of the situation in the development of a togetherness situation into a group situation is the emergence of shared expectations about how group members should act. These expectations, which are called social *norms*, are similar to roles in that they are enforced by sanctions. They differ from roles in that they are expectations which apply to all members of a social grouping, not just to those occupying certain positions. While there are differences in the behavior expected of the chairman of a group and other group members—differences in role—there are some expectations which apply to all members, such as that they should wear clothes to meetings. Because these expectations are enforced by rewards and punishments by group members, they are one of the main forces accounting for group influence on individuals.

Group expectations about the behavior of group members have been referred to in many of the studies cited in this book. That Bennington students should espouse the political left, that soldiers in the Wehrmacht should be loyal to their comrades, that residents in the integrated-housing-project studies by Deutsch and Collins should interact with their neighbors regardless of skin color, and that members of one of Blau's work groups should cooperate with each other are all social norms, for they are all enforced by sanctions on the part of group members.

Let us now look more closely at these group standards which have such a great influence on our lives.

One of the most important properties of norms is that they are generally enforced by all group members regardless of their personal preferences. This is dramatically demonstrated in a study by Merei.[13] Merei first observed boys in a free play situation and observed some who were dominant. When one of these boys (who might be called either a leader or a bully) made a suggestion to one of the other boys, it was generally carried out. Merei then formed the less dominant boys into small groups to facilitate the development of shared standards. The dominant boys were excluded from these groups for from three to six meetings of 30 or 40 minutes each in order to allow the group to establish traditions about what games were played with the toys provided.

After this period, one dominant boy was introduced into each group. Instead of being able to assert his dominance as before, he was now forced by the group to conform to its traditions. He engaged in the activities which the group had established in his absence, while his own suggestions were either ignored or needed to be modified to conform to the group's norms. This change from the previous relationship of the boy to the group came about because all the members of the group enforced its new norms. Before, a command from a dominant boy might be opposed only by the person to whom it was directed; after the establishment of norms, the members of the group all united in opposing the violation of their traditions.

Once the groups had established social norms, very few of the dominant boys ever succeeded in reestablishing their dominance over the groups. The formerly dominant boy might obtain use of some of the toys and might even give commands; but the group structured his activity rather than him structuring its. The one strategy which was successful in reasserting dominance is especially interesting. If the formerly dominant boy played the role of a "diplomat" and accepted the new group traditions, it was possible for him to become an interpreter of those traditions. Once established in the position of the chief authority on the traditions, he could interpret them so as to structure the activities of the group. In this case change was initiated by using the norms rather than by changing them.[14]

The importance of social norms as a force resisting change was perhaps most clearly revealed in a series of studies by Kurt Lewin[15] and his students. The initial studies were concerned with the changing of food preferences during the Second World War. Lewin reasoned that if forces to bring about changes in food preference, such as attempts to get mothers to give their babies orange juice and cod-liver oil or to get adults to eat cuts of meat such as kidney, had no effect, then they must be calling out forces opposing change. If social traditions or norms dealing with how babies should be fed or whether kidneys are a proper food for human consumption were preventing change, then change could be brought about more effectively by changing the norms than by simply opposing them with more propaganda. Lewin and his students thus did a number of studies contrasting different ways of inducing change.

Group decision was used as a method of changing social norms. In a lecture situation, norms cannot be changed because individuals cannot communicate with each other about the ideas given in the lecture. Even if convincing arguments were presented that kidneys could be cooked in ways that made them very appetizing (an idea which would be considered as obvious in Britain as it was considered absurd in the United States), a woman who heard the lecture would still wonder what other people might think if it were known that she fed kidneys to her family. If, on the other hand, the members of a group should decide that kidneys were a suitable food, they would have the social support of their fellow group members in their new norm.

Lectures were thus contrasted with group discussions in their effect on use of cod-liver oil, orange juice, and new meats. In all cases the group-discussion techniques had greater effects. In the case of using new meats, for example, only 3 percent of the subjects tried one of the new meats after the lecture, while 32 percent of those who had participated in the group discussion did so. The mothers were more willing to give their children orange juice—55 percent did so after the lecture and 100 percent after the group discussion.

Unfortunately, the exact variables which made the group discussions a more effective method of social change than the lectures were not made completely clear by the research. The group and lecture situations differed in a number of ways—in that discussion took place, that a decision was reached, that a public commitment was made to try the innovation, and that there was complete group consensus on the decision. Which of these factors was responsible for the difference, or are all of them necessary? Although a study has been done by Edith Bennett Pelz[16] to answer this question, the answer still remains in some doubt. In the Pelz study, in contrast to those of Lewin, there were no significant overall effects. That is, as many members of control groups who were not exposed to any influence attempt engaged in the suggested behavior as did subjects in lecture or group-decision treatments. Since within the varieties of group-decision treatments which were used there were significant differences, it would seem that some of the influence attempts had negative effects. Why should this be the case?

The answer may lie in the topic of the persuasion attempt and the experimenters and subjects who were used. The decision which the subjects had to make was whether to participate in psychology experiments; the experimenters were psychology graduate students with teaching experience, and the subjects were psychology students. In these circumstances, it would not be surprising if some of the subjects at least should suspect that they were being coerced rather than convinced. Whatever the reasons, Lewin's discussion leaders seem to have been more like the "diplomats" in Merei's experiment, who managed to be accepted by the groups and then change the norms, while Pelz's seem to have failed as completely as the majority of Merei's formerly dominant boys to change group standards. Further research is still necessary to make clear the conditions under which group discussion is an effective method of changing group norms.

Dealing with Self-oriented Needs

In our treatment of motivation the existence of motives which are not fully admitted to awareness and the role of group support in bolstering the individual's perception of himself have been emphasized. The relationships between lack of social support and one motive, aggression, have been explored in the chapter on prejudice. Both these emphases point to potent sources of disruption of the interaction of problem-solving groups. The expression of motives which are not socially acceptable, such as aggression or dependency, would call out negative reactions in others and weaken attraction to the group. As indicated in the discussion of the work of Bion and of Schachter, individuals may even be chosen as leaders on the basis of their effective interference with the tasks in which the group is nominally engaged. Sufficient interpersonal hostility would eventually lead to the disintegration of the group. We would thus expect the maintenance of individual self-esteem and mutual attraction to be major problems with which any group must cope.

These tasks would be made more difficult simply because group members generally disagree about the task decisions which confront them. Let us look at an example in terms of balance theory. Mr. Smith and Mr. Jones are friends who are members of the planning commission of their city, which is considering the case of Mr. Wilson, who has just built a carport on his property. The city laws state that any construction with a roof must be set back 5 feet from the side property line of a lot, and Mr. Wilson, who has built the carport himself without obtaining a building permit, has built to within 1 foot of the line dividing his land from that of Mr. West. The question before the planning commission is whether Mr. Wilson will be required to tear down his illegal construction or it will be made legal after the fact by the planning commission giving him a variance for it.

Since Mr. West does not object to the carport coming so close to his lot, Mr. Smith is in favor of letting it stay up. Mr. Jones, on the other hand, notes that some of the people who live on the street do object and feel that construction right up to lot lines "ruins the neighborhood." Mr. Jones does not want to set a precedent of legalizing illegal construction done without a building permit for fear that many similar cases will arise, and thus he favors making Mr. Wilson tear the carport down again.

Both Mr. Smith and Mr. Jones will suffer from imbalance, for each has a high opinion of the other but a low opinion of the ideas which the other is advancing. While the issue on which they disagree might at first glance seem a trivial one, it can involve important ideological differences. Whether an individual favors letting Mr. Wilson keep his carport is likely to depend on conceptions of the nature of private property and of the rights of individuals versus obligations to the community as a whole. Discussion is liable to be lengthy and heated, and if Mr. Smith and Mr. Jones wish to remain friends, each will have a difficult time deprecating the ideas of the other without saying anything which might be considered a personal attack. It is easy to make the transition from "He is attacking my ideas" to "He is attacking me," and balance could always be restored by the two men lowering their evaluations of each other.

The importance of dealing with the disruptive emotions aroused in group situations is clearly revealed in studies of group interaction. It may be seen in the types of leadership positions in groups found by Bales and his colleagues, for the "social specialist" is essentially a person who specializes in dealing with problems in this area. In his interaction, such categories as "shows solidarity," "shows tension release," and "shows agreement" are especially high.

The stages of problem solving observed by Bales also show the importance of maintaining group cohesion. After a decision is made on a problem or at the end of a meeting, the group typically engages in social interaction irrelevant to the task. Joking and laughing together serve to reestablish the social relations which have been strained by the interaction on the task.

Perhaps the strongest evidence of the importance of self-oriented needs, however, comes from a study of decision-making conferences in business and industry carried out by Fouriezos, Hutt, and Guetzkow.[17] The use of real-life decision-making groups meant that there was necessarily a good deal of variety in the composition of the groups and the nature of the tasks with which they were confronted. Despite these important sources of variation due to other sources, sizable correlations were found between behavior expressing self-oriented needs and the presence of group conflict, low group solidarity, and lack of satisfaction on the part of the participants. Group productivity was also measured by a very crude index based largely on the proportion of the items on the agenda which each group managed to deal with. Though this index could only be a very rough indication of productivity, since items would differ widely in their difficulty and importance, even it showed a relationship to the expression of self-oriented needs. Groups in which individual members expressed more personal needs finished less of their business.

From studies of group interaction, then, we may see the importance of personal motives to the functioning of groups and the efforts made by organized groups to deal with their disruptive effects. Like the other characteristics of groups which we have considered in this chapter, the ways of dealing with these needs point to the existence of important differences between togetherness situations and group situations. Individuals in a togetherness situation are less dependent upon their fellow members for support to the self. On the other hand, they have not developed the interpersonal relations, norms, and leadership structures for dealing with their needs which exist in an organized group.

The Selection of Environments

In Chapter 10 the question of why people change so little was raised. The material considered in this chapter makes this question even more puzzling. We have seen, from research by Asch and Milgram, that even togetherness situations can have important effects on individuals, and we have seen that real-life groups differ from these situations in ways which should make their impact upon individual members even greater. How, then, do people manage to remain reasonably constant over a period of years? For an answer to this question, let us now return to the Bennington girls. What happened to them over a period of 20 years after leaving Bennington?[18]

If we look at their demographic characteristics, we see that in terms of financial success they came to resemble their well-to-do parents. The follow-up study revealed that of the 117 respondents who were or had been married, 77 percent had annual incomes of twenty thousand dollars or more. This income was also reflected in their style of life. Of those who were parents, 65 percent had sent some of their children to fee-paying private schools.

In terms of their political beliefs, on the other hand, they had not on the whole returned to the views of their parents. In the 1960 presidential election, for example, more than 75 percent of the voters with the income and religious preferences of the Bennington graduates preferred Nixon over Kennedy. Yet of the Bennington graduates, only 40 percent preferred Nixon. Their political differences from others of their socioeconomic status were shown in other ways— 76 percent of them were in favor of Medicare, and 61 percent in favor of admitting Red China to the United Nations.

The effects of their experiences at Bennington were thus clearly evident after a period of 20 years. This is even more clearly shown by a look at individual differences. If attitude scores on political and economic progressivism (PEP) obtained while they were at Bennington are compared with political preferences in 1960, a strong relationship is apparent, as shown in Table 11–1. Of the girls who were least conservative when they left Bennington, thirty out of thirty-three favored Kennedy in 1960. Of those who were most conservative on leaving Bennington, twenty-two out of thirty-three favored Nixon. This is surely strong evidence for the stability of attitudes and the predictive value of attitude scales.

Why did the women change less in 20 years after leaving Ben-

Table 11–1 *Presidential preferences in 1960, according to quartiles of PEP scores on leaving college in the late 1930s*

PEP QUARTILE	NIXON PREFERRED	KENNEDY PREFERRED	TOTAL
1 (least conservative)	3	30	33
2	8	25	33
3	18	13	31
4 (most conservative)	22	11	33
Total	51	79	130

SOURCE: Newcomb[19]

nington than they did in the 4 years while they were there? The answer was hinted at in our discussion of *Elmtown's Youth* and of the initial Bennington study, for in both these discussions it was emphasized that individuals select those with whom they will have close personal relations. While at Bennington the majority of the girls had been placed in an environment where their previous political beliefs had little support, after leaving Bennington they were able to select groups which supported their political ideology. Especially important in this respect were the men they married, for we have seen evidence that the family is the most important reference group for most individuals.

The husbands of the women who went to Bennington turn out to be an unusual group. They have highly paid jobs, and half of them went to Ivy League colleges, yet to a great extent they share their wives' political preferences. There is even a highly significant correlation between the husband's voting record over the period from 1940 to 1960 and the wife's political and economic progressivism score before marriage. On the whole, then, the women married men who had the economic characteristics of their parents but the political preferences which they themselves had learned at Bennington. These men, in turn, were able to support their wives' political views and keep them from changing over time. The women who married men whose political views differed from their own were the women who most changed their political views over time.

This fascinating long-term study does much to explain the paradox that individuals may be dramatically changed by their reference groups, yet usually remain much the same over long periods of time. With some exceptions, such as prisons, the armed forces, hospitals, and prisoner-of-war camps, individuals generally have a good deal of freedom to choose their environments. While groups may have great influences on us, by choosing the groups we are able to select the influences to which we will be exposed.

Summary

Small groups are both important in their own right and the smallest units in which the basic processes of social interaction may be observed. It is small groups which shape the individual personality, on the one hand, and which serve as the building blocks of social institutions, on the other. In this chapter we have looked at five inter-related processes taking place as an arbitrary collection of individuals develops into a functioning social group. In doing so, we have reviewed much of the content of the book from a new perspective.

One of the first tasks of individuals meeting together is defining the nature of the situation. As discussed in the preceding chapter, it is necessary for the interacting individuals to agree both on who each of them is and on what role each of them is playing. A variety of alternate definitions of any situation could be drawn from the same cultural heritage, but the individual is likely to import definitions from his own experience. Cooperative and competitive work groups in an employment agency studied by Blau provide examples of similar situations being differently defined by different groups.

Even in small informal groups where there are not named positions such as "production manager" and "copywriter," different individuals come to specialize in playing different roles. Some leadership roles are more concerned with the external production of the group, while others are more concerned with maintaining internal social relations. Different situations place different demands on a group and require different types of leadership. There is thus no such thing as a "natural leader," for the attitudes and personal characteristics which make a person a leader of one group might lead to his being rejected or put to death by another.

Besides developing a division of labor which is generally recognized by all members of the group, the participants also develop personal relations with each other which may not be widely known or recognized. Friendship ties serve as channels of communication, a role that is apparent in French's experiment in which the subjects thought the building was on fire. This function becomes especially important in understanding larger-scale organizations, where informal friendship ties may be as important as formally defined relationships in communicating information in the organization. Friendship ties also provide a basis for interpersonal influence, for attraction is one basis of social power.

Social power is used to enforce the norms or traditional ways of doing things arrived at by the group. The tendency of group members to uphold norms whether they represent their personal preferences or not gives norms great power to influence behavior. As they are transmitted from one generation to another, it is norms which make true the statement, "The dead are more powerful than the living." In the creation of new norms by the group we see the prototype of the evolution of cultural institutions.

For a group or culture to succeed, it must evolve norms which enable its members to satisfy their needs. Especially difficult for the group to cope with are the needs of its members to preserve their self-esteem. Disagreement about a task is easily interpreted as personal attack, and one of the major leadership functions is maintaining harmony within the group. As the group constantly faces new situations which must be defined and dealt with, the social processes described in this chapter are continuing ones.

Notes and Acknowledgments

1. Sherif, Muzafer, and Carolyn Sherif. *An Outline of Social Psychology.* New York: Harper & Row, Publishers, Incorporated, 1956.
2. French, J. R. P., Jr. "Organized and unorganized groups under fear and frustration" in University of Iowa Studies: Studies in Child Welfare. Vol. 20. *Studies in Topological and Vector Psychology* III, 1944, pp. 229–308.
3. Blau, Peter. *The Dynamics of Bureaucracy.* Chicago: The University of Chicago Press, 1955.
4. *Ibid.,* Copyright 1955 by The University of Chicago. p. 59. By permission of The University of Chicago Press.
5. Bion, W. R. *Experiences in Groups and Other Papers.* New York: Basic Books, Inc., Publishers, 1961.
6. Bales, Robert F. "Task roles and social roles in problem-solving groups" in Eleanor Maccoby et al. (Eds.), *Readings in Social Psychology.* New York: Holt, Rinehart and Winston, Inc., 1958, pp. 437–447.
7. Schachter, Stanley. "Deviation, rejection and communication." *Journal of Abnormal and Social Psychology,* 1951 (46), pp. 190–207.
8. Thibaut, John W., and Harold H. Kelley. *The Social Psychology of Groups.* New York: John Wiley & Sons, Inc., 1959, pp. 64–79.
9. Vidich, Arthur J., and Joseph Bensman. *Small Town in Mass Society: Class, Power and Religion in a Rural Community.* Garden City, N.Y.: Anchor Books, Doubleday & Company, Inc., 1960.
10. Back, Kurt. "Influence through social communication." *Journal of Abnormal and Social Psychology,* 1951 (46), pp. 9–23.
11. French, J. R. P., Jr., and Bertram Raven. "The bases of social power" in D. Cartwright (Ed.), *Studies in Social Power.* Ann Arbor, Mich.: Institute for Social Research, 1959.
12. Thibaut, John, and Harold Kelley. *Op. cit.,* p. 109.
13. Merei, Ferenc. "Group leadership and institutionalization." *Human Relations,* 1949 (2), pp. 23–39.
14. *Ibid.,* p. 25.

15. Lewin, Kurt. "Group decision and social change," in E. Maccoby et al. (Eds.), *op. cit.*, pp. 197–211.
16. Pelz, Edith B. "Discussion, decision, commitment and consensus in 'group decision.' " *Human Relations,* 1955 (8), pp. 251–274.
17. Fouriezos, N. T., M. L. Hutt, and H. Guetzkow. "The measurement of self-oriented needs in the discussion situation, and their relationship to satisfaction with group outcome." *Journal of Abnormal and Social Psychology,* 1950 (45), pp. 682–690.
18. Newcomb, Theodore M. "Persistence and regression of changed attitudes: Long-range studies." *Journal of Social Issues,* October, 1963 (19), pp. 3–14.
19. *Ibid.,* p. 7. By permission of the author and of the publisher.

GLOSSARY

A-B-X model: a balance model devised by Newcomb relating two people and a thing.

acceleration principle: the economic principle that slight changes in demand for a consumer good cause great changes in the demand for the machinery to make the consumer good.

achievement motive: a desire to accomplish things which are valued in one's culture.

acquired: developing only through exposure to certain environmental conditions. Speaking the English language is an acquired characteristic, for example.

ACTH: adrenocorticotropic hormone.

ad hoc group: individuals brought together for a particular purpose, such as to participate in an experiment.

adrenal cortex: the outer portion of the adrenal gland, an endocrine gland found at the end of the kidney.

adrenal medulla: the inner portion of the adrenal gland, an endocrine gland found at the end of the kidney.

adrenocorticotropic hormone: a hormone secreted by the pituitary and controlling production of corticosteroids.

aerial perspective: increased haziness of something which is farther away.

afferent: carrying impulses toward the brain.

affiliation motive: a desire to have close interpersonal relations with others.

amnesia: a person's inability to remember a period of his life experience.

analyzer: in Deutsch's model of motivation, a perceptual system responding to a particular set of environmental stimuli. Similar to a releasing mechanism except not innate.

androgen: male sex hormone.

anomie: the lack of norms.

anticipatory socialization: taking on the apparent characteristics of a group or class one desires to join.

anxiety: a state similar to fear except that the cause of the fear is not known. A central concept in a psychoanalytic theory of personality.

artificial pupil: a hole in a surface placed in front of the eye eliminating many depth cues.

assimilable discipline: discipline which is not highly threatening to the child.

assimilation: perceiving something as more similar than it actually is to something the perceiver expects or is familiar with.

associationist: a member of a school of philosophy which explained the succession of ideas in consciousness through their having acquired connections with each other.

assumptive context: the assumptions made about what in the real world is most likely to be causing the stimulation of the sense organ.

asthenic reaction: a reaction to anxiety characterized by feelings of fatigue.

attention: the selection of some of the available stimulation for central processing.

attitude: a relatively enduring readiness to respond to an object in some way, composed of both beliefs about the object and sentiments toward it.

attitude scaling: the development of questionnaires composed of sets of interrelated opinion items, yielding more extensive information than opinion polling.

authoritarianism: a constellation of attitudes and personality factors related to sympathy toward fascist ideology.

authority: anyone seen as having a legitimate right to apply sanctions.

balance theory: a theory proposing that people modify their perceptions to make them more internally consistent. Consistent perceptions are called balanced and inconsistent ones imbalanced.

behavior: what an organism does from the point of view of an external observer.

behaviorism: a school of psychology maintaining that psychology is the study of behavior.

belief: a cognition about the nature of the world.

binocular parallax: the difference in the retinal images of objects resulting from the two eyes being located at slightly different points in space.

bit: the amount of information needed to divide the number of alternatives in half. If a person was trying to guess the name of one resident of the United States, telling whether the person was a male or a female would give approximately one bit of information.

blank-slate hypothesis: the idea that no important components of human thought and behavior are innate.

Bogardus social-distance scale: a device for measuring attitudes toward members of a minority group by finding out how close a relationship to them the subject is willing to accept.

brightness constancy: seeing an object as remaining the same in brightness even though the amount of light reflected from it varies.

capon: a castrated rooster.

carpentered world: a world in which there are many straight lines and rectangular corners because it is filled with man-made structures.

caste: a rigid and endogamous social class.

catalyst: a substance which helps a chemical reaction to take place although it is not permanently changed in the reaction.

cathexis: a learned liking or aversion.

centrality: the number of similar items to which an item is related. A central personality trait is related to many other traits, and a central member of a group has interpersonal relations with many members of the group.

central nervous system: the brain and the spinal cord.

cerebral cortex: the surface of the two large hemispheres of the brain which lie immediately under the skull. The portion of the brain which is most enlarged in man as compared with other animals.

chance: factors having no relationship to those under investigation. Drawing cards and selecting the person who draws the highest one is a way of leaving the selection to chance, for example.

character disorder: a wide variety of different types of symptom having in common that the individual does not live up to the expectations of his society.

chronological age: what is usually meant by age, the length of time since the person was born.

closure: a gestalt principle of perceptual organization indicating that stimuli which form closed forms are likely to be seen as going together.

cochlear nucleus: a collection of cell bodies within the brain processing auditory stimulation.

cocktail-party effect: filtering of stimulation so that one voice is attended to and others are ignored.

coding: changing the form in which information is transmitted or stored.

coercive power: the ability of one person to influence another by being able to punish or compel him.

cognitive: concerning ideas.

cognitive balance: mutual consistency among one's beliefs and sentiments, in a series of theories proposed by Heider, Rosenberg and Abelson, and others.

cognitive dissonance: an unpleasant state resulting from discrepancy between a person's beliefs and his behavior. The central concept in a theory by the same name first proposed by Festinger.

cognitive learning theory: a theory taking the position that not all learning is the learning of responses to stimuli, but that instead some learning involves associating stimuli or ideas with each other.

cognitive structure: a person's ideas

about the world and their relationships to each other.

cohesion: forces holding a group together, such as mutual attraction.

completion effect: perceiving an object as being continued behind something which is interposed between the observer and the object.

compulsion: a feeling that one must do something without understanding of the underlying motives.

concept: a class of stimuli which may be described in general terms so that a person could recognize a novel example.

conditional reflex: a type of learning first studied by Pavlov, in which a new stimulus comes to call out a response similar to a reflex response.

conditional response: a response similar to an unconditional response which comes to be called out by a stimulus paired with the unconditional stimulus.

conditional stimulus: a stimulus which is paired with the unconditional stimulus and comes to call out the conditional response.

conditioned avoidance: a learning task in which the organism learns to make a response to a stimulus in order to avoid unpleasant stimulation.

conditioned reflex: conditional reflex.

conditioned response: conditional response.

conditioned stimulus: conditional stimulus.

confederate: a helper of the experimenter posing as a subject.

conflict: parts of something being in opposition to each other.

conformity: modifying one's perceptions or behavior to achieve more similarity to the perceptions or behavior of others.

congenitally: from birth.

conscience: one's standards of what one ought not to do.

conservation of energy: the principle, now superseded, that energy cannot be created or destroyed but only changed into different forms.

conservation of mass: the principle, now superseded, that matter cannot be either created or destroyed.

consolidation hypothesis: the idea that it takes some time for memories to be permanently stored.

consonant: consistent, given the individual's assumptions about the world. Campaigning for a political candidate and having a high opinion of him are consonant.

constancy phenomena: tendencies for objects to be perceived as remaining the same even though the stimuli coming from them change. See **brightness constancy, shape constancy, size constancy.**

contact comfort: Harlow's term for the motive which made baby monkeys prefer contact with a soft surrogate mother to contact with a wire surrogate mother.

content analysis: the categorization of verbal materials so that the proportion of materials falling in different categories will provide a relatively objective measure of the content of the materials.

contiguity: closeness together, in time or space.

contiguity theorist: a learning theorist believing that learning can take place without reinforcement.

control group: a group similar to the experimental group in all respects except the level of the independent variable.

conversion: a radical change in a person's most important beliefs and values, usually accompanied by a re-interpretation of the person's past.

conversion reaction: the development of a specific physical symptom as a way of dealing with anxiety. The name stems from an earlier view that the anxiety was somehow converted into the symptom.

corpus luteum: a yellow mass which develops in the ovary at the point where an ovum was released if pregnancy has resulted. It is a source of hormones.

correlation: the extent to which things tend to go together. There is a correlation between how tall boys are and how many points they make in a basketball game.

cortex: the outer layer, as of the brain or adrenal gland.

cortical: concerning the cortex.

corticosteroid hormones: numerous chemical substances produced by the outer layer (cortex) of the adrenal glands with diverse functions such as control of water and salt balance, production of carbohydrate from fat and protein, and various responses to stress.

CR: conditional response.

criterion: a standard. A common criterion of learning is one errorless repetition. A person who can recite the material without error has reached the criterion and is presumed to know the material.

critical experiment: a single experiment making possible a choice among theories. Thought seldom if ever to exist.

cross pressures: influences acting on an individual to influence his vote, but acting in different directions.

CS: conditional stimulus.

culture: patterns of thought and behavior transmitted from generation to generation by learning, and the mate-rial products of those ways of behaving.

data: the actual observations on which theories are based.

decision tree: a series of questions the answers to which enable one to characterize concepts.

defended hostility: aggression expressed in an indirect or disguised manner.

defense mechanism: a way of protecting the self from anxiety.

defining the situation: deciding what concepts one's culture would apply and hence what norms should be followed. One of the main functions of leaders.

dependency: a state of needing another.

dependent variable: a variable observed to see what effect the experimental conditions had.

depressive psychosis: a variety of severe mental illness especially characterized by self-hatred and negative emotions.

developmental quotient: a measure, similar to an intelligence quotient, of how well a child performs for his age.

deviant: a person who is atypical of the group. In Schachter's study, a confederate who took a position considerably different from that adopted by other members of the group.

differentiation (as a way of reducing imbalance): coming to see something as made up of different parts which are evaluated differently.

digit span: how many numbers a person can correctly repeat back immediately after hearing them.

diluted water: a solution of salt and water having a higher osmotic pressure than pure water.

direction: a gestalt principle of perceptual organization indicating that stimuli which line up with each other are likely to be seen as going together.

discriminated operant: behavior which has come to be called out by a stimulus by being reinforced only when that stimulus is present.

discrimination: responding differently to slightly different stimuli.

discrimination learning: acquiring different responses to different stimuli, such as learning to approach a triangle but not a circle.

displacement: expressing a motive toward a substitute object.

dissociative reaction: a splitting off of some of a person's memories from consciousness. The most extreme cases would involve alternation of personalities.

dissonance: See **cognitive dissonance.**

dissonant: inconsistent, given the individual's assumptions about the world. Perceiving that one was out campaigning for one political candidate while actually hoping that his opponent would win would generally be dissonant, for example.

division of labor: breaking a task down into different subtasks so that different people perform different roles.

dominance hierarchy: an ordering of organisms from the most successful fighter to the least successful fighter.

dorsal: toward the back of an organism.

drive: a motive, often a motive presumed to be based on a need of the organism.

ecological validity: accuracy of perceptions because the world is such that the perceiver's assumptions about it are usually justified.

ECS: electroconvulsive shock.

EEG: electroencephalogram, a record of the electrical activity of the brain.

efferent: carrying impulses away from the brain.

ego: processes in the personality most in contact with the real world.

ego-alien: largely unconscious and unrecognized by the ego. Either impulses or moral standards may be ego-alien.

ego ideal: one's long-range goals and aspirations.

electra complex: in psychoanalytic theory, the attraction of a girl to her father and its psychological consequences.

electroconvulsive shock: the causing of unconsciousness and convulsions by means of an electric current.

electroencephalograph: a device to amplify and record small changes in electrical potential, such as those occurring spontaneously in the brain.

embryology: the study of the development of an organism prior to birth or hatching.

emotional leader: an expressive leader, one who expresses emotions which other members of the group are feeling. Almost synonymous with **socio-emotional leader.**

empathic: understanding others, presumably at least partly through identification with them.

empiricist: a member of a school of philosophy holding that all knowledge comes from experience.

endocrine gland: an organ secreting substances directly into the bloodstream.

endogamous: marrying within, rather than outside, the group.

environment: conditions external to the organism. Includes the intrauterine environment as well as conditions to which the individual is exposed after birth.

enzyme: an organic catalyst.

epinephrine: a hormone produced by the adrenal medulla or produced artificially. Among its effects are increases in heart rate and blood pressure.

equal-appearing intervals: a method of attitude scaling developed by Thurstone and depending on judges who sort opinion statements into categories.

equivalent-stimulus technique: a way of discovering what an organism has learned by testing new stimuli to see which ones the organism will respond to in the way it has responded to the previous stimulus.

ethnic group: individuals sharing a common culture or subculture.

ethologist: biologist specializing in the study of animal behavior, frequently under naturalistic conditions.

expedient: in the Gross et al. study, a school superintendent who seldom said that a superintendent should always or never do a certain thing, but instead said that it depended on the circumstances.

experience: consciousness as viewed by the conscious organism.

experimental control: elimination of alternate explanations of experimental results through the study of control groups.

experimental group: a group exposed to the conditions the effects of which are being investigated.

experimentation: a research method in which conditions are actively manipulated.

expert power: the ability of one person to influence another through having knowledge or ability which the other lacks.

externalization: perceiving one's difficulties as being due to something in the external world when in reality they are due to one's own characteristics.

extinction: ceasing to give a learned response when the response is no longer reinforced.

facilitation of consolidation: an improvement in the efficiency of the process by which material is stored in long-term memory.

fanning: circulation of water over eggs by movements of the tail as shown by the stickleback.

feedback: information on the state of a system used in the control of the system.

field expectancy: a learned idea about relations of different parts of the environment to each other.

figure-ground relationship: the tendency for a portion of what is perceived to stand out more clearly in consciousness.

fistula: a tube or opening, such as into the throat or stomach.

fixed-interval schedule: reinforcement of the organism for the first response after a certain period of time has elapsed since the last reinforcement.

fixed motor pattern: an organized motor response which is innate.

fixed-ratio schedule: a pattern of reinforcing the organism once every time it makes a certain number of responses.

forced compliance: an approach to attitude change in which behavior is changed in the belief that attitudes will then change also in order to become consistent with the behavior.

formal organization: the structure of a social grouping as it exists on paper. Many informal groups and relationships arise within any organization which are not provided for in the organization's table of organization and are thus not part of the formal organization.

fractional anticipatory goal response: in Hullian learning theory, a partial response of the type made at the goal which is made before the goal is reached and acts both to motivate and to reinforce behavior.

frame of reference: all those things a person considers in judging a particular stimulus.

fraternal twins: individuals who are born at the same time but are no more similar genetically than any brothers or sisters.

frustration: failure to achieve a goal or an individual's reaction to such a failure.

functional equivalents: behaviors which serve the same motive for an individual.

functionalism. a school of psychology seeing the central problem of the field as discovering how mental activity helps the organism to survive.

general adaptation syndrome: a complex reaction of the whole body to stress, with both adaptive and maladaptive consequences.

generalization: transferring previous learning to a similar situation, either by stimulus generalization or by response generalization. If used without qualification, usually means stimulus generalization.

gestalt theory: a theoretical approach to psychology which emphasized the extent to which things are influenced by their context.

gonadotrophin: a hormone secreted by the pituitary and stimulating hormone production by the gonads.

gonads: the glands secreting the most important of the sexual hormones.

gram molecular weight: a weight in grams of a substance equal to the molecular weight of the substance.

habit-family hierarchy: a learned set of alternate ways of achieving the same goal.

halo effect: perceiving a person as good in other ways when something favorable is known about him.

Hansen's law: the generalization that second-generation Americans stress their Americanism while the third generation again becomes interested in its cultural origins.

hedonism: the theory that individuals seek pleasure.

higher-order conditioning: conditioning in which a previously acquired conditional reflex plays the role usually played by the unconditional reflex.

homeostasis: the maintaining of a relatively constant internal environment.

homeostatic drive: a motive to behave in a way which will help maintain a constant internal environment.

hormone: a chemical formed in one organ of the body and having effects in one or more other organs.

hyperthyroidism: having an excess of the secretions of the thyroid gland.

hypertonic: having a higher osmotic pressure than blood.

hypochondriacal reaction: an anxiety reaction in which the anxiety is focused on particular physical symptoms.

hypothalamus: a structure at the base of the brain playing important roles in motivation and emotion.

hypothyroidism: having an insufficient amount of the secretions of the thyroid gland.

hypotonic: having a lower osmotic pressure than blood.

hysteria: conversion reactions and dissociative reactions.

id: the unsocialized impulses of the individual.

identical twins: two children who have developed from the same fertilized ovum, and thus have exactly the same heredity.

identification: responding as if the self and another were one.

ideographic approach: an approach to theory construction in which generalizations are drawn which would only apply to a restricted population of individuals or a single individual.

ideology: a view of the world which it is in the interest of some group to have generally accepted.

illusion: an inaccurate perception.

impression formation: the way in which strangers develop perceptions of each other. Includes both studies of what causes individuals to act in different ways and studies of how the behavior is perceived.

imprinting: a type of one-trial learning which is highly resistant to extinction.

incentive: a goal object.

incentive effect: a change in performance brought about by changing the expectations of the organism about the rewards it may obtain for the performance.

index of political predisposition: a predictor of how a person is likely to vote based on his socioeconomic status, religious affiliation, and rural or urban residence.

informal organization: groupings and relationships which are not provided for in the official structure of the organization. Compare **formal organization.**

innate: not dependent on specific experiences, but instead developing from hereditary causes in any normal environment.

innate releasing mechanism: a perceptual system responding to certain types of stimuli without previous learning.

insight learning: learning in which the solution to a problem appears suddenly and completely rather than developing gradually on the basis of trial and error.

instinct: a complex, stereotyped, unlearned pattern of behavior shown by all members of a species (or of one sex of a species) under the appropriate circumstances. Used by earlier theorists in a more general way as roughly equivalent to **drive.**

interaction: mutual influence on each other.

interaction (social): the sequence of events by which two or more individuals influence each other.

interaction (statistical): the additional effect which one variable has when another is at a particular level.

interference theory of forgetting: the idea that learning some material causes other material to be forgotten because in some way the memories interfere with each other.

intergroup: between groups.

internalization: making the standards of another a part of the self through identification.

interposition: something coming between the observer and what he is observing.

interrole conflict: different things being expected of someone because he simultaneously occupies more than one status.

intraception: a concern with subjective phenomena.

intracranial: within the skull.

intragroup: within the group.

intrarole conflict: different things being expected of the holder of one status.

introspection: reporting on experience by trained observers.

IQ: intelligence quotient. A measure of intelligence deriving its name from initially being calculated by dividing mental age by chronological age.

just-noticeable difference: the least change in stimulation which is, on the average, noticeable to an observer.

killing bite: the specific motor response used by polecats in killing prey.

kilogram: A unit of weight equaling approximately 2.2 pounds. Its abbreviation is kg.

kinesthesis: the sense which tells individuals the positions of their limbs by means of receptors in muscles, tendons, and joints.

latent learning: learning which is not apparent in performance.

lateral geniculate body: a collection of cell bodies within the brain processing visual stimulation.

law of effect: Thorndike's principle that the tendency for a stimulus to call out a response will be increased if the response leads to a satisfying state of affairs and decreased if the response leads to an annoying state of affairs. Later considerably modified.

law of exercise: a principle, first proposed and then later abandoned by Thorndike, indicating that learning takes place through the simple repetition of responses.

legitimate power: the ability which one person has to influence another through holding a position which people see as giving him a right to make certain decisions and perform certain acts.

leveling: a failure to perceive or forgetting of details in the thing perceived.

level of aspiration: the performance for which an individual is striving.

limited central processing capacity: a person's inability to actively deal with very much information at any one moment in time.

linear perspective: the apparent convergence of parallel lines receding in the distance.

link: in Deutsch's model of motivation, a unit which conducts excitation into the motor system when the analyzer associated with it is activated.

long-term memory: ability to remember events which are in the more distant past. Because of the great length of time that things may be remembered, it appears that long-term memories may be stored by means of structural changes in the nervous system.

Machiavellianism: the extent to which a person espouses the manipulative orientation to politics which Machiavelli advocated in *The Prince*, as measured by an attitude scale.

manic-depressive psychosis: a severe personality disturbance characterized by states of wild excitement, states of withdrawal and self-hatred, or both in alternation.

manipulative strategy: a way of trying to get someone to do what you want him to do.

maturation: development of innate potentials with time.

mental age: the average age of children who perform as well as the child being tested. If a child performs as well as the average six-year-old, his mental age is six.

metabolism: the chemical processes by which protoplasm is formed and food is broken down.

mnemonic device: an aid to memory.

mode: the score or category which is most frequent. In Schachter's study of communication to the deviant, a confederate who adopted the position taken by the largest number of members of the group.

molar: organized or studied in terms

of large rather than small units of analysis.

molecular: organized or studied in terms of small rather than large units of analysis.

moral anxiety: a disturbed state based on fear that one will feel guilty about one's behavior.

moralist: in the Gross et al. study, a school superintendent who frequently made categorical judgments that a superintendent should always or never do certain things.

motion parallax: the apparent movement of the world when the head is moved. It may be used as a depth cue, since objects nearer the observer seem to move more than those farther from him.

motivation: the internal forces producing behavior.

motivational pathway: in Deutsch's model of motivation, a conductor of excitation from the point where the motive originates to the links and motor systems which initiate motivated behavior.

motor area: a portion of the brain which, when stimulated, gives rise to a muscular response.

motor-impairment study: an experiment in which an animal is trained to give a response and then is made unable to make that response so that the response it makes instead may be studied.

multiple T-maze: a maze made of a number of sections, each one shaped like the capital letter T.

nativism: the position that much is inherited and little is learned.

natural experiment: an experiment in which the independent variable is not actively manipulated, but changes in its level which occur naturally are used as the basis for learning its effects.

negative reinforcement: a state of affairs which, when it follows a response being given to a stimulus, will decrease the probability of that response being given to that stimulus in the future.

neurosis: a mental disorder which does not involve as great disturbance of emotion, perception of reality, and behavior as does a psychosis.

neurotic anxiety: a disturbed state based on fear that one's impulses will get out of control.

neurotic depression: a disturbed state characterized by negative emotional reactions similar to those found in mourning. Characterized by more anxiety but less self-hatred than depressive psychosis.

nomothetic approach: an approach to theory construction in which generalizations are drawn which would apply to all normal individuals.

nonsense syllable: two consonants with a vowel between them not forming a word.

norm: a standard applied to members of a culture regardless of the specific positions they hold within their society, and enforced by sanctions.

object choice: the expression of a motive on a particular object, with resulting learning of preferences for this type of object.

observer bias: categorizing data so as to either prove or disprove a point, either consciously or unconsciously.

obsession: the recurrence of a thought or image, often a highly unpleasant one. A person who kept imagining scenes of airplane crashes, for example, would suffer from an obsession.

obsessive-compulsive reactions: obsessions and/or compulsions. They are classed together as they frequently occur in the same individuals.

occupational mobility: the extent to which a person is moving upward to a job generally regarded as more desirable or downward to a job regarded as less desirable.

Oedipus complex: in psychoanalytic theory, the attraction of a boy to his mother and its psychological consequences.

operant behavior: behavior for which no unconditional stimulus is known.

opinion: a quite specific idea about something. Similar to an attitude except more specific and limited in scope.

opinion polling: the asking of isolated questions, such as "Do you favor re-election of the President?" Yields less extensive information than attitude measurement, where a series of related questions is asked about each topic.

organic therapy: the treatment of a disorder by physical means.

osmotic pressure: a measure of the tendency of a fluid to pass through a semipermeable membrane into a more salt solution.

ovary: the organ producing female germ cells.

overactive deviant: a member of a group who initiates a great deal of interaction but is not seen by other members of the group as being either productive or likable.

overlearning: continuing to study material after it is apparently learned.

paired comparisons: a highly precise method of attitude scaling devised by Thurstone, but an extremely laborious method to use.

paleontology: a branch of geology studying the fossil remains of earlier forms of life.

panel design: a study in which certain individuals, called the panel, are interviewed repeatedly. Multiple control groups are used to guard against artifactual results.

paradoxical sleep: the stage of sleep in which dreaming generally occurs. It is characterized by great relaxation but a pattern of electrical activity of the brain similar to that found when the person is awake.

parathyroidectomized: having had the parathyroid glands removed.

parathyroid gland: a gland controlling the level of calcium in the blood.

parsimony: giving the simplest explanation which can account for the phenomena.

partial correlation: the extent to which two things would go together if a third thing were held constant.

partial reinforcement: only rewarding an organism for a portion of its correct responses. There are several varieties of partial reinforcement—fixed-ratio, in which the organism is reinforced for perhaps every tenth correct response, fixed-interval, in which it is reinforced for the first correct response after a given period of time, etc.

perception: experience based on information coming in through the sense organs. See also **sensation.**

peripheral: not central.

phobic reaction: the externalization of anxiety by fixing it on certain objects or situations. An unreasonable fear.

phylogenetic scale: an ordering of organisms in terms of their evolutionary development.

pituitary gland: a structure attached to the base of the brain and influencing many other glands.

placebo: a treatment which has no effect except through the suggestibility of the patient.

place learning: learning to go to the same place even though doing so requires different muscular responses.

placenta: the organ of communication between the mother and the embryo.

pleasure centers: areas of the brain in which positive reinforcement seems to be localized.

positive reinforcement: a state of affairs which, when it follows a response being given to a stimulus, will increase the probability of that response being given to that stimulus in the future.

poulard: a spayed hen.

prejudice: a judgment made without evidence, usually a negative one.

prestige suggestion: making something more acceptable by linking it to something or someone that is highly thought of.

primacy effect: being most influenced by material presented first.

primary process thinking: irrational thinking characterizing both young children and fantasy and humor of adults.

principle of least interest: the generalization that the person who cares least about maintaining a relationship is in the best bargaining position.

proactive inhibition: interference with learning of later material by earlier learned material. If knowing your old telephone number made it more difficult for you to learn your new telephone number, this would be an example of proactive inhibition.

probability: the proportion of the time that the event will occur in a long series of trials.

process (applied to mental disorder): developing gradually without the precipitating conditions being clear.

projection: attributing qualities to others which are not there but which explain one's own emotional reactions.

proximity: nearness. A gestalt principle of perceptual organization indicating that stimuli which are close to each other are likely to be perceived as going together.

psychiatrist: a medical doctor specializing in the treatment of mental illness.

psychiatry: a branch of medicine specializing in the treatment of mental disorder.

psychoanalysis: a theoretical approach to the study and treatment of personality disorder initiated by Sigmund Freud.

psychoanalytic approach: an approach to personality and mental illness initiated by Sigmund Freud.

psychopathic: violating the laws and customs of one's society without apparent guilt.

psychophysics: the study of the relationships between variations of physical energy and experience.

psychosis: a serious mental disorder involving major disturbances in the perception of reality, in speech and thought, and in mood and social relations.

psychosomatic disorders: illnesses in which physical symptoms are partially or entirely due to psychological causes.

psychotherapist: a psychologist specializing in the treatment of mental illness.

psychotherapy: the treatment of mental disorder by psychological means.

psychotic: having or characterizing a psychosis.

purposive: oriented toward a goal.

RAS: Reticular activating system.

rationalization: giving a reason other than the real one for doing something.

reaction formation: acting on the basis of a motive which is unacceptable to the self, although giving the superficial impression of acting on the opposite motive.

reaction potential: the tendency to give a particular response at a particular time. Depends, in Hullian theory, on both the strength of the habit and the amount of motivation.

reactive (applied to mental disorder): characterized by sudden onset, as if in reaction to a particular situation.

reality anxiety: a disturbed state in which one fears punishment from the world for behavior which is unacceptable to himself.

recall: the reproduction of a stimulus in awareness.

recency effect: being most influenced by material presented last.

receptor cell: a cell responding to some aspect of its environment by altering the frequency with which it fires.

rcognition: the identification of a stimulus with one perceived previously.

reference group: a group whose possible judgments of him a person cares about. It may be a group, such as "literary critics a hundred years from now," to which the person does not himself belong.

referent power: the ability of one person to influence another because the other identifies with him.

reflex: a simple, stereotyped, innate response given to a particular stimulus by any normal member of the species.

regression: a return to an earlier mode of adjustment.

reinforcement: in a broad sense, anything which alters the probability of a response being given to a stimulus. In a narrow sense, satisfaction or frustration of motives.

reinforcement pathway: in Deutsch's model of motivation, a conductor of

impulses to the pleasure centers in the brain.

reinforcement theorist: a learning theorist believing that some reinforcement, in a narrow sense, is necessary to all learning.

reintegration: remembering the context in which a stimulus was previously encountered.

relearning: learning something again, generally with the expenditure of less time than was required to learn it the first time. The amount of time saved is the most sensitive measure of previous learning.

reliability: the extent to which a measuring instrument gives consistent results.

replication: a repetition of a research study to establish whether following the specified procedures will reliably produce the expected results.

representative sample: a number of cases selected from a population in such a way that the proportions of various characteristics in the sample and the population will be approximately the same.

repression: actively keeping material out of consciousness.

respondent behavior: behavior for which an unconditional stimulus is known.

response generalization: giving somewhat different responses than those that were learned.

reticular activating system: a complex formation of neurons which is involved in attention.

retina: the layer of the interior of the eyeball containing the receptor cells.

retroactive inhibition: interference with memory for things learned earlier by things learned later. If learning a new telephone number made a person forget one he had learned before, this would be retroactive inhibition.

retrograde amnesia: backward loss of memory.

reward power: the ability of one person to influence another by being able to offer him something he wants.

rigidity of behavior: continuing to do the same thing under conditions where it is inappropriate.

role: the behavior expected of a person holding a certain position in a given society.

role playing: taking on the behavior of a position other than that actually held in society. A boy who pretends to be an airplane pilot is role playing, for example.

routinization of charisma: a change in the nature of the leadership of a religious movement from leaders who are accepted on the basis of divine inspiration to leaders accepted on the basis of meeting formal criteria of selection.

rule of law: general agreement on the rules of the political game. Proposed by Dicey to necessarily include acceptance of government as legitimate and freedom from arbitrariness or favoritism on the part of government.

rules of correspondence: statements of what characteristics of the world correspond to what entities in a theory.

sampling bias: comparing groups which differ in ways other than the level of the independent variable, or generalizing from cases to a population which they are not representative of.

sanction: a reward (positive sanction) or punishment (negative sanction) administered to one who does or does not comply with social expectations.

saving score: how much less time it takes to learn something after it has been learned before, expressed as the proportion of the original time saved.

scalogram analysis: a method of attitude scaling developed by Guttman. Has the advantage that no judges are needed to sort the items, but other disadvantages.

scapegoat: a substitute object for the expression of aggression.

schizophrenia: a psychosis especially characterized by disturbances of language, thinking, and attention.

secondary process thinking: the realistic thinking which characterizes rational problem solving in the adult.

secondary reinforcer: a stimulus which, through association with a reinforcer, acquires the property of also acting as a reinforcer.

self-oriented needs: motives to defend the ego.

semicycle: in directed-graph theory, a series of lines which, if followed, will lead back to the point of origin.

sensation: awareness of energy impinging on a sense organ. While a distinction used to be made between sensation, which was thought to involve no interpretation of the stimulation, and perception, which was thought to involve interpretation, it now appears that pure sensation is probably never experienced.

sense organ: a portion of the body specialized in the perception of stimuli of a given type. The eye is the sense organ of vision, for example.

sensory area: a portion of the brain which, when stimulated, gives rise to a sensation, such as that of light, sound, or taste.

sentiment: a positive or negative feeling toward something.

septal area: a region of the brain near the band of nerve fibers connecting the two cerebral hemispheres.

serial-position effect: the tendency, when a series of items is presented to be learned, to learn the first and last items best and the middle items least well.

set: readiness, either to perceive something or to respond in a certain way.

shape constancy: seeing an object as remaining the same shape even though the retinal image of it changes in shape.

sharpening: exaggerating the differences between something perceived and other things which the perceiver expects or is familiar with.

short-term memory: ability to remember events which are in the immediate past. It is so easily disrupted that it seems to depend on an ongoing process.

significant results: results which would occur by chance less than some arbitrarily set proportion of time, frequently one time in twenty.

similarity: a gestalt principle of perceptual organization indicating that stimuli which are similar to each other are likely to be perceived as going together.

situational factors: influences on behavior which are environmental rather than personal.

size constancy: seeing an object as remaining the same size even though the size of the retinal image changes.

Skinnerian methods: the shaping of operant behavior by providing positive reinforcement for successively closer approximations to the desired response. A pigeon might be taught to peck a lever, for example, by reinforcing it every time it moved closer to the lever than it had been before.

slider: in Schachter's study of communication to the deviant, a person who initially took a position quite different from that taken by most members of the group but then allowed himself to be won over to the majority position.

social class: a position in a prestige hierarchy to which a person is assigned more on the basis of the roles he plays in society than on the basis of how well he plays them.

social group: used loosely to apply to any aggregation of individuals or even a class of individuals, such as "men over the age of forty." Used strictly to apply to an enduring organization of few enough individuals that they are responded to on the basis of their personal characteristics.

social institution: the traditional ways in which a particular culture provides for a given area of human activity. All cultures, for example, have certain institutionalized ways of raising children.

socialization: induction into a role or roles which a person will play in society.

social power: relative ability to influence. In Thibaut and Kelley's theoretical approach, the range of costs and rewards through which one individual can move another.

social reality: the nature of the world according to the views of a particular social grouping.

social role: the behavior expected of a person holding some particular status, or position, in a society.

socioeconomic status: social class as judged by those indicators, largely economic, most readily rated by an interviewer.

socioemotional leader: the person most effective in dealing with the emotional tensions and conflicts arising in a group.

source of data: what it is that is studied. Used more specifically to refer to what organisms, living under what conditions, are studied.

spontaneous recovery: the reappearance of an extinguished response after a period of time during which the conditional stimulus is not present.

standard stimulus: one provided so that others may be compared with it.

statistical control: the elimination of alternate explanations of experimental results by the study of the relative effects which different variables have when more than one are allowed to vary at a time.

status: (1) any position in a society which has a role or set of expected behaviors associated with it. (2) Position in a hierarchy of class, prestige, or power.

stereotype: a widely held idea not supportable by evidence. Frequently a negative view of a group to which the person holding the view does not belong.

stimulus: a feature of the environment which may influence an organism.

stimulus error: in classical introspection, reporting perceptions rather than sensations.

stimulus generalization: responding to a new stimulus in a way similar to that in which the organism has learned to respond to a similar stimulus in the past. Initial generalization occurs without reinforced practice with the new stimulus, while conditioned generalization occurs after positive reinforcement for generalization.

stimulus-response theory: a learning theory maintaining that what is learned is to give certain responses to certain stimuli.

structuralism: the first formal school of psychology. It saw the basic task of the field as finding the elements of experience.

subcortical: areas of the brain reached by afferent stimulation before it reaches the cortex.

subliminal: below the threshold, or limen. The limen is the amount of stimulation which will be reported on the average.

successive-comparison system: learning a list by visualizing images which combine each successive pair of stimuli.

successive intervals: a method of attitude scaling more refined and accurate than equal-appearing intervals. The task of the judges is the same as in equal-appearing intervals, but the data are analyzed differently.

superego: the individual's internalized moral standards.

synthesis: the combination of elements to form a more complex whole.

task leader: the person most effective in enabling a group to be productive.

TAT: Thematic Apperception Test.

testosterone: a male sex hormone.

Thematic Apperception Test: a test of personality and motivation based on telling stories about pictures.

theory: a set of symbols and rules for their manipulation.

thoracic ganglion (plural **ganglia**): a nerve center in the chest.

thymus gland: a gland involved in immune reactions of the body.

thyroid gland: a gland regulating metabolism.

togetherness situation: a situation in which people come together for only a short time or a special purpose. A situation in which an ad hoc group is assembled.

total institution: a social structure attempting to provide for all the needs and activities of its members.

transposition effect: responding to a stimulus on the basis of its relations to other stimuli. See **transposition experiment.**

transposition experiment: an experiment in which an organism is trained to respond to one stimulus rather than another and then tested on a different pair of stimuli. The name derives from the transposition of a melody into a different key. An example of a transposition experiment would be one in which an animal was trained to go toward a bright light rather than a dim one and then tested with a bright light and a still brighter one.

traumatic anxiety: a disturbed state which is based in the actually present situation rather than memories of earlier situations.

traumatic discipline: discipline which is highly anxiety-inducing for the child, either because it is unclear what behavior is being punished or because of the harsh and unusual nature of the punishment.

UCR: unconditional response.

UCS: unconditional stimulus.

unconditional positive regard: the total acceptance of the patient by the therapist thought necessary in the school of psychotherapy founded by Carl Rogers.

unconditional response: a response which is always called out by a particular stimulus, without training. See also **unconditional stimulus.**

unconditional stimulus: a stimulus which always calls out a particular response, without training. The stimulus and the response make up the unconditional reflex.

unconditioned response: unconditional response.

unconditioned stimulus: unconditional stimulus.

unconscious: not present in consciousness for any one of several reasons, including lack of appropriate sense organs and motivated unconsciousness.

unit of analysis: the size element into which the data are broken down in being studied.

unit relation: in Heider's balance theory, a relationship between people forcing them to associate with each other regularly.

value: a positive or negative view of something broad enough to help the individual evaluate many other things. Similar to an attitude but more general.

ventral: toward the abdominal side of the organism.

visual cliff: a drop-off covered by strong glass so that it appears to be a cliff even though it is not possible to fall off it.

visual-deprivation experiments: studies in which organisms are kept from having normal opportunities to see.

von Restorff effect: learning better a stimulus which differs from the others.

word salad: a highly disturbed use of language characteristic of schizophrenia.

Zeigarnik effect: remembering uncompleted tasks better than completed tasks under nonthreatening conditions.

NAME INDEX

Page numbers in *italics* indicate quotation.

SUBJECT INDEX

Acquaintance, 77, 78, 269–271, 345, 352–355
  (*See also* Perception, of people)
Acquisition, 91
Aerial perspective, 55, 58
Aggression, expression of, 286–305, 331, 332
  (*See also* Motives, aggressive)
Alcoholism, 188, 189, 195, 290, 291
Amnesia, 153, 154, 193–195, 228, 231–235

Analysis, opposition to, 15, 19
  in perception, 32–35
Anxiety, effects of, 136, 165, 289
  sources of, 166, 179, 292, 333, 340
  theoretical discussion of, 165–174, 190–192
  types of, 166, 167
  ways of coping with, 167, 182, 189, 204, 212, 303–305, 333, 340
Assimilation, 67–72, 84, 239